REAL PROPERTY LAW

Real Property Law

DISCLAIMERS

This Course Has Been Approved By The Registrar Under The *Real Estate And Business Brokers Act, 2002.*

Real Estate Council of Ontario
3300 Bloor Street West
Suite 1200, West Tower
Toronto, ON M8X 2X2

International Standard Book Number: 978-0-9780344-6-7
Content Development: Ontario Real Estate Association and Acronamic Learning Systems Inc.
Design and Graphics: Automation Plus Ltd.

Printing and Binding: MediaLinx Printing Group

Reprint: September, 2016

ROLE OF THE REGISTRAR UNDER REBBA 2002 IN EDUCATION

The Registrar under the *Real Estate and Business Brokers Act, 2002* (REBBA 2002) is responsible for setting the educational requirements for individuals who wish to obtain and maintain registration as a real estate salesperson or broker. In order to trade in real estate in Ontario, real estate salespersons, brokers and brokerages must be registered with the Real Estate Council of Ontario (RECO) under REBBA 2002. Before beginning a career as a real estate salesperson, individuals are required to complete the required pre-registration courses.

The Registrar, through an Educational Services Agreement, had designated the Ontario Real Estate Association as the organization authorized to provide the pre-registration, articling and broker educational program. All registration-related courses of study, including associated course content, must be approved by the Registrar prior to being offered to students.

DESIGNATE

The Ontario Real Estate Association, through its OREA Real Estate College, takes great pleasure in delivering this program on behalf of the Registrar pursuant to an Educational Services Agreement between the Real Estate Council of Ontario and the Ontario Real Estate Association.

The course curriculum supports the Real Estate Council of Ontario's mandate to protect the public interest through the development of skilled and educated real estate professionals by providing students with timely, comprehensive, accurate and up-to-date education that will allow them to succeed in the real estate marketplace. The OREA Real Estate College fulfills many of its responsibilities to the Registrar, the public of Ontario and the real estate profession by providing learning opportunities so that individuals, either contemplating registration or currently holding registration, can receive appropriate and timely training.

The real estate profession makes a valuable contribution to the economy of Canada and the welfare of its people. Congratulations on taking the first step towards real estate registration in Ontario. The Real Estate Council of Ontario and the Ontario Real Estate Association hope that the successful completion of *Real Property Law* will inspire and motivate you to pursue advanced educational offerings throughout your career.

ACKNOWLEDGEMENTS

A course of this scope is only possible with the assistance of many dedicated professionals committed to the advancement of real estate skills and knowledge. A special note of thanks is owed to the Ontario Real Estate Association for its ongoing forty-year commitment to excellence in real estate education.

A further debt of gratitude is owed to various government departments and agencies who assisted with information and published materials. Appropriate references are included within text materials.

The terms REALTOR® and MLS® are identified as design marks in this publication. No attempt has been made to designate all words or terms in which proprietary rights might exist. The inclusion, definition, or description of a word or term is provided for general information purposes only and is not intended to affect any legal status associated with the word or term as a trademark, service mark or proprietary item.

HOW TO CONTACT OREA

Address	99 Duncan Mill Road Don Mills, ON M3B 1Z2
Instructor Support Line	(866) 444-5557 Clarification regarding *course content only.*
Missing Course Materials	(416) 391-6732 (866) 411-6732 Course Administration Services
College Education Centre	(866) 411-6732 (Toronto)

My OREA Community—Education Forums

OREA encourages the use of the Education Forums as a learning tool. This can be found on our website at **www.orea.com**. Log in to "My Portfolio" using your student ID and password. Once logged in, click on the *My OREA Community (Discussion Forum For Courses)* link. If you do not already have a "My Portfolio" password, please contact the College Education Centre. This positive exchange of content information with an expert who will answer posted questions can be practical and extensive. Participation in the forum is specific to each course and fellow students are encouraged to join the discussions. Privacy is protected.

REAL PROPERTY LAW
CONTENTS AT A GLANCE

TABLE OF CONTENTS

TABLE OF CONTENTS (continued)

TABLE OF CONTENTS (continued)

TABLE OF CONTENTS (continued)

TABLE OF CONTENTS (continued)

TABLE OF CONTENTS (continued) 

TABLE OF CONTENTS (continued)

CHAPTER 12
Residential Tenancy 382

APPENDIX

INTRODUCTION

ABOUT THIS TEXT

Learning Features

Chapter content summaries and **learning outcomes** detail the learning journey in each chapter.

Illustrations simplify and summarize complex topics. A picture is worth a thousand words. Detailed subject matter often requires visual enhancements to ensure complete understanding.

Curiosities offer novel ideas or explanatory details, while satisfying the inquisitive nature in us all. The element of discovery can expand awareness and consolidate subject matter.

Perspectives bring fresh outlooks and consolidate complex topics, usually using a story line. Everyday occurrences of real estate practitioners often complement the subject matter.

Cautions identify special concerns including situations where prudence is required and practices that can lead to dire consequences if pursued.

Each **Focus** concentrates on additional details for a particular topic. These informative descriptions bridge the gap between academic discussions and today's realities.

Study Aids

Notables highlight key topics in each chapter to assist students with review and study efforts, along with a summary of key glossary terms.

A **Chapter Mini-Review** is provided with each chapter for personal review and assessment. The mini-review is a warm up for active learning exercises.

Active Learning Exercises are included at the end of each chapter. Various testing formats are used including multiple choice, fill-in-the-blanks and short answer exercises.

The **Appendix** contains *all* solutions (including solutions for case law, chapter discussion, chapter mini-reviews and active learning exercises).

Additional Resources

Web Links are provided for general interest regarding selected chapter topics. Knowledge of website content is not required for examination purposes.

Case Law includes relevant residential and commercial cases to expand on topics addressed in specific chapters. Case law solutions are located in the *Appendix.*

Chapter Discussion allows for consolidation of key legal concepts within the framework of real estate trading. Chapter discussion solutions are located in the *Appendix.*

SECTION I

OVERVIEW OF PROPERTY OWNERSHIP

The activities of real estate brokers and salespersons go far beyond the basics of showing properties and negotiating the terms of an agreement. The trend towards consumerism and the proliferation of laws and regulations that can affect a real estate transaction require specialized knowledge on the part of a broker or salesperson. The history of property and the modern concepts of property form the basis for all real estate transactions. To understand how law was created over time, originating with custom and tradition and modified by statute and court decisions, is to gain an insight into the importance of this history to a modern real estate transaction. This same process is continuing today, with laws related to real estate changing at a rapid pace, and brokers and salespersons must understand the importance of keeping up-to-date with these changes.

In the usual course of business, salespersons are confronted with a variety of documents and terminologies: deeds, metes and bounds descriptions, terms such as joint tenancy, matrimonial home, etc. While salespersons should not provide legal opinions, they must have a basic knowledge of these legal concepts when listing, selling or leasing property. Brokers and salespersons must verify information with respect to ownership, the existence of easements and deed restrictions, and a variety of issues that can affect the negotiating process and even the value of a property. Knowledge of these issues is essential for a broker or salesperson to provide a professional service to consumers.

CHAPTER 1

History and Concepts of Property Ownership

Introduction

Real estate practitioners must be familiar with a number of terms and concepts with respect to property ownership. A knowledge of the history of property law will help the practitioner understand the meaning and importance of these concepts. The present day system of land holding flows from English medieval law and the development of tenure and the subsequent doctrine of estates.

Various estates have evolved in Canadian law ranging from the highest form of ownership in fee simple to more limited forms such as life estates and leasehold estates. To properly understand ownership of real property, chapter materials delve into the bundle of rights that are guaranteed by law. Of course, such rights are subject to government limitations.

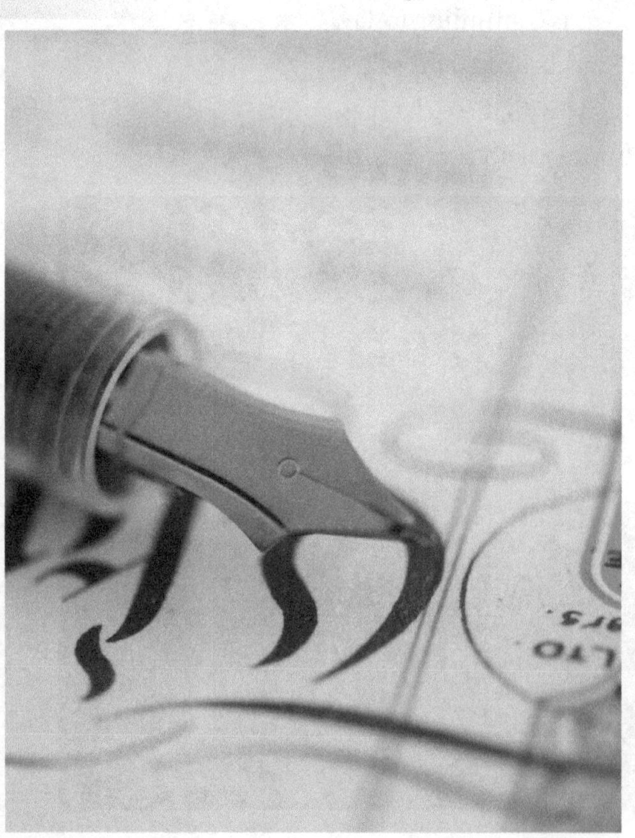

Concurrent ownership is then detailed with reference to both joint tenancy and tenants in common. Of particular note to practitioners are regulatory requirements found in the *Family Law Act* that impact concurrent ownership arrangements. These limitations associated with the matrimonial home are important considerations when listing and selling such property.

Learning Outcomes

At the conclusion of this chapter, students will be able to:

- Outline the evolution of property ownership, from tenure to the modern concept of estates.
- Demonstrate an understanding of the history of the law of property and how laws are created over time.
- Identify and describe different estates and the rights of ownership attached to such estates.
- Describe and differentiate between joint tenancy and tenancy in common.
- Explain how statutes can change existing common laws, with specific reference to the *Family Law Act.*
- Apply ownership concepts to typical situations encountered by real estate practitioners.

HISTORICAL BACKGROUND

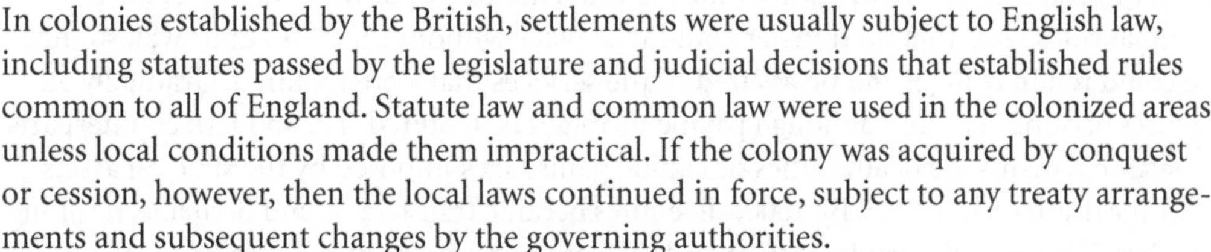

In colonies established by the British, settlements were usually subject to English law, including statutes passed by the legislature and judicial decisions that established rules common to all of England. Statute law and common law were used in the colonized areas unless local conditions made them impractical. If the colony was acquired by conquest or cession, however, then the local laws continued in force, subject to any treaty arrangements and subsequent changes by the governing authorities.

Ontario was affected by these general concepts in its early years, and in 1792, the Upper Canada Legislature passed an important statute called *The Property and Civil Rights Act.* It brought to Ontario the laws of England as of 15 October, 1792, as a basis for legal decisions. Even today, unless there is some specific current Ontario legal provision, court decisions still rely on English precedents.

In 1867, the *British North America Act* was passed, dividing legislative power between the federal government and the provinces. In Section 92, the provinces were given exclusive jurisdiction over property and civil rights. The land law of Ontario is thus a blend of English common law and Ontario statute law as modified and interpreted by the courts. Some law in Ontario may resemble English law or British Columbia law or New York law, while Quebec law may resemble laws of France or Louisiana.

Recent constitutional legal history involves the *1981 Constitution Act* and its *Charter of Rights and Freedoms* and other provisions. It adopted the *British North America Act of 1867* while stipulating that no future act of Parliament of the United Kingdom shall extend to Canada as part of our law.

Tenure vs. Estate

In the history of Canada, two doctrines of law relating to land ownership have arisen: the original doctrine of tenure, and the subsequent doctrine of estate. For the majority of provinces, the present-day system of land holding has its roots in English medieval law.

THE FEUDAL SYSTEM OF TENURE

After the fall of the Saxon empire in 1066 to King William of Normandy, a military regime was imposed on the entire English countryside. Under this regime, a land-holding system was instituted known as *feudalism.* Through this system, King William appointed approximately 1,500 tenants-in-chief who became the King's principal tenants of all England, thus becoming in turn the lords of the land (or landlords) of the entire domain. The tenants-in-chief, who were the principal lords of the realm, did not own the land, but were merely tenants of their king. (This method of "*holding*" land rather than "*owning*" it was called a system of tenure.) Payment by services of different kinds was demanded by the sovereign for allowing the lords to occupy these large tracts of land. The lords, in their turn, were allowed to sublet.

A system of parcelling land was established that allowed the respective tenants to pay with goods and services. This system was one of tenure, or the holding of land subject to some superior right rather than ownership. The type of tenure held was related to the duties owed to the landlord, the payment exacted became traditional with each type of tenure so that if one knew the nature of services due, one could identify the type of tenancy held. These "*incidents*" of tenure were the forerunners of modern concepts of taxes, levies, conscription to war service and other payments to the Crown in return for the protection of the state.

One matter of significance was the concept of alienability. Alienability refers to the power to transfer tenure to another during one's lifetime or at the time of death. The original rules were that no transfer could take place without the lord's approval, so that he could retain control and be assured of the services that were required. Gradually all tenures became heritable, although payments might be required. The modern counterparts of such payments are death duties or capital gains taxes imposed by the state on assets after the death of an owner. By 1600, all tenures became transferable and heritable, resulting in a breakdown of the feudal system and the commencement of modern concepts of ownership recognized as "*estates*" in land.

DOCTRINE OF ESTATES

The earliest use of the word *estate* is found in the medieval *Year Book*, where lawyers of the time were found to use this term in their reports to describe the interest that a tenant held in his land. *Estate*, connected with the Latin word *status*, was used to convey the legal position. The recognition of estates in land law arose through legal action that brought disputes over ownership before the royal courts. Before the Norman conquest of 1066, the jurisdiction of the royal courts was rather narrow, since the administration of local justice was left to the lords of the realm who made it a very profitable business. After 1066, King William saw fit to intervene frequently between the tenants-in-chief and their subtenants, thereby establishing a more or less uniform system of rights, which is said to have led to the establishment of the principle of common law.

Modern law was developed as a result of the many disputes brought before the royal courts. These actions, where interests in the property were recognized, became known as real estates, thus leading to the phrase *real estate* in modern usage to define interest in, or rights to, land.

Development of Canadian Law

At one time, every part of Canada was a colony under English law. The method of establishing English law depended entirely on how those lands became colonized. If a territory became a colony because of direct British settlement, English statute and common law was established immediately as a general rule, unless local conditions made this impossible. Following the establishment of a local legislature, power was granted to enact laws of a local nature under some form of control by Britain.

If a colony was acquired by conquest or cession, laws in force at the time were generally adopted until altered or modified. With cession, these alterations or modifications were subject to treaty. The various colonies that now comprise Canada were acquired in all three ways. Ontario was mainly a settlement, but at one time it belonged to Québec, which in turn, according to one's view of history, was acquired either by cession or conquest.

In 1774, the *Quebec Act* greatly enlarged the boundaries of the province, including what was to become Upper Canada (now Ontario). One part of the Act provided that the then laws of Canada (i.e., French law) applied to civil rights and matters of property. At the separation of Canada in 1791 into Upper and Lower Canada under the *Constitutional Act*, French law with some minor exceptions still took precedence. Since the great majority of Upper Canada was settled by the British, steps were taken to alter this situation. The new legislature of Upper Canada enacted *The Property and Civil Rights Act* of 1792, and noted that the province had been principally settled by British settlers unaccustomed to French law. Among other things, the Act repealed that particular provision of the *Quebec Act.*

The enactment of *The Property and Civil Rights Act* meant that Upper Canada acquired all the laws related to real property developed in England over centuries. Although these laws had developed from the feudal system, by 1792 the incidence of feudal tenure had long since been abolished or ceased to exist. Thus, while influencing the development of Canada's real property laws, the English feudal system as such has never directly been part of them.

By the *Constitution Act* of 1867 (formerly the *British North American Act 1867*) Canada became a confederation of provinces in which legislative power was divided between federal and provincial governments. Section 92 of the Act gave the provinces exclusive jurisdiction over property and civil rights, except those aspects of law that could be enacted by federal parliament. English law, adopted by most provinces, has obviously been modified by statutes passed into law by provincial legislatures, and by the common law decisions of courts, coupled with the provisions of the *Constitution Act.*

Common Law

Common law is the part of the law that is formulated, developed and administered by the common law courts, mostly unwritten and founded originally on common customs. Common law is based on principles more so than specific rules and has developed over the centuries using legal precedents as opposed to statutory provisions set out by parliamentary decree.

TYPES OF ESTATES

In Ontario, we came to recognize many different forms of estates in land such as ownership (fee simple), or limited forms of estates such as life estates or future estates. The degree of ownership or extent of the rights to the land defined the type of estate held. There are a number of ways an individual can hold title to property, including the concept of concurrent ownership as evidenced by the estate of tenancy in common or joint tenancy.

The term estate describes an interest in land or more specifically the degree, quantity, nature and extent of interest that a person has in real property. As previously discussed, the historical background of an estate lies in the development of British law. The status of the person holding a land interest (a tenant) for a lord of the land (a landlord) became known as an estate in the land.

When disputes arose involving interest in property, traditionally, they were brought before the royal courts and decisions ultimately formed part of common law. Property disputes specifically became known as real actions involving real estates. In modern language, the term *estate* is now used to define concepts of interests in, or rights to deal with, land and its components. Estates can be classified under several general headings.

Estate to Uses

The estate to uses concept was at one time a method of holding ownership. Normally, such ownership was obtained by deed, will or possession. Estate to uses flowed from trust ownership in which title was in the name of a registered owner who may have held title as a trustee for the real or beneficial owner.

This concept gave rise to *estate to uses* where ownership was held for a future buyer and was often used to avoid a dower right. Dower right has been largely replaced by provincial legislation concerning spousal rights in regard to land ownership and, consequently, estate to uses has fallen into disuse.

Fee Simple

Fee Simple is the highest estate or absolute right in real property. Fee simple provides the most rights with the fewest limitations and is generally considered absolute ownership. However, this bundle of rights (the right to use, sell, lease, enter, give away or refrain from any of these rights in regard to property) is subject to various restrictions imposed by laws of governing authorities. The bundle of rights is discussed later in this Chapter.

EXAMPLE *Fee Simple*

Mr. and Mrs. Jones acquired a property in fee simple and are now convinced that as owners they are free to do whatever they want on the property. The lawyer points out that fee simple is subject to important restrictions. For example, the Criminal Code of Canada permits peace officers to enter Mr. and Mrs. Jones' lands if a crime is committed. Further, as owners, they cannot alter lands (e.g., drainage) to adversely affect a neighbouring property; the Crown may have reserved various mineral and timber rights with the original Crown grant; municipal regulations may set out minimum construction standards and the right of inspection; and the owner cannot create a nuisance in law by bringing dangerous chattels (dynamite, wild animals, etc.) or obnoxious uses (smelter, glue processing, etc.) onto the property. Such uses might be permitted, depending upon local municipal requirements and provided that various governmental regulations and procedures are followed.

FEE SIMPLE WITH CONDITIONS

Fee simple can be created so that it terminates under certain conditions. A determinable fee simple is one that automatically terminates on the occurrence of some event, which may never happen. While prevalent historically, such arrangements are infrequently found and may be considered contrary to law and public policy.

For example, a tract of land might be dedicated for educational purposes and would revert back if such use was ever terminated. Another example of fee simple with conditions would be a grant from the grantor to Smith and his heirs so long as the property is used as a farm. The fee simple interest will cease and the land will revert to the grantor or the heirs if the land ceases to be used as a farm.

EXAMPLE *Estate—Condition Contrary to Public Policy*

Fee simple may be granted subject to a condition, and if the condition is breached then the grantor can put an end to the estate. Assume that the deed provided a tract of land to Jones and his heirs on condition that Jones does not marry Smith, then on Jones' marriage to Smith the grantor could re-enter the property. However, as earlier referenced, many such historical restrictions would now be in contravention of public policy and/or law.

FEE TAIL

An historical fee that restricted the inheritability of land to a limited class of heirs, such as the eldest male. Such provisions, often found in old deeds/wills, are no longer valid.

Future Estate

Future estates normally arise with life estates. Since a life estate is not everlasting, a large portion of the fee simple remains when the life estate ends. This remaining portion is called a reversion when the grantor of the life estate reserves the balance for himself. If, however, the grantor gives the balance to a third party, the remaining portion is called a remainder.

The life estate and the estate in remainder co-exist. The life tenant and the person entitled to the remainder both have an interest in the property from the beginning of the life estate. The difference is that the person with the remainder cannot use the property so long as the life estate exists, while the life tenant is restricted in what he/she can do with the property. In a general sense, the life tenant is responsible for current obligations and has the benefit of current assets while the ultimate owner has the capital benefits and obligations. If, however, the life tenant and the person with the remainder are in agreement, the property may be dealt with in any manner they choose; e.g., sell the property, tear down buildings or dig up the land, because their combined interests form the entire fee simple.

Leasehold Estate

A leasehold estate is an interest in land for a definite period of time—a week, a month, a year, 99 years or any other specific period of time. The estate cannot, however, be longer than the estate from which it was granted. In a leasehold estate, the person to whom the interest is granted is called the lessee or tenant, and the grantor of the interest is called the lessor or landlord. These individuals are governed partly by old established rules of common law and partly by provincial tenancy legislation.

Life Estate

A grantor in a deed or will may grant an interest in the lands to someone for a lifetime period. That interest will cease on the death of the named individual: for example *to Jones for his life*. The grantor may specify rights and obligations that affect the life tenancy; e.g., use of the land, limitations on alterations/improvements, and payment of usual expenses such as taxes and maintenance. This type of estate often arises under the terms of a will.

EXAMPLE *Estate—Life Estate*

Seller Smith wishes to provide a life estate but wants to codify various rights and obligations that affect the life tenancy. Jones, the life tenant, has exclusive right of possession, use, profits, enjoyment and rents derived from the land. The land can be leased, but the lease will terminate upon the life tenant's death, as a higher ownership interest than that which is enjoyed cannot be granted.

Jones cannot commit waste and, therefore, cannot cut down trees, except for incidental general maintenance. He cannot cut down the apple tree in the back yard, but he can enjoy the apples. If valuable minerals exist below the surface, Jones could not mine on that property. If Jones elected to plant a crop, he could reap that crop including the last crop by his heirs upon his death. Jones cannot remove fixtures but is required to pay realty taxes and all maintenance.

Smith will pay capital expenses such as fire insurance and the principal amount of any mortgage against the property. Jones pays the mortgage interest. In a general sense, the life tenant is responsible for current obligations and has the benefit of current assets, while Smith as the ultimate owner has the capital benefits and obligations.

Heir **CURIOSITY** 

An individual who inherits or who has the right to inherit the property of another upon the death of that person.

Agreements/contracts for real estate typically include a clause indicating that the agreement/contract shall be binding on all respective successors, heirs, assigns, administrators and personal representatives.

Two wordings are provided for illustration purposes.

- The heirs, executors, administrators, successors and assigns of the undersigned are bound by the terms herein.
- This agreement shall be binding upon and shall enure to the benefit of the Vendor and Purchaser and each of their respective successors, assigns and personal representatives.

BUNDLE OF RIGHTS

The theory underlying the *bundle of rights* holds that the ownership of real property can be compared to a bundle of sticks, with each stick representing a distinct and separate right or privilege of ownership. These rights are inherent in ownership of real property and are guaranteed by law including the right to: use real property, sell it, lease it, enter it, give it away and finally the right to refuse to exercise any of these rights. The highest level of ownership rights is fee simple.

Property

Property is either real or personal. The distinguishing factor is mobility, with personal property being movable. Real property is the freehold ownership of land, including the tangible elements (physical elements) and the intangible elements (rights that accrue from the ownership of the physical real estate). Real estate usually refers to the physical tangible property, while real property is the more all encompassing term that includes both real estate and rights of ownership.

EXAMPLE *Bundle of Rights (Property)*

Salesperson Martin is trying to understand the difference between real and personal property. The broker provides a straightforward example. When a property is listed, the land, house and all improvements (e.g., garages, decks and accessory buildings) represent the real estate, but are also viewed as the tangible items of real property. The rights associated with the land, (e.g., the right to occupy, mortgage or sell the property) are the intangible items. In combination, the tangible and intangible items make up what is referred to as real property. All the chattels or moveable possessions of the seller are personal property (e.g., furniture, automobile).

Government Limitations

The legal definition of land implies complete ownership of the land and everything attached to it, under it or over it. However, legal title to land does not imply unrestricted exercise of the bundle of rights. Such rights and privileges are limited by the following four government powers.

Police Power	The right of government to regulate property for promotion of public safety, health, morals and general welfare. Zoning by-laws, building codes, traffic regulations and sanitary regulations are also based on police power.
Power of Expropriation	A right reserved by the government to take private property for public benefit provided that *just* compensation is paid. This right has been extended to quasi-public bodies such as housing authorities and public utilities.
Power of Taxation	Right of all levels of government to generate revenue through the taxation of land. The most common and direct form being property taxation at the municipal level.
Escheat	Right to have ownership of the property return to the state if the owner dies having no will and no known or ascertainable heirs.

Government limitations on the bundle of rights can be far-reaching. For example, the *Criminal Code* permits law enforcement officers to enter one's lands if a crime is committed. An owner cannot create a nuisance in law; e.g., bring dangerous chattels such as dynamite onto the land. Although owners may excavate, lateral support to the neighbour's land must be retained. Riparian rights affect an owner's ability to interfere with the quality or quantity of water and taking action that might have a detrimental effect on other property owners sharing the waterway.

Private restrictions can limit the use, manner of development or even the ownership that may be conveyed concerning real property. Encumbrances may require that the buyer be obligated to use the property subject to restrictions; e.g., deed restriction, easement, right-of-way, party wall agreement and mortgages.

Various bundling of rights can produce a wide range of ownership options, as well as offering flexibility of use. While most immediately think of leasehold interests, real property has many ownership dimensions; e.g., life estates, sub-leasehold estates, and partial and fractional interests. In fact, fractional interests can be a significant value in an increasingly complex society; e.g., real property can be divided into different planes: subsurface rights, surface rights and air rights.

EXAMPLE *Bundle of Rights*

An owner can sell or lease mineral rights while retaining the rights to use the surface area of his/her property. An absentee owner can rent the surface rights to one party and lease the sub-surface rights to another. The remaining rights in the bundle can be sold, leased, transferred or otherwise disposed of. In establishing a property's value, the rights remaining with the property and the effect of the loss of any of these private rights on its value must be taken into consideration.

CONCURRENT OWNERSHIP

In brief, concurrent ownership arises when two or more persons have a right of ownership at the same time. Concurrent interests normally fall into two primary categories:

- Joint tenancy; and
- Tenants in common.

Concurrent ownership can be disposed of by agreement of the owners. If concurrent owners cannot agree as to the disposition of the property, an application can be made to the court that then leads to the forced sale of the property and distribution of proceeds.

EXAMPLE *Concurrent Ownership*

The buyers, James Jones and Judy Jones, purchase a home as joint tenants and draft the offer in both names. Accordingly, the deed is prepared showing both parties as owners in joint tenancy. As such, Mr. and Mrs. Jones have concurrent ownership of the property.

Joint Tenancy

Joint tenancy involves ownership of land by two or more persons whereby, on the death of one, the surviving tenant(s) acquire the whole interest in the property.

CREATION

In joint tenancy, all the owners have the same size of interest, the same possession and the same title to the land. Described alternatively, joint tenants between themselves have equal rights, but against everyone else they are in the position of a single owner. A joint tenancy arises only when expressly created in the grant of the estate or afterwards by an express agreement between the holders of the estate. For example, a will could state:

I leave my fee simple in 123 Main Street to my five nephews equally.

However, stating that the five nephews are to hold the interest in the property equally is not enough to create a joint tenancy. A presumption exists, typically spelled out in provincial legislation, that a grant of land to two or more people will be a tenancy in common unless clear intent is evident that it be a joint tenancy. Where co-owners exist on a deed, the assumption is that they are tenants in common unless the title specifies otherwise.

FOUR UNITIES

Even though a clear intention exists to create a joint tenancy, one will not be formed unless the *four unities* are satisfied. If these conditions are not satisfied, then a tenancy in common has been created.

TITLE

All joint tenants must derive their title from the same instrument; e.g., deed or will.

EXAMPLE *Unity of Title*

Buyer James Jones acquires an interest in a home and subsequently transfers one-half interest in the property to his spouse, Judy. If the ownership is not obtained at the same time by the same document, Jones and his spouse will own the property as tenants in common.

However, James Jones can transfer the title of the property to "James Jones and Judy Jones as joint tenants and not as tenants in common."

TIME

The interest of each joint tenant must begin at the same time.

EXAMPLE *Unity of Time*

Buyer James Jones acquires one-half interest in the home on Monday and his wife Judy receives the remaining portion on Tuesday. In this case, James Jones and his wife will be tenants in common, not joint tenants, as their interests were not received at the same time.

POSSESSION

Each joint tenant is entitled to undivided possession of the whole of the property and none holds any part separately to the exclusion of the others. Perhaps a clearer way to explain unity of possession is to say that it gives all joint tenants an interest in all of the property, but an exclusive interest in none of the property.

EXAMPLE *Unity of Possession*

If Jones and Smith own two acres of land as joint tenants, they both own two acres—not one person one acre and the other person the other acre. In addition, neither has an exclusive right to any particular part of the land as they both together own the whole. Accordingly, one joint tenant cannot maintain an action in trespass against the other.

INTEREST

The interest of each joint tenant must be identical in nature, extent and duration.

EXAMPLE *Unity of Interest*

If three brothers hold the fee simple in a property as joint tenants, each has a one-third interest in the fee simple.

Additional Considerations

If any of the four unities are missing, or cease to exist during joint tenancy, then the owners will automatically become tenants in common. If these four unities are present and there is a clear intention that a joint tenancy should exist, then a joint tenancy will be created.

EXAMPLE 1 *Additional Considerations*

Buyers James Jones and Judy Jones purchase a duplex at the same time and by the same document. However, James insists that the lower unit be specifically owned by Judy and that he will hold title to the upper unit. In this case, joint tenancy cannot apply as both parties must have an undivided interest in the property. Neither can specifically point to one portion of the lands and improvements and claim ownership to those specific areas.

EXAMPLE 2 *Additional Considerations*

Buyers James Jones and William Jones are purchasing an investment property and want to create $2/3$ and $1/3$ interest, as they are not contributing equally to the purchase. They also inform the lawyer that they would like to acquire title as joint tenants. The lawyer explains that joint tenancy is not possible in this situation as the same quantity of ownership would not be demonstrated.

SURVIVORSHIP

The right of survivorship is an important aspect of joint tenancy in that the interest of the deceased tenant (owner) is automatically transferred to the surviving tenant (owner). This means that, if one joint tenant dies, his/her interest does not pass to his/her estate (such as a personal representative or to heirs) but passes directly to the surviving joint tenant or tenants.

Joint tenancy is often encountered when a husband and wife obtain title to the family home as joint tenants. In such cases, on the death of either spouse, the survivor is automatically entitled to immediately receive full title to the property. The joint tenancy is thus an advantage to the surviving spouse because the house does not form part of the deceased's estate where it could become entangled in problems of settling the estate.

A joint tenant cannot bequeath his or her interest by means of a will because the transfer to the other joint tenant is automatic at death. Effectively, the deceased joint tenant's interest ceases to exist.

EXAMPLE *Joint Tenancy—Survivorship*

If James and Judy Jones are joint tenants in fee simple, and Judy dies, James immediately becomes the owner of the whole interest. This is true even if Judy tries to dispose of it by will. The right of survivorship takes precedence.

SPOUSAL INTEREST

The general rule concerning right of survivorship in a joint tenancy is subject to an important exception. Under applicable provincial legislation, if a married person dies owning an interest in a matrimonial home jointly with someone other than his/her surviving spouse, the joint tenancy is deemed to be severed immediately before the time of death. Consequently, the interest becomes a tenancy in common and thereby provides a basis for the appropriate spousal interest in the assets of the deceased spouse's estate. This topic is explored in more detail under the heading ***The Family Law Act*** later in this Chapter.

TERMINATION

If joint tenants sever their joint tenancy relationship, they automatically become tenants in common. Obviously, if both parties agree to sever voluntarily, then the parties become tenants in common as a result of that agreement.

A joint tenant may destroy the right of survivorship before his/her death without the consent of the other joint tenant(s). This process, called *severance*, turns the joint tenancy into a tenancy in common with the other tenant or tenants. Even after an act of severance, if there are two or more other tenants remaining, they still remain joint tenants with each other, but are tenants in common with the person who holds the severed interest. The most common method of severance is by a joint tenant granting his/her interest to a third party. The grant has the effect of turning the interest transferred into a tenancy in common with the remaining interests.

Other modes of severance exist, such as when all the joint tenants mutually agree to end the joint tenancy and instead hold their interests as tenants in common. For example, with a marriage separation, the joint tenancy termination can be mutually agreed upon as part of the separation agreement. A joint tenancy may also terminate by partition; i.e.,splitting the land by means of an application to a court. If proper grounds exist, the court will order that the property be divided according to the joint tenancy. When it would be impractical to divide the property into different sections, as the case would be for a residential home, the court can order that the property be sold and the proceeds divided up.

The termination or severance of a joint tenancy has a significant impact on property ownership and must be done properly. A lawyer should always be consulted.

EXAMPLE *Joint Tenancy—Termination*

Jones, Smith and Taylor are joint tenants. If Jones sells his share to Wilson, then Wilson becomes a tenant in common (one-third) with Smith and Taylor (two-thirds). Smith and Taylor remain as joint tenants. If Smith dies, Taylor will become the owner of the two-third interest and will hold it as a tenant in common with Wilson (two-third ownership by Taylor and one-third ownership by Wilson).

Tenants in Common

Tenants in common involves ownership of land by two or more persons, however, unlike joint tenancy the interest of a deceased person does not pass to the survivor, but is treated as an asset of the deceased's estate.

Tenancy in common requires only the unity of possession as opposed to joint tenancy that has four unities. Each tenant in common is entitled to the same rights over the property and the use of the whole property. Since the only unity that is required is that of possession, tenants in common may hold different interests and acquire those interests in different ways. It is quite possible to have two tenants in common each owning ¼ of the property and the third tenant in common owning the balance, namely ½ of the property.

No right of survivorship exists under a tenancy in common as the tenants/owners hold separate interests. Therefore, upon the death of one of the owners in a tenancy in common arrangement, the interest in the land passes to that individual's estate and does not automatically transfer to the remaining tenants.

Each tenant in common may sell or lease his/her undivided interest to another or dispose of it by will. A tenancy in common arrangement can therefore be terminated by the sale of one tenant's interest to the other tenant(s), the sale of the entire property to another party or the dissolution of the tenancy in common relationship by a court order.

RIPARIAN RIGHTS

Real estate practitioners will typically encounter riparian rights in the listing, marketing and selling of recreational properties. Riparian rights are more specifically described as the rights of the owners of lands on the banks of watercourses, to take advantageous use of the water on, under or adjacent to their land.

Such rights are deemed to be natural rights by reason of ownership, as they arise from the natural state of the property in conjunction with the abutting watercourse. Riparian rights can be grouped under the following two categories.

Rights Concerning the Body of Water	• Right of access to water. • Direct exclusive access from owned land. • Right of increase in shore area by natural growth. • Right of navigation.
Rights Concerning Flow of Water	• Right to enforce water flow. • Right to unpolluted water. • Right to use water.

Riparian rights are frequently subject to provincial legislation concerning public lands under bodies of water and other environmental legislation impacting shoreline property.

THE FAMILY LAW ACT

There have been a number of changes in family law in recent years, recognizing marriage as an equal partnership and providing protection for individuals in a number of situations, including the death of a spouse and a marriage breakup.

These changes in Ontario law have reinforced the concept of spousal rights regarding real property. Notably, the *Family Law Act* has instituted the concepts of:

- The matrimonial home.
- Net family property.
- Equalization payments.

As a result of these changes, the medieval concept of dower has been abolished. Also, in situations where property could fall into the category of family assets over time and where family assets are not to be owned equally, "*domestic contracts*" have become an essential part of spousal relationships.

Matrimonial Home

This distinct status is afforded to selected properties pursuant to provincial legislation. The *Family Law Act* recognizes the concept of an equal partnership-marriage relationship and provides a code for the orderly and equitable settlement of the spouses' affairs when a marriage breaks down, or when a spouse dies, by an equalizing of the net family properties.

Practitioners require a general knowledge of legislative provisions concerning matrimonial homes and related matters, as issues regarding spousal rights often arise in the listing and selling of residential property. According to the *Family Law Act*, there can be more than one matrimonial home, (e.g., a home in the city and a home in the country). Registrants should not attempt to advise their clients, but rather ensure they are directed to seek qualified legal advice, as per their obligation under Code, Sec. 5 and 6(1). Four topics are addressed, but salespersons and brokers are encouraged to refer to the Act directly and seek legal counsel for additional information.

DESIGNATION

A designation of a home as a matrimonial home essentially means that the property is deemed to be the family residence at the time of designation. Any property can be designated by both spouses as a matrimonial home by joint registration. All other matrimonial home property is then released from the protection of Part II of the *Family Law Act* and issues concerning possession and the consent of the non-owner spouse are eliminated. The designation does not remove such property from the calculations of net family property and the resulting equalization payment in the case of divorce. If only one spouse completes a designation, all of the remaining matrimonial homes retain their status despite that registration.

The *Family Law Act* effectively alters common law. In joint tenancy, the interest of a joint tenant passes immediately upon the death of that individual to the other tenant(s). However, where a spouse dies owning an interest in a matrimonial home as a joint tenant with other person(s), the joint tenancy is deemed to be severed immediately before the time of death. Consequently, a tenancy in common is created that requires the inclusion of the deceased person's interest in his/her estate.

A seller of real property will usually make one of nine statements concerning the issue of a spousal relationship in the deed. Five of the nine statements are included for illustration purposes only:

- I am not a spouse.
- We are spouses of one another.
- The person consenting below is my spouse.
- The property is not ordinarily occupied by me and my spouse, who is not separated from me, as our family residence.
- I am separated from my spouse and the property was not ordinarily occupied by us at the time of our separation as our family residence.

A mortgage also includes a choice of various statements regarding spousal rights under the *Family Law Act* when the mortgagor is an individual.

EXAMPLE ***Matrimonial Home: Designation***

Sam and Trisha have agreed to separate and have put their residence up for sale with ABC Realty Inc. Meanwhile, they have equalized net values as required by the *Family Law Act* with the exception of one property. Trisha owned a duplex before marrying Sam and an agreement was signed concerning this matter at the time of the marriage. The value of the property was estimated at $389,000 and, in the event of divorce, Sam would only receive his proportionate share of any increase from that value. Sam and Trisha lived in this property before acquiring their new house.

For purposes of the divorce action, their current home is the matrimonial home. The duplex, while having the matrimonial home status for a specified period, reverted to its prior status once the new home was purchased. However, for purposes of an equalization payment, the duplex has increased in value by approximately $60,000. Accordingly, a payment of $30,000 from Trisha to Sam would be factored into the final equalization process.

FAMILY PROPERTY

The Act sets out procedures for the equal division of property on marriage breakdown or death. Property acquired during the marriage is equally divided between the spouses, subject to the provisions of any valid domestic contract signed by the spouses and subject to any court order. Each calculates the value of his/her own property, after deducting the net value of the property that he/she brought into the marriage, excluding the matrimonial home. The spouse with the greater net value pays the other an amount to equalize their holdings. The right to equalization also occurs on the death of a spouse. The surviving spouse does not have to accept the benefits under the will or intestacy and has six months to elect to take the equalizing payment instead.

Exclusions apply to the net family property concept:

- Property excluded in a valid domestic contract.
- Amounts received during marriage from court awards.
- Amounts received during marriage from insurance proceeds.
- Property inherited or received as a gift.
- Increases in the prior listed items may be included unless the donor specifically made provision that the increase would not form part of the recipient's net family property.

Although spouses are considered separate in regard to property ownership during the marriage, they are subject to this equalizing payment, but may contract out of this system with a valid domestic contract. However, this contract cannot affect the spouse's possessory rights to the matrimonial home. This right relates only to possession and does not affect ownership. The right to possession by the non-owner spouse continues until the spouses have agreed to the contrary or until the court orders otherwise.

NON-OWNER RIGHT TO POSSESSION

Both spouses have an equal right to possession of a matrimonial home. The Act confirms the rights of the non-owner spouse to equal possession of a matrimonial home. This right is a personal one and is not an interest in land. The Act further provides that the spouse has the right to be notified of any proceedings by a third party that could affect that possessory right. The registered owner cannot dispose of, or encumber, the matrimonial home without the consent of the other spouse.

EXAMPLE ***Matrimonial Home: Non-Owner Right to Possession***

Sam and Trisha have recently separated and are obtaining a divorce. The matrimonial home is owned by Sam and is currently valued at $250,000, less an outstanding mortgage of $180,000. The couple have agreed to list the property at $259,900, with Trisha retaining possession until the point of sale. If the property does not sell within three months, the listing price will be reduced in line with recommendations from the listing salesperson. At the point of sale, the equity remaining following discharge of the mortgage and all related costs, will be added to their net family property. The fact that Trisha was neither a tenant-in-common nor a joint tenant with her husband in the matrimonial home is irrelevant. The *Family Law Act* protects the rights of non-owner spouses in this situation.

OTHER PROVISIONS

- Part III of the Act addresses support obligations that go beyond the scope of this text. The definition of a spouse for this purpose is expanded to include those who have cohabited for more than three years or who cohabit and are the natural or adoptive parents of a child or children. Same-sex partners are also included under provisions of Part III.

- Part IV relates to agreements between those who are married, are to be married, are cohabiting or are separating. Basically, a contract can deal with ownership in, or division of, property. However, a domestic contract cannot limit a spouse's possessory rights in the matrimonial home, except in a valid separation agreement.
- Part V addresses claims by dependents for remedies covering losses suffered through the injury or death of the spouse upon whom they are dependent.
- Part VI should be highlighted as it deals with changes to some doctrines of common law that are no longer appropriate. A spouse, married or common-law, can bring a court application for support to determine ownership rights and to restrain the other spouse from depleting the property. The court can determine the ownership and order property sold or transferred to a spouse. Consequently, the prudent practitioner will have all parties sign legal documents such as a listing agreement, agreement of purchase and sale, a waiver and other forms dealing with real property, to ensure that all possible parties are consenting to the transaction.

EXAMPLE ***Matrimonial Home: Other Provisions***

Sam and Trisha have recently separated and are obtaining a divorce. Both brought approximately $25,000 in value to the marriage and have established their net values for the divorce at $100,000 and $140,000 respectively, excluding the matrimonial home. Following deduction of the initial contributions of $25,000 each, the net value for equalizing purposes is $75,000 (Sam) and $115,000 (Trisha). Accordingly, Trisha will pay Sam $20,000 to equalize their values. Trisha did inherit property from her parent's estate amounting to $50,000 but this is not included, as per Part I of the Act. Sam and Trisha also entered into a domestic contract at the time they were married which excluded that eventuality.

While awaiting the final divorce, Sam leaves the matrimonial home and attempts to secure a loan against the property for $20,000 to assist with unexpected costs. His lawyer advises that it is not possible owing to provisions of Part II of the *Family Law Act.* Alternatively, he wants to sell the property, but Trisha refuses. The lawyer advises Sam that he cannot disrupt Trisha's possession of the property even though her name may not be on title to the property. Ultimately, the spouses arrive at a mutual agreement that permits the property to be offered for sale. The listing salesperson has both Sam and Trisha sign the listing agreement before marketing the property.

CASE LAW

Case Synopsis

DEBORA V. DEBORA ONTARIO COURT OF APPEAL DECEMBER, 2006

At issue in this appeal is whether a cottage owned by a corporation should be considered as a matrimonial home in a marriage breakdown or, alternatively, since one spouse owns all of the shares in the corporation, whether the shares of the corporation should be included in the net family property. The FLA regards a matrimonial home as a unique asset and gives it special treatment. If the property is considered as a matrimonial home, the entire value of the one million dollar asset would be subject to equalization of the net family property.

If the corporation's ownership of the cottage prevents it from being considered as a matrimonial home, only the increase in value of the shares of the corporation that owned the cottage during the time period of the marriage would be subject to equalization in the net family property, that amount being approximately $160,000.

There was no dispute as to the fact that the cottage owned by the numbered company was ordinarily occupied as a family residence. The cottage was ordinarily used as an all season recreational residence at both the date of the civil marriage and the date of separation. They entertained family and friends at the cottage and it was maintained from their joint bank account.

The husband claimed that as a shareholder of the corporation, he has no interest in the assets of the corporation and had no interest in the cottage, therefore it is his ownership of the shares of the company that should be subject to equalization. The husband was the sole shareholder of the corporation that owned the cottage.

The court noted that Section 18 of the FLA provides:

(1) Every property in which a person has an interest and that is or, if the spouses have separated, was at the time of the separation, ordinarily occupied by the person and his or her spouse as their family residence is their matrimonial home.

(2) The ownership of a share or shares, or of an interest in a share or shares, of a corporation entitling the owner to occupy a housing unit owned by the corporation shall be deemed to be an interest in the unit for the purposes of subsection (1).

In *Mancini v. Mancini* [1982] it was held that legal control over the corporation amounts to legal control over the residence for the purposes of the matrimonial home provisions.

The Court of Appeal upheld the trial judge's decision that the cottage property was a matrimonial home and that the entire value of the cottage was to be considered in determining the equalization of the net family property.

Case Questions

1. In what way is a matrimonial home treated differently from the other net family property in the event of a marriage breakdown?	**2.** Describe 2 other provisions in the *Family Law Act* that could have prevented the full value of the cottage from being included in the net family property.

CASE LAW

Case Synopsis — *MCLENNAN V. MEYER* — ONTARIO SUPERIOR COURT OF JUSTICE COURT FILE #81/95 PEMBROKE

The owners of a 100-acre farm experienced flooding on their property due to a neighbour's dam that disrupted the natural water flow. In 1984, they had purchased the property as vacant land with plans to build a home, operate a plumbing business and manage a race horse boarding operation. For approximately ten years after the purchase, a long-established, natural watercourse flowed through the front field from a higher property, drained onto the neighbour's farm to the west at a lower elevation and then proceeded to a river.

In 1993, the westerly neighbour filled in the creek at the boundary line (easterly side of his property) causing the water to back up and flood the owners' front field. During heavy rains, the water reached the horse paddocks and caused basement flooding in the newly-constructed house. The owners installed two culverts to access their house by the front laneway during such rains. Further, the front field tile drains ceased operating, as water backed up the drains rather than flowing to the original watercourse. In 1994, the neighbour added more fill and compounded the flooding problem. The owners sought legal recourse to remove the dam and pursued damages for the flooding.

The issue at law centred on whether a natural watercourse was involved or the matter related solely to the mere flow of surface water. If the former, then an obstruction would have to be removed. If the latter, the neighbour at the lower elevation (who built the dam) had no obligation to accept surface water drainage and could take necessary action to protect his lands. The Court determined (based on photos, supporting documentation and testimony) that a natural watercourse had been in existence for many years and the lower property owner should not have interfered with its natural flow.

The Court ordered that the property be returned to its natural state with costs borne by the lower neighbour who constructed the dam. In regard to damages, the cost associated with culvert installations had to be paid by the neighbouring owner. Damages involving loss of income (relating to flooding that impacted the plumbing and race horse boarding businesses), boarding costs (boarding the horses elsewhere) and punitive/aggravated damages were not allowed.

Case Questions

1. What proactive strategy would you recommend to buyers planning on purchasing land with shoreline, a natural watercourse flowing through the property or wetland located on the property?

2. What relevant questions should a listing salesperson ask a potential seller whose property includes, or is impacted in some way by, a natural watercourse?

CHAPTER DISCUSSION

1. HISTORICAL BACKGROUND

a. What significant rights for the landholder became recognized by the royal courts as the concept of "*tenure*" evolved into the concept of "*estates*" in land?

b. "*History only tells us what happened and it has little importance in my day-to-day real estate business.*" Comment.

CHAPTER DISCUSSION

2. CONCURRENT OWNERSHIP

List the main similarities and differences between joint tenancy and tenancy-in common.

3. THE FAMILY LAW ACT

According to the *Family Law Act*, what special provisions for the matrimonial home do not apply to the balance of the family property?

KNOWLEDGE INTEGRATION

Notables

- The history of land ownership plays a significant role in how modern day society deals with estates in land.
- Individuals can hold title to a property in various ways.
- Fee simple is the highest estate or absolute right in real property.
- A grantor can grant an individual an interest in land for a lifetime period. This interest will cease upon the death of the named individual.
- The bundle of rights transcends ownership of real property and is guaranteed by law.
- Legal title to land does not imply unrestricted exercise of the bundle of rights, because such rights are limited by the four government powers.
- The two primary categories of concurrent ownership interests involve joint tenancy and tenants in common.
- Four unities for joint tenancy include title, time, possession and interest. If these conditions are not satisfied then a tenancy in common is deemed to be created.
- Only the unity of possession is required to create tenants in common. Unlike joint tenancy, the interests of a deceased person, in the case of tenants in common, does not pass to the survivor.
- Riparian rights involve the ownership of lands on watercourse banks and restrict the activities of such owners which may affect water flow, access, navigation and other important factors.
- Provisions of the *Family Law Act* protect interests in a matrimonial home when a marriage breaks down or a spouse dies.

Chapter Mini-Review

Solutions are located in the Appendix.

1. A life estate involves an interest in land granted to someone for a lifetime period.

   ○ True ○ False

2. The concept of concurrent ownership applies to joint tenancy, but not to tenants in common.

   ○ True ○ False

3. An owner having riparian rights relating to a watercourse abutting his or her property has a right to access the water and alter the shoreline to suit personal needs.

   ○ True ○ False

4. Even if a wife is the only registered owner of the matrimonial home, the husband is entitled to live there.

   ○ True ○ False

Chapter Mini-Review (continued)

5. If there is no marriage contract and a marriage breakdown occurs, the husband is entitled to claim half of the increase in value of his wife's rental property that she owned before they got married.

   ○ True ○ False

6. If I own a house that my husband and I live in as our matrimonial home, he automatically owns half based on requirements set out in the *Family Law Act.*

   ○ True ○ False

7. A husband and wife own a matrimonial home as joint tenants. Upon the husband dying, the interest in this home would automatically transfer to his wife.

   ○ True ○ False

8. Property inherited or received as a gift is excluded under the net property family concept.

   ○ True ○ False

Active Learning Exercises

Solutions are located in the Appendix.

Exercise 1

John Smith transferred title to his son Joseph. The deed was to "Joseph Smith so long as the said land and premises are used as a farm." John Smith, the father, died two years later. His will gave everything to his son Joseph Smith and to his daughter Mary White. Joseph continued to farm the land until a few months ago at which time he listed the property with ABC Realty Inc. and the property was sold to Developer Reed. After the deal closed, Joseph got his money, ABC Realty Inc. received their commission and Developer Reed started excavations for a plaza. The lawyer for Mary White then wrote a letter to the developer claiming that Mary owns half of the site. The developers claim that all the land is owned by them, and is to be developed as they require.

a. Did Joseph Smith convey a fee simple interest when he sold the property to the developer? Explain.

b. Who is the owner of the property? Explain.

Exercise 2

Charles Emeritus Chan left a Will that leaves everything to his wife stating that on her death everything is to go to his first son. The wife does not want to live on the property so she rents it out for ten years to George Tenant.

a. Can she rent it for ten years?

b. Who is entitled to the rent?

c. What if the wife dies next year?

d. What happens if the buildings burn down tonight?

e. You have been asked to list the property. Who must sign the listing?

Exercise 3

Smith provided for various owners of his real estate. Who should sign a Listing under the following circumstances?

a. The Deed is to Mary Smith until her son, David Smith, reaches his 30th birthday, when it goes to him. David is now 26.

b. The Deed is to Mary Smith for her life and then to her children. There are three children: David, 26, Bill, 21 and Sarah, 19.

c. The Deed is to Mary Smith and David Smith as joint tenants.

d. The Deed is to Mary Smith for life and, on her death, will go to her daughter Sarah. Sarah is married to Adam Black and they live on the property.

Exercise 4

A property can be designated as a matrimonial home under *The Family Law Act.* Explain why this may be done and what the effect would be of such designation.

Exercise 5

Before they were married, John and Mary signed a marriage contract. That contract provided that if the marriage was not successful, Mary would get 10% of John's assets. John owns a Villa in Spain, a house in Ontario and a condominium in Hawaii. They spend several months each year living in each place. Mary now wants a divorce. What interests does she have in the real estate?

Exercise 6

Richard Brown owns a small house on First Time Drive where he lived with his wife Jane until 1980, when they divorced. Brown kept the house as part of the divorce settlement. However, he vacated the house and rented it to Frank Jones and Sally Jones. Richard then bought another house on Better Street, and resides there with his second wife, Susan, who insisted that this house be registered in her name only. They want to sell both houses and want to give you the Listings for both of them. Who should sign each Listing?

Exercise 7

Harry Short bought a house in 1960. It is currently mortgaged to Lender Inc. Harry married a year ago. The mortgage is now three months in arrears. The lawyer for the mortgagee wishes to notify Harry's wife, but the manager says she didn't sign the mortgage because Harry wasn't married at the time the mortgage was arranged. Besides that, the manager doesn't even know her name and insists she is not involved. The lawyer insists that she is. Discuss.

Exercise 8

Smith owns land across which flows a creek. He decides to change the flow of the creek to create an artificial pond. Can down-creek neighbours object? Why? Assume that Smith redirects the creek so that by the time the flow leaves his land, it returns to the natural creek-bed. Does this make a difference?

CHAPTER 2

Leaseholds and Property Interests Other Than Ownership

Introduction

Real estate practitioners frequently market properties that are rented or may arrange leases. A knowledge of the law related to leaseholds is essential. Issues related to easements and deed restrictions frequently arise in the listing of properties, the drafting of agreements and the valuation of property. In addition, when an agreement is negotiated, disputes are inevitable unless the issue of fixtures and chattels is addressed. It also must be recognized that parties other than the owner may have an interest in the property. For example, real estate practitioners may encounter liens on the property, fixtures that are leased or power of sale situations.

Learning Outcomes

At the conclusion of this chapter, students will be able to:

- Differentiate between commercial and residential tenancies.
- Discuss selected topics involving leases including creation, essential elements and subletting.
- Discuss selected topics involving commercial tenancies that are commonly encountered by practitioners in the marketplace.
- Identify the main characteristics of easements and other non-ownership interests.
- Apply concepts involving leaseholds and other property interests to typical situations encountered by real estate practitioners.

COMMERCIAL VS. RESIDENTIAL TENANCIES

The line between commercial and residential tenancies is often blurred by legislative considerations impacting both landlords and tenants. Practitioners must first understand the *Residential Tenancies Act* to gain a full perspective on the issue of whether a lease falls to residential tenancy legislation or to the *Commercial Tenancies Act.* This determination can have significant impact, as the *Residential Tenancies Act* affords tenants a wide range of rights not found in its commercial counterpart.

A commercial lease can be identified as any lease involving a property that is principally used for business activity. The operative word principally should be emphasized and, in most instances, common sense prevails. For example, a small home office within a residential structure would not affect the residential status of the property. A structure containing a main level commercial enterprise and two upper apartments would be identified as commercial for the lower units and residential for the upper units.

Practitioners should normally determine if a property is residential and subject to the *Residential Tenancies Act.* However, certain hybrid situations can cause problems. For example, consider a tenant renting a home located on 30-acre rural property and also renting the barns and balance of the property as a riding stable. If the individual occupied the home prior to the riding stable operation and leased the business operation under a separate lease, the *Residential Tenancies Act* would undoubtedly apply to the residential tenancy. If the person became a tenant coincident with renting the barns for a riding stable operation under a single lease (in other words the occupancy of the house was required to carry on the business) the property would undoubtedly be judged as principally used for commercial purposes. Establishing whether a residential or commercial tenancy exists can have a significant impact particularly in regard to notices concerning termination, rent charged and rights of access by the landlord (or his/her agent) to show the property and to make repairs.

Practitioners should also be aware of exclusions for certain types of rental arrangements provided in the *Residential Tenancies Act.*

- Living accommodation intended to be provided to the travelling or vacationing public or occupied for a seasonal or temporary period.
- Living accommodation when the occupancy is conditional on the occupant continuing to be employed on a farm, regardless of where the accommodation is situated.
- Living accommodation provided by a non-profit housing co-operative to tenants in member units, occupied by a person in a penal or correctional facility, governed by selected legislation (e.g., *Public Hospitals Act*), provided as emergency shelter or provided by an education institution (subject to certain qualifications).
- Living accommodation located in a building or project and the occupancy is required relating to a function performed by the tenant in that building or project.

- Living accommodation whose occupant or occupants are required to share a bathroom or kitchen facility with the owner (including spouse, same-sex partner or child or parent of one of them) and the owner resides in the building.
- Premises occupied for business or agricultural purposes with living accommodation attached if the occupancy for both purposes is under a single lease and the same person occupies both.
- Selected types of living accommodation provided for the purpose of receiving rehabilitative or therapeutic services.

LEASE

In its simplest form, a lease is a grant of an interest in land. The relationship of a landlord and tenant originated from ancient feudal doctrines but in modern practice, these doctrines are altered by contractual arrangements between the parties and recent statute law. Since a landlord is giving up rights to the land for some term, there are few obligations left upon the landlord to perform. The two most notable ones are quiet enjoyment and an obligation not to become involved in derogation from the grant.

The tenant is given possession of the property and must treat the property as would a careful and prudent owner. There are a number of remedies available to either party should a breach of the lease occur.

Definition

Essentially, a lease is a contract between a landlord (lessor) and a tenant (lessee) for the occupation or use of the landlord's property by the tenant, for a specified time and for a specified consideration. Under the terms of a lease, the lawful owner of the property (the landlord) transfers the rights of use, possession and enjoyment to another (the tenant) for a specified period of time or at will for a consideration (rent). A lease may also be referred to as a tenancy agreement.

The purpose of a lease is to establish a written record of an agreement between the parties for a tenancy arrangement within a defined period. A lease can be verbal or written, express or implied. A lease document, whether residential, commercial or industrial, is a detailed document setting out the responsibilities of the parties, rents payable and obligations of both landlord and tenant, along with a wide range of provisions concerning notices, remedies and termination.

Assignment

An assignment involves the assigning of rights, ownership and interest in a lease whereby the assignor or lessee, transfers the entire remainder of the term created by the lease.

The tenant, as assignor, may transfer all of his/her leasehold interests to a new tenant but, unless he/she is released by the landlord, the assignor remains liable for the lease obligations to the landlord. It should be noted that the assignor may not remain liable for performance under the lease if such is specifically set out in the terms of the lease pertaining to assignment. If the tenant transfers something less than an entire interest, he/she sublets it. This may be either the subletting of part of the term or part of the premises. Again, the tenant remains liable to the landlord, unless otherwise stipulated in the lease.

A tenant may assign or sublet at will without the approval of the landlord unless the lease stipulates otherwise or provincial legislation establishes certain requirements or procedures. In fact, most leases contain an express covenant that the tenant will not assign or sublet or a qualified covenant that there will not be any assignment or subletting without the prior written consent of the landlord. This clause may be further qualified so that the landlord's consent will not be withheld arbitrarily. In these circumstances, the tenant can apply to a judge to obtain approval for an appropriate tenant who intends to use the premises in a reasonable manner. Usually both the tenant and the assignee or subtenant will sign a form agreeing to be bound by the main lease and the landlord will consent to this agreement. The parties will pay the landlord's reasonable costs in arranging for this consent and they will include any legal expenses. There may be other requirements concerning subtenants for residential tenancies in government-subsidized housing or government-owned projects.

Creation/Registration

A lease can be written or verbal, express or implied by a person's conduct. Its terms are found in common law and in provincial statutes concerning commercial or residential tenancies. Normally, the parties will enter into a written signed lease or tenancy agreement in order to precisely describe their relationship. A wide range of lease forms and associated wordings are found in the marketplace.

When a property owner agrees to lease property, the tenant acquires an interest in that property and may register applicable documents in the land registration office giving notice of this interest. Methods will vary based on whether the property is registered under land titles or registry and upon specific registration requirements set out in individual provincial jurisdictions.

Elements

Lease forms differ substantially, but whether for residential or commercial purposes, all must contain the following elements to make them legally enforceable:

- Statement of the correct names and signatures of legally competent parties.
- The full legal name, correctly spelled, of the individual(s) and/or corporation(s) that are party to the lease must appear.
- The person signing must be legally competent. This is particularly important in the management of retirement and nursing homes, and the signatures of spouses and guarantors are obtained, where applicable.
- Legal description of the leased premises should ideally be entered. However, as long as the description allows the space and specific property to be readily identifiable (including address, dimensions and a floor plan) this requirement can be considered fulfilled.
- Consideration, that is, the exchange of something of value. In a lease, the amount of rent, method of payment and to whom the payment is due are detailed.
- A lease must include a description of the legal purpose for which the premise is to be used. By virtue of this clause, for example, tenants can be controlled in the particular type of business being carried on, thereby permitting exclusive use within a retail complex and providing assurance that other tenants will not be in direct competition.

- Commencement and expiration dates must be included since, if these two dates were omitted, the lease would be so vague as to be unenforceable. Any renewal privileges should be spelled out in detail.
- Rules and regulations, policies, procedures and generally what is expected of each party must be clearly delineated.

Chattels vs. Fixtures PERSPECTIVE

When selling property, it is important to know what is included with the property in addition to the lands and the buildings. Real estate practitioners need to be able to differentiate between chattels and fixtures and be aware of possible liens which can exist against chattels affecting ownership rights.

CHATTELS

Chattels can be described as moveable possessions and personal property (usually items that may be removed without injury to the freehold estate).

Practitioners should be aware that the legal nature of a chattel changes when it becomes fixed to the real property. Whether chattels become fixtures depends largely on circumstances. No set rule exists, but the deciding factor tends to be degree and object of annexation.

EXAMPLE Thomson is selling his recreational property and advises Salesperson Lee that various items are not included in the sale. While understanding that chattels are moveable and fixtures are fixed to the property and improvements thereon, Lee must ensure that there is no confusion in relation to these items with either Thomson or a potential buyer. He prepares and attaches a schedule to the listing itemizing all excluded chattels. This list includes a 14 foot aluminum fishing boat, two outboard motors (5 HP and 10 HP), fishing tackle boxes, assorted rods/reels, two space heaters in the guest cabin, various lawn ornaments and outside furniture.

FIXTURES

An improvement or item of personal property on the real property becomes a fixture when it is so attached to the real property or building that it becomes part of it.

Whether a chattel becomes a fixture depends largely on the circumstances, with particular emphasis placed on the method of how the item is affixed, the intent of the party(ies) and degree of importance to the property. A chattel designed for temporary use or convenience could remain as a moveable item. However, if its purpose was to enhance the property and is affixed thereto, it might well become a fixture. As with chattels, practitioners must clearly identify in any agreement/contract what *is* and *is not* included. The general rule is that fixtures are part of the real property and go with the sale unless specifically excluded.

Rented items must also be listed and acknowledged by the buyer as excluded from the purchase price. In commercial tenancies, the tenant can remove trade fixtures at the end of the lease term, repairing any damage caused by their removal.

EXAMPLE *Excluding Fixtures*

Seller Smith wants to retain the dining room chandelier, that is now permanently affixed to the ceiling, and the decorator rods in the living room. Salesperson Lee informs Smith that both fixtures should be clearly excluded in the listing as well as in the agreement/contract.

EXAMPLE *Chattels vs. Fixtures*

In a simpler time, real estate practitioners confidently separated chattels from fixtures; the former were always detached and movable, while the latter remained affixed as improvements. While common sense should prevail, doubt can arise.

- A 500 lb. Grecian urn adorning the patio, is it movable or not?
- An intricate interlocking paved drive; looks permanent, but is it attached?
- The pool equipment, some are attached and some are not. Which are chattels and which are fixtures?

The list goes on and on: indoor vacuum cleaning attachments, wall-to-wall carpeting (fitted but not stapled) and satellite dishes.

History

For centuries, the law recognized freehold estates as property interests and permitted only a person who possessed a freehold estate to bring an action to protect his/her real estate. All other interests were less significant and considered personal in nature. The introduction of leasehold interests into law and the increasing use of this land holding method required a change in legal concept.

Leaseholds became known as estates that were less than freehold, but as estates nevertheless. One major distinction between freehold and leasehold estates is that, while both are a measurement of time, the freehold is for an uncertain time, whereas a leasehold is for a time that is certain or capable of being made certain.

In discussions of feudal doctrines and concepts, the relationship of landlord and tenant was of major significance. The courts were called upon to decide disputes between the two and the results often favoured the landlord by strict interpretation of principles of land law. The land and its right of occupancy were the major assets of most aristocracy and land was prized for the wealth and power it bestowed.

In its simplest form, the lease is a grant of an interest in land. In practice, it is usually a grant by way of a contract whereby the owner, called the lessor or landlord:

- Transfers exclusive use and possession of real property to another person, called the lessee or tenant;
    - For a period of time, called the term; and
    - For valuable consideration, called the rent.

While there are various requirements in a lease, the most important aspect involves the granting of exclusive possession. If the parties contract for something less than that, the law might not recognize the arrangement as a lease, but as some other legal personal arrangement, such as a licence. The distinction has practical significance, in that a lessee may enforce entitlement to rights against a subsequent owner while a licensee may not be able to do so. Therefore, a contract that may not grant exclusive possession is not a lease and the occupant does not have the right to exclude all other persons from the premises.

Such contracts may involve mall kiosks or residential roomers/ boarders. The latter can be complex, since landlord and tenant law historically did not consider roomers to be tenants, whereas modern statutes, such as those of rent control, may consider them to be covered by specific legislative protections. In a leasehold arrangement, the landlord retains an interest called a reversion. The tenant's estate is a lesser one than that of the landlord. If it were otherwise, the arrangement would amount to a transfer of entire interests and constitute a sale.

Landlord

A person or company who owns tenanted real property is referred to as a landlord. The typical statutory definition for landlord is illustrated:

> *A person who is a lessor, owner, the person giving or permitting the occupation of the premises in question and these persons' heirs, assigns and legal representatives.*

The duties of a landlord, set out statutorily and by common law, vary depending on both the type of property and the tenant. Basically, the landlord is required to guarantee possession to the tenant for the duration of the lease period. If this covenant is broken, the

tenant may pursue legal damages. The landlord cannot use the premises retained in such a way that the tenant is unable to use his/her leased premises (derogation from the grant).

Landlord duties are often detailed in the lease document as the following example for a commercial property illustrates.

EXAMPLE ***Landlord***

Salesperson Lee has just leased a 3,000 square foot office to a new real estate brokerage opening in the west end of the city. When asked about the landlord's obligations, the salesperson detailed a list of items taken from a standard lease used by the landlord.

The landlord will:

- Pay realty taxes;
- Provide heating, ventilating and cooling to the common elements and the leased premises;
- Maintain and repair the common elements;
- Provide janitorial service in keeping with standards appropriate to the building; and
- Control the management and operation of the building, including employing personnel, making changes or improvements and such other acts as deemed prudent, using good business judgement.

Offer/Agreement to Lease

An offer sets out material terms regarding a proposed tenancy arrangement between landlord and tenant that, once agreed by the parties, becomes the reference document for drafting a lease.

In most lease transactions, the practitioner is involved in two steps:

- An offer to lease is signed, setting out the basic terms of the agreement between the parties.
- Terms in the offer to lease flow to a detailed lease agreement that must be signed by the parties.

Practitioners frequently attach a preprinted blank lease to the offer as an assurance that all parties are aware of terms set out in the agreement that will be subsequently completed and signed.

Sublet

Practitioners should clearly differentiate subletting from the assignment of a lease. When an entire interest is transferred, it is said to be assigned. Thus, the tenant as assignor may transfer all of his/her interest to a new tenant, the assignee. The original tenant remains liable for the lease obligations to the landlord.

As a general statement, a tenant may assign or sublet at will without the approval of the landlord unless the lease stipulates otherwise. In reality, most commercial leases contain an express covenant that the tenant will not assign or sublet or a qualified covenant that there will not be any assignment or subletting without the prior written consent of the landlord. This clause may be further qualified so that the landlord's consent will not be withheld arbitrarily. If this occurs, the tenant may be able to apply to a judge and obtain approval for an appropriate tenant.

Usually both the tenant and assignee or subtenant will sign a form agreeing to be bound by the main lease and the landlord will consent to this agreement/contract. The parties will pay the landlord's reasonable costs in arranging for this consent including the legal expenses, credit investigations and similar expenses.

Subletting provisions apply to all tenancies whether periodic (e.g., month-to-month), fixed (e.g., lease with exact term), contractual (specifically detailed by contract) or statutory (provided under the Act, for example, a fixed tenancy becomes a periodic tenancy if the tenant remains following the term).

The *Residential Tenancies Act* sets out various requirements and restrictions concerning subletting. Selected items are highlighted for descriptive purposes only. Practitioners should access the Act directly for exact wordings.

- Subletting provisions do not apply to the tenant of a superintendent's premises.
- The tenant may sublet with consent of the landlord for a term ending on a specified date before the end of the tenant's term, giving the tenant the right to resume occupancy after that date.
- The landlord cannot arbitrarily or unreasonably withhold consent to a sublet.
- The landlord may charge reasonable out-of-pocket expenses relating to the consent.
- The tenant remains entitled to benefits and liable for breaches under the tenancy agreement during the subtenancy period.
- The subtenant is entitled to benefits and is liable to the tenant for breaches of the subtenant's obligations.
- The subtenant has no right to occupy the rental unit after the end of the subtenancy.
- The tenant may apply to the Tribunal for an order for compensation from an overholding subtenant, if the subtenant is in possession of the rental unit at the time of the application.
- Various rights given to the landlord concerning termination apply to the tenant/subtenant relationship as if the tenant were landlord and the subtenant were tenant (e.g., damage, reasonable enjoyment and too many persons).
- If a subtenant overholds and the original tenant has vacated the rental unit, the landlord can (within 60 days of discovering the unauthorized occupancy):
    - negotiate a new tenancy agreement with that person.
    - apply to the Tribunal for an eviction order.

The unauthorized occupation shall be deemed to be an assignment with landlord consent if:

- a new tenancy agreement is not entered into within 60 days; and
- no application is made to evict the person or the subtenant.

Be Up-To-Date CAUTION 

Information contained in this chapter is summary in nature only. The *Residential Tenancies Act* is a complex piece of legislation. Always check the Act for current requirements at ***www.e-laws.gov.on.ca*** and the Landlord and Tenant Board regarding Landlord/Tenant Applications, Rules of Practice and Interpretation Guidelines (***www.ltb.gov.on.ca***).

COMMERCIAL TENANCIES

A commercial tenancy can be generally described as any property subject to a leasehold interest that involves land and/or building used for business activity. Commercial tenancies are governed by the provisions of the *Commercial Tenancies Act*. The name of the Act, previously the *Landlord and Tenant Act* (Parts I, II and III) was formally changed in 1997. Part IV of the *Landlord and Tenant Act* was repealed and replaced with a separate, but more all-inclusive Act titled the *Tenant Protection Act*, which was then replaced by the *Residential Tenancies Act*.

Commercial tenancies are complex for several reasons. Commercial properties are inherently diverse and require specialized wordings relating to industrial, office, retail, investment and vacant land leases. Requirements concerning such tenancies require an interplay of legislative as well as legal precedents. In fact, debates concerning commercial leases can require detailed reviews of legislative requirements, principles set out in contract law and case law often dating from both the 19th and 20th centuries.

The structure of the *Commercial Tenancies Act* is somewhat disjointed in comparison to its residential counterpart. Part I generally addresses the landlord/tenant relationship, Part II focuses on distrain (seizing and holding goods) for arrears in rent and Part III concerns overholding tenants. This text includes a limited range of topics commonly encountered by practitioners. Salespersons and brokers seeking additional information are advised to consult appropriate legal counsel.

Fortunately, commercial real estate is heavily influenced by national and international practices. Consequently, a wide range of commercial leasing terminology is used in the marketplace. Selected topics are included in this course book for descriptive purposes only. Practitioners are reminded that no standard commercial lease wordings are used in Ontario and that every real estate transaction is unique.

Assigning & Subletting

The legal distinction between *assigning* and *sub-letting* in commercial leases is based on privity. Privity generally refers to the legal proposition that a contract including rights and obligations is only enforceable upon the parties to that contract.

Practitioners need not fully understand legal complexities associated with assignments, subletting and privity, but should be aware of basics. At the end of a lease term, the tenant is required to reconvey the leasehold estate to the owner of the freehold estate. This creates a privity of estate between the tenant and the landlord. If, for instance, the tenant assigns all of its lease to a third party, then that third party (known as the assignee) has established a privity of estate with the owner/landlord. The former tenant or assignor of the lease has no privity of estate remaining with the landlord.

On the other hand, if a tenant conveys a portion of its leasehold estate to a third party such that the tenant retains a period of time at the end of the term, then the tenant remains in a privity of estate relationship with the landlord. The subtenant so created would have no privity of estate with the landlord.

In a contractual context, if a tenant sublets its premises, no privity of contract exists between the occupying subtenant and the landlord. Therefore, the landlord will not have any legal relationship in the form of privity of estate or contract with the occupier of the premises. However, the landlord retains its privity of contract and estate with the original tenant. Accordingly, leases normally provide that a subtenant must directly covenant with the landlord, in order to ensure that the landlord may then pursue its action either against the tenant or the subtenant.

With an assignment, the assignee and the landlord may have privity of contract, provided that the assignment to the assignee includes language to the effect that all of the benefit and the burden of the lease is assumed by the assignee. In that case, the obligations to the landlord flow through to the landlord and a privity of estate continues between the landlord and the assignee. The landlord also retains his/her privity of contract with the original tenants, unless otherwise agreed.

Landlords should be careful in preparing the assignment and sub-letting provisions of the lease. In the first instance, the landlord should require that any assignment or sub-letting is subject to the landlord's consent and that the new party, be it an assignee or a sub-tenant, must agree to covenant directly with the landlord with respect to the tenant's obligations pursuant to the lease. Additionally, the former tenant would not be released by the landlord unless the landlord, for other reasons, may elect to do so.

The landlord is entitled to withhold its consent only upon reasonable grounds. For that reason, many commercial leases allow the landlord, when faced with an assignment or sub-letting situation, to terminate the lease. This gives the landlord certain control over the premises, particularly in a strong market; i.e., the rent chargeable at the time of the assignment or subletting is substantially higher than that currently being paid by the existing tenant.

Further, the landlord often includes a provision whereby the tenant is not permitted to sublet or assign the premises and receive rents higher than that which would otherwise be payable to the landlord pursuant to the lease. The tenant, from a landlord's perspective, should not be in a position of obtaining extra funds should the demand for rental space increase after the execution of the original lease.

The landlord should also take care at the time of the assignment or subletting to ensure that adequate documentation is in place to obtain sufficient covenants from the new assignee or tenant, as well as preserving the rights to pursue any and all legal remedies against the original tenant.

Continuous Use

A continuous use clause requires that the tenant must continuously occupy the rented space during the currency of the lease. Typically, a continuous use clause is accompanied by covenants that the tenant will maintain a substantial merchandise stock and fully staff the operation.

Landlords are increasingly concerned with dark space. If a lease does not contain a continuous use clause, the tenant may move out of the premises, while continuing to pay rent. A landlord might be left with dark space in a retail centre, which cannot be re-let to third persons. Landlords have found it necessary to include a continuous use clause in the lease, particularly with respect to large tenants.

Anchor tenants may use this technique to control the marketplace, most notably in small suburban or rural areas. If, for instance, only two malls service a community and a large retail outlet leases space in both malls, the tenant can leave one dark and essentially control the retail market in that community. The value of market share is simply offset against the rent cost for the other mall location.

The landlord with dark space is left in the uncomfortable position of leasing to other tenants in a mall, which is not attractive due to the lack of an anchor. A carefully-drafted continuous use clause provides the landlord with options to prevent such a scenario.

Guarantor vs. Indemnifier

A third party, guarantor or indemnifier, undertakes to be responsible for tenant's obligations upon default.

Real estate practitioners involved with commercial leases often encounter landlord requirements concerning guarantors or indemnifiers. In leasing, a guarantor is requested to sign appropriate documents assuring the landlord that, in the event of default, he/she is responsible for the default of the lessee. Landlords may request that an individual agree to an indemnification agreement rather than simply being a guarantor. A person signing an indemnification agreement becomes an indemnifier. As such, he/she assumes a broader scope of liability.

Historically, a landlord would seek a guarantee when a corporate tenant lacked sufficient assets to fund any default. However, such a guarantee involving a third party is limited, as it extends only to the tenant's obligation. If the tenant is deemed by law to have no obligation, then the guarantor is released as well from its obligation. For instance, if a tenant is adjudged bankrupt, then the tenant has no on-going obligations pursuant to the lease. If the guarantor has simply guaranteed the obligations of the tenant and the tenant becomes bankrupt, then the guarantor is not required to pay (as the tenant no longer has liability pursuant to the lease).

In recent years, indemnities have grown in popularity. This arrangement provides that the indemnifier agrees to indemnify and hold harmless the landlord against any damages that may result from the tenant's failure to perform its obligations pursuant to the lease. Indemnity agreements normally go further and imply that the indemnifier is a covenantor pursuant to the lease in the same sense as the tenant and that this indemnity survives any bankruptcy or insolvency of the tenant.

Such agreements also typically provide that the indemnifier, upon the failure of the tenant to perform pursuant to the lease, is deemed to be the tenant and subject to all the covenants contained in the lease. Accordingly, the prudent landlord will have, where appropriate, an indemnity agreement in place with the proposed guarantor, as opposed to a straight guarantee.

Another method to protect the landlord is the creation of a co-tenancy. Essentially the proposed guarantor becomes a co-tenant with the tenant and is jointly and severally responsible for all obligations of the tenant pursuant to the lease. The landlord can then look to the co-tenant in the case of the bankruptcy or insolvency of the main tenant.

Interest on Rent Deposits

Under the Act, a landlord is not required to pay interest on a commercial tenant's security deposit. However, a lease agreement may require a landlord to pay interest on a security deposit or last month's rent.

Landlord

For purposes of the *Commercial Tenancies Act*, a landlord is deemed to include a person who is the lessor, owner, the person giving or permitting the occupation of the premises in question and these persons' heirs, assigns and legal representatives. In Part II and Part III, a landlord also includes the person entitled to possession of the premises.

Lease

A lease is a contract between a landlord (lessor) and a tenant (lessee) for the occupation or use of the landlord's property by the tenant, for a specified time and for a specified consideration.

Real estate practitioners commonly negotiate with landlords and tenants through the use of an agreement to lease. The agreement to lease establishes the substantive terms, conditions and other material matters that flow to the lease documents.

Wordings of commercial lease documents will vary significantly based on the type of property. While no universal lease form prevails in the marketplace, legal publishers typically provide standard wordings to cover multi-residential, retail, industrial, office and retail properties along with supporting forms and notices; e.g., assignments, terminations, affidavits and liens. Practitioners should note that a signed lease agreement may take precedence over the *Commercial Tenancies Act.*

Lease vs. Agreement to Lease

An agreement to lease is technically referred to as an agreement for lease without settled form of lease. An agreement to lease generally sets out fundamental, material aspects of the agreement between the parties, but contemplates the execution of a formal, detailed lease. An agreement to lease covers substantive issues and is best described as a consensus leading to final agreement (the lease).

Practitioners, when drafting an agreement to lease, must ensure that all essential elements of the lease are included, namely, the parties, a description of the premises to be leased (often formally referred to as the demised premises), the commencement of the lease, the term of the lease and the amount of rent. All other material matters in a lease, other than specific exceptions, reservations, covenants or special conditions, are implied by law.

The agreement to lease must also address all other material issues in order that a lease can be correctly drawn as a consequence of the agreement. Salespersons are well advised to ensure that every agreement to lease is complete in all respects. Any confusion can result in legal ramifications. A clause can be inserted in an agreement to lease stating that the lease will include other reasonable conditions and terms as the landlord may require. The issue of what constitutes reasonable will ultimately fall to judicial interpretation should problems arise. While courts would undoubtedly strictly interpret this term as being anything of a non-substantive nature, the entire matter is best avoided by practitioners. Prudence suggests that a blank copy of the lease be attached to eliminate any confusion and ensure that the tenant fully appreciates the true scope of the document. Landlords dealing with complex leases often require this procedure.

Fixtures/Trade Fixtures

Commercial leases often refer to tenant's fixtures or trade fixtures. The general theory of common law was that any fixtures belonged to the person who owned the real estate. Thus, a landlord would own the building and the landlord would also own any fixture which became part of the building, whether that fixture was placed by the tenant or not.

Common law further developed to permit a tenant to remove such fixtures from the real estate as were necessary for it to conduct its business. Such fixtures became known over time as trade fixtures.

Unless a lease states otherwise, a tenant who affixes an item to the realty is entitled to remove that item at the end of the term (if it is an item necessary for the tenant to carry on its trade). The difficulty arises in that any particular item may, in one situation, be a trade fixture and not in another. An example would involve sinks in a barber shop. The sinks that are in the barber shop portion of the premises would be trade fixtures, which the tenant is entitled to remove at the end of the term. On the other hand, the sink (although exactly the same sink) which is in the bathroom, could be retained by the landlord.

Most leases provide that any fixture fastened to the real estate becomes the property of the landlord at the time of the affixation. After the lease term is expired (and provided that the tenant has paid all of the rent) the tenant may remove only the trade fixtures. Landlords may insert a provision in the lease to ensure that the tenant may not take goods unless all the rents have been paid. Also, landlords may provide in their leases that the tenants, at the landlord's option, may be required to bring the premises back to its original condition (bare walls and bare floors) at the end of the term. This represents a substantial lever for the landlord at the end of the term, as the necessary repairs may be costly for the tenant.

Tenants should exercise caution regarding such a provision in a lease or at least be aware of the costs associated with the removal of items at the end of the term.

Commercial leases may also provide that the tenant repair the premises when tenant fixtures are removed at the end of the term. Further, a lease may include a provision outlining the implications of the tenant leaving the goods on the premises for any considerable period after the end of the term.

License vs. Lease

A license is a right or permission granted to an individual, while a lease is both a matter of contractual arrangement and also the conveyance of an estate in land.

The issue of license vs. lease is best illustrated by concessions in a retail shopping mall. Disputes can arise as to whether the tenant or the landlord may seek legal remedies pursuant to the *Commercial Tenancies Act*, as well as case law in support of landlord/tenant relationships. Often, a concession stand (e.g., a food stand or cosmetics counter) within the common area of a mall or within a large department store is not granted exclusive possession and the business is simply located in a particular spot subject to the landlord's rights and ultimate control.

While such matters fall to judicial interpretation, the courts generally look to the issue of whether exclusive possession has been given and whether signed agreements are couched in terms usual to leases; e.g., landlord, lessor, tenant, lessee, lease and demised premises. However, other factors beyond the scope of this text may also be taken into consideration.

Non-payment of Rent

When a tenant has failed to pay the rent, the landlord has two options available under the *Commercial Tenancies Act*.

OPTION 1: **Change the Locks**	A landlord may change the locks of the unit and evict on the 16th day after the day rent was due. The landlord is not obligated to notify the tenant that the locks will be changed. For example, if the rent is due on January 1st, the locks can be changed without notification on January 17th. As a cautionary note, landlords and/or tenants should not force their way into the premises. Also, after the locks have been changed, landlords should allow tenants reasonable access to the rental unit to remove their property.
OPTION 2: **Seize and Dispose of Tenant's Property**	A landlord may seize and dispose of a tenant's property that is contained within the rented premises. The landlord is not required to give advance notice of seizing the tenant's property, unless the lease provides for such notice. However, landlords are required to notify the tenant of the distress and the sum of monies required to cure the default before proceeding to sell the seized property. Prior to disposing of seized property, the landlord must hold such property for five days. If the proper payment is made by the tenant in this five-day period, the landlord is not permitted to sell the tenant's property. Otherwise, after the proper appraisals are made, the property can be sold. **EXAMPLE** *Seizure/Disposal* If rent is due and not paid on January 1st, the landlord may seize the tenant's property and notify the tenant of his/her intent to dispose of same. Five days following the seizure, the landlord can obtain appraisals and dispose of the tenant's property, if the proper payment is not made by the tenant.

NOTE: Landlords and tenants are advised to seek legal advice regarding their specific situations.

Disposing of Tenant's Property CAUTION 

- The Act requires two appraisals before selling or disposing of a tenant's property.
- The proceeds from the disposal of a tenant's property are to be applied to the rental arrears. In the event that proceeds exceed the amount of the arrears, a landlord is obligated to reimburse the excess amount to the tenant.
- Certain types of tenant property cannot be seized; e.g., property that is leased or co-owned.
- Sub-tenants who continue to pay the full rent cannot have their property seized if the head tenant failed to pay the rent to the landlord. In the event that a sub-tenant's property is seized, the landlord would be required to return the goods.
- Commercial tenants who wish to dispute their landlord's actions may apply to the Superior Court of Justice.

Quiet Enjoyment

This clause provides for non-interference by the landlord with the tenant's occupation of the premises, which generally protects the tenant from any direct or indirect actions or threatened actions by the landlord that disturb the tenant.

Practitioners should exercise due caution in all matters concerning this topic. Quiet enjoyment does not generally mean undisturbed by noise or other disturbances; e.g.,

sounds and odours from adjoining tenants, temporary maintenance activities by the landlord or renovations undertaken by the landlord.

If the landlord effectively deprives the tenant of the use and enjoyment of the rented premise, a breach of the covenant can result. This breach, if significant, effectively results in constructive eviction, which can entitle the tenant to abandon the premises and not pay rent. That said, practitioners should be aware that issues concerning quiet enjoyment and rights of landlord and tenant are complex.

Rent Increases

Most commercial tenancy agreements outline in detail issues such as the amount of rent charged and frequency of rental fee increases. In the event of a tenancy agreement, the landlord may increase the rent by any amount at any time. The Act does not regulate rent increases.

Restrictive Use

A restrictive use clause within a lease limits or in some way restricts the activities of either the landlord or the tenant pursuant to a lease agreement.

The landlord may insert a restrictive covenant regarding the specific use. For example, a retail establishment may be permitted to sell donuts and coffee, but not sandwiches. A tenant should ensure that the clause is broad enough to cover all activities; i.e., both upon entering the lease as well as contemplated within the term or lease renewal. Further, the defined use should not be too narrow so as to obstruct finding another tenant to assume the lease obligations, should the need arise.

Landlords will typically introduce restrictive clauses to ensure a proper mix of tenants within a shopping centre. Restrictions may be even more specific to address the particular makeup of the trading area or immediate neighbourhood in which the mall is located.

In some instances, a tenant may request exclusive use (particularly in a shopping centre context) to better ensure business volumes. To protect the tenant's interests, such clauses should apply to the lease term and any renewals thereof, apply to the benefit of the premises (i.e., be enjoyed by any assignee of the tenant) and apply to any expansion of the shopping centre.

Rights and Obligations

LANDLORDS	TENANTS
• Must notify tenants in writing of specific breaches of the lease and allow a reasonable period of time for them to comply.	• Must notify landlords in writing of specific breaches of the lease and allow a reasonable period of time for them to comply.
• May have the right to terminate a tenancy when the tenant fails to fulfill obligations as outlined in the lease.	• Cannot hold back rent because a landlord has failed to fulfill their obligations as outlined in the lease.
• Have the right to apply to the Superior Court of Justice (or depending on the amount, Small Claims Court) to seek damages from the tenant for the loss of rental income owed for the balance of the term of the lease.	• Must fulfill their obligations as outlined by the lease agreement.

LANDLORDS	TENANTS
	• Have the right to take their disputes with the landlord to Small Claims Court for disputes concerning money or personal property under $6,000. Otherwise, an application must be made to the Superior Court of Justice.

Signing Authority

Commercial leases usually involve corporations, partnerships and, in some instances, associations or societies. In each case, care must be taken to ensure that such organizations have the authority to enter into contractual arrangements and that appropriate individuals have signed the lease documents.

Corporations Corporations may be restricted in their ability to enter into leases either through incorporation documents or by statute restrictions. If the corporation does not have capacity to enter into a lease, the lease will probably be deemed void and not enforceable against the tenant.

The landlord should obtain from the tenant's solicitor an opinion that the corporate entity has sufficient capacity and power to enter into the arrangement. Further, assurances should be sought that the parties who have executed, on behalf of the corporate entity, have obtained the necessary approval to do so.

Partnerships Partners are typically bound jointly and severally to obligations entered into by the partnership. Accordingly, each partner is solely responsible for all obligations to the lease. Despite this implied obligation, all partners should execute the lease on behalf of the partnership, in order to ensure acknowledgement of individual obligations. The lease wording will also typically provide that each and every partner remains jointly and severally liable for the lease, unless otherwise specified by the landlord.

Partnerships may request that retiring partners be released by the landlord. The landlord will generally only release such partners if deemed appropriate and at its sole discretion. Otherwise, if retiring partners leave and if the lease deems that they are automatically released, too few partners may be left to retain sufficient strength of covenant.

If all partners are not available to sign the lease, the partners who do sign should covenant that they have the authority to bind the partnership and each of the partners individually with respect to execution of the lease.

Associations and Societies Associations and societies may be limited by their incorporation documentation regarding powers that can be exercised; e.g., the leasing or purchase of real property. The lease document should acknowledge that the association or society has the capacity to enter into the agreement and that the parties who are executing the documents have the authority to do so. A confirming letter from the association's or society's solicitor should be obtained.

Tenant

For purposes of the *Commercial Tenancies Act*, a tenant includes a person who is lessee, occupant, sub-tenant, under-tenant and the person's assigns and legal representatives.

Termination

Month-to-Month Under the Act, either a landlord or a tenant can terminate a month-to-month tenancy with a minimum one-month written notice. The last day of the tenancy would be the last day of the rental period. For example, on March 31st, written notice is delivered by one party to the other, the next rental period begins on April 1st and the tenancy can be terminated on April 30th.

The written notice of termination should include:

- Landlord's name,
- Tenant's name,
- Address or description of the rental unit,
- Date that the tenancy should terminate; and
- Date the notice is served.

Fixed-Term Fixed-term tenancy agreements specify the length or term of the lease. Under the Act, once the tenancy ends, the tenant no longer has the right to occupy the premises. For example, under a three-year lease agreement, the tenant is expected to leave the premises at the end of the three years.

If a tenant continues to occupy the rental premises after the landlord has requested that the tenant move out, that tenant may be subject to a penalty of two months rent for every month they remain on the premises, plus applicable costs.

In addition to imposing a financial penalty, the landlord may also apply to the Ontario Superior Court of Justice to obtain an eviction order.

Trade Fixtures

Trade fixtures are articles installed by a commercial tenant usual to the tenant's business and removable by the tenant before the lease expires. Under the terms of a lease, trade fixtures typically remain personal property and are not true fixtures.

In a commercial lease involving new premises, the landlord will normally have developed the design of the buildings, the landscaping and common areas and established the elements of the areas to be leased, such as washrooms, electrical devices, HVAC, floor finishes and store fronts. The balance of the work to be completed is usually at the tenant's cost, subject to the landlord's approval as to design and finish and of course to building codes and other governmental requirements and restrictions.

All alterations, decorations, additions and improvements made by the tenant or by the landlord on behalf of the tenant become the property of the landlord, provided that the tenant shall be responsible for the insuring of such affixed alterations, decorations, additions and improvements. Commonly, the lease specifically references tenant trade fixtures as excluded under the provision and to remain the property of the tenant unless the tenant abandons such fixtures at the expiration of the lease.

EXAMPLE *Trade Fixtures*

Developer Reed is negotiating with Tenant Jones concerning a 5,000 square foot retail space for the operation of a restaurant. Given the possibility of a ten-year lease, Reed has agreed to complete various interior improvements for the restaurant, while Jones will install extensive kitchen and related facilities. Under the terms of the lease, all such facilities are deemed to be tenant trade fixtures and as such remain the property of the tenant at the expiration of the lease. Reed and Jones agree to precisely detail such trade fixtures as a schedule to the lease to avoid any future potential confusion.

Following is an excerpt to that effect taken from the lease document:

> *Upon the expiration of this lease, the alterations, decorations, additions and fixed improvements excepting the Tenant's trade fixtures as detailed in Schedule A will remain the property of the landlord as part of the reversion.*

EASEMENT

An easement is a right enjoyed by one tenement over another tenement (see Curiosity), for example, one land owner with a right over another land owner, usually granted for a special purpose rather than for the general use and occupation of the land. An easement is an interest that runs with the land.

Once granted, an easement attaches to the land and binds subsequent owners. An easement must have both a dominant tenement (land that benefits from the easement) and a servient tenement (land that serves or is subject to the easement). Separate ownership of the dominant and servient tenements must exist and the right must confer a benefit on the dominant tenement. The two tenements need not be adjoining.

Agreements relating to easements are usually registered against titles to both properties. However, such is not always the case, for example, when statutory easements are involved (see subsequent details). The title to an adjacent property may have to be searched before determining if a particular property benefits from a registered easement over another's land. These agreements may be registered as instruments on their own and appear on the title under that particular name or they may be registered by way of a caveat (a warning or notice on title) in some provincial jurisdictions.

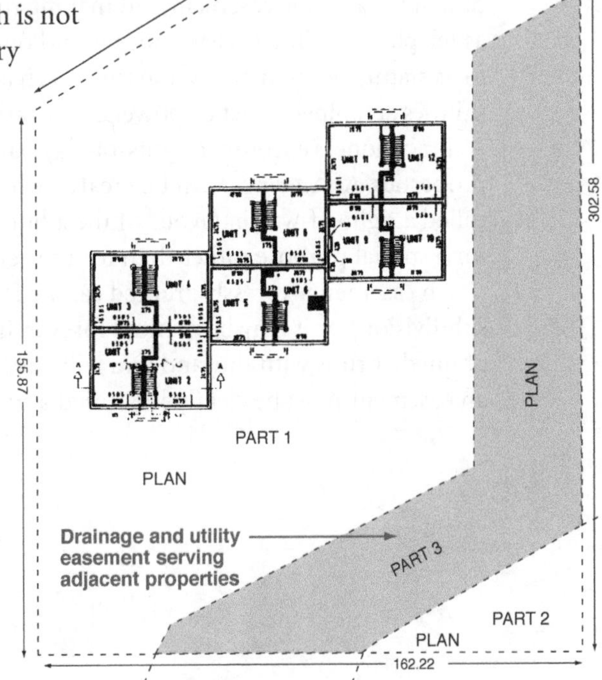

Typical Easements

Real estate practitioners encounter a wide range of easements including a party wall agreement such as in a duplex or semi-detached home, an encroachment agreement; e.g., when one owner has inadvertently built a fence over the adjoining owner's land, a right-of-way for pedestrians or vehicles or a utility agreement granting a utility company the right to place and maintain utility lines, pipes or equipment.

Party wall agreements and rights-of-way warrant further discussion. Registered owners of adjoining parcels of land; e.g., semi-detached houses in which each side has a separate title, may enter into a party wall agreement. The agreement will declare the dividing wall between the dwelling units a party wall and set out the rights, privileges, easements and covenants that exist in respect of the party wall. These will usually be the same for both parties. Therefore, a party wall agreement is similar to a mutual easement. Legal descriptions and characteristics of party walls varies by provincial jurisdiction.

EXAMPLE *Easement—Typical Easements*

Seller Smith wants to list his property with ABC Realty Inc. Upon inspecting the survey supplied to Smith (received by Smith when originally purchasing the property), Salesperson Lee, a representative with ABC Realty Inc., noticed a storm sewer easement cutting diagonally across the rear yard.

The easement, according to the owner's recollection, contains an underground storm sewer that services higher portions of the subdivision in which his home is located and drains into the sewer network in the lower part of town. In this instance, the municipality is the dominant tenement (benefits from the easement) and Smith's property is the servient tenement (subject to the easement).

RIGHT-OF-WAY

The right-of-way is also a frequently encountered form of easement; e.g., the right to pass over the land of another or make use of a designated strip of land. While a right-of-way is seemingly distinct from an easement, in reality, it is only a matter of terminology as both possess the same legal characteristics. A right-of-way is an easement that includes the right to enter upon the lands of the servient tenement (the dominant tenement enjoys the right-of-way over the servient tenement to which the easement applies) for the purpose of maintaining the easement and making repairs as in cases involving public utilities such as telephone, railway, telegraph, gas and oil rights. Often such rights-of-way are referred to as statutory easements if the right is created by the authority of a statute; e.g., a public utilities act, pipeline act or power corporation act.

Practitioners encounter rights-of-way particularly in the listing of rural and recreational properties. An *easement* can be created whenever an owner decides to grant a privilege called a right-of-way in favour of the adjoining property owner. An easement is obtained for a special purpose rather than for the general use and occupation of the land.

An easement expressly granted can be for a limited period (e.g., until completion of a subdivision) or it may be granted forever. In the latter instance, once the right-of-way is granted, it runs with the land and will pass from owner to owner. When listing property, an easement must be clearly identified and described.

Dominant/Servient Tenement CURIOSITY

Dominant Tenement

The estate or interest in land that derives benefit from an easement over a servient tenement, as in a right-of-way.

An easement must confer a benefit on the dominant tenement. As long as the easement properly serves the dominant tenement, the dominant and servient tenements need not be adjoining. The owner of the dominant tenement has no right to enlarge the use for which the easement was granted.

The following diagram illustrates a right-of-way over **Lot 2** (the servient tenement) as an interest attached to **Lot 1** regarding access to the lake.

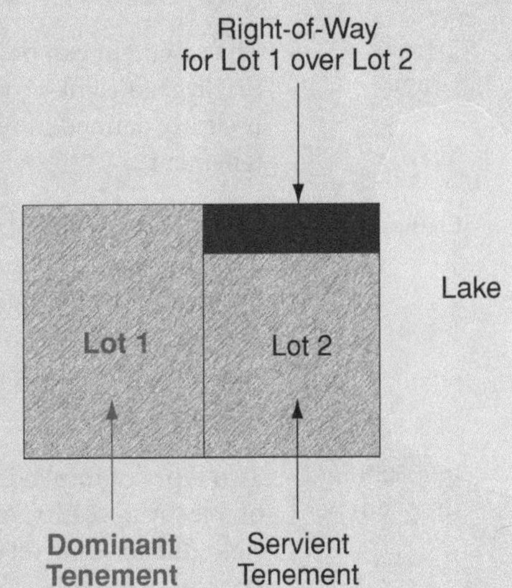

Servient Tenement

Land over which an easement exists in favour of a dominant tenement.

EXAMPLE *Servient Tenement*

Seller Smith owns a cottage on Big Lake. The listing salesperson noted that access to the property was by way of a private easement over an adjacent property owned by Williams. The right-of-way forms part of the title. In this instance, Williams' property is the servient tenement and Smith's property is the dominant tenement. The precise wording for the servient tenement easement follows:

> *Subject to an easement in, over and along the most westerly 40 feet of even width through Lot Number 9 and running southerly from the road allowance between Concession IX and X in the said Township of Anytownship to the waters of Big Lake.*

Creation

Easements can be created by express grant, prescription, implication or statute.

Express Grant	The easement can be created whenever an owner decides to grant a privilege (a right-of-way or easement), in favour of another owner and is clearly defined in registered documents of the dominant and servient tenement.
Prescription	An individual can obtain a right-of-way or easement by adverse possession, also known as *by prescription* or *squatters' rights*, in certain circumstances if the usage of the right-of-way was open and continuous for a specified period of time. The onus of proof is always on the person claiming the right and various legal complexities arise concerning easement by prescription.
Implication (Implied)	Two types of implied grants exist: a right of mutual support and a right-of-way by necessity. As the name suggests, implied is a naturally inferred right due to some related circumstance. With mutual support, a shared docking area with access rights by both owners would naturally preclude the ability of one party to destroy his/her portion of the docking facility to the detriment of the other's structure. In an urban setting, this would also apply in semi-detached units. The second form of implied grant relates to access and rights-of-way that are necessary for the reasonable enjoyment of a property. The essential elements of an implied grant involving access are three-fold: • The owner used the right-of-way as though it was appurtenant to the property. • The use was both apparent and continuous. • The right-of-way was necessary for the reasonable and convenient use of the property.
Statute	Easements created by statute involve groups such as public utilities and telephone companies who gain the right to string wires, install equipment and maintain services by virtue of various provincial statutes. A statutory easement is created by the authority of the statute and does not require a dominant tenement.

Registration

An easement is most commonly registered on title by inserting the appropriate reference in Box 7 of the Transfer/Deed of Land (Form 1). Detailed descriptions can be attached by way of a Schedule (Form 5). A Document General (Form 4) is required to delete an easement from a property.

Salespeople and brokers should be aware that many historical documents produced by a seller may lack precision in regard to an easement. Following is an example relating to an older, recreational deed with a vague wording that lacks a detailed metes and bounds description for the easement:

TOGETHER WITH a right of way in, over and along a certain parcel of land 30 feet in width, being the most westerly 30 feet of road through Lot Number 9 and running southerly from the road allowance between Concession IX and Concession X in the said township of Northside to the waters of Big Lake.

In particular the phrase: **30 feet of road through Lot Number 9 and running southerly** would prove problematic.

This description can cause considerable confusion in the process of listing and selling a property. An easement should be fully described in terms of metes and bounds and clearly identified on a survey. According to Section 23 of the *Registry Act*, any instrument registered after January 1, 1967 describing an easement must provide either a reference plan or an accurate metes and bounds description outlining the extent of such easement. The land registrar reserves the right to waive this requirement under certain circumstances. Following is a detailed easement using metes and bounds:

Together with a right of way unto the grantee, his heirs and assigns, over, along and upon the following described lands:

Commencing at the most southerly angle of the herein described parcel and being distant south 43 degrees 21 minutes east, 1489.7 feet from the north-westerly angle of the said lot 20;

Thence south 10 degrees 46 minutes east, 20.0 feet;

Thence north 79 degrees 14 minutes east, 279.64 feet, more or less, to the westerly limit of a public road leading through the said lot 20;

Thence north 26 degrees 48 minutes west along the last mentioned limit to its intersection with a line drawn on a course of north 79 degrees 14 minutes east from the point of commencement;

Thence south 79 degrees 14 minutes west a distance of 273.51 feet to the point of commencement.

Practitioners should be aware that the Agreement of Purchase and Sale (OREA Form 100) contemplates the existence of easements. Clause 10 states:

Provided that the title to the property is good and free from all registered restrictions, charges, liens and encumbrances except as otherwise specifically provided in this Agreement...

The purchaser agrees to assume encumbrances, such as easements that are described in the agreement. The agreement does, however, provide for the assumption of:

...minor easements for domestic utility or telephone services to the property or adjacent properties and any easements for drainage, storm or sanitary sewers, public utility lines, telephone lines, cable television lines or other services which do not materially affect the present use of the property.

TERMINATION OF EASEMENT	
MERGE An easement is extinguished if the ownership of both dominant and servient tenements merge.	EXAMPLE Seller Smith, a cottage owner, has an easement over his neighbour's vacant piece of land for purposes of accessing a road, without which Smith could only get to his property by boat. Uncomfortable with this situation, Smith approaches the neighbour offering to buy the property to make one large cottage lot. Upon closing the sale, Smith's original easement is extinguished as the properties merge into one parcel of land.
RELEASE The person entitled to the benefit of an easement may release it to the servient tenement by removing the easement from the title.	EXAMPLE Seller Smith has a precisely described easement across a neighbour's property for purposes of accessing a rear lane. With the passage of time, the lane has become unuseable and Smith no longer requires access. Further, neighbour Jones wishes to build a garage on the rear of his property that would obstruct the easement. The neighbours agree to extinguish the easement by signing and registering appropriate documents.
CEASING OF PURPOSE If the purpose of the easement disappears, so does the easement.	EXAMPLE Seller Smith owns a right-of-way to a cottage. The right-of-way subsequently becomes a public thoroughfare and the easement ceases to exist given this change. The easement would also disappear if it is abandoned by an actual intention to abandon (not merely by non-use).

NON-OWNERSHIP INTERESTS

Appurtenance

This form of non-ownership interest is a right that goes with a property. Something that is outside the real property, but belongs to the land, is joined thereto and adds to greater enjoyment of the land.

A right-of-way is one example of an appurtenance that allows access over a property. Most commonly, a right-of-way involves one landowner that has access over another, usually adjacent, property. In the aforementioned illustration contained within the Dominant/Servient Tenement Curiosity, the owner of Lot 1 has been granted a right-of-way over Lot 2 in order to access the lake.

Appurtenance can also apply to other rights that are outside the property but add to greater enjoyment, for example, riparian rights or access to dock facilities in the case of recreational properties.

Encroachment

Encroachment is described as the unauthorized intrusion onto the lands and property by one individual over that of another.

The right to an encroachment by one landowner over an adjoining owner's property is sometimes granted by express written agreement; e.g., when a window sill, eave, deck, porch or chimney extends over a side yard area. This is particularly common in older urban areas where side yards can be particularly narrow. When the overhang is no longer present, the encroachment ceases to exist. No right to substitute an encroachment exists if one is lost, except by further agreement.

EXAMPLE *Encroachment*

Salesperson Lee, when listing Smith's property, is reviewing various documents and notes an apparent encroachment involving one of the accessory buildings. Smith acknowledges that the garage encroaches a few feet on a public right-of-way. However, he adds that the municipal by-law enforcement officer has acknowledged the fact and felt that the municipality would not require its relocation. In any event, a local contractor would do the job for approximately $1,000 if it was necessary.

After some discussion, Lee insisted that a reference to the encroachment be included in the listing. The Remarks section read as follows:

Beautifully maintained and upgraded home only 10 minutes drive from Southville. Note: Single-car garage encroaches on right-of-way. Estimated cost to move: $1,000. Call listing salesperson for further information.

ENCROACHMENT AGREEMENT

This agreement permits the encroachment of an improvement onto an adjoining parcel of land that may be registered against the title of both properties affected by the encroachment.

Under an encroachment agreement, the owner whose land has been encroached upon by the improvement essentially forebears from exercising his/her legal right to require the improvement be removed from the land. Encroachment agreements are often encountered where one owner has inadvertently built a building, fence or driveway over adjoining land.

An encroachment agreement may contain provisions that call for the removal of the offending improvement upon the happening of a future event; e.g., destruction by fire or wind or by a specific time. The market value of the property may be adversely affected to the extent that a risk exists and/or that the offending improvement might have to be removed at a certain time or in the event of partial or full destruction by fire or other cause.

Encumbrance

An encumbrance is an outstanding claim or lien recorded against property or any legal right to the use of the property by another person who is not the owner.

Encumbrances are frequently referred to in relation to mortgages registered against the title to a property. However, the term has a much broader scope including anything that places a burden on property title including a lien, mortgage or other registered interest (e.g., rights-of-way, restrictions and covenants). Preprinted agreements/contracts contain standard wordings (as illustrated) concerning the acquisition of property free of encumbrances except minor encumbrances or those specifically referenced. Exact wordings vary by provincial jurisdiction.

TITLE: Provided that the title to the property is good and free from all registered restrictions, mortgages, liens and encumbrances except as otherwise specifically provided in this agreement...

Lien

A lien is a right of encumbrance affecting any property. Generally, a lien can be either in the form of an agreement between two parties, namely, the party owing the money (lienor) and the party to whom those funds are due (lienee) or by statutory provision as in the case of a tax lien imposed by the Canada Revenue Agency.

In real estate, liens are most commonly associated with statutory provisions to protect and give priority to work performed and materials furnished in constructing, repairing or modifying a structure. Terminology will vary by province; e.g., construction lien, mechanic's lien and builder's lien. Issues regarding purchaser's and vendor's liens in relation to agreements/contracts for real property go beyond the scope of this text.

Mineral Rights

Minerals can be broadly described as including gas, oil, gold, silver and precious metals but not generally deemed to include sand, gravel or stone. Mineral rights include the right to enter or use lands for the purpose of removing such minerals located therein. Typically, such rights involve a range of activities including exploring, drilling, extracting or otherwise removing such materials. Practitioners involved in recreational properties may encounter titles in which mineral rights are sold or reserved by the Crown. Legal advice is required.

MINING LEASES/CROWN LAND LEASES

The Ministry of Natural Resources (MNR), in addition to patenting Crown lands, grants mining leases and crown land leases. In both instances, leases are recorded by a numeric recording system unique to the Ministry. If a legal description is available (as it is for most areas of the province except certain northern regions) the MNR can cross reference the information and locate property by the registry or land titles description.

Mining leases issued after 1940 can be found, as is the case with Crown patents, in the Official Documents Section of the Ministry. All pre-1940 mining documents were registered in the appropriate land registration office as is the case with land leases on Crown land.

Mutual (Shared) Drive

This strip of land is shared by adjoining neighbours and used as a joint driveway by both parties, created by an easement on each property.

Mutual drives are a potential source of confusion or worse, litigation. As a listing salesperson, the best approach involves a clear understanding of the exact location of the mutual drive, any obstructions related thereto and careful inquiry if there have been any difficulties or disputes with the drive. Analysis of errors and omissions claims show that many problems start with simple confusion of material facts and later become major obstacles.

Private Access

Private access is a right of entry most commonly associated with private roads leading to cottage and other types of rural properties. Salespeople should be particularly wary of private rights-of-way or other access arrangements.

Difficulties arise because of vague or non-existent descriptions concerning the extent of such private accesses. Ambiguous, obscure wordings are of particular concern. Further, buyers may be unaware that maintenance and repair obligations normally rest with the user of the private access. Lastly, in some instances, the actual access road may take a different route than that which is described in legal documents. Corrective action may prove costly.

EXAMPLE *Private Access—By Prescription*

Salesperson Martin is concerned that the buyer fully understands the implications of using an unregistered easement for purposes of accessing a listed cottage. The seller has already stated that his family has used the access for the past 40 years with no problems whatsoever. He cannot recall whether or not the easement was registered on title.

The salesperson inserts the following clause in the agreement:

> *The buyer acknowledges that the road to the said property may be an unregistered easement. The seller shall provide to the buyer, on or before completion, a statutory declaration or declarations establishing that the existing road has been used by the seller to gain access to the said property on an uninterrupted basis for the last 40 years.*

Profit A Prendre

Profit a prendre is the right to enter upon a property based on a written agreement and take something from it, such as crops, minerals or timber. This right can, in some instances, pass with title upon the sale of the property.

EXAMPLE *Profit A Prendre*

Owner Smith has entered into a lease arrangement with Jones for 200 acres of farmland that is currently being used for the production of corn. Originally, Smith had planned to harvest the crop, but instead has decided not to pursue farming and returned to his city employment. Jones, already possessing the necessary harvesting equipment, leases the property as of July 20xx for five years. The lease specifically provides that Jones, for an agreed annual rental sum, shall remove the existing crop during the current year and thereafter harvest crops for the remaining four-year period.

Restrictive Covenant

A restrictive covenant is a limitation placed on the use of property contained in the title for that property. More specifically, a restrictive covenant is a contract between two land owners, by which the person obtaining the promise (the covenantee) acquires the right to restrain the covenantor from putting the land to certain specific uses. Such contracts between landowners run with the land and can involve a wide array of limiting conditions regarding a property.

Restrictive covenants have certain characteristics:

- A dominant tenement (benefited land) and a servient tenement (burdened land) must exist.
- The covenant must be negative in nature and represent a burden on the covenantor's land. No positive or affirmative covenant can be imposed on the land, unless by statute.
- The covenant must directly benefit or enhance the value of the covenantee's land.
- Both the covenantee's and covenantor's land must be clearly defined, the agreement between the owners should state that a covenant is being imposed and titles to both benefited and burdened lands must be registered (unless provided otherwise by statute).

- The covenant must be reasonable in nature and not arbitrary or contrary to the public interest.

Historically, restrictive covenants were widely used in residential areas to regulate the uses to which land could be put. Typical restrictive covenants prohibited the use of land for other than residential purposes, limited building on the land to one-family dwellings and required minimum frontage per house.

A prudent buyer who intends to use the lands for a specific purpose would be wise to do some preliminary title investigations and zoning enquiries before completing his/her offer to purchase. This research is particularly important because, if the restriction is being complied with at the time of purchase, it cannot be used as an objection to title unless appropriate provisos are added to the agreement to protect the buyer.

Restrictive covenants are usually created by express promises contained in the grant of the property to the buyer who has previously agreed to accept title subject to these covenants. Restrictive covenants are often found in subdivisions, where all the owners are obliged to conform to various stipulations. These served as the forerunners of municipal by-laws. Real estate practitioners should be aware of all restrictions that affect any subdivision in which they are marketing homes so that they can provide accurate information to buyers.

EXAMPLE *Restrictive Covenant*

Buyer Jones is considering a resale property owned by Seller Smith. Various restrictive covenants were imposed on buyers within this subdivision when the new homes were first marketed. These restrictive covenants run with the land and must be assumed by Jones. The following is a brief list for example purposes:

- Six foot maximum height for fences and only permitted in side and rear yard subject to front yard setback requirements.
- Prohibited use of television antennas.
- All fuel to be supplied by pipeline as opposed to individual fuel tanks.
- No unauthorized removal of trees or other significant vegetation or alterations to drainage.
- Prohibition of clothes lines.
- Property restricted to single-family residence.
- Prohibition against the storage of motor homes, except in enclosed areas.
- No alteration to front elevations of houses or exterior colours on houses, without approval.
- In the case of alterations to vegetation, house elevations and exterior colours on house, such plans must be first approved by the developer or his nominee; such approval not to be unreasonably withheld.

Running with the Land

This covenant extends beyond the original parties to the agreement and binds all subsequent owners to liability concerning the requirement to perform or the right to take advantage of, that covenant.

CASE LAW

Case Synopsis

GORDON S. RIDGELY, APPLICANT LIEF NIELSON, RESPONDENT
ONTARIO SUPERIOR COURT APRIL, 2007

A buyer applied to the Ontario Superior Court for a declaration allowing him to rescind an Agreement of Purchase and Sale and for the return of the deposit of $60,000. The Buyer argued that the Seller has failed to show good title because of a 20 foot wide easement for storm and sanitary sewers. The area affected by the easement represents 26% of the property and an elaborate two-storey gazebo encroaches on the easement.

The Seller quoted the wording of the standard Agreement of Purchase and Sale and argued the requirement that easements "*do not materially affect the present use of the property*" applies only to easements for "*other services*". The court decided that this requirement also applies to easements for storm and sanitary sewers.

The Seller also argued that, while the easement may restrict the future use of the property, the present use is not affected.

The court identified four considerations as relevant in determining materiality of the easement: (1) the location of the easement, (2) the size of the easement, (3) the point of access; and, (4) the owner's enjoyment of the property.

The court also held that "*present use*" with respect to easements is to be interpreted as "*reasonably intended use*". The judge quoted *Dennis v. Hockin* [1993] in which the court considered an easement that bisected the backyard and consumed 20% of the backyard and 10% of the total property. "*All quibbling apart, no one reasonably suggested that a property owner reasonably advised would erect any structure, including a swimming pool, in the backyard. It is beyond question that the easement significantly compromises the use that the purchaser could make of the backyard.*" The judge concluded in that case that the easement was "*major*" and the buyer was entitled to rescind.

The court held that the easement significantly compromises the owner's present use of the property. The Buyer's application to rescind the agreement was granted and the deposit was ordered returned to the Buyer.

Case Questions

1. How large must an easement be for the salesperson to be concerned?	2. What steps should a salesperson take to avoid such a loss of a sale?

CASE LAW

Case Synopsis

COUNTRY STYLE FOOD SERVICES INC. V. 1304271 ONTARIO LTD
SUPERIOR COURT OF JUSTICE COURT FILE # 01-CV-219404CM2

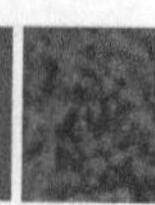

During 1998, two individuals entered into agreements with a franchisor to acquire a retail fast food franchise. The $300,000 franchise included licensing rights, the purchase of necessary equipment and the completion of required leasehold improvements.

The franchisor then entered into a head lease with the landlord who, in turn, constructed a free-standing restaurant with a drive-thru facility. The site was located within a new shopping centre being developed subject to a site plan. The site plan included the fast-food operation, another free-standing establishment and a proposed L-shaped building. The site plan was set out in the head lease with appropriate cross-reference to the franchisee's sublease. The franchisee carefully reviewed the site plan and associated documents prior to signing the sublease as parking facilities, internal road layout and accessibility were critical to the business venture.

The fast food franchise opened in 1998. Approximately one year later, the landlord began developing the balance of the mall in line with a revised site plan that materially altered the plaza configuration. The amended plan directly impacted automobile traffic flow and accessibility to the fast food operation. Interestingly, as evidence would prove, the landlord was underway with revised plans when the head lease (along with the original site plan attached) was signed by the franchisor.

The franchisee and franchisor took immediate action claiming that the new site plan was a breach of the agreement. While some minor changes were made, the overall negative impact on the franchisee was significant and seemingly irreversible. Further, the franchisor appeared to do little to assist the franchisee in the dispute. Ultimately, the franchisor took over the operation when the franchisee vacated. The franchisor obtained judgement against the franchisee for default, but a stay of execution was granted as the franchisee took legal action for damages against both the franchisor and landlord.

Based on evidence presented, the Court found that:

- The landlord owed a duty of care to the franchisee, as the franchisee was reliant on representations made regarding the site.
- The landlord should have realized that the franchisee would reasonably rely on its representations.
- The landlord, by attaching the initial site plan while simultaneously planning proposed changes, acted in a negligent manner.
- The franchisor, while initially supportive of the franchisee, gradually appeared to side with the landlord and, in effect, left the franchisee to its own resources.

Detailed evidence confirmed that the site changes adversely affected the franchisee's sales volumes and the business viability. The Court awarded the franchisee $400,000 in damages.

Case Questions

1. In this instance, the Court found that the landlord had negligently misrepresented facts to the franchisee. What is the difference between fraudulent and negligent misrepresentation?

2. What evidence supported the franchisee's claim that the landlord made a negligent misrepresentation?

CHAPTER DISCUSSION

1. LEASEHOLDS

Under common law, the creation of a lease imposes various duties on the parties involved. Briefly describe the main duties of both Landlord and Tenant.

Landlords Duties

Tenants Duties

2. A STUDY OF HISTORY

A study of the history of landlord and tenant relations provides an interesting insight into the way law changes over time in society. Provide at least three examples from Ontario statutes to show how the law relating to tenancy has changed dramatically to reflect the needs of modern society.

CHAPTER DISCUSSION

3. ELEMENTS OF A LEASE

Briefly describe the main basic elements for a lease to be enforceable.

4. DEROGATION FROM THE GRANT

Using a specific example, explain the meaning of the term "*derogation from the grant*".

CHAPTER DISCUSSION

5. OTHER INTERESTS IN PROPERTY

You are listing an older two-storey home in an established part of the city. The seller mentions the property has a "*mutual drive*".

a. What two provisions with reference to the mutual drive would you expect to find in the deed to this property?

b. As listing salesperson what steps would you take in the marketing of this property as a result of your knowledge of the mutual drive?

CHAPTER DISCUSSION

6. CHARACTERISTICS OF AN EASEMENT

List the major characteristics required for the creation of an easement.

7. RESTRICTIVE COVENANTS

With the introduction of zoning by-laws in the twentieth century, does this make the concept of a restrictive covenant obsolete? Explain.

CHAPTER DISCUSSION

8. ENCROACHMENT

A few days ago you placed a sold sign on one of your listings. Today you received a call from the seller's lawyer who informs you that the seller's detached garage is an encroachment on the neighbour's property. For a property in the Registry system, what does this mean and how can it affect the transaction?

9. FIXTURES AND CHATTELS

Many items do not readily fall into the category of either chattels or fixtures. Build a list of items that may cause problems or result in disputes either before or after an Agreement of Purchase and Sale is arranged.

KNOWLEDGE INTEGRATION

Notables

- A commercial lease is best described as any lease involving a property that is principally used for business activity.
- Practitioners need to be aware of important exclusions under the *Residential Tenancies Act* to more accurately differentiate between commercial and residential tenancies.
- A lease is described as a grant of an interest in land that can be written or verbal, express or implied by a person's conduct.
- Commercial tenancies are regulated under the *Commercial Tenancies Act*, but many requirements flow from legal precedents established over many years.
- A lease should be clearly differentiated from an agreement to lease. An agreement to lease is technically referred to as an agreement for lease without settled form of lease.
- An easement is a right enjoyed by one tenement over another.
- A right-of-way is a frequently encountered form of easement.
- Other non-ownership interests include encroachments, encumbrances, liens, mineral rights, restrictive covenants and profit a prendre. Each creates a unique right onto the lands and property by one individual over that of another.

Web Links

Web links are included for general interest regarding selected chapter topics.

Residential Tenancies Act	Go to ***www.e-laws.gov.on.ca*** for information concerning residential tenancy issues.
Landlord & Tenant Board	Go to ***www.ltb.gov.on.ca*** for information concerning Landlord/Tenant Applications, Rules of Practice and Interpretation Guidelines.

Chapter Mini-Review

Solutions are located in the Appendix.

1. Living accommodation intended for the travelling or vacationing public is regulated by the *Residential Tenancies Act.*

   ○ True ○ False

2. A lease must include a description of the legal purpose for which the premise is to be used.

   ○ True ○ False

3. An agreement to lease sets out material matters regarding a proposed tenancy arrangement, which can then be included in a formal lease document.

   ○ True ○ False

4. The term *dark space* refers to a situation in which a commercial tenant moves out of a rented premise while still paying the rent.

   ○ True ○ False

Chapter Mini-Review (continued)

5. A license to occupy a space, such as a concession in a retail shopping centre, is legally considered to be a contractual arrangement that involves the conveyance of an estate in land.

   ○ True ○ False

6. A restrictive use clause within a commercial lease can be used to ensure a proper mix of tenants within a shopping centre, but cannot be used when leasing other retail establishments.

   ○ True ○ False

7. An easement, once granted, attaches to the land and binds subsequent owners.

   ○ True ○ False

8. A restrictive covenant might involve a prohibition on the use of clothes lines and satellite dishes within a particular subdivision.

   ○ True ○ False

Active Learning Exercises

Solutions are located in the Appendix.

Exercise 1

You are asked to help in drafting an Offer to Lease that will permit the tenant to operate a restaurant with a liquor licence. The landlord will not permit any video games or live entertainment. The tenant wants to be certain there are no other similar operations in the plaza that will be in competition. Draft an appropriate clause you could insert into such an Offer.

Exercise 2

"A commercial tenant can remove trade fixtures at the end of the lease term." What are trade fixtures? Give several examples.

Exercise 3

Terry Tenant rents office space from Investor McKay on a five-year lease that ends December 31, 2010. There are no special clauses in the lease and the rent is $500 per month.

a. On June 30, 2007, Terry Tenant vacates. McKay advises that Tenant will be responsible for the remainder of the lease. However, on November 15, 2007, the same space is leased to Mary Newcombe. How much can McKay claim from Tenant by way of damages?

b. The facts are the same as in a) except that the tenant told the landlord that he could no longer pay the rent but had arranged for Jane Connors to take over the lease. McKay refused to permit this and then rented to Mary Newcombe. Discuss any difference this would make to the landlord's claim for damages.

Exercise 4

Peter owns Blackacre. Linda, the owner of Whiteacre, uses part of Blackacre for access in accordance with a registered easement.

a. Which is the dominant tenement?

b. What happens if Linda buys Blackacre?

c. Under what other circumstances could the easement cease to exist?

Exercise 5

Your neighbour agrees to give you an easement over her land so that you can have access to your rear yard. The easement is to be on a strip of land four feet by eighty feet. You want to be certain she does not change her mind. What will the agreement between you and your neighbour have to include?

Exercise 6

You own the lots on both sides of your large home with its manicured lawn, award-winning gardens, designer pool and sparkling pond. You decide to sell one lot but you want to be certain that the buyer does not do anything that would reduce the value of your property or make it difficult for you to sell the other lot.

a. How would you accomplish this?

b. List the topics about which you might have concerns.

Exercise 7

You are about to prepare an offer on Lot 10, Registered Plan 190 (Registry System). Carefully examine the information in the sketch below and explain any concerns you will have to deal with when drafting the offer.

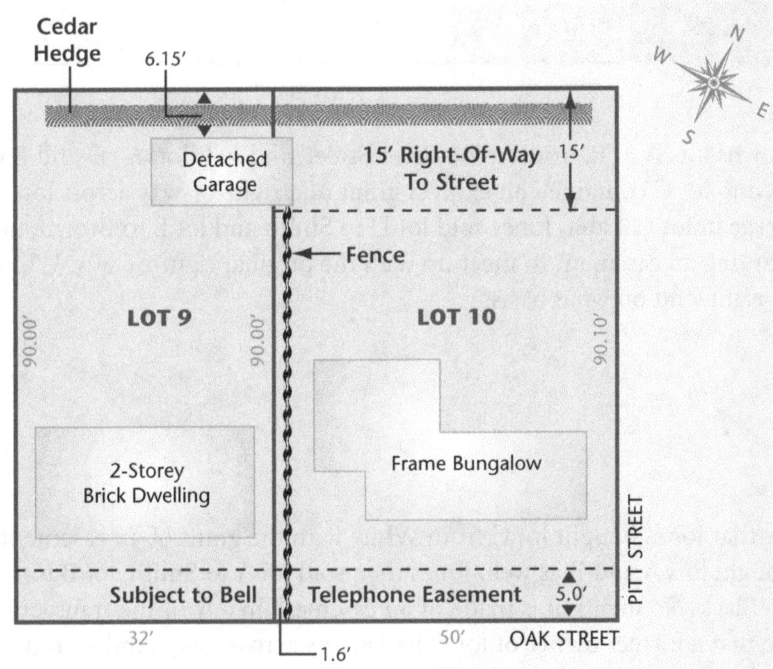

Exercise 8

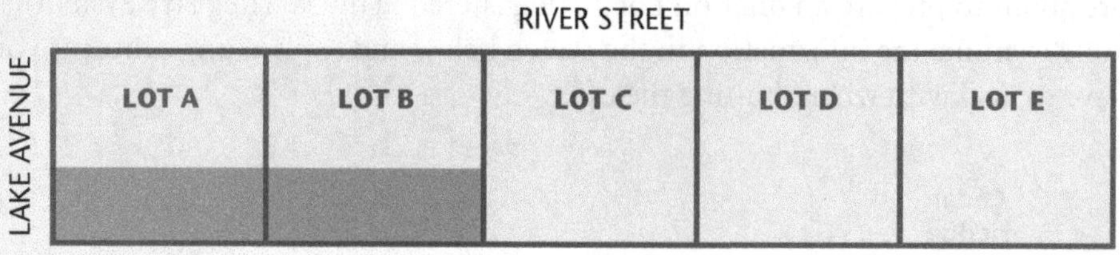

LAKE AVENUE	RIVER STREET				
	LOT A	LOT B	LOT C	LOT D	LOT E

a. White owns lots A to E, fronting on River Street, and sells lots C, D and E to Jones. The deed to lot C contained an express grant of a right-of-way across lots A and B to a garage in lot C. Later, Jones sold lot D to Smith and lot E to Brown, in each case granting an easement to meet up with the original right-of-way. White objects. Who is right, and on what basis?

b. Assume that Jones bought lot C from White with the grant of an easement, but later bought lots A and B as well. Jones then sold lot A to Smith, lot B to Brown and lot C to Black. No mention is made of an easement in any of the transactions. Black is aware that a former owner of lot C had access across lots A and B, and claims the same right. What results from this? Would your answer be different if the lots did not front on any street and Black had no other access for lot C? Explain.

c. Assume that when lot C first acquired an easement across lots A and B, River Street did not exist. Later, River Street opened, but because of traffic direction, Jones found it more convenient to use the old driveway off Lake Avenue. White put up a fence, preventing Jones from using it. What are Jones' rights, assuming the fence was erected before River Street opened?

d. What are Jones' rights if the fence was erected after River Street opened?

CHAPTER 3

The Recording Acts

Introduction

Land registration systems provide for the orderly ownership of land in Ontario. Real estate practitioners require knowledge of the registration process and the types of documents involved. Land registration in Ontario involves both the Registry and Land Titles system. Currently, the province is undergoing significant changes from paper-based to electronic systems. A long range province-wide conversion from Registry to Land Titles is underway. Also, initiatives involving Teranet and Polaris make automated electronic title information accessible from computer terminals throughout the province. A real estate salesperson should also be familiar with closing procedures after the agreement has been negotiated, including the role of the lawyers for the parties and the adjustments and disbursements involved.

In Ontario, all land is registered either under the *Registry Act* or the *Land Titles Act.* Under the registry system, claims are registered in the form of instruments or documents and in chronological order, which establishes priority. The Registrar takes no responsibility for the truth or legality of the statements contained in any of the documents registered. The *Land Titles Act* is drastically different in that it operates on the principle that the Land Titles Register is the source of information for buyers and that the government is prepared to guarantee the interests as set out in the register.

Learning Outcomes

At the conclusion of this chapter, students will be able to:

- Discuss how ownership of land in Ontario can be acquired in various ways with specific reference to grants, quit claim deeds and agreements for sale.
- Briefly summarize the basic operation of the registry system, which is currently being phased out in the Province of Ontario.
- Outline the main features of Land Titles including the operation of the Land Titles Assurance Fund.
- Describe major changes that came about with the *Land Registration Reform Act* with particular emphasis on standardized forms.
- Discuss how land is described for legal purposes and then used for registration.
- Identify the types of title insurance policies offered, the range of coverages provided and title insurance benefits from a listing and selling perspective.
- Detail closing procedures from the purchaser's perspective involving a residential property, including title and non-title searches, requisitions and closing.
- Discuss closing procedures from the seller's perspective involving a residential property, including responses to requisitions, closing and the closing statement.
- Discuss how electronic closing procedures are now replacing traditional closing methods.
- Apply concepts involving title registration to typical situations encountered by real estate practitioners.

LAND OWNERSHIP

Ownership of land in Ontario can be acquired in a number of ways, including:

- Inheritance.
- Deed.
- Agreement for sale.
- Mortgage remedy.
- Court order.
- Possession.

When conveying title, the seller's solicitor is involved in the preparation of the necessary documents to convey title and will respond to requisitions from the buyer's solicitor. The buyer's solicitor, on the other hand, is primarily involved in a title search and preparation of documents such as the Land Transfer Tax affidavit, directions as to title, new mortgages, etc.

Whether the property is registered in the Registry or the Land Titles system, the buyer's solicitor will likely recommend that the buyer obtain title insurance.

With respect to adjustments and disbursements, real estate salespersons are required to make sure that all parties to a real estate transaction are made aware of their financial obligations and commitments.

Grant

For real estate purposes, grant is a legal term used in deeds of conveyance to indicate a transfer of an interest or estate in real property by the grantor to the grantee.

Methods used to transfer land have developed over hundreds of years. By the middle of the 19th century, a comparatively uniform method had evolved in the use of a grant. The grant contained a description of the grantor, the grantee and the interest being transferred, and was signed and sealed by the grantor before a witness. Since the document was under seal, it was often called a *deed of conveyance*, frequently shortened to deed.

The most common way of disposing of interests in land is by transfers between living persons, such as the voluntary grant in the performance of a contract for the sale of land. Another way includes the compulsory transfer of land known as expropriation. A transfer of an interest in land can have two results. If the transfer is of the whole interest, then the interest remains unaltered but it is in the hands of another person. If the transfer is of only part of the interest, the interest is divided into two parts with two holders—the grantee with the interest he/she has obtained under the grant, and the grantor with the interest he/she has retained as it was not transferred by the grant.

The equivalent of a grant or deed under the land titles system is a transfer and is effective without being made under seal. The term *grant* also refers to the allocation of rights, powers or monies by the Crown or other authority to particular persons or for particular purposes.

Quit Claim Deed

The Quit Claim Deed is a legal document wherein a person agrees to release any right that he/she may possess in a parcel of land. In the case of a mortgagor, the release involves the equity of redemption.

A quit claim deed can be an expedient process when mortgagee and mortgagor arrive at the conclusion that no practical way exists by which the mortgagor can keep the property.

This approach is typically quick, inexpensive and pragmatic in the resolution of an otherwise awkward situation. A quit claim deed does not involve either covenants or undertakings and is a simple relinquishing of whatever rights or interests are vested in the mortgagor. If equity exists, the mortgagor could potentially bargain with the mortgagee for a payment to satisfy equity in return for giving the quit claim deed.

A quit claim deed is most easily effected if no other encumbrances exist on title, otherwise action may be taken to remove such interests in the property through other remedies or the mortgagee may elect to assume these encumbrances. Even in the absence of any equity, this approach may prove best given time and cost considerations. However, the mortgagee, in accepting a quit claim deed, not only acquires rights concerning the property but also any problems associated with it and has no further recourse against the mortgagor.

Agreement for Sale — PERSPECTIVE

An agreement for the purchase of real property wherein the seller retains title to the property while permitting the buyer to occupy the premises without becoming the owner. Title is not conveyed until some future stipulated date or until some future event occurs:

- When payment for the property is made in full.
- When sufficient payments are made to pay the difference between the price and the existing mortgage.
- When the buyer has built up sufficient downpayment and the seller feels comfortable in taking back a mortgage on the property.

Until one of these occurrences takes place, the buyer is said to have a contractual interest in the property. If payment default occurs, the buyer immediately relinquishes any right to the property. The seller has no need to foreclose as title still rests with that individual.

In most provincial jurisdictions, no standard form exists for an agreement for sale to be used by real estate practitioners, but forms are provided by legal publishers. An agreement for sale is infrequently used but could be viewed as a financing alternative for a buyer with limited downpayment when the seller is seeking the best possible security. This agreement should be clearly differentiated from the preprinted agreement/contract that is commonly used in the transacting of real estate. In such agreements, title passes on the payment of the purchase price.

The agreement for sale can be used in various circumstances: where existing mortgages cannot be discharged for a specified period, when the deposit is small or where it is impractical to have a sale with a mortgage back to the seller.

EXAMPLE *Agreement for Sale*

Buyer Jones agrees to pay $3,000 downpayment with 12 installment payments of $3,000 and takes possession of the property. Upon receipt of the full $39,000, Seller Smith takes back the balance of the purchase price as a seller-take-back mortgage. Once Jones has made all payments in full, he will get the normal transfer/deed. If Jones defaults in payment prior to receiving the full sum of $39,000, Seller Smith can terminate the agreement and proceed with eviction, unless a court orders the reinstatement of the agreement.

REGISTRY

The registry system is the older of the two land registration systems in Ontario. The first *Registry Act* was passed in 1795 to give evidence of interests that exist with respect to a particular plot of land and to establish priority of those interests. This Act, as with the *Land Titles Act*, promotes prompt and accurate registration to clearly indicate what interests are claimed in the land, thus facilitating the orderly sale of real property.

Under the *Registry Act*, the registry system records title documents on a geographic basis. A separate record is kept in an abstract book for each lot or part of a lot of land as originally patented by the Crown or as appears on any registered plan of subdivision or other type of registered plan. Given the growing complexity of real estate interests, this indexing system has grown to include a wide range of abstract books involving condominiums, subdivision plans, leaseholds, wills, probates, highways and sundry lots. Given inherent weaknesses and complexities in the registry system, property records throughout Ontario are being converted to land titles.

Land Titles Conversion Project FOCUS

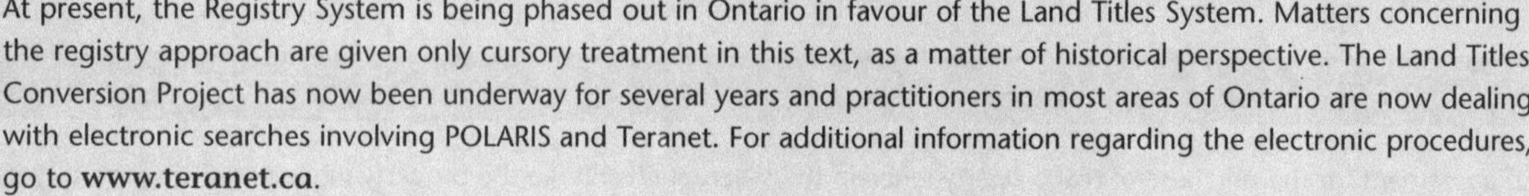

At present, the Registry System is being phased out in Ontario in favour of the Land Titles System. Matters concerning the registry approach are given only cursory treatment in this text, as a matter of historical perspective. The Land Titles Conversion Project has now been underway for several years and practitioners in most areas of Ontario are now dealing with electronic searches involving POLARIS and Teranet. For additional information regarding the electronic procedures, go to **www.teranet.ca**.

Abstract

Abstract is a written history of the title, but not assurance of good title, to a parcel of real estate as recorded in a land registry or land titles office. Abstracts (abstract pages) include a condensed history of the title to individual parcels of land and include a synopsis of all recorded instruments affecting the title; e.g., deeds/transfers of land, mortgages, discharges of mortgages, encumbrances, easements and restrictive covenants. Abstract pages have undergone modifications in format, information required and method of recording within provincial jurisdictions utilizing the registry system.

Abstract Book

An abstract book is a central reference source within a registry system. Historically, these books (also referred to as *abstract indexes*) began as a compilation of patented lots in numeric order by lot and concession, but ultimately expanded to include a variety of books including subdivisions and condominiums. Individual ownership was detailed by way of abstract pages within a wide range of abstract books. The terms *abstract* and *abstract book* are most commonly associated with the registry system (as opposed to terms such as *parcel registers* found in land titles). During the past decade, cumbersome abstract books and associated manual recording systems have given way to computerized record keeping.

Adverse Possession

Adverse possession arises When an individual, not the owner, takes possession of the property, hostile to, and without the consent of the owner and remains in exclusive possession using the land like an owner and ignoring the claims of other persons including the owner. It is possible, by adverse possession, for an occupier of land to extinguish the title of the owner. The possessor then becomes, in effect, the owner of the land.

Title by adverse possession began in medieval times, given the number of large estates and the fact that absentee landowners and squatters often entered and stayed on those lands for long periods. With the introduction of more accurate surveys, the number of squatters has become smaller. Under common law, a person can acquire possessory title

to lands under certain circumstances by taking possession of the lands for a period of time as set out in the applicable provincial law of limitations. The possession must be open, exclusive and continuous for a period, without the consent of the owner, but with the owner's knowledge. Adverse possession ceases to be effective if interrupted by the owner before the limitation period has elapsed, or if the adverse possessor abandons the land before the limitation period has expired, as the law considers that possession has returned to the owner.

EXAMPLE *Adverse Possession*

Buyer Jones acquires a one acre rural lot in Ontario based on measurements and a survey provided by Seller Smith. Without precisely measuring the property, both parties assume that the lot includes a small laneway on the westerly edge of the lot. The abutting neighbour, next to the laneway, is also under the same impression and consequently no formal consent is required as everyone assumes that Smith owns the property in question. In fact, the laneway is not owned by Smith, but by the neighbour. A few days following closing, Jones erects a fence between the lane and the neighbour. Under common law, the lands in question might be acquired by Jones through adverse possession if such possession was open, exclusive and continuous for a time period as set out in provincial legislation, without the consent of the owner but with the owner's knowledge.

Practitioners must exercise caution in all matters regarding adverse possession. As background, possessory title in Ontario is only granted under the *Registry Act.* No title by adverse possession can occur under land titles. In Ontario, for those areas under the registry system, statutes set out limitation periods beyond which an owner loses the right to regain possession of his/her land. That period, as set out in the *Limitations Act* is ten years.

The principle behind the law of limitations is that a person who has a right of action against another must pursue it within a time period or lose the right. He/she must not keep the other party in indefinite jeopardy of being sued.

Expert legal advice is strongly recommended regarding such matters.

Chain of Title

A chain of title is a sequence of conveyances and encumbrances affecting a title pursuant to the applicable property legislation within provincial jurisdictions. The term *chain of title* is most commonly associated with land registry. Practitioners may refer to the history of a property for a 40-year period (the typical statutory requirement) but chain of title actually extends to the Crown Patent.

LAND TITLES

The first *Land Titles Act* in Ontario was passed in 1885. With limited exceptions, all provincial crown patents must now be registered under the Act. In addition, all land to be subdivided by a registered plan of subdivision and all land on which condominiums are developed under the *Condominium Act* must be registered under the *Land Titles Act,* if that system of land registration is available in the applicable land registration office.

Land registered under the *Registry Act* may be brought under land titles by the owner through a process called first application. The large-scale conversion of registry records into land titles has been underway within the province for several years. The land titles conversion project involves the conversion of registry records into land titles coincident with the move to electronic registration systems.

Practitioners increasingly rely on land titles searches as the land titles conversion project extends beyond larger urban centres. While registry operates under a tract indexing system using geographic location, all land titles entries are by way of assigned parcel numbers. A separate parcel record is kept in a register of title for each unit of ownership. The actual title searching process involves identifying outstanding entries on the most recent parcel register for a specific property.

Features/Principles

The primary features of the land titles system are:

- A method of government registration of title to land in which the government, subject to certain limitations, guarantees the title and operates the registration process.
- All transactions must be registered against the title in the provincially-operated land titles office and are not valid in the form of mere instruments executed by parties as against other competing registered interests.
- The certificate of title is intended to be a complete and accurate reflection of the result of all preceding transactions affecting the property. Persons dealing with a registered property do not need to look elsewhere, except to search a few statutory exceptions to indefeasibility (that which cannot be annulled or terminated).
- An assurance fund is provided that is intended to provide compensation to those persons who suffer loss due to errors or omissions of the registrar in the operation of the system.
- No title to land registered under the Act that is adverse to the title of the registered owner can be acquired by any length of possession or prescription.
- Each parcel of land is recorded in the register at the land titles office as a unit of property. The land is surveyed and accurate boundaries in parceled descriptions are available that facilitate the recording of land dispositions.
- A land titles office is officially referred to as: The Land Registry Office for the Land Titles Division of the Regional Municipality [or county] of [name]. Each land titles division is overseen by a land registrar.
- The Act provides that documents are effective on registration and that priority of registration prevails. The parcel register page is abstracted and, therefore, examining the actual registered documents is usually necessary to gain proper perspective on the extent of ownership.
- The land registrar is empowered to make rulings as to the sufficiency of documents, subject to certain avenues of appeal.
- Detailed, uniform procedures must be followed in the preparation of all documents, either manually or electronically, for registration under land titles.

The land titles system operates in accordance with three principles:

THE MIRROR PRINCIPLE	THE CURTAIN PRINCIPLE	THE INSURANCE PRINCIPLE
The register of title is a mirror that accurately and completely reflects, beyond all argument, the current facts that are material to a person's title.	The register is the sole source of information for proposed buyers, who need not and indeed must not, concern themselves with trusts and equities that lie behind this curtain of information.	The mirror (register) is deemed to give the absolute correct reflection of title, but if through human error a flaw appears, anyone who suffers loss must be put in the same position, so far as money can do, that he would have been in had the reflection been a true one.

Land Titles Act

The *Land Titles Act* is divided into parts as illustrated.

THE LAND TITLES ACT	
PART I	Preliminary (Definitions)
PART II	Organization and Administration
PART III	Jurisdiction of the Court
PART IV	Application for First Registration
PART V	Assurance Fund
Part VI	Part Owners
Part VII	Subsequent Registrations
Part VIII	Descriptions of Land and Registered Plans
Part IX	Fraud
Part X	Rectification of the Register
Part XI	Regulations and Procedure

Land Titles Assurance Fund

The land titles assurance fund, established under Part V of the *Land Titles Act*, provides that persons deprived of ownership through selected errors or fraud are entitled to compensation, provided such compensation cannot be obtained from other sources. (More specifically, the fund is designed to provide financial compensation for persons wrongfully deprived of land or some interest therein, due to the land being brought under this Act or by reason of some other person being registered as owner through fraud or, by reason of any misdescription, omission or other error in a certificate of ownership or charge, or in an entry on the register.) The compensation is subject to various qualifications.

The person claiming to be entitled to payment for compensation must apply to the Director of Titles. The amount of compensation will be determined by the Director of Titles, subject to certain rights by the claimant.

EXAMPLE *Land Titles Assurance Fund*

Owner Smith owns a dilapidated home in the village of Westend and has not occupied the property for a considerable period of time. Unknown to Smith, Jones forges various documents and successfully has the property registered in his own name. Following the forgery, he sells the property to an innocent buyer for fair market value.

The new owner tears down the dilapidated house and builds a new, modern two-storey home on the property. Smith ultimately uncovers the situation and legally pursues both Jones and the new owner. The new owner may have no involvement as the property was acquired in good faith at fair market value. Further, if Jones turns out to have no money or has disappeared in the process, Smith would then look to the land titles assurance fund for settlement. Smith has lost an interest in land, cannot recover that interest and has suffered loss as a consequence of fraud. An owner's success in dealing with the assurance fund would depend on specific circumstances.

LAND REGISTRATION REFORM ACT

This Act, consisting of three Parts, came into force on April 1, 1985, and was instrumental in the introduction of standardized records while paving the way for electronic registration. Part I of the *Land Registration Reform Act* (LRRA) is devoted primarily to the implementation of standard registration documents for both registry and land titles:

- Transfer/Deed of Land (Form 1);
- Charge/Mortgage of Land (Form 2);
- Discharge of Charge/Mortgage (Form 3);
- Document General (Form 4); and
- Schedule (Form 5).

Part II authorizes the automation of records and property mapping, including the storage and retrieval of such documentation.

Part III outlines procedures for electronic registration including the use of electronic formats. Part III also sets the stage for various regulations relating to the conversion of land registration records to an automated format. The Regulations provide detailed requirements concerning direct electronic transmissions to the land registration office and requirements regarding the content of electronic documents. Currently, the conversion of all land registry records is taking place and will ultimately include electronic access, retrieval and registration services throughout the province.

Transfer/Deed Of Land (Form 1)

A standard form, also referred to as Form 1, used to register a deed under either the registry or the land titles system. Standardized forms were introduced during the mid-1980s under the *Land Registration Reform Act* with a particular view to create uniformity in registry records. Prior to that time, various document formats were utilized. The Transfer/Deed of Land is normally registered along with the Land Transfer Tax Affidavit.

Practitioners will encounter the Deed/Transfer of Land when reviewing instruments concerning the title to property. This form is used to convey title or an interest in real property and includes the full names of both sellers (transferors) and buyers (transferees) along with birth dates. Any other person who has an interest in the estate being conveyed would also join in the document; e.g., third parties such as a life tenant, a spouse releasing matrimonial home possessory rights and heirs or beneficiaries of an estate.

Transfer/Deed of Land

Source: Dye & Durham Co. Inc.

DYE & DURHAM CO. INC.—Form No. 970
Amended NOV. 1992

Province of Ontario

Transfer/Deed of Land

Form 1 — Land Registration Reform Act

A

FOR OFFICE USE ONLY

New Property Identifiers — Additional: See Schedule ☐

Executions — Additional: See Schedule ☐

(1) Registry ☐ Land Titles ☐

(2) Page 1 of pages

(3) Property Identifier(s) Block Property — Additional: See Schedule ☐

(4) Consideration — Dollars $

(5) Description — This is a: Property Division ☐ Property Consolidation ☐

(6) This Document Contains — (a) Redescription New Easement Plan/Sketch ☐ (b) Schedule for: Description ☐ Additional Parties ☐ Other ☐

(7) Interest/Estate Transferred — Fee Simple

(8) Transferor(s) The transferor hereby transfers the land to the transferee and certifies that the transferor is at least eighteen years old and that

Name(s)	Signature(s)	Date of Signature Y	M	D

(9) Spouse(s) of Transferor(s) I hereby consent to this transaction

Name(s)	Signature(s)	Date of Signature Y	M	D

(10) Transferor(s) Address for Service

(11) Transferee(s)

Transferee(s)	Date of Birth Y	M	D

(12) Transferee(s) Address for Service

Planning Act — OPTIONAL

(13) Transferor(s) The transferor verifies that to the best of the transferor's knowledge and belief, this transfer does not contravene section 50 of the Planning Act.

Signature. . . . . Date of Signature Y M D — Signature. . . . . Date of Signature Y M D

Solicitor for Transferor(s) I have explained the effect of section 50 of the Planning Act to the transferor and I have made inquiries of the transferor to determine that this transfer does not contravene that section and based on the information supplied by the transferor, to the best of my knowledge and belief, this transfer does not contravene that section. I am an Ontario solicitor in good standing.

Name and Address of Solicitor — Signature. . . . . Date of Signature Y M D

Affix Statement by Solicitor for Transferee(s) here if necessary

(14) Solicitor for Transferee(s) I have investigated the title to this land and to abutting land where relevant and I am satisfied that the title records reveal no contravention as set out in subclause 50 (22) (c) (ii) of the Planning Act and that to the best of my knowledge and belief this transfer does not contravene section 50 of the Planning Act. I act independently of the solicitor for the transferor(s) and I am an Ontario solicitor in good standing.

Name and Address of Solicitor — Signature. . . . . Date of Signature Y M D

(15) Assessment Roll Number of Property

Cty.	Mun.	Map	Sub.	Par.

(16) Municipal Address of Property

(17) Document Prepared by:

FOR OFFICE USE ONLY

Fees and Tax	
Registration Fee	
Land Transfer Tax	
Total	

Electronic Transfer/Deed of Land

Source: Teranet

****** NOT VALID - TO BE USED FOR TRAINING PURPOSES ONLY ******

The applicant(s) hereby applies to the Land Registrar. yyyy mm dd
LRO # 20 **Transfer** **Receipted as HH198** on 2006 06 16 at 10:15

Properties

PIN 07014 - 0500 LT *Interest/Estate* Fee Simple
Description LT 48 , PL 1361 ; HAMILTON
Address 05000 IDLEWOOD CR
HAMILTON

Consideration

Consideration $ 259,000.00

Transferor(s)

The transferor(s) hereby transfers the land to the transferee(s).

Name JONES, MARIANN JOYCE
Address for Service 123 Main St.
Toronto, Ont
M7T 5R4

I am at least 18 years of age.

JONES, JOHN WILLIAM and I are spouses of one another and are both parties to this document

This document is not authorized under Power of Attorney by this party.

Name JONES, JOHN WILLIAM
Address for Service 123 Main St.
Toronto, Ont
M7T 5R4

I am at least 18 years of age.

JONES, MARIANN JOYCE and I are spouses of one another and are both parties to this document

This document is not authorized under Power of Attorney by this party.

Transferee(s) *Capacity* *Share*

Name SMITH, JOHN FRANKLIN Joint Tenants
Date of Birth 1969 06 04
Address for Service 05000 IDLEWOOD CR
HAMILTON, ON
L8N 5R4

Name SMITH, ELEANOR JOYCE Joint Tenants
Date of Birth 1978 08 07
Address for Service 05000 IDLEWOOD CR
HAMILTON, ON
L8N 5R4

Signed By

Paul P. Lawyer(TCD) acting for Transferor(s) Signed 2006 06 16

Tel
Fax

Paul P. Lawyer(TCD) acting for Transferee(s) Signed 2006 06 16

Tel
Fax

Submitted By

TRAINING COMPANY D 2006 06 16

Tel
Fax

Fees/Taxes/Payment

Statutory Registration Fee $60.00
Land Transfer Tax $2,360.00
Total Paid $2,420.00

IMPLIED COVENANTS

Section 5 of the *Land Registration Reform Act* sets out the implied covenants for a transfer of freehold or leasehold land by the transferor. Additional covenants apply to release by a trustee or a settlor. Only freehold covenants are included below:

- The seller's (transferor's) right to convey the land and the buyer's (transferee's) right to quiet enjoyment.
- The assurances that both seller and buyer will execute such further assurances and do such other acts as may be reasonably required.
- The assurance that the seller has not done, omitted or permitted anything whereby the land is, or could be, encumbered (other than as per the land registration records).
- The seller transfers to the buyer all existing claims that he/she has upon the land except as noted in the land registration records.

Implied covenants can be changed through an amending schedule or by setting out an appropriately amended covenant. When the deed or transfer is submitted for registration and accepted by the land registrar, the transaction is said to be closed or completed. Ownership normally changes at that time and typically possession and payment occur simultaneously, unless otherwise provided in the agreement of purchase and sale.

Charge/Mortgage Of Land (Form 2)

A Charge/Mortgage of Land (Form 2) is a standard form used to register a mortgage under either the registry or land titles system. Standardized forms were introduced during the mid-1980s under the *Land Registration Reform Act* with a particular view to develop uniformity in registry records. Previous to that time, various document formats were used.

The Charge/Mortgage of Land provides important information to practitioners concerning mortgage financing on property being listed or sold. Salespeople and brokers will find the form relatively straightforward to analyze and extract relevant information. Selected portions of the form are briefly described.

Box 4 sets out the principal amount of the mortgage that was originally placed on the property. Box 5 provides the legal description of the mortgaged property. Box 7 outlines the type of estate; e.g., fee simple, leasehold or life estate. Box 8 identifies the standard charge terms that apply between mortgagee and mortgagor. Standard charge terms provide detailed terms of the mortgage and are assigned a number in the land registry office when filed.

Box 9 outlines the payment provisions including last payment. A balance due date is provided as Canadian mortgages typically have long amortization periods combined with short terms (often referred to as Canadian roll-over mortgages) resulting in a balance due amount and an appropriate balloon payment is required. Box 10 provides for any special provisions agreed between mortgagee and mortgagor; e.g., prepayment privileges. If insufficient space, a schedule is used. Boxes 11-13 set out details concerning the chargor (mortgagor) with Boxes 14-15 relating to the chargee. The balance of the form involves property details including assessment roll number, who prepared the form and fees associated with the mortgage registration.

Charge/Mortgage of Land

Source: Dye & Durham Co. Inc.

Province of Ontario

Charge/Mortgage of Land

Form 2 — Land Registration Reform Act

Form No. 975

B

FOR OFFICE USE ONLY

New Property Identifiers

Additional: See Schedule ☐

Executions

Additional: See Schedule ☐

(1) Registry ☐ Land Titles ☐

(2) Page 1 of pages

(3) Property Identifier(s) Block Property

Additional: See Schedule ☐

(4) Principal Amount

Dollars $

(5) Description

(6) This Document Contains (a) Redescription New Easement Plan/Sketch ☐ (b) Schedule for: Description ☐ Additional Parties ☐ Other ☐

(7) Interest/Estate Charged Fee Simple

(8) Standard Charge Terms — The parties agree to be bound by the provisions in Standard Charge Terms filed as number and the Chargor(s) hereby acknowledge(s) receipt of a copy of these terms.

(9) Payment Provisions

(a) Principal Amount $ (b) Interest Rate % per annum (c) Calculation Period

(d) Interest Adjustment Date Y M D (e) Payment Date and Period (f) First Payment Date Y M D

(g) Last Payment Date (h) Amount of Each Payment Dollars $

(i) Balance Due Date (j) Insurance Dollars $

(10) Additional Provisions

Continued on Schedule ☐

(11) Chargor(s) The chargor hereby charges the land to the chargee and certifies that the chargor is at least eighteen years old and that

The chargor(s) acknowledge(s) receipt of a true copy of this charge.

Name(s)	Signature(s)	Date of Signature Y	M	D

(12) Spouse(s) of Chargor(s) I hereby consent to this transaction.

Name(s)	Signature(s)	Date of Signature Y	M	D

(13) Chargor(s) Address for Service

(14) Chargee(s)

(15) Chargee(s) Address for Service

(16) Assessment Roll Number of Property Cty. Mun. Map Sub. Par.

(17) Municipal Address of Property

(18) Document Prepared by:

FOR OFFICE USE ONLY

Fees	
Registration Fee	
Total	

Electronic Charge/Mortgage of Land

Source: Teranet

****** NOT VALID - TO BE USED FOR TRAINING PURPOSES ONLY ******

The applicant(s) hereby applies to the Land Registrar. yyyy mm dd

LRO # 20 **Charge/Mortgage** **Receipted as HH199** on 2006 06 16 at 10:55

Properties

PIN	07014 - 0500 LT	*Interest/Estate*	Fee Simple
Description	LT 48 , PL 1361 ; HAMILTON		
Address	05000 IDLEWOOD CR HAMILTON		

Chargor(s)

The chargor(s) hereby charges the land to the chargee(s). The chargor(s) acknowledges the receipt of the charge and the standard charge terms, if any.

Name	SMITH, JOHN FRANKLIN
Address for Service	05000 Idlewood Cr. Hamilton, ON L8N 5R4

I am at least 18 years of age.

Eleanor Joyce Smith and I are spouses of one another and are both parties to this document

This document is not authorized under Power of Attorney by this party.

Name	SMITH, ELEANOR JOYCE
Address for Service	05000 Idlewood Cr. Hamilton, ON L8N 5R4

I am at least 18 years of age.

John Franklin Smith and I are spouses of one another and are both parties to this document

This document is not authorized under Power of Attorney by this party.

Chargee(s) *Capacity* *Share*

Name	MONEY BANK
Address for Service	144 Constitutional Dr. Burlington, ON B9T 5R2

Provisions

Principal	$ 259,000.00	*Currency*	CDN
Calculation Period	half yearly, not in advance		
Balance Due Date	2010/11/01		
Payments	$ 1,681.00		
Interest Adjustment Date	2006 12 01		
Payment Date	first day of each month		
First Payment Date	2006 12 01		
Last Payment Date	2011 11 01		
Standard Charge Terms	9412		
Insurance Amount	full insurable value		
Guarantor			

Additional Provisions

The chargor shall have the privilege of prepaying, at any time, without notice, the whole or any part of the principal hereby secured without notice or bonus.

Signed By

Paul P. Lawyer(TCD)	acting for Chargor(s)	Signed	2006 06 16
Tel			
Fax			

Submitted By

TRAINING COMPANY D	2006 06 16
Tel	
Fax	

Fees/Taxes/Payment

Statutory Registration Fee	$60.00
Total Paid	$60.00

IMPLIED COVENANTS

The *Land Registration Reform Act*, coincident with the introduction of standardized forms for registry and land titles, permitted the inclusion of standard charge terms. This provision was designed to ensure that certain covenants were included, which might otherwise be omitted from a mortgage document. In effect, a mortgage under land titles or registry could be registered with nothing more than the basic information included in the standard Charge/Mortgage of Land form. Consequently, certain covenants (originally implied in the *Mortgages Act*) were included in the *Land Registration Reform Act* and deemed to be implied upon registration of the mortgage document.

First Implied Covenant	• The mortgagor will make payments including interest and also pay taxes. • The mortgagor has the legal right to give the mortgage. • The mortgagor will provide insurance on the buildings. • The mortgagor has no other encumbrances other than those currently registered on the specific property. • The mortgagee, when the mortgagor is in default, has the right to take possession, collect rents/profits or sell the land. • The mortgagee in possession by default shall be granted quiet possession. • Upon default, total monies due shall become payable. • Interest in arrears may be collected. • The mortgagor in default agrees to do such things as reasonably requested by the mortgagee in possession relating to the land.
Second Implied Covenant	• The mortgagor covenants that the land held in fee simple is owned with good title.
Third Implied Covenant (relates to leasehold property)	• The mortgagor covenants that the lease is valid and up-to-date and, further, that reimbursement to the mortgagee will be made by the mortgagor for non-payment or non-performance of other covenants under the lease.

EXAMPLE ***Charge/Mortgage of Land: Implied Covenant***

Seller Smith and Buyer Jones are attempting to close a transaction without legal counsel. In preparing the Charge/Mortgage of Land (Form 2), Jones doesn't understand the reference to Standard Charge Terms (Box 8) and leaves it blank. Smith overlooks the missing information. As no set of standard charge terms is referenced, the document is registered lacking important provisos, remedies and procedural matters. Regardless, the implied covenants as set out in the *Land Registration Reform Act*, at minimum, assure Seller Smith that certain significant covenants are addressed.

STANDARD CHARGE TERMS

Standard charge terms were introduced under the *Land Registration Reform Act* of 1984. This Act provided that, effective April 1, 1985, a person or corporation had the right to file standard charge terms with the land registrar. The registrar assigns a number to this unique set of charge terms and circulates the set to all land registry offices. This number can then be included in a Charge/Mortgage of Land and the mortgage is deemed to automatically include that particular set of terms.

Standard charge terms can be amended by filing a new set with a new number. In reality, a mortgagee may have several sets of standard charge terms registered with the land registrar at any particular point in time, each with a unique reference number. Should any information within the set of standard charge terms conflict with the Charge/Mortgage of Land, then the latter will prevail. If specific prepayment or other privileges are inserted in the appropriate space provided on the mortgage form, these also preempt any terms outlined in the set of standard charge terms.

The Director of Land Registration can require the filing of standard charge terms in electronic format pursuant to Part III of the *Land Registration Reform Act.*

The conversion to automated land registration in Ontario has eliminated the need for extensive paper documentation. Standard charge terms can now be attached electronically to mortgages as part of the registration process using Teraview software. Currently, most lenders provide PDF versions for that purpose.

Discharge of Charge/Mortgage (Form 3)

A Discharge of Charge/Mortgage is executed by the mortgagee and given to the mortgagor verifying that a mortgage loan has been repaid in full before, at or after the maturity date. This document is registered at the land registration office as a permanent record of the discharge. Merely paying of the debt is not sufficient, as a Discharge of Charge/Mortgage must be registered to give evidence of the removal of the original claim made by way of a Charge/Mortgage of Land.

Document General (Form 4)

Practitioners will encounter the Document General (Form 4) in a variety of circumstances associated with property titles; e.g., caution, notice of lien, discharge of lien, power of attorney, judgment and notice of survivorship. Any Document General registered on title should be carefully analyzed as the contents can significantly impact the title to the property and consequently buyers and sellers. The Document General is relatively straightforward to read as either the provisions are fully described in Box 8 or an applicable schedule is attached. Legal advice should be sought in all matters relating to title.

LAND DESCRIPTION

Land is described for legal purposes in a precise manner, according to a formula, so that one piece of land cannot be mistaken for another. As such, the difference between land description and legal description is somewhat blurred and, in fact, both terms are generally viewed as synonymous for purposes of real estate discussions. In a legal document, descriptions such as the lot with the white stucco house or 43 Enroy Court are not sufficient. Land description, therefore, must include the most complete legal identification of the property. This wording is then used for registration in the appropriate land registration office.

Discharge of Charge/Mortgage Source: Dye & Durham Co. Inc.

DYE & DURHAM CO. INC.—Form No. 980
Amended NOV. 1992

Province of Ontario

Discharge of Charge/Mortgage

Form 3 — Land Registration Reform Act

C

FOR OFFICE USE ONLY

New Property Identifiers

Additional: See Schedule ☐

(1) Registry ☐ **Land Titles** ☐ **(2)** Page 1 of pages

(3) Property Identifier(s) Block Property Additional: See Schedule ☐

(4) Description

(5) Charge to be Discharged

Registration Number | Date of Registration Y M D

(6) This is a

Complete Discharge ☐ Partial Discharge ☐ Final Partial Discharge ☐

(7) Description (cont'd.), Recitals, Assignments

Continued on Schedule ☐

(8) Chargee(s) I am the person entitled by law to grant the discharge and this charge is hereby discharged as to the land described herein.

Name(s)	Signature(s)	Date of Signature Y M D

Additional: See Schedule ☐

(9) Chargee(s) Address for Service

(10) Document Prepared by:

FOR OFFICE USE ONLY

Fees	
Registration Fee	
Total	

Document General

Source: Dye & Durham Co. Inc.

DYE & DURHAM CO. INC.—Form No. 985
Amended NOV. 1992

Province of Ontario

Document General

Form 4 — Land Registration Reform Act

D

FOR OFFICE USE ONLY

New Property Identifiers — Additional: See Schedule ☐

Executions — Additional: See Schedule ☐

(1) Registry ☐ **Land Titles** ☐

(2) Page 1 of pages

(3) Property Identifier(s) Block Property — Additional: See Schedule ☐

(4) Nature of Document

(5) Consideration Dollars $

(6) Description

(7) This Document Contains: (a) Redescription New Easement Plan/Sketch ☐ (b) Schedule for: Description ☐ Additional Parties ☐ Other ☐

(8) This Document provides as follows:

Continued on Schedule ☐

(9) This Document relates to instrument number(s)

(10) Party(ies) (Set out Status or Interest)

Name(s)	Signature(s)	Date of Signature Y	M	D

(11) Address for Service

(12) Party(ies) (Set out Status or Interest)

Name(s)	Signature(s)	Date of Signature Y	M	D

(13) Address for Service

(14) Municipal Address of Property

(15) Document Prepared by:

FOR OFFICE USE ONLY

Fees and Tax	
Registration Fee	
Total	

Lots/Concessions

The basis for modern methods of land description lies in the original survey of the province completed in 1792. At that time, Governor Simcoe divided Ontario into counties. He hired teams of surveyors to trek through the bush to mark out the actual boundaries. The county boundary often followed a river or lake, but in most cases was a straight line through the bush. The counties were then divided into smaller parcels referred to as townships. Many townships were square, although topography sometimes necessitated a rectangle, or an irregular line on one or more township sides due to natural boundaries.

Each township was in turn divided into strips of land known as concessions, numbered in Roman numerals beginning with I. Each concession was separated from the next one by a road allowance. The road allowance was not always converted into an actual road, but remained as public property. Each concession was further divided into lots, running at right angle to the concessions and numbered in Arabic numerals from 1. The lots were sometimes divided by a road allowance (usually every 5th lot) or simply by a lot line. A parcel of land could then be described as the entirety of the lot and concession, for example:

> *Lot 5 in Concession III in the Township of Anytownship, in the County of Anycounty.*

Townships

Practitioners should be aware of special considerations regarding the development of townships. The single front and double front township configurations were introduced in 1783 and 1818 respectively, with sectional townships following in 1835. Single front townships normally contained 200 acre lots, while double front townships were usually patented in 100 acre half-lots.

Single Front Township The single front township, the oldest of the township systems, was laid out in southern Ontario between 1783 and 1818 and was found generally on the banks of navigable lakes and rivers. The sizes of the lots in this system varied from time to time. In the example provided, the lots were intended to be 20 chains (1,320') by 100 chains (6,600') and to contain 200 acres. A standard road allowance is 1 chain wide (66 feet).

In this system, only the township boundaries and the fronts of the concessions were run with posts generally planted at the front corners of the lots. No provisions existed for check ties across the concessions in the original survey. Consequently, the road allowances between lots, when later surveyed, were usually found to jog at the fronts of the concessions.

Double Front Township The term *double front* refers to a township where the original survey laid out the township in lots to be 30 chains (1,980') by 66.67 chains (4,400') and were usually patented in half-lots containing 100 acres. The township boundaries and the centre-line of the road allowances between the concessions were run with posts planted on each side of the road to mark the front corners of the lots. As with single front townships, no provisions existed for check ties across the concessions in the original survey. Thus, the road allowances between lots, when later surveyed, were usually found to jog at the fronts of the concessions.

Sectional System Township This system of land division involved 1,000-acre sections and was introduced in 1835. In this arrangement, lots were designed to be 20 chains by 50 chains and to contain 100 acres. This system was the first township system in which an attempt was made to check the survey by means of cross ties between concessions. Not only were the centre-lines of the road allowances between concessions surveyed but also the centre-lines of the road allowances between every fifth lot, thus forming surveyed sections of 10 lots with each section containing a total area of 1,000 acres.

Measurements

The measurement of land was based on the old chains and links system. A chain is 66 feet, 100 links make a chain and 80 chains equal one mile. Each concession was 100 chains across, or 1 ¼ miles. As time passed, many farmers divided the land among their sons. Such divisions could be easily described as long as the parcel was ½ or ¼ of an overall lot; e.g., land could be described as:

> *the South East 1/4 of Lot 5, Concession III, Township of Anytownship, in the County of Anycounty.*

This system of describing land as part of a concession lot is still the basis for land descriptions in Ontario today. The system can be used to describe a lot containing as few as 50 acres. However, this description would only be approximate, and to comply with present-day conveyancing standards, property normally must be re-surveyed and measured more accurately. To describe smaller parcels, further refinements were necessary.

Fractional Descriptions As the provincial population grew, the demand for smaller divisions of land increased with land registration systems gradually encountering more and more fractional parts of lots. Initially, legal descriptions were based on dimensions without concern for precise directions and descriptions were prepared without benefit of surveys.

An excerpt from a typical description dating from the early 1800s follows:

> *ALL AND SINGULAR that certain parcel or tract of land and premises situate, lying and being in the Township of Anytownship in the County of Anycounty and being composed of part of Lot 7, Concession IV in the said Township and being more particularly described as follows:*
>
> *COMMENCING at a point in the northern limit of the road allowance between concessions III and IV distance 198 feet measured westerly there along from the South East corner of said Lot 4...*

The lack of exact directional bearings could cause conflict between the printed word and what existed on the ground. Metes and bounds descriptions and associated surveys helped eliminate a great deal of confusion through improved wording precision:

> *Commencing at a point in the northern limit of the said road allowance distant 198 feet measured on a bearing of South 60 degrees 10 minutes thirty seconds West there along from the South East corner of said Lot 4...[partial description only]*

The reader now possessed sufficient details to confirm boundaries exactly by means of a re-survey of the property. Unfortunately, written metes and bounds descriptions were often complex and surveys lacking sufficient reference to abutting properties could prove confusing. As a result, various requirements were added to recording acts and regulations associated with registry and land titles systems.

Detailed surveys with improved standards are now required in support of fractional descriptions and new developments require formal surveys of the entire subdivision including all lots. A severance of land in rural areas now must be fully described by means of a reference plan identifying the severed property as a PART. The legal description, while still referring to lot and concession, is now supported by a visual reference plan filed in the land registration office. A typical description might read as follows:

> *Part of Lot 25, Concession IV, more particularly described as PART 2 on Reference Plan 99R-1832, Township of Anytownship.*

In the case of subdivision lots, the entire plan is allocated a number based on when it was registered and individual lots are simply described numerically. For example, Mr. Smith purchases Lot 27 in the Anycity Heights subdivision. The legal description would be:

> *Lot 27, Plan 99M-165, City of Anycity*

The lot number designates his property and the plan number informs the searcher of the following: the land registration office is identified by the number (in this case 99), the plan can be found under land titles (frequently indicated by the letter M) as opposed to registry and the plan number being #165 (the 165th plan registered in that land registration office) is filed accordingly within the land titles records for that land registration office. This example is provided for illustration purposes only. Variations exist across the province.

TITLE INSURANCE

Title insurance relates to a loss or liability for loss due to the invalidity of title to a property or instrument related thereto, or a defect in a title or instrument.

Title insurance in Ontario is issued by companies licensed under the *Insurance Act*. Policies include coverage for the type of property (actual loss incurred) and the payment of legal expenses (costs associated with the duty to defend). Current insurers operating within the Ontario marketplace include Chicago Title Insurance Company, First Canadian Title Company Limited, Lawyer's Professional Indemnity Company and Stewart Title Guaranty Company.

Types of Policies

Title insurance policies are designed primarily for two audiences: lenders and owners. Title insurers in Ontario offer a range of policies to address these audiences and policy terms/coverages will vary. The structure and form of title policies, whether for lender or owner, are more or less standardized keeping in mind that separate policies are targeted to commercial and residential properties. Commercial policies follow one of several more or less standard wordings. In the case of residential, standardized basic policy wordings have given way to various extended coverage policies making direct comparison more complex. Title insurers may offer combined policies with coverage for both the lender and the owner.

Most title policies include a general statement of coverages, specific types of title risks covered, exclusions and exceptions from coverage and policy conditions/stipulations. Beyond pre-printed policy wording, individual policies are also subject to specific terms set out in attached schedules; e.g., amount of insurance for a particular property, along with any endorsements attached to the policy that modify the preprinted wording of the basic policy. Obviously, any title policy should be carefully read to fully appreciate the scope of insurance provided. Further, any review must include the total policy along with all attachments as exclusions, exceptions, conditions, stipulations and endorsements can affect any general coverage statement found at the start of the title policy.

Range of Coverages

Any detailed comparison of either owner or lender policies as well as residential or commercial packages goes well beyond the scope of this text. For descriptive purposes, title risks for residential property (owner's policy) provide some indication of the scope of such coverage. The following is not an exhaustive list, but includes the typical risks that are covered when the condition of title is other than stated in the title documents.

- A document relating to the title is not properly signed or is otherwise defective; e.g., not sealed or delivered.
- A document was defectively registered on title; e.g., a defect in a lien, charge or other encumbrance.
- Some form of forgery or fraud in documents affects title to the property.
- An inability to access the property is uncovered; i.e., the legal right for pedestrian or vehicular access.
- The title is unmarketable for a number of reasons that result in a person refusing to perform a contract, lease or make a loan.
- A contravention of a municipal by-law occurs; e.g., the owner is forced to move or otherwise remedy a structure (or any part thereof) due to a violation of zoning by-laws.
- A contravention of a subdivision, development agreement or other agreement relating to the development of the property.
- Construction liens are discovered on title (that had not been previously agreed to be paid).
- Other individuals claim rights over the property not identified in the title documents arising from leases, contracts, options or some other possessory right.
- A lien on title is discovered that may have a priority; e.g., arising from a judgment, a mortgage or a public utility account.
- Certain restrictive covenants may exist that affect the use of the land.
- Someone else owns an interest in the title.

A detailed review of individual policies is required along with expert advice. Practitioners should also be aware that title insurance is a relatively new concept in the Canadian marketplace. Consequently, many policy wordings and issues surrounding title insurance lack interpretation through Canadian courts.

Benefits

Real estate practitioners should be aware that title insurance may provide certain benefits from both a listing and selling perspective. Traditionally, buyers relied on a letter of opinion from a lawyer as assurance that the title was good and marketable. A lawyer's letter of opinion was typically qualified, at least to some degree, concerning such marketability. If a subsequent problem arose, the onus rested with the buyer to prove that the lawyer failed to do something and/or that legal services failed to meet an acceptable standard.

Title insurance provides a means to not only address qualifications within a reporting letter, but also to protect against various errors that could potentially occur through fraudulent activity, or simply errors made in documents prepared by others. Lenders, in particular, take great comfort in the value of title insurance to address issues that might be missed despite the diligent efforts of the solicitor. Once again, prudence is advised as title policies do not solve all issues given exclusions, conditions and stipulations affecting the scope of coverage.

Survey	An attractive aspect of title insurance is the possible avoidance of a new survey. The elimination of the survey requirement can represent significant savings as well as eliminate a possible delay in the closing process. Coverages vary and any policy should be read carefully. Practitioners should NOT in any way lead buyers to believe that the survey cost will be avoided, but rather that it might be avoided depending on specific property circumstances and the policy under consideration.
Title Problems at Listing	Sellers can take advantage of title insurance at the point of listing. For example, a problem relating to title may crop up in the listing process when a real estate practitioner identifies a circumstance such as a deck that extends beyond the approved setback in the municipal zoning by-laws. The seller may be able to secure title insurance and confirm that the property will be insured against any losses that may occur due to this problem. The seller is then in a position to assure any potential buyer that this situation has been resolved through insurance coverage.
Marketing Incentive	The seller may agree to purchase title insurance as an incentive in the marketing of his/her property. The seller's commitment translates into cost savings at the point of negotiations with a potential buyer. Even during negotiations, the seller may offer to pay this cost.
Title Problems at Closing	Title policies have proven particularly effective by insuring over certain title problems that crop up at or near closing. As an example, a minor encroachment may exist that could otherwise delay or cancel a sale. Alternatively, a minor issue regarding final inspection of an addition or improvement to the property may not have been completed by the municipality. The title insurer, after an investigation of the risk involved, may elect to insure over the problem allowing the transaction to close on time.

Legal Disclosure Requirements

The Law Society of Upper Canada (LSUC) sets out various disclosure requirements for lawyers concerning title insurance pursuant to the Rules of Professional Conduct.

2.02 Quality of Service
Title Insurance in Real Estate Conveyancing

(10) A lawyer shall assess all reasonable options to assure title when advising a client about a real estate conveyance and shall advise the client that title insurance is not mandatory and is not the only option available to protect the client's interests in a real estate transaction.

(11) A lawyer shall not receive any compensation, whether directly or indirectly, from a title insurer, agent or intermediary for recommending a specific title insurance product to his or her client.

(12) A lawyer shall disclose to the client that no commission or fee is being furnished by any insurer, agent or intermediary to the lawyer with respect to any title insurance coverage.

(13) If discussing *TitlePlus* insurance with the client, a lawyer shall fully disclose the relationship between the legal profession, the Society and the Lawyers' Professional Indemnity Company (LPIC).

CLOSING PROCEDURES

Purchase (Residential Transaction)

The closing, from a legal perspective, is the culmination of a residential sale traditionally completed by lawyers of the buyer and seller at the land registry office. Presently, electronic closings are most frequent as solicitors utilize new online document preparation and registration facilities.

Practitioners require a fundamental understanding of closing steps to appreciate what procedures and forms are used from the buyer's perspective. The following brief narrative is based on the traditional paper-based system outlining major steps carried out by the buyer's solicitor following preliminary discussions, receipt of an accepted agreement of purchase and sale and related consultations with his/her client. It is intended for information only, and is not exhaustive given the wide range of issues faced by a buyer's solicitor when addressing unique properties and transactions.

TITLE SEARCH

The buyer's solicitor undertakes a title search at the appropriate land registry office in which the property is situated. An existing survey, if available, is normally requested before the title search. If in land titles, the search involves all current information concerning the property as shown on the parcel register. In registry, the search is for a period of at least 40 years and involves an examination of the chain of title describing all transactions along with any gaps, errors or missed parties.

In both instances, the solicitor is looking for items such as outstanding encumbrances, restrictive covenants, non-resident parties, expropriations and matrimonial home status. He/she will also investigate adjoining lands to ensure compliance with the *Planning Act*. The date of the search is recorded in anticipation of a sub-search at point of closing. The solicitor will report to the client on title, conditions and other matters significant to the title.

NON-TITLE SEARCHES

The buyer's solicitor will search various non-title records including but not limited to:

- Zoning (to ensure that the present use conforms to zoning by-laws).
- Work orders or deficiency notices.
- Executions.
- Unregistered easements; e.g., hydro easements.
- Personal property pursuant to the registration system established under the *Personal Property Security Act*.
- Outstanding amounts relating to a local utility company owed by the owner of the property.
- Status of real property taxes including any special assessments/local improvements and surcharges.
- Survey documentation concerning setbacks, encroachments and related matters.
- Compliance with subdivision or site plan agreements and registered restrictive covenants.
- Status concerning Ontario New Home Warranty Program (if applicable).

The range of non-title searches varies by property and individual circumstance. For example, a rural property may require searches involving the local health unit and/or municipal records concerning the waste disposal system, conservation authority requirements for properties within regulated areas, approvals required from the Ministry of Natural Resources under the *Public Lands Act* and, in some instances, Parks Canada in relation to federally-controlled canals concerning waterfront improvements.

REQUISITIONS

The Agreement of Purchase and Sale (OREA Form 100) provides for a specified date (requisition date) to complete the title search. The buyer may examine the title to the property at his/her own expense until a stipulated requisition date, and the earlier of (i) 30 days from the later of the requisition date or the date on which the conditions in the agreement are fulfilled or otherwise waived; or (ii) five days prior to completion, to ensure that no outstanding work orders or deficiency notices exist affecting the property, to verify the property is insurable and to confirm the present use is legal.

Typical Requisition Letter

VIA FAX AND ORDINARY MAIL
January 5, 20xx
FROM PURCHASER'S LAWYER

To: ________________ Re: Purchase From ________________ Closing Date: January 12, 20xx
VENDOR'S LAWYER PROPERTY ADDRESS

Dear Sir/Madam:

Further to the above matter, we act as solicitors for the purchaser and understand that you will be acting for the vendor. We now have completed our search of title with respect to this property and we submit herein the following requisitions, without prejudice to our rights to submit further and other requisitions as we may require:

- On or before closing—draft Transfer/Deed of Land in joint tenancy in the following manner:

  ____
  PURCHASER'S NAME BIRTH DATE

  ____
  PURCHASER'S NAME BIRTH DATE

  ____
  ADDRESS FOR SERVICE

- Satisfactory evidence by way of a Statutory Declaration that the Transferor(s) is not a non-resident of Canada within the meaning of The Income Tax Act or, alternatively, we will require the Certificate of the Minister of Revenue, pursuant to the provisions of The Canada Income Tax Act.
- Declaration of Possession covering the vendor's period of ownership of the property.
- Direction for payment of funds on closing should be made payable to a person other than the vendor herein.
- Statement of Adjustments, in duplicate.
- Vendor's Undertaking with respect to the following:
  (a) To pay all levies, charges and penalties collectible as taxes owing to the date of closing, except those allowed to the purchaser on the Statement of Adjustments, forming a lien prior to the mortgage or incurred on its own account.
  (b) To pay all hydro-electric, water and gas accounts to the date of closing except those allowed to the purchaser on the Statement of Adjustments forming a lien prior to the mortgage or incurred on its own account.
  (c) To deliver vacant possession of the premises.
- On or before closing, satisfactory evidence of the following:
  (a) That there are no executions in the hands of the Sheriff of the County of ________________ against the vendor, or their predecessors on title.
  (b) That the vendor has not contravened the provisions of Section 50 of the Planning Act, and amendments hereto. We wish to utilize the provisions of Section 50 (22) of the Planning Act and we therefore request that the Transferor(s) and the solicitors for the Transferor(s) complete Box 13 of the Transfer/Deed of Land. Please advise us immediately if you are unable or unwilling to cooperate with this request.
  (c) That there are no unregistered liens, right-of-ways, restrictive covenants, easements or restrictions or encumbrances of any kind against the said property and that possession has been consistent with the registered title.
  (d) That there are no arrears of taxes nor penalties for arrears of realty taxes and/or charges for water, hydro, electricity, gas or oil with respect to this property.
  (e) That as at the date of closing herein, no part of the said lands have been taken or expropriated by any competent authority.
  (f) That the Transfer/Deed of Land from the vendor(s) to the purchaser(s) herein has the proper statement of compliance regarding spousal status under The Family Law Act, PART II.
  (g) That on or before closing, satisfactory evidence that there are no liens arising by virtue of The Construction Lien Act, as amended. In this regard, a Statutory Declaration executed by the vendor(s) to this effect will suffice.
- On or before closing, production and registration on title of valid discharges of any liens, mortgages and/or encumbrances whatsoever registered or unregistered other than those mortgages which may be assumed by our client in accordance with the Agreement of Purchase and Sale.
- On or before closing, satisfactory evidence that all buildings on the said lands and premises have been erected in accordance with the appropriate statutes and by-laws of the municipality in which the property is situated and any other provincial, municipal or federal governmental authority, having jurisdiction therein.
- Statement of Certificate of Status from the vendor(s) certifying that the sale of the above lands and premises to the purchaser(s) is/are exempt from Harmonized Sales Tax.
- An opportunity for final inspection of the property on the evening before or the morning of the date of closing to determine if any substantial or other damage has occurred to the premises since the date of signing of the Agreement of Purchase and Sale. In this regard, we would refer you to the decision of HARKNESS V. COONEY (1979) 131 d.l.r. (3rd.) 765.

CLOSING

The buyer's lawyer, upon arrival at the land registry office, will commence a sub-search. This completes the chain of title from initial search date to closing date including a review of the daybook for instruments that are not yet abstracted; i.e., items that have not yet appeared in parcel or abstract registers. In offices with electronic registration, the day book is no longer required as abstracted entries occur coincident with registration of documents.

The solicitor for the buyer then meets with the seller's representative to compare any last minute details, provides items as requested in closing memoranda and discusses problems and/or gives undertakings as required for unresolved issues. At the registration counter, the documents are presented in correct order for registration and the funds are released at point of registration.

The lawyer will provide a final reporting letter after closing that includes his/her opinion regarding title, all qualifications, limitations, exceptions and provisos concerning that title, title insurance details (if applicable), references to any documents received from the seller's solicitor, the statement of adjustments, trust account entries and any other documents as required; e.g., mortgage details and documents, tenancies, new home warranty documentation and any report concerning chattels pursuant to the *Personal Property Security Act.* Occasionally, an interim reporting letter is forwarded in advance of the final report if certain payments or actions are required immediately after closing.

Sale (Residential Transaction)

The closing of a residential sale involves a series of steps traditionally completed by lawyers of the buyer and seller at the land registry office. This brief narrative of closing steps involves a traditional, paper-based system. Increasingly, electronic closings are occurring as solicitors utilize new online document preparation and registration facilities in Ontario. This discussion focuses on major steps by the seller's lawyer following any preliminary discussions, receipt of an accepted agreement of purchase and sale and related consultations with his/her client.

Practitioners require a fundamental understanding of closing steps to appreciate the range of procedures and forms used from a selling perspective. The following, intended for information only, is not exhaustive given the wide range of issues faced by a seller's solicitor when addressing unique properties and transactions.

Lawyers involved in closing procedures typically rely on a detailed checklist that can be complex particularly regarding requisitions and pre- and post-closing considerations.

DOCUMENT PREPARATION

The seller's lawyer is responsible for preparing a draft Transfer/Deed of Land (Form 1) with the buyer(s)' names, birth date(s), type of ownership (joint tenancy or tenants in common) and the statement of adjustments in duplicate. He/she will also complete any declarations or directions necessary for the transaction; e.g., a bill of sale (if chattels are being sold), seller's undertaking concerning the payment of utility bills (rendered following closing) and directions for proceeds of the sale. If a mortgage is being taken back, directions concerning that mortgage, confirmation of fire insurance from the buyer's lawyer, amortization schedule and a review of draft documents are also completed.

REQUISITIONS

The seller's lawyer will respond to requisitions from the buyer's solicitor provided that such are consistent with the agreement of purchase and sale and within the time limits specified. Requisition items may include:

- Statutory declaration concerning not being a non-resident.
- Declaration of possession covering the seller's period of ownership.
- Direction for payment of funds on closing.
- Seller's undertaking to pay tax levies, charges, penalties, utility accounts and provide vacant possession.
- Evidence of no executions, no contravention of the *Planning Act*, and no unregistered liens, rights-of-way, tax arrears, expropriations and construction liens.
- Discharges of any liens, mortgages or encumbrances other than those to be assumed by the buyer.
- Compliance of buildings and other improvements with zoning by-laws.
- A statement certifying that the sale of the land and premises is exempt from harmonized sales tax, or otherwise, depending on the circumstances.

DOCUMENT REVIEW

The seller's solicitor reviews all draft documents provided by the buyer's lawyer to ensure compliance with the terms of the agreement and discusses any items requiring clarification and/or resolution with the buyer's solicitor.

CLOSING

The seller's lawyer will attend the land registry office and exchange documents with the buyer's lawyer. He/she will typically review any last minute details, provide items as requested in closing memoranda, discuss problems and/or give undertakings as required for unresolved issues. At the registration counter, the buyer's lawyer presents the documents in correct order for registration and the funds are released at the point of registration.

Following closing, the seller's lawyer delivers funds to obtain discharges of mortgages and any other payments (e.g., taxes, utilities and brokerage commission) and other distributions unique to that particular sale (e.g., mortgage take-back documents and undertakings concerning the sale) and then forwards net proceeds to the client. The lawyer will also provide a final reporting letter referring to any documents received from the buyer's solicitor and generally summarize the transaction and disposition of funds, along with any remaining items that must be diarized.

CLOSING STATEMENT (STATEMENT OF ADJUSTMENTS)

A statement is prepared itemizing the financial history of the transaction including such items as the deposit, down payment, balance due on closing and mortgage amount. Typical fees and disbursements for a residential property are provided on the following page for illustration purposes only. Significant cost variations are encountered in the marketplace.

COST GUIDE—FEES AND DISBURSEMENTS

Urban Residential Transaction

ITEM	ESTIMATED COST	EXPLANATION/NOTES
		Only selected costs have been itemized. The range of fees and disbursements is by no means exhaustive, and is limited to expenses usual to a typical urban residential transaction. Costs can vary significantly.
REALTOR® Fee/Commission	*	
Survey *(Range for typical location survey)*	$500.00–$950.00	Survey cost varies according to size, type and location of property.
Title Insurance *(Range for average condo/single family)*	$150.00–$350.00	Insurance coverage regarding title. Survey cost may be avoided.
Mortgage Financing	*	Mortgage financing cost varies and may include application fee, mortgage insurance fee, mortgage broker's fee and discharge costs for existing financing.
Land Transfer Tax *(Four examples are provided for illustration purposes)*		Land transfer tax is computed as follows: .005 x the first $55,000, plus .01 x from $55,000.00 to $250,000, plus .015 x remainder of purchase price, plus .005 surcharge on single family homes and duplexes for the amount over $400,000
Sale Price of Home	*Tax Payable*	
$ 40,000	$ 200.00	
200,000	1,725.00	
400,000	4,475.00	
500,000	6,475.00	
Legal Fees	*	Lawyer's statement of account will normally include fee plus disbursements listed below.
Typical List of Disbursements		**Title Search** Title search fees and sheriff's office search. **Letter Searches** Building clearance, tax certificate, water and hydro certificate, natural gas status, subdivision agreement clearance, *Personal Property Security Act* searches. **Registration Costs** Transfer/deed, charge/mortgage and other documents requiring registration. **Pro-rated Adjustments** Property taxes, fuel, mortgage interest adjustments, holdbacks (taxes, repairs), any special assessments/levies. **Miscellaneous** Photocopies, fax transmissions, courier, long distance telephone, travelling costs, subsearch on closing, inspection fees.
City Tax Certificate	$ 20.00	
Zoning Reports	70.00	
Engineering Reports	40.00	
Sheriff's Certificates	154.00	
Registry Office Searches	125.00	
Utility Searches	20.00	
Register Deed	50.00	
Register Mortgage	50.00	
Copies, Fax, Postage, Courier	45.00	
Total Disbursements	$574.00	
Add (as required)		
Adjustment for Municipal Taxes		
Fuel (i.e., Oil: $350.00 for 910 litres)		
Ontario New Home Warranty Plan Fee		
Mortgage Interest Adjustment		
Mortgage Holdbacks (Repairs or Taxes)		
Home Inspection Fee		
Fire Insurance Premium		
Applicable Taxes (HST)		Harmonized sales tax as applicable.

* Indicates estimate unavailable due to wide variances resulting from unique factors and local market practices.

ELECTRONIC CLOSING PROCEDURES (RESIDENTIAL TRANSACTION)

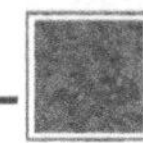

The traditional system of registration at closing involves manual submission of prescribed forms over the registration counter at the land registry office. A mailing option also exists if distance is an issue or if the transaction is of a non-urgent nature. The Ministry of Consumer and Business Services, recognizing inherent weaknesses and the ever-expanding needs of the land registration system, began the process of electronic land registration during the mid-1980s.

Several interrelated projects are moving the province to full electronic record keeping for the benefit of all users. For those involved with closings, the automation process ultimately eliminates the need for signatures on documents and permits remote access to electronic records by solicitors for the buyer and the seller. Consequently, the traditional requirement to attend the land registry office is gradually being eliminated. Persons involved can create, amend or retrieve information as required. Recent initiatives have further broadened this perspective to include links (e.g., assessment, planning and building departments) thereby allowing access to various documents involving requisitions and other needed information in pre-closing activities.

Practitioners require general knowledge of automated records both to appreciate the types of procedures used in real estate closings as well as the benefits for listing, marketing and appraising functions. Presently, real estate salespeople and brokers will find differing levels of electronic conversion as the province moves through the process. The ultimate goal is the creation, approval, exchange and registration of electronic documents combined with electronic transfer of funds.

Overview

Electronic conversion is primarily driven by two systems: POLARIS and Teraview. POLARIS (an acronym for **P**rovince of **O**ntario **LA**nd **R**egistration and **I**nformation **S**ystem) is an automated land registration system based on title index (description of property ownership) and property mapping (surveys and plans) databases. The province-wide conversion involves the lengthy reorganization of documents and data under individual parcels with unique identifiers, referred to as property identification numbers (PINs). Teranet Inc. is responsible for enhancements to the POLARIS system as well as providing an electronic, user gateway called Teraview. The process of electronic conversion is further complemented by the land titles conversion project in which records are not only automated but also moved from the cumbersome registry system into land titles.

Access

Teraview users must be registered with Teranet. Each user must have a removable computer storage device with individual security credentials. The user creates a unique password and establishes an account for access charges and other disbursements; e.g., land transfer tax can be electronically calculated, deducted at closing and forwarded to the Ministry of Finance. Teranet requires that a sufficient balance remain in the user's account at all times to handle charges and disbursements.

From a lawyer's perspective, Teraview operates on four levels:

Search	Allows the lawyer to view documents registered under POLARIS.
Create/ Update	The lawyer can create, view or alter documents for registration; e.g., transfers, mortgages and mortgage discharges. The system contains data entry fields that parallel information required in the manual system.
Complete/ Approve	The lawyers confirm that documents are acceptable for registration by means of an electronic complete signature.
Release/ Registration	The lawyers then provide a release electronic signature and the document is released for registration. Both complete and release signatures must occur before acceptance by the land registration office. Teraview provides various levels of security that may be assigned by the lawyer to others; e.g., legal assistant and/or conveyancer.

CASE LAW

Case Synopsis

FIFE V. COHAN ONTARIO SUPERIOR COURT JULY, 2007

Two neighbouring property owners at 203 and 205 Roslin Avenue have been using a mutual drive amicably for more than 20 years to access their backyard parking areas. However, the sale of 203 Roslin Avenue has resulted in the new owner disallowing the owner of 205 to continue this use. This case is an application by the owner of 205 for an order granting an easement that will allow the owner to continue to use the mutual drive between the two houses to access the backyard parking area, and for an injunction prohibiting the owner of 203 from erecting a fence that would block this access.

This case is somewhat complicated since there is a legal right of way 76 feet long and 7 feet wide registered on the title of both properties. The right of way was created in 1923 to allow the owners of 203 and 205 to encroach upon each other's land for 3.5 feet for the length of the 76 foot easement in order to access the backyard parking areas.

The source of the problem began in 1985 when the owner of 205 built a frame addition to the house that required the owner to travel an additional 39 feet beyond the registered 76 foot right of way to reach the backyard parking. The owner of 205 has been traveling on the additional 39 feet openly and continuously for more than 20 years.

In 2005, the property at 203 sold and the builder erected a new home with a front-facing garage that made it no longer necessary for the owner of 203 to use the right of way to access the backyard. The buyer of the new home decided to fence the backyard right to the end of the registered 76 foot right of way, thus blocking the owner of 205 from using the additional 39 feet necessary to access the backyard parking.

The issue in this application is whether the owner of 205 will be allowed to continue to use the additional 39 feet to access the backyard, something that the owner has been doing for more than 20 years.

The court noted that if the properties had been registered under the *Registry Act*, rather than Land titles, there would be no difficulty in granting the application. However, both properties are registered under the *Land Titles Act* and no title can be acquired by length of possession or by prescription.

Counsel for the applicant also argued that the easement should be granted, even though registered under Land titles, because of "*necessity*".

The court noted that a finding of "*necessity*" generally requires that the property would be landlocked or otherwise inaccessible without the implied grant of an easement. While the loss of access to the parking area is a "*serious inconvenience*", this consideration does not meet the requirement for an easement to be granted.

The application to grant the easement and an injunction preventing the erection of the fence was dismissed by the court, however a non-binding comment was added to the decision suggesting it would be appropriate for the owner of 203 to allow the owner of 205 to use the 76 foot right of way to park his car.

Case Questions

1. How long must a property owner have continuous use of a right of way to claim the right by prescription (under the Registry system)?

2. If the issue in this case was the ownership of a strip of occupied land, rather than a right of way, what would be the required time frame for continuous use for title to be granted?

CHAPTER DISCUSSION

1. THE RECORDING ACTS

List and briefly explain the major differences between the two systems of land registration in Ontario.

REGISTRY	LAND TITLES

Explain, in full, any differences in the meaning of the following terms.

DEED	TITLE

CHAPTER DISCUSSION

1. THE RECORDING ACTS (continued)

Explain, in full, any differences in the meaning of the following terms.

AGREEMENT OF PURCHASE AND SALE	AGREEMENT FOR SALE

MORTGAGE	CHARGE

CHAPTER DISCUSSION

1. THE RECORDING ACTS (continued)

Explain, in full, any differences in the meaning of the following terms.

ABSTRACT OF TITLE	CHAIN OF TITLE

RIGHT-OF-WAY	EASEMENT

CHAPTER DISCUSSION

1. THE RECORDING ACTS (continued)

Describe the main responsibilities and activities of the solicitors in the completion of the transaction.

THE BUYER'S SOLICITOR	THE SELLER'S SOLICITOR

2. COMPLETION

a. Once the Agreement of Purchase and Sale has been arranged, what role should the real estate salesperson have in the completion of the transaction?

CHAPTER DISCUSSION

2. COMPLETION (continued)

b. "It is possible for a seller or buyer of real property in Ontario to complete the purchase themselves without the assistance of a solicitor." Comment.

KNOWLEDGE INTEGRATION

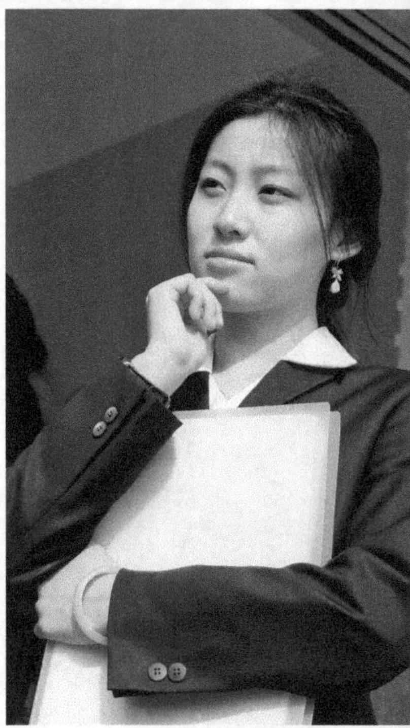

Notables

- In Ontario, all land is registered either under the *Registry Act* or the *Land Titles Act*.
- Registry is the older of the two systems and is now being phased out.
- Land Titles operates under three principles referred to as the mirror, curtain and insurance principles.
- The *Land Registration Reform Act* introduced standardized forms, as well as paving the way for electronic registration.
- The Transfer/Deed of Land and the Charge/Mortgage of Land both have implied covenants.
- Standard charge terms can be filed with the Land Registrar and referred to in the Charge/Mortgage of Land.
- Land description was originally designed based on townships and lots/concessions, but has undergone many changes to meet today's needs.
- Title insurance policies typically involve provisions both for the property covered (actual loss incurred) and the payment of legal expenses (costs associated with the duty to defend).
- Title insurance coverages vary. A summary of typical coverages is provided in the text, but a detailed review of individual policies is required.
- The closing process, culminating the residential sale, was typically completed by lawyers of the buyer and seller at the land registry office, until the introduction of electronic closing procedures.
- The closing procedure, from the buyer's perspective, is focused on title and non-title searches along with requisitions.
- The closing procedure, from the seller's perspective, is focused on preparing the draft Transfer/Deed of Land, answering requisitions and preparing the closing statement.
- Electronic closing procedures are now in place for most of Ontario, with the balance scheduled for completion in the near future.

Chapter Mini-Review

Solutions are located in the Appendix.

1. A quit claim deed can be an expedient method to resolve a mortgagor's financial difficulties by vesting all rights associated with the property to the mortgagee.

   ◯ True ◯ False

2. Under land titles, the curtain principle states that the register of title accurately and completely reflects current facts about a property title.

   ◯ True ◯ False

3. The Charge/Mortgage of Land can only be used to register mortgages under land titles and not registry.

   ◯ True ◯ False

4. While the basis for modern land description was originally based on lots and concessions, this approach is no longer used as electronic registration requires that properties be identified by lot and plan number.

   ◯ True ◯ False

Chapter Mini-Review (continued)

5. Title insurance policies are primarily designed for two target markets: lenders and owners.

   ○ True ○ False

6. A survey is not required when a buyer obtains title insurance.

   ○ True ○ False

7. The seller's solicitor must undertake a title search of the property and provide a list of outstanding encumbrances to the buyer.

   ○ True ○ False

8. Non-title search items could include compliance with zoning and the existence of any work orders.

   ○ True ○ False

9. The seller's lawyer is responsible for preparing a draft Transfer/Deed of Land in preparation for closing a residential transaction.

   ○ True ○ False

10. The electronic conversion of land registry records is driven by two systems: Teraview and Teranet.

   ○ True ○ False

Active Learning Exercises

Solutions are located in the Appendix.

Exercise 1

The Land Titles System was designed in Australia by a man named Torrens. It is superior to the Registry System because:

Exercise 2

Under what circumstances might an Agreement for Sale be an appropriate method to sell a property for a seller? Explain why.

Exercise 3

Yolanda Landrich owns a farm which she obtained by deed from her father. The land is registered under the Registry System. She began grazing her cattle on another property across the creek where there was a ten-acre parcel of vacant land. She did that for four years. At the end of that time she put up a fence enclosing the ten acres of land and continued to use it with her farm for the next nine years.

Last week the registered owner of the ten acres came to the farm and, for the first time, told Landrich to "*get your cows off my land.*" Landrich was concerned so she phoned her son, a real estate broker, who advised her that "*you own all the property either by Deed or by Possession.*"

a. On the basis of these facts, do you agree?

b. What other facts would you want to know before you gave any opinion?

c. Would it make any difference if the properties were registered in the Land Titles System? Explain.

d. What would have been the effect if Landrich had been told to get her cows off the land when she first put up the fence?

e. What should her son, the real estate broker, have done?

Exercise 4

Your grandfather was the owner of an irregular shaped piece of property, registered under the *Registry Act*, for many years. When he died, that property went to your father under the grandfather's will. Your father continued to use the property and gave the deed to you before his death. No survey has ever been done. You now sell the property and the buyer obtains a survey for the new first mortgagee. That survey shows some concerns about the boundary lines of your land. What can you do to satisfy the concerns of the buyer and mortgagee?

Exercise 5

Broker Dibbs and lawyer Dobbs occupy offices on the same floor of an office building. They frequently lunch together and have become friends. Broker Dibbs gets an offer from Tom Angelo who is moving from Montreal, and the offer is accepted. A friend of Angelo in Montreal has recommended that he use Lawyer Whaffle. Dibbs honestly believes that Dobbs would be a better lawyer for Angelo than Whaffle. Discuss.

SECTION II

AGENCY REPRESENTATION, CONTRACT LAW AND THE AGREEMENT OF PURCHASE AND SALE

The real estate profession in Ontario is based on the relationship of principal and agent, a relationship most commonly created by a representation agreement. While the basic concepts of agency law remain unchanged, there have been a number of recent changes in the way these concepts are now being applied, as a result of the trend in Ontario towards buyer representation along with various regulatory changes. Equally important for a real estate practitioner is a knowledge of contract law. Agreements between parties negotiated by real estate practitioners must be legally enforceable and free of problems. This section reviews the law of agency and contract law, and applies these concepts to the creation of a binding Agreement of Purchase and Sale.

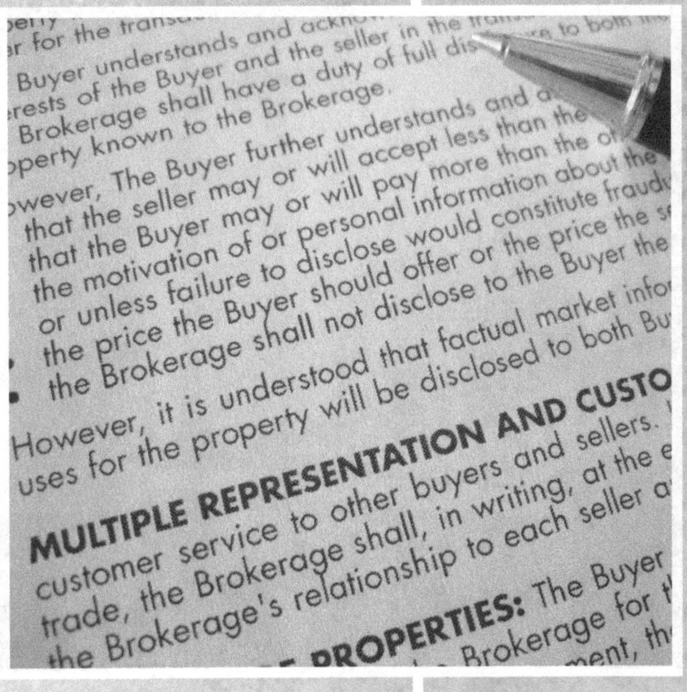

The basis for all communication between a real estate practitioner and a buyer or seller depends upon agency representation and the nature of the service being provided. This requires the agent to be knowledgeable about the law of agency and the application of agency concepts in the market today. A knowledge of every detail of the Agreement of Purchase and Sale is also required. There is no room for error when an agreement is being negotiated between buyer and seller.

CHAPTER 4

Agency Representation

Introduction

The agency relationship between broker and principal involves certain duties and obligations that are unique in law, unlike those experienced in the typical employer/employee scenario based on a master/servant relationship. In reality, an agent (brokerage) falls somewhere between a servant and an independent contractor, in that the agent is expected to carry out the lawful instructions of the principal. The agent does, however, have some latitude in deciding how these instructions are expedited. This chapter provides you with a number of case studies to illustrate how agency relationships operate in the marketplace.

IMPORTANT: The Agency Task Force of the Canadian Regulators Group has advanced various refinements and clarification concerning agency. For example, agency obligations owed by an agent to a principal are now grouped under three categories: *general*, *fiduciary* and *regulatory*. Changes are scheduled for the next printing of this text. Further, the term '*agency*' is no longer used from a regulatory perspective in Ontario and has been replaced with '*representation*.' Applicable materials have been inserted at the end of this chapter.

Learning Outcomes

At the conclusion of this chapter, students will be able to:

- Describe how agency relationships are formed.
- Outline and differentiate between various types of agency relationships common in the Ontario marketplace.
- Discuss duties owed by an agent to principal and a principal to an agent.
- Summarize key considerations in establishing an agency authority and preparing appropriate documentation.
- Outline key provisions in REBBA 2002 concerning representation and its relationship to agency as established by common law.

OVERVIEW: LAW OF AGENCY

If someone acts on behalf of another, the law considers that person as being an extension of the principal, and the law governing the relationships between them and their relations with other persons is called the law of agency. There are a number of ways in which the principal-agent relationship might be established, but the most common is by express agreement.

A number of duties arise under the law of agency for which a real estate agent (brokerage) is responsible to the principal (client). The agent must honour the obligations that are inherent in an agency agreement. The agent must perform these duties:

- Good faith and full disclosure.
- Competence.
- Obedience.
- Accounting.
- Confidentiality.
- Loyalty.

It is possible for an agent to delegate the agency responsibilities to another, but this can only be done under certain circumstances. An agent who fails to carry out those duties owed to the principal is liable to the principal, the agent's profession and local board, the registration authorities and those responsible for prosecution. The principal, in return, owes the agent these responsibilities:

- Remuneration.
- Indemnification.

The typical agency agreement between an owner of property as principal and the real estate brokerage as agent is the Seller Representation Agreement. Regardless of the listing form used, it will establish the agency relationship. If an agent is to represent a buyer as principal, the agent should have a specific representation agreement with the buyer that sets out the terms of their understanding.

Master/Servant

A master directly controls and supervises the work of the servant, who is bound to comply with all of the master's reasonable orders. The master is responsible to third parties for the servant's actions in the performance of that work. Although this relationship may have originated with the ancient doctrines of servitude, the concept persists today in relationships involving most employees in the typical business situation, including a registered real estate salesperson employed by a broker.

This employment relationship is often contrasted with an agency relationship created between principal and agent. The degree of control and direction by an employer is greater than in the relationship between principal and agent. The contrast is even greater with the independent contractor relationship, which will only be recognized when little or no direct control is exercised over the ongoing activities of the employee.

EXAMPLE *Master/Servant*

Broker/Owner Brown, of XYZ Real Estate Ltd., is expanding her brokerage. She wants to hire approximately eight salespeople particularly to service the new housing market. The salespeople will be registered under the applicable regulatory act as employees. However, each new registrant will work as an independent contractor. Accordingly, Brown is creating employee status in line with provincial statutory requirements, but each salesperson will have considerable independence in their day-to-day activities.

AGENCY

An agency relationship arises in a real estate transaction when a person, wishing to sell his/her home, seeks the assistance of a real estate brokerage through discussions with a real estate broker or salesperson employed by that brokerage. The principal is the seller of the property and the brokerage is the agent. Alternatively, the brokerage may be engaged by a buyer to assist in the purchase of a property. In this situation, the buyer is the principal and the brokerage is the agent. The agency relationship, in either case, exists between the brokerage and the buyer or seller despite the fact that a broker or salesperson actually secures the agency agreement.

Agency has grown into a complex topic beyond traditional seller agency because of the evolution of client/customer relationships. To complicate matters, agency practices and associated disclosure procedures currently vary by province as well as within brokerages and real estate boards across Canada. Further, terminologies differ based on individual provincial registration requirements.

Many situations involve agency relationships; e.g., executors acting as agents for estates, guardians acting as agents for minors, union representatives acting as agents for worker members and brokerages acting as agents for buyers and sellers.

Creation

An agency relationship is created between principal and agent when an agent is authorized by the principal to act on the principal's behalf in business transactions with a third party. The agency relationship results from mutual consent between principal and agent. Formalities, such as compensation or a written agreement are not necessary to create agency; nor does agency have to be intended, it can be created accidentally.

Agency can be established through various methods.

By Express Agreement	The most common method of creating an agency relationship. An express agreement should set out the definite understanding of client and brokerage (principal and agent) regarding the relationship. Common law does not require the agency relationship to be expressed in writing; however, it is obviously better for both principal and agent that a written agreement exists. In the real estate profession the practice of written authority is commonplace through the use of listing and buyer agency forms.
By Ratification	Agency is created by ratification if the principal accepts the benefits of an agent's previously unauthorized act. For example, Seller Smith adopts the actions of ABC Realty Inc., although the actions of ABC Realty Inc. were carried out without the express authority of Smith. Ratification can occur when a salesperson is attempting to obtain listings and the homeowner will not sign an agreement but advises the salesperson that if he/she has interested buyers to *bring them over.* When the salesperson does introduce a buyer and secures a sale, the seller has accepted the benefits and liabilities of that sale and thereby becomes the principal. When the agent expects to create agency retroactively, the agent must act on behalf of the principal even before agency has been ratified.
By Estoppel or Conduct	Occurs when a principal gives the impression to a third person that another person is acting on his/her behalf as an agent. For example, Smith, by deeds or conduct authorizes Jones, to act as his/her agent. Smith is then prevented from denying the existence of Jones' agency to a third party who dealt with Jones on the basis of Smith's words and conduct. In real estate, if a seller indicates to prospective buyers that they should contact a specific salesperson about the purchase of the seller's home, the seller may be legally barred from denying that the agency existed, even though a listing was not signed. Agency may also be created when an agent gives the impression to a third party that the agent is protecting and promoting the interests of the third party.
By Operation of Law (By Necessity)	Occurs when an emergency situation exists whereby the agent has the authority to bind his/her principal, although under normal circumstances this right would not exist. For example, an agent might be required to save goods of a client in his/her absence when unable to reach the principal for a decision given the need for immediate action. This type of circumstance could occur to the master of a ship or carrier of perishable produce, but is unlikely to happen in matters surrounding real estate transactions.
By Implied Authority	The authority to act on behalf of another may be implied, under certain circumstances. For example, if Smith had given ABC Realty Inc. express authority to do something, the courts would imply (in the absence of evidence to the contrary) that Smith has also given ABC Realty Inc. the authority to do those things necessary to carry out the express authority.

Disclosure

Agency disclosure has become complex with the advent of various agency relationships. While agents owe principals the duty of good faith and full disclosure, more precise guidelines were required in addition to common law requirements. Consequently, codes of ethics and provincial regulatory procedures and controls have been developed requiring specific disclosure procedures concerning the role and nature of agency services.

Most disclosure requirements, above those dictated by common law, concentrate on the timing and completeness of disclosure along with the informed consent of the client. Disclosure requirements are detailed in the Code of Ethics established by The Canadian Real Estate Association and the Code of Ethics established by way of regulation under the *Real Estate and Business Brokers Act, 2002.*

Representation CAUTION 

The *Real Estate and Business Brokers Act, 2002* and associated Regulations (collectively referred to as REBBA 2002) introduced new terminology based on the concept of representation. Common law agency terms used in this text (e.g., agent, agency relationship and dual agency) do not appear in REBBA 2002.

The legislation focuses on representation including the use of representation agreements. The term *represent* generally applies to situation where the brokerage owes fiduciary duties to the client. While terminologies have changed, certain underlying premises remain. For example, a buyer agency agreement and a buyer representation agreement are viewed as analogous to minimize any potential conflict between traditional common law terminology (agency) and regulatory requirements (representation).

A section has been added at the end of this chapter highlighting relevant definitions and descriptive materials found in REBBA 2002. Cross references are provided in the text. Chapter materials will be modified at next printing to integrate these regulatory changes.

Code of Ethics: The Canadian Real Estate Association Members of organized real estate are required to fully disclose the existence and nature of a member's agency relationship in accordance with the Code. The CREA Code of Ethics was updated as of January 1, 2008.

> ***Article 2: Disclosure of Role–Agency***
>
> *A REALTOR® shall fully disclose in writing to, and is advised to seek written acknowledgement from, his or her Clients and those Customers who are not represented by other Registrants regarding the role and nature of the service the REALTOR® will be providing. This disclosure shall be made at the earliest possible opportunity and in any event prior to the REALTOR® providing professional services which go beyond providing information as a result of incidental contact by a consumer.*

Real Estate and Business Brokers Act, 2002 and Regulations Detailed agency (representation) disclosure requirements have also been established for registrants by the Real Estate Council of Ontario. (See additional discussion under *REBBA 2002: Information Before Agreement* and *Multiple Representation*).

Duties

The agent is considered in law to represent the principal and to bring the principal into legal relationships with other parties. The needs of individuals are so complex that, to a large extent, such needs are fulfilled not by their own efforts but by the efforts of others on their behalf. If someone acts on behalf of another, he/she is considered in law to be an extension of that person. The law governing relations between these individuals and other persons is referred to as the *law of agency*. (See additional discussion under *REBBA 2002: Agency* and *Agent*.)

Agents owe principals (e.g., clients) their primary allegiance, including such duties as good faith and full disclosure, competence, obedience and accounting. Classifications and terminology regarding these duties generally fall under the term *fiduciary responsibilities* and vary somewhat in printed materials. (See additional discussion under *REBBA 2002: Client* and *Fiduciary Duties*.) Fiduciary duties are best explained using the following six categories.

Disclosure	The agent must disclose to his/her principal any information relevant to the transaction in which the agent has been engaged to assist. This includes any facts affecting the value or desirability of the property and all known relevant and material information.
Competence	The agent must exercise a degree of competence when representing his/her principal such as would be expected from an average person in that occupation or profession. In all agency relationships, the law sees the agent as an extension of the principal. Thus, the principal is liable for the agent's actions. Therefore, the agent will be under a duty to use superior skill and knowledge while pursuing the principal's affairs. An agent who claims to be a specialist must exercise competence in that specialty.
Obedience	An agent is obligated to obey the principal's lawful and reasonable instructions, even if the agent doesn't agree with them.
Accounting	An agent is obligated to account for all monies or property entrusted to his/her care that belongs to the principal; i.e., safeguard any money or documents relative to the principal's transactions or affairs.
Confidentiality	An agent must not use information acquired as the principal's agent for any purpose that is likely to cause the principal harm or to interfere with the principal's business, now or in the future. The duty of confidentiality should not be confused with a real estate professional's responsibility to disclose known material facts about the property to non-principals. The obligation to disclose such facts, including defects, is based on the professional's duty to treat all persons fairly and honestly.
Loyalty	The most important duty an agent has toward the principal is loyalty. The agent must place the interests of the principal above all else except the law in carrying out his/her functions as an agent.

Agents owe third parties (e.g., customers) the ethical duty to be honest, the legal duty not to misrepresent and the responsibility to exercise due care when answering inquiries or giving information. (See subsequent discussion under *REBBA 2002: Customer*). In real estate, the agency relationship can be established between the agent and either the buyer or the seller. The relationship can arise out of an agreement either expressed or implied, or written or oral. Agency relationships should be in writing and real estate brokerages should ensure that all activities fall within the limits of that authority. Agency will be implied when agents treat customers as principals (clients) even though no written agreement/contract exists.

Termination

The act of terminating a relationship between principal and agent will not affect any rights of either party that arose during the agency relationship. Several methods can be used to terminate an agency relationship.

Mutual Consent	Since the agency relationship is created by an agreement between parties, it is clear that the relationship can be terminated by the parties if they agree to do so.
Revocation	Generally, a principal has the absolute right to revoke any authority given to an agent at any time. However, in the majority of real estate scenarios, the principal has agreed to certain obligations until a specific date. The principal is not required to contract with anyone as a consequence of the agency agreement and may remove the property from the market by refusing to enter into any agreement. However, the principal may be liable for damages for breach of the agency, if the terms of that agency agreement are satisfied. Similarly, an agent may terminate the agency agreement, but may remain liable for damages for breach of the agreement if there was a fixed expiry date.
Expiry	The agency relationship will terminate at the date agreed to by the parties; i.e., the expiry date set out in the listing or buyer agency agreement. This may be replaced by either a new or renewal agreement and a true copy of this agreement must be given to the seller. The agreement may continue for purposes of commission resulting from a sale in a holdover period as provided in the listing agreement or buyer agency agreement.
Completion/ Performance	When the agent completes what was agreed to and the ultimate purpose is achieved, the relationship will terminate. The parties hope that the relationship will end with the successful completion of an agreement; e.g., the sale of the principal's property or the acquisition of property by the buyer.
Impossibility	Termination will occur if the agreement involves material that no longer exists; e.g., a building destroyed by fire. A listing agreement may provide for a continuation to permit the sale of the vacant land. An agency agreement concerning the sale of property may also be disrupted if the property is expropriated or foreclosed and neither commission nor damages may be payable, depending on the terms of the agency arrangement.
Death, Mental Incapacity or Bankruptcy	The agency agreement will be terminated in the event of the death, bankruptcy or mental incapacity of either the agent or the principal. Limited circumstances may exist where the agency agreement will continue despite the principal's death. For that reason, agreements may provide for an irrevocable provision and the requirement that such agreements be binding on the estate of the principal.
Registration Cancellation	Termination of agency will result if the agency agreement becomes void due to the cancellation of a brokerage's registration.

Types of Agency

BUYER AGENCY

Under buyer agency, a real estate brokerage represents the interests of the buyer. Buyer agency can be established by implication, as well as by written agreement. Buyers seeking exclusive representation usually do so through a representation agreement. This relationship is the counterpart of seller agency with the same agency principles and practices applying.

A representative of the buyer must use professional negotiation skills, seek appropriate properties that meet the buyer's needs, describe the merits and defects of any selected property, keep information confidential concerning the buyer and generally act in the buyer's best interests. The hallmarks of this relationship are good faith, full disclosure, competence, obedience, accounting and loyalty. The buyer and the brokerage will enter into a signed buyer representation agreement that details their relationship.

The seller usually pays all commission to the listing brokerage who, in turn, forwards the appropriate portion to the buyer's brokerage. Alternatively, the buyer's brokerage can be paid directly by the buyer and, therefore, this amount does not form part of the sale proceeds. In most transactions, the commission to the buyer's brokerage is paid via the listing brokerage from the proceeds of the sale. Payment procedures for the payment of commission will vary by provincial jurisdiction.

DUAL AGENCY

Under dual agency, the same brokerage has an agency relationship with both the buyer and the seller in a real estate transaction. Dual agency also occurs when different salespeople represent buyer and seller, and are employed by the same brokerage. Dual agency includes those who work in different branch offices. The brokerage or its representatives must advise the seller and the buyer of the dual aspect of representation and must be impartial when representing both parties. Both buyer and seller must give their informed consent to this form of representation. Dual agency is now referred to as multiple representation under the *Real Estate and Business Brokers Act, 2002.* (See additional discussion under *REBBA 2002: Multiple Representation*).

> *The law does not allow a person to assume relations so essentially inconsistent and repugnant to each other without the authority and consent of both principals.*
>
> *Source:* Mr. Justice Hughes, New Brunswick Court of Appeals, Cec MacManus Realty Ltd. vs. Bray, 1979

Extreme care must be exercised if a brokerage practises dual agency representation. If a dispute develops and remains unresolved, the brokerage and its representatives cannot continue to act for both parties. In the simplest situation, dual agency involves the seller signing a listing agreement with the brokerage and a buyer authorizing a buyer representation agreement with the same brokerage, with both parties understanding the inherent duality of function being performed by the brokerage. While legally permissible, The Canadian Real Estate Association has traditionally discouraged this practice. Dual agency can be awkward and potentially dangerous both legally and ethically for a brokerage and its representatives.

> *The Canadian Real Estate Association (CREA) has taken the position that it does not encourage the practice of dual agency representation. Therefore, CREA has not developed materials (clauses, forms and procedures) for dealing with unique situations that might necessitate the practice. Therefore, check with management before committing the brokerage to any situation that might contemplate dual agency representation.*
>
> Source: Sample Office Policy Manual, CREA

Proponents of dual agency advocate that full and complete disclosure, precise guidelines for conduct in a dual agency situation, and proper documentation will all but eliminate any risks. However, a strong cautionary note must be voiced.

> *Although disclosed dual agency relationships are technically lawful, there are compelling reasons real estate brokers (agents) should avoid creating them.*
>
> Source: *Who is My Client?* A REALTORS® Guide to Compliance with the Law of Agency, National Association of REALTORS®.

Implied (Unintended) Dual Agency The real danger with dual agency lies not so much with expressed agency, which can be largely remedied through proper procedures, but rather with implied dual agent relationships. In an expressed, fully disclosed relationship, the brokerage and its representatives can, in fact, represent both buyer and seller if the terms and responsibilities are clearly understood and agreed to by both parties in advance, through informed consent. With unintended dual agency, no formal document exists. Such duality arises when a brokerage or salesperson inadvertently represents two parties or unwittingly works on both sides of the transaction.

EXAMPLE ***Implied (Unintended) Dual Agency***

Salesperson Lee completed a listing agreement with Seller Smith. During the conversation, Lee was very explicit regarding his duties to Smith as a client and stated that all buyers would be treated as customers and owed honesty and fairness. Buyer Jones got an entirely different impression from Lee at an open house. Lee was forthright in providing information about Smith's circumstances concerning the sale and assured Jones that he could get the property for a low price.

While the listing authority created an express agreement with the seller, given Lee's actions, an implied dual agency relationship was established with both the buyer and seller.

Limited Dual Agency Limited dual agency has proven popular given inherent conflicts that arise with dual agency. Procedures, including variations found in individual brokerages, have generated considerable discussion. Most concerns centre on the issue of confidentiality and loyalty owed to the seller that conflicts with the same duties owed to the buyer. Generally, *limited dual agency* sets out procedures regarding:

- Non-disclosure of the price that either party is prepared to pay the other.
- Non-disclosure of the motivation of either buyer or seller.
- Non-disclosure of the terms of competing offers.
- Not disclose personal or financial information unless authorized.
- Not represent the interest of the buyer over the seller (or vice versa).

Undisclosed Dual Agency This situation arises when a professional is found to be acting in an agency role for conflicting interests without prior approval, understanding and agreement of the parties. The results may have serious consequences including forfeiture of commission, discipline by a local board or regulatory body, punitive or exemplary damages and possibly the loss of salesperson or broker registration. The broker and/or manager who is responsible for the activities of the sales force may also be at risk.

SELLER AGENCY

Seller agency is a relationship in which the brokerage and its salespeople represent the interests of the seller exclusively.

Sellers typically give authority to a brokerage to sell their property by signing a listing agreement that establishes a formal agency relationship between the seller and the real estate brokerage. This agreement sets out what the seller instructs the brokerage to do and what services are provided under seller agency. Further, it provides that representatives of the seller will use their professional negotiation skills to seek qualified buyers and generally promote the listed property, while keeping information concerning the seller confidential and always acting in the seller's best interests. The hallmarks of this relationship are good faith, full disclosure, competence, obedience and accounting. The seller has traditionally paid a commission directly to the agent. The listing agency then pays any brokers or salespeople within its employ and, if applicable, any co-operating brokerages involved in the transaction.

SINGLE AGENCY

Single agency is a relationship between a seller or buyer and an agent wherein the agent is considered in law to represent only the principal.

Agents owe principals their primary allegiance, including good faith and full disclosure, competence, obedience and accounting. Single agency is to be differentiated from dual agency in which the same agent has an agency relationship with both the seller and the buyer in the same real estate transaction. With the rise of buyer agency, the term *single agency* is sometimes used to refer to brokerages that only work with either buyers or sellers. For example, a brokerage dealing only with buyers and not offering agency services to sellers is referenced in certain jurisdictions as being a single buyer brokerage.

SUB-AGENCY

Sub-agency is a relationship whereby an individual is empowered by an agent to act on behalf of a principal of that agent.

The sub-agency concept extends to the authorization of co-operating brokerages to work on behalf of the seller. Traditionally, Multiple Listing Services® were based on the automatic offering of sub-agency by the listing broker to all other members of the real estate board. The use of subagency has gradually diminished given the growing popularity of buyer agency.

EXAMPLE ***Sub-Agent***

Salesperson Lee, of ABC Realty Inc., has recently entered into an exclusive listing agreement with Seller Smith to sell Smith's property. However, ABC Realty Inc., with Smith's permission, will also work with sub-agents to sell the property. In other words, other brokerages and their representatives will be provided the opportunity to sell the property and as such will owe the same duties to the seller as ABC Realty Inc. and Lee in the sale of the property.

AGENT

An agent is authorized by a principal to represent that principal in business transactions with another party. An agent acts on behalf of a principal as an extension of that person and can bring the principal into legal relationships with others.

Role

The agent must obey the principal's lawful instructions, although not necessarily subject to detailed and direct control or supervision as to how work is to be done. In many cases, an agent is authorized to bring the principal into contractual relations with other persons referred to as third parties. A typical example is the relationship between an owner of real estate and the real estate broker engaged to sell the property.

An agent in a real estate transaction is a special class of agent who may negotiate contracts for the principal, while not entrusted with the possession of the title documents or the sale article. To assist in understanding the role of an agent, the relationship may be compared with two variations, namely that of master and servant, and of employer and independent contractor. All three relationships are easier to define in theory than to identify in practice. In modern business, each may assume complicated and overlapping forms.

EXAMPLE *Agent—Role*

ABC Realty Inc. is asked to exclusively list Seller Smith's property. The listing agreement is signed and Salesperson Lee, a representative of ABC Realty Inc., proceeds to market the home, along with other properties currently listed with the firm. ABC Realty Inc. has established an agent/principal relationship and owes fiduciary duties to that principal. In effect, the agent becomes an extension of the seller.

Real estate agency is somewhat different from the traditional agent/principal relationship. For example, the seller exercises much less control over the agent than might be the case in other agency arrangements. In fact, the brokerage has various principals (buyers and sellers) to which it owes fiduciary duties at the same time. Further, the brokerage is not entrusted with the property, but rather only the marketing of the home. As a result, brokerage agency is often viewed as a special class of agent given the uniqueness associated with buying and selling real estate.

Delegation of Duties

As a rule of law, agents are expected to carry out their duties personally, since the principal expects them to accomplish allotted tasks for which they were engaged. However, exceptions to the rule apply to real estate brokerage.

EXPRESS AUTHORITY

The most common form of delegation is granted in a typical multiple listing agreement, where the principal authorizes the listing brokerage to co-operate with other brokerages in marketing the property. If a co-operating brokerage acts as a sub-agent, the duties of the agent to the principal are delegated to the sub-agent.

EXAMPLE *Agent—Delegation of Duties— Express Authority*

Seller Smith signs an MLS® agreement with ABC Realty Inc. to market his property at a price of $249,000 for a period of 90 days. By signing the listing agreement, Smith has agreed, by express authority, that ABC Realty Inc. is authorized to co-operate with other members of the real estate board in marketing the property. If a co-operating brokerage is acting as a sub-agent, ABC Realty Inc.'s duties are delegated to the sub-agent by express authority.

IMPLIED CONSENT

The second form of delegation is by way of implication. If an agent is involved in a profession in which it is common public knowledge that delegation of duties is necessary and standard practice, then it may be argued that the principal has given implied consent to delegate; e.g., the listing of a property.

EXAMPLE *Agent—Delegation of Duties— Implied Consent*

Seller Smith signs an exclusive listing agreement with ABC Realty Inc. and agrees to pay a commission based on an agreed upon percentage of the selling price. A commonplace arrangement in Smith's particular community is for brokerages to co-operate with other brokerages as sub-agents in selling the property regardless of whether or not the property was listed on the Multiple Listing Service®. In fact, it is common knowledge that such co-operation assists the seller, as the property gets much broader exposure to the market. Salesperson Lee, a representative of ABC Realty Inc., immediately calls various brokerages in the area in the hopes of finding a prospective buyer. In this instance, it could be claimed that Smith gave implied consent to the delegation of agency.

Traditionally, the listing brokerage was the agent and a co-operating brokerage was the sub-agent owing the same duties to the seller as the listing brokerage. Since the mid-1990's, the co-operating brokerage has taken on the role of a buyer agent in which allegiance is owed to the buyer while allegiance of the listing brokerage is owed to the seller. Consequently, the above example has limited applicability in the current marketplace.

STATUTORY

Statutory is the final form of delegation whereby real estate brokerages are permitted to delegate duties to registered salespeople under REBBA 2002. Therefore, if ABC Realty Inc. hires a salesperson who is registered under the Act, then that salesperson can work on behalf of the brokerage to secure listings and sell property for the brokerage.

The typical real estate transaction involves a listing brokerage that is the agent for the seller and any co-operating brokerages are assumed to be agents for the buyer unless otherwise agreed to. Thus, the co-operating brokerage's allegiance is toward the buyer and the listing brokerage's allegiance is toward the seller with both commissions being paid from the proceeds of the sale.

Duties to the Principal

A real estate agent under the law has numerous responsibilities to the principal including general duties at common law and specific provisions of provincial statutes. The fundamental duties of an agent to a principal are:

- Good faith and full disclosure;
- Competence;
- Obedience;
- Accounting;
- Confidentiality; and
- Loyalty.

The agent has an obligation to perform all duties personally unless otherwise authorized by express consent, by implication or by statute. If an agent does not carry out his/her duties, the principal has remedies that include dismissal, damages, action to recover property, action for an accounting, action to resist payment, prosecution and indemnity.

Duties to Third Parties

When the agent represents a client, that principal is owed complete loyalty. However, where do the brokerage and its salespeople stand in relation to the third party when there is no client relationship with that individual?

Legally, the brokerage and salespeople have specific duties failing which liability for damages can result.

- Make no misrepresentation regarding the property to the third party.
- Be fair and ethical.
- Take care in answering third party inquiries to ensure complete and accurate information.

EXAMPLE *Agent—Duties to Third Parties*

Buyer Jones advised Salesperson Martin that she could afford a monthly mortgage payment of $1,000. Martin knew that Jones was relying on her expertise and advice. The MLS® listing showed a mortgage at 7% with monthly payments of $1,032.34, amortized over 25 years, but due in one year. Martin did not explain to Jones that the interest rate might change the following year and in fact stated that the rate would apply for the full term of the mortgage. The buyer assumed that the term was 25 years and Martin said nothing to correct this assumption.

At renewal date, nine months following closing, the rate increased to 8.5%. Jones sued Martin and the judge held that Martin and the brokerage were negligent for failing to confirm and fully explain the listing information relating to the mortgage. The judge stated that an agent is under a duty to avoid negligent misrepresentations.

PRINCIPAL

For agency purposes, a principal is an individual who authorizes the agent (brokerage) to act on his/her behalf in an agency (principal/agent) relationship.

Principal/Agent Relationship

A principal/agent relationship is created by express or implied agreement or by law, whereby one party delegates the transaction of some lawful business, with more or less discretionary power, to another who undertakes to manage the affair and render an account thereof.

EXAMPLE ***Principal (Agency)—Principal/Agent Relationship***

Salesperson Ward has just completed a listing agreement with Owner Jones. This exclusive authority to sell Jones' home is for a period of 90 days at a listing price of $149,000. As such, Jones and XYZ Real Estate Ltd., have entered into a principal/agent relationship. The creation of this relationship is best described in the wording of the listing:

> *I hereby give you the exclusive and irrevocable right to act as my agent to lease or sell the property until 11:59 p.m. on the 1st day of May, 20xx for the price of One Hundred and Forty-Nine Thousand Dollars ($149,000), and upon the terms particularly set out herein or at such other price or terms acceptable to me. It is understood that the price set out above is at my personal request, after full discussion with your representative regarding potential market value of the property.*

Duties: Indemnity and Remuneration

The primary duties owed to an agent by a principal are remuneration and indemnification. In terms of remuneration, the principal is obligated to pay the agreed upon amount. Where no specific agreement exists, the agent is entitled to a reasonable sum, based on compensation for similar services within that particular locale. The principal must also provide indemnification in respect of all acts undertaken or liabilities incurred by the agent, provided that the agent has acted competently and within the lawful instructions of that principal.

See *Agency* regarding responsibilities and duties owed to a principal by an agent.

EXAMPLE ***Principal (Agency)—Duties***

A salesperson obtained a listing agreement for the sale of two adjacent properties. Negotiations commenced immediately on the smaller property, following the buyer's introduction to both parcels. An agreement was ultimately entered into between the buyer and seller. At a later date, the buyer proceeded to enter into another agreement with the seller for the second property through a corporation owned by the buyer (without involving the real estate brokerage). The brokerage sued, arguing that the seller knowingly and deliberately evaded the contractual understanding between the seller and the named brokerage. The Judge agreed.

The court agreed that a contractual understanding did occur that involved both properties. The brokerage was awarded a commission based on the prevailing rate for the area.

Indemnity

The obligation to indemnify involves the assurance of one party to make financial compensation or repair and make good for any loss or damage that has been incurred or may be incurred on another party. Alternatively, the right of one party to claim damages against another.

The specifics of an indemnity are often detailed in an indemnification agreement between the parties or a clause set out within a contract between the parties.

EXAMPLE *Indemnity*

ABC Realty Inc. is contemplating a move to a larger office within a commercial office tower. The brokerage specializes in commercial and industrial property sales and leasing and the new location will be conveniently close to several important corporate customers.

The landlord of the property is concerned about the brokerage's overall financial strength and seeks some form of indemnification, failing which, lease negotiations will be at an end. Fortunately, Broker/Owner Johnson owns a successful development company with a proven ten-year financial track record.

The landlord insists on an indemnity agreement with Johnson's development company stating that, in the event of default by ABC Realty Inc., the company will:

- Pay all rent if the tenant, ABC Realty Inc., fails to do so.
- In the event of an early termination, be responsible and effectively become the landlord's tenant (at the landlord's option), in terms of obligations under early termination.

The landlord is not required to notify the indemnifier that the tenant has failed to fulfill any obligations under the lease. In the case of a default, the landlord may pursue the indemnifier directly. The indemnity agreement can only be altered by mutual agreement of landlord and indemnifier as it is absolute and unconditional.

INDEMNITY BY A PRINCIPAL

The principal must indemnify the authorized agent against losses, liabilities and expenses incurred in the lawful performance of the undertaking. The agent must have acted within the authority granted. The principal has no duty to indemnify an agent who acts unlawfully or negligently or is in breach of duty.

EXAMPLE *Indemnity by a Principal*

Salesperson Lee lists Seller Smith's house exclusively for $155,000 after carefully inspecting the property and preparing the listing agreement.

At the point of signing and in the presence of another salesperson from the brokerage, Lee asks Smith specifically if he has had any problems with basement leakage. The question was posed because of a faint water stain on part of the downstairs panelling. Smith explained that he had inadvertently left an outside hose running for several hours. Satisfied with the answer from his client and seeing no further evidence, Lee highlighted the water stain on his notes but disregarded any reference to it in the listing.

Later, when a buyer acquired the property, the true extent of water damage and ongoing leakage was discovered. The buyer sued both seller and agent. The agent proceeded with a counterclaim against the principal arguing that he was operating under the authority granted, was misled by the principal and was seeking indemnification for any damages successfully pursued by the buyer.

INDEMNITY BY AN AGENT

The agent is liable to indemnify the principal for any acts undertaken personally or delegated to that agent's employees, salespeople or sub-agents. The principal may be liable to third parties for acts carried out by the agent under the doctrine of vicarious responsibility. The principal will then claim indemnity from the agent, who will be responsible for all losses resulting from the breach of duty. The third party may claim compensation that includes legal costs. The principal may recover monies paid out, legal expenses and interest on all such payments.

Real estate practitioners, in carrying out their function, encounter various situations that can give rise to litigation involving indemnity; e.g., representations made on behalf of a client (buyer or seller), failure to correctly carry out duties in listing and marketing a property, and matters involving the drafting and presentation of offers.

EXAMPLE *Indemnity by an Agent*

Salesperson Ward listed a property adjacent to a river. Seller Green advised Ward that the rear part of the property was within a flood risk area and subject to applicable provincial legislation. Several years ago, Green had been unable to put an addition on the property owing to restrictions relating to the flood risk area. Ward, while making a mental note of the situation, forgot to mention anything in the listing. Due to an unexpected interruption during the listing process, Green had to leave and agreed to meet again the following day. Salesperson Ward, unable to attend, sent another salesperson to complete the documentation. As an incentive, the salesperson would split any listing commission. No further mention of rear yard restrictions appeared on the listing.

The salesperson placed several ads about the property. The heading for one read: Pool-Sized Yard. A prospective buyer, seeing the panoramic view and wishing to fully landscape the rear yard, acquired the property only to discover that his plans for a deck, swimming pool and other improvements were not possible owing to flood area restrictions.

The buyer sued the seller. The seller in turn sought indemnification from the agent and sued the brokerage, claiming that the agent was liable for misrepresentations made to the buyer.

Remuneration

An agent is entitled to payment for services rendered as agreed between the parties. In a real estate transaction, this normally takes the form of an agreement, such as an exclusive listing agreement or a buyer agency agreement. If no agreement exists, but the agent acts on behalf of the client and fulfills a duty that is ratified, the agent will be entitled to remuneration, subject to compliance with the applicable provincial real estate act.

EXAMPLE *Remuneration*

Owner Smith wants to sell his property and has agreed to a five percent commission on any sale effected by ABC Realty Inc. during the currency of an exclusive listing. The list price was $159,900 and the property sold for $155,000. Accordingly, Smith as the principal, owes ABC Realty Inc., the agent, the sum of $7,750 (0.05 x $155,000). If a real estate brokerage other than ABC Realty Inc. sells Smith's property, ABC Realty Inc. would forward the selling portion of the commission to the selling brokerage pursuant to local real estate board procedures in the case of an MLS® listing, or as agreed between the brokerages.

FINDER'S FEE

A finder's fee is paid to a person or other entity for information that initiates a business transaction. Various types of finders' fees or referral fees can be generated from real estate transactions, the most common involving listing or selling properties (e.g., client referrals) and arranging financing. The Code of Ethics under REBBA 2002 sets out guidelines concerning disclosure of such fees or other money received, other than from the client. (See additional discussion under *REBBA 2002: Finder's Fee.*)

Remedies

Remedies available to a principal in the event that an agent does not carry out his/her duties include dismissal, damages for breach of contract, action to recover property in the agent's possession, action for an accounting of all that has been received on the principal's behalf, action to resist payment (i.e., refuse to pay the commission), prosecution and indemnity.

The final remedy bears special mention. The agent can be liable to indemnify the principal for any acts undertaken personally or delegated to employees or sub-agents when that agent does not carry out his/her duties. While the principal may in fact be liable to third parties for such acts (doctrine of vicarious responsibility) the principal will then claim indemnity from the agent for all losses flowing from the breach of duty. As the example shows, the principal may successfully pursue remedies, regardless of whether the agency relationship was formally agreed and documented between the parties.

EXAMPLE *Principal (Agency)—Remedies*

The salesperson was approached by an individual wishing to invest personal funds in the mortgage market. The approach was made based on the salesperson's apparent knowledge of mortgage investments in that particular suburban marketplace. Sometime following this discussion, the same salesperson sold a property conditional upon the sale of the buyer's property. As events unfolded, however, the closing date of the new property was fast approaching with no sale of the prior home. As a result, the salesperson contacted the investor referenced earlier and recommended that his investment funds be placed by way of a second mortgage on the new property. The investor, trusting the salesperson, delivered the funds as promised and the transaction closed.

As an aside, the salesperson also committed funds to assist in the closing. In fact, according to the full text of the judgment, the first and second mortgages exceeded the purchase price.

Ultimately a default occurred and the investor sued the mortgagors (buyers), the real estate brokerage and the salesperson. Without delving into all aspects of this case, one focal point is relevant to all real estate practitioners. The Judge, while conceding that the courts have had difficulty defining fiduciary duty, found that the investor relied upon the professionalism of the salesperson and that the investor was dependent upon that individual. While acknowledging that a customer/brokerage relationship need not be a fiduciary one, this circumstance did fall within accepted definitions of fiduciary duties. Because a fiduciary duty did exist, the salesperson failed to provide full disclosure regarding various matters, including but not limited to the merits of investing monies in the property and the salesperson's undisclosed role in contributing funds to facilitate the closing. The Judge ordered that the defendant (salesperson) be responsible for the return of the plaintiff's (investor's) money.

AUTHORITY

Authority is the legal power or right given by a principal and accepted by the agent to act on the principal's behalf in business transactions with a third party.

The listing agreement is the most common form of authority delegated to real estate brokerages. Wordings for this authority vary as no standard form prevails throughout the province. However, most set out similar basic responsibilities concerning the marketing of the property, payment of commission for its sale, lease, exchange or option and authority to co-operate with other brokerages.

A typical introductory wording for an exclusive listing authority is provided:

I [the seller] hereby give you the exclusive and irrevocable right to act as my agent to lease or sell the Property until 11:59 p.m. on the __ day of _______, 20xx for the price of ______________________ Canadian Dollars ($Can), and upon the terms particularly set out herein or at such other price or terms acceptable to me. It is understood that the price set out above is at my personal request, after full discussion with your representative regarding potential market value of the property.

Most listing forms then detail various responsibilities and obligations flowing from this authority, such as:

- Commission payable for the marketing of property on terms and conditions as set out in the listing or as otherwise accepted.
- Agency relationship including the right to co-operate with any other brokerage.
- Referral of inquiries by the seller from any source whatsoever to the brokerage.
- Permission to show prospective purchasers and market the property including the placement of a *for sale* sign.

Estoppel

An estoppel is a bar to alleging or denying a fact because of one's own previous actions or words to the contrary.

The concept of estoppel comes into play with agency relationships and authority granted by a principal. Such a relationship can arise when a person's conduct is such that another person acts upon a reasonable inference that the relationship exists. The person is then estopped from denying the relationship. The relationship cannot be denied if it was the person's own conduct that led to a reasonable, but inaccurate conclusion. For example, a principal may be estopped because the principal's conduct of allowing that person to be his agent prevents the principal from denying that he/she gave the authority. Estoppel may also arise:

- When no actual authority was given to an agent;
- When only a limited authority was given; or
- Where the authority has been terminated but the circumstances lead others to believe that the agent has full authority.

This gives the agent an apparent or ostensible authority to act. The principal will be bound by contracts made with third parties who acted in good faith.

The apparent authority that an agent may have in a specific instance will depend on the nature of the business involved, local laws and trade customs. For example, a mercantile agent who has possession of goods may have authority to pledge them for credit. A stock broker may be able to borrow against bearer certificates in his/her possession. A real estate broker, in some jurisdictions, may be able to sign an agreement on behalf of the seller, however, a real estate broker is usually empowered to trade in real estate by assisting in the formation of contractual relationships between a seller and buyer. This apparent authority is not as extensive as that of other types of agents.

Ratification

Ratification is a process in which a person may initially purport to act for someone as his/her agent knowing that authority to do so has not been granted or that the limits of authority have been exceeded. The subsequent adoption of the agent's acts by the principal is called *ratification.* This affirmation of the conduct of the agent after the fact is usually considered to put the parties in the same legal position as if the agent always had authority to represent the principal.

Certain conditions must exist before this doctrine applies. The principal must have been in existence and capable of adopting a legal contract. The principal must have been in the contemplation of the agent, and the relationship must have been disclosed to the third party. The principal must be aware of the acts of the agent and adopt them unconditionally.

Although these rules generally apply, exceptions may exist. For example, in common law, a limited company does not normally become a legal person until it is incorporated. It, therefore, cannot ratify an act purportedly made on its behalf before it was created unless statutory law provides for this eventuality. In Ontario, this situation has been altered by statute so that a company can adopt a pre-incorporation contract made on its behalf. The words used in a typical agreement are:

> *X, as trustee only, on behalf of a company to be incorporated.*

The efficiency and speed with which an Ontario numbered company can now be created, sometimes in one day, has also largely eliminated certain underlying concerns.

Express Authority

An express authority is a precise instruction, either in writing or orally, in which an authority is granted. In real estate terms, express authorities normally apply to listing situations. An authority delegated by the principal clearly sets forth in exact, plain, direct and well-defined limits those acts and duties that the agent is empowered to perform on behalf of the principal.

If there is a definite understanding between the principal and agent, then the agency relationship has been established by express agreement. This may be oral, in writing or in writing under seal. An exclusive listing agreement between an owner of real estate and a real estate brokerage is an obvious example of written express authority.

Exclusive Authority

An exclusive authority is one in which a brokerage has the exclusive rights to sell, lease or exchange the property owned by another for a fixed period. The exclusive authority is granted to the real estate brokerage named in the listing agreement.

An MLS® exclusive listing agreement has a similar wording but provides an additional authority for the brokerage to co-operate with other brokerages who are members of that real estate board or as otherwise defined, to assist in the marketing of the property.

The authority, along with other preprinted clauses within the listing agreement, normally provides that all marketing of the property, negotiations with the seller and other matters relating to the marketing process be conducted through the exclusive agent until expiry of the listing. An exclusive authority is contrasted with a non-exclusive or open listing in which any number of brokers might be involved in marketing the property with a commission paid to the successful brokerage upon an agreement being signed and the completion of that sale.

The increased use of buyer agency representation in a real estate transaction has given rise to exclusive agency relationships with the buyer. Wordings for both listings and buyer representation agreements vary by real estate board as well as provincial jurisdiction.

EXAMPLE *Exclusive Agent*

Salesperson Lee has completed an exclusive listing agreement with Seller Smith. The authority granted by the listing is exclusive. Following is an excerpt from the preprinted listing form:

> *In consideration of your listing my property known as 123 Main Street in the City of Anycity, I hereby give you the exclusive and irrevocable right to act as my agent to lease or sell the property until 11:59 p.m. on the 23 day of May, 20xx...*

AGREEMENTS

Listing Agreement

A listing agreement is an oral or written agreement under which the owner appoints a real estate brokerage for a designated period of time to sell, lease or exchange a property based on the owner's stated terms, and under which the owner agrees to pay the brokerage a commission.

The listing agreement performs several basic functions. As the basis for the agency relationship between the seller and real estate brokerage, the listing establishes well-defined limitations on the agent's authority and provides detailed information regarding the property for assistance when answering inquiries from prospects' buyers. This listing agreement also provides the foundation for offer negotiations, the drafting of an offer and, if necessary, a mortgage application.

Most listing agreements consist of two essential parts. The authority involves the appointment of the agent and includes the agreement to pay commission. The data input form provides detailed information on the property. A seller property information statement may or may not be used in conjunction with the listing. Accuracy and care in completing a listing agreement are crucial. The listing agreement is a legal document and must be completed with due regard and consideration for its completeness and accuracy. (See additional discussion under *REBBA 2002: Seller Representation Agreement*).

HOLDOVER PROVISION

The holdover provision is a provision in an agreement remaining from a former period and is found in practically all listings used by real estate brokerages. Under this provision, while the listing brokerage's authority ends upon the expiry date, if the brokerage introduces a person to the property during the term of the listing who effects a private sale with the owner during a specified period after the expiry, the owner is liable for a commission payment to that broker. A similar provision is included in buyer agency agreements concerning property introduced to the buyer during the currency of the agreement.

EXAMPLE 1 *Buyer Introduced During Listing Period*

Seller Smith signs a 90-day listing with ABC Realty Inc. that contains a holdover provision. Following expiration, a buyer originally introduced to the property by a salesperson in ABC Realty's employ returns to negotiate directly with Smith. The buyer clearly wants a lower price to gain the benefit from Smith not paying any commission. Smith, uncertain as to his position, takes the exclusive agreement to his lawyer. The lawyer confirms that if Smith sells the property to this buyer, then a commission is payable to ABC Realty Inc.

EXAMPLE 2 *Subsequent Listing and Holdover Clause*

Seller Smith was unhappy with Salesperson Lee because the property did not sell within the 60-day listing period despite several showings. While Lee insisted that a price reduction was necessary, Smith elected not to renew the listing but rather to select XYZ Real Estate Ltd.

Interestingly, within the first month of this new 120-day listing authority, Smith agreed to reduce the price. Two months later, it was sold unconditionally by a co-operating brokerage to a buyer who was introduced to the property when ABC Realty Inc. was the listing agent. Smith, alluding to the holdover clause, expressed concerns that he might have to pay two commissions. XYZ Real Estate Ltd. assured him that such was not the case as the original listing provided that the holdover did not apply if the property was subsequently listed and sold by another brokerage pursuant to a new listing agreement.

The exact wording and time limit of the holdover period in a listing or buyer agency agreement can vary.

Buyer Agency Agreement

A buyer agency agreement is an oral or written agreement in which the buyer typically appoints a real estate brokerage for a designated time period to locate property meeting certain general characteristics, for which the broker receives a commission either from the listing brokerage or the buyer. Wordings and terms will vary in the marketplace.

The buyer agency agreement performs several functions. The agreement establishes agent authority, commission arrangements, agency responsibilities and other relevant items including the buyer's obligation to refer found properties to the agent. The agreement provides the foundation for offer negotiations and offer drafting. The buyer agency agreement, as a legal document, must be accurate and completely prepared setting out the exact understanding of the client and the agent. (See additional discussion under *REBBA 2002: Buyer Representation Agreement*).

Option to Buy/Purchase

An option to buy/purchase is a right given by the owner of property to another (for valuable consideration) to buy certain property within a limited time at an agreed price. An option to buy, referred to in some jurisdictions as an *offer to purchase*, allows a seller and buyer to enter into an option that gives the buyer the right to buy the seller's property at an agreed price at some future date.

An option to buy is not normally used in residential transactions, but would have application in transactions dealing with industrial, commercial and investment properties; e.g., a developer wishes to option certain lands for a period of time to obtain development approvals and/or adjoining lands.

An option to buy is distinct from an agreement/contract in that the latter creates immediate mutual rights and obligations on both seller and buyer. The option to buy only gives the buyer a right to purchase the property within a specified period without imposing any obligation to purchase. An option is not to be confused with a conditional contract; i.e., one that depends on the occurrence of some specified event. When a condition is inserted in an agreement, the courts have determined that an obligation exists for the party to make a reasonable effort to satisfy the condition. The option to purchase gives the buyer the right to purchase but does not impose any obligation to do so. If the option is not exercised, the contract will be at an end.

If the option is exercised by the buyer, then a binding agreement will result. The seller must understand that, while the option period is in existence, he/she cannot sell the property to a third party. All terms of the option to purchase must be completed in the same detail as one would with any agreement.

REBBA 2002

The *Real Estate and Business Brokers Act, 2002* and Regulations uses the term *representation* and makes no reference to *agency*, as described in common law. Selected sections from REBBA 2002 have been reprinted to illustrate significant topics including representation and service agreements, multiple representation and customer/client relationships.

NOTE: References to the Act & Regulations cite the appropriate section using the following abbreviations.

REBBA	Real Estate and Business Brokers Act, 2002
GEN	General, Ontario Regulation, 567/05
OTH	Education Requirements, Insurance, Records and Other Matters, Ontario Regulation 579/05
CODE	Code of Ethics Ontario Regulation 580/05

Agency

The common law term *agency* and associated terms; e.g., *agent, agency relationship* and *dual agency* do not appear in the Act or the Regulations. The legislation focuses on representation and agreements between brokerages and buyers/sellers.

While REBBA 2002 does not explicitly define the term *represent*, it generally applies to situations where the brokerage owes fiduciary duties to a client. As such, the brokerage must act in the best interests of that person when providing advice and services as in the case of a representation agreement.

The legislation also clearly differentiates between a representation agreement involving a client and non-representation (non-fiduciary) services offered to a customer by way of a service agreement.

Agent

The term *agent*, which is derived from common law, does not appear in REBBA 2002 or the Regulations. Registration categories under REBBA 2002 include brokerage, broker and salesperson. As background, an agency relationship is established when an agent (real estate brokerage) accepts responsibility to act for another (principal/seller) in negotiations with third parties.

REBBA 2002 (CONTINUED)

Buyer Representation Agreement

- CODE, Subsec. 1(1) and Sec. 14

A buyer representation agreement involves a written, oral or implied agreement between a brokerage and a buyer in which the brokerage represents the buyer as a client relating to a trade in real estate (CODE, Subsec. 1(1)). See ***Representation Agreement*** for additional discussion.

The Code of Ethics requires that such an agreement must be reduced to writing, signed by the brokerage and submitted to the buyer for signature prior to that buyer making an offer (CODE, Sec. 14). The Code does not require the buyer's signature, but registrants need to be aware of practical issues and risks associated with an unsigned representation agreement. In particular, proving entitlement to commission may become a problem.

The Code of Ethics also refers to any agreements registrants have with buyers or sellers (be they clients or customers) as *agreements for purpose of trading*. For requirements regarding information that must be contained within such agreements (i.e., effective and expiry dates), see ***Agreement (For Purpose of Trading)***.

See also ***Information Before Agreement*** outlining information that must be provided to either buyer or seller before that individual enters into an agreement in respect of trading in real estate.

Client

- GEN, Subsec. 1(1)
- CODE, Sec. 3, 4, 5, 16, 23, 24 and 27

A client is someone who is represented pursuant to a representation agreement with a brokerage. Brokers and salespersons employed by that brokerage offer services to that client and represent that person on behalf of that brokerage (GEN, Subsec. 1(1)).

Representation, while not defined in the Act or Regulations, applies to situations where the registrant is acting as a fiduciary agent from a common law perspective. The registrant in such a relationship has fiduciary duties to the client and must act in that client's best interests.

A client is clearly differentiated from a customer who is not represented by a brokerage. A customer may, however, enter into a service agreement with a brokerage. The Code of Ethics address obligations to clients and customers, as well as fiduciary duties owed specifically to clients.

The Code states that registrant loyalty ultimately rests with the client by protecting and promoting his/her best interests (CODE, Sec. 4). However, it also requires that registrants deal fairly, honestly and with integrity (CODE, Sec. 3) and provide conscientious service (CODE, Sec. 5) to all clients and customers.

Other examples of duties owed to clients are:

- Written consent is required for multiple representation (CODE, Sec. 16).
- A client must be informed of all significant steps taken in representing that person (CODE, Sec. 23).
- Registrants must convey offers to the client at the earliest practicable opportunity (CODE, Sec. 24).
- Registrants must use their best efforts to ensure that agreements are written and legible (CODE, Sec. 27).

Finder's Fee

- CODE, Sec. 18

A registrant must disclose to the client any direct or indirect financial benefit received from another person arising from services provided to the client; e.g., a finder's fee or referral fee. See also ***Registrar's Bulletins–Mortgage Finder's Fee and Referral Fees.***

REBBA 2002 (CONTINUED)

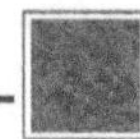

Information Before Agreement

- CODE, Sec. 10

The Code of Ethics requires that buyers and sellers be provided certain information as early as is practically possible and before entering an agreement in respect of trading in real estate. Further, the brokerage must use its best efforts to obtain a written acknowledgement that such information has been received.

Information to be provided includes:

- Service alternatives available through the brokerage and types of services provided under the agreement (e.g., a representation agreement or other agreement such as a service agreement).
- The fact that circumstances could arise where multiple representation might occur involving the same trade, a discussion of services that would be provided to each client in such an instance and the need for client consent to this arrangement.
- The fact that circumstances could arise where services might be provided to more than one customer for the same trade.
- The fact that circumstances could arise where clients might be represented and services are provided to customers for the same trade, including the restricted nature of services provided to the customer under that situation.

Multiple Representation

- GEN, Sec. 22
- CODE, Subsec. 10(1) and 16

A significant addition in the new legislation concerns rules regarding brokerage conduct in multiple representation situations.

Multiple representation refers to any situation where two or more clients in a real estate transaction are represented by a single brokerage. Possible scenarios include a single broker or salesperson representing both the buyer and seller; different salespersons or brokers employed by the same brokerage representing both the buyer and seller; or a registrant representing multiple buyers in the same transaction.

Provisions included in the legislation are intended to minimize potential problems by ensuring that registrants and clients are both clear about the nature of services being provided.

Informed, Written Consent (GEN, Sec. 22)
Registrants must not represent more than one client in respect of a real estate trade unless all of the clients represented by the registrant consent in writing to the multiple representation.

Nature of Services (CODE, Subsec. 10(1))
Sec. 10 of the Code of Ethics identifies information that must be discussed with buyers and sellers prior to entering into an agreement in respect of trading in real estate.

Subsec. 10(1) 3 specifically addresses two requirements regarding multiple representation. First, a brokerage must inform the buyer or seller that their written consent is required for such representation. Second, the brokerage must outline the nature of services provided to each client.

See ***Information Before Agreement*** for other information that must be provided before entering into an agreement with a buyer or seller in respect of a trade in real estate.

Disclosure to Clients (GEN, Sec. 22; CODE, Sec. 16)
The Code also addresses multiple representation in Sec. 16 which indicates that a brokerage shall not represent more than one client in a trade unless certain disclosures are made. The brokerage must indicate that it proposes to represent more than one client and outline the differences in its obligations when representing one client, in comparison to multiple clients, including any differences relating to information disclosed and services provided.

See ***Registrar's Bulletins–Representation*** for a detailed discussion of representation, multiple representation and associated disclosures.

REBBA 2002 (CONTINUED)

Purchase/Sale By Registrant

- REBBA, Sec. 32

Disclosure by a registrant when acquiring or disposing of any interest in real estate has undergone only minor changes from the previous Act. As before, registrants must deliver a notice to all other parties and receive signed acknowledgements from those parties prior to making any offer.

The written notice, when acquiring or disposing of an interest in real estate, must state that the registrant is a brokerage, broker or salesperson. This statement must include full disclosure of facts known by the registrant that may affect the value of the real estate.

When acquiring an interest in real estate, the Act also requires disclosure of any negotiations by the registrant for the subsequent disposition of such real estate.

Representation Agreement

- GEN, Subsec. 1(1)
- CODE Sec. 13 and 14

A representation agreement can be written, oral or implied. The key determinant is that the brokerage and the person have agreed that the brokerage will represent the person as a client in relation to a trade (GEN, Subsec. 1(1)).

The Act and Regulations do not specifically define *represent*, but the term refers to a brokerage and its employed brokers and salespersons acting in a fiduciary capacity (i.e., performing various fiduciary duties to protect and promote the interests of the buyer or seller as a client).

The Code of Ethics states that representation agreements with buyers and sellers must be reduced to writing, signed by the brokerage and submitted to the buyer or seller client for signature (CODE, Sec. 13 & 14). The Code does not require a signature, but registrants need to be aware of practical issues and risks associated with an unsigned representation agreement. In particular, proving entitlement to commission may become a problem.

Representation agreements must be clearly distinguished from other agreements between brokerages and customers, such as a service agreement. Services to customers do not include the fiduciary duties that registrants owe to clients.

See ***Registrar's Bulletins–Representation*** for a detailed discussion of representation, multiple representation and associated disclosures.

Seller Representation Agreement

- CODE, Subsec. 1(1) and Sec. 13

A seller representation agreement involves a written, oral or implied agreement between a brokerage and a seller in which the brokerage represents the seller as a client relating to a trade in real estate (CODE, Subsec. 1(1)). See ***Representation Agreement*** for additional discussion.

The Code of Ethics requires that such an agreement must be reduced to writing, signed by the brokerage and submitted to the seller for signature prior to the buyer making an offer (CODE, Sec. 13). The Code does not require the seller's signature, but registrants need to be aware of practical issues and risks associated with an unsigned representation agreement. In particular, proving entitlement to commission may become a problem.

The Code of Ethics also refers to any agreements with buyers or sellers (be they clients or customers) as *agreements for purpose of trading*. For requirements regarding information that must be contained within such agreements (i.e., effective and expiry dates), see ***Agreement (For Purpose of Trading)***.

See also ***Information Before Agreement*** outlining information that must be provided to either buyer or seller before that individual enters into an agreement in respect of trading in real estate.

REBBA 2002 (CONTINUED)

Service Agreement

- GEN, Subsec. 1(2)
- CODE Sec. 10 and 15

The General Regulation refers to agreements *other than representation agreements* in which the brokerage provides services to the customer, as distinct from a representation agreement with a client. The Code of Ethics also refers to a representation agreement or *another type of agreement.*

While many types of *other* agreements are possible, the most common contemplated by the legislation is a service agreement. This agreement with a customer sets out specific services offered to that individual, but does not involve the greater number of obligations required when representing a client (GEN, Subsec. 1(2)).

The Code of Ethics requires that an agreement in respect of a trade in real estate must be reduced to writing, signed by the brokerage and submitted to the customer for signature (CODE, Sec. 15). The Code does not require the signature, but registrants need to be aware of practical issues and risks associated with an unsigned service agreement. In particular, proving entitlement to commission may become a problem.

Registrants must fully understand obligations set out in the Code of Ethics and review the Code, clause by clause, to determine how each provision applies when representing clients and providing services to customers.

See also ***Information Before Agreement*** outlining information that must be provided to either buyer or seller before that individual enters into an agreement in respect of trading in real estate (CODE, Sec. 10).

REBBA 2002 (CONTINUED)

Published by the Real Estate Council of Ontario

Representation

The *Real Estate and Business Brokers Act, 2002* (the "Act") contains a number of provisions related to disclosures registrants must make to the buyers and sellers they represent in real estate transactions. In general, registrants are required to be clear about the nature of services they are providing when they enter into agreements to represent or provide services to others in real estate transactions.

Three definitions that registrants need to fully understand to meet their obligations toward buyers and sellers are the definitions of "*client*", "*customer*" and "*representation agreement*". Under the Act a client is someone who is represented under a representation agreement with a brokerage. With respect to brokers and salespersons, persons are clients if the person has a representation agreement with the brokerage that employs the broker or salesperson and they are providing services to the person or representing the person on behalf of the brokerage in the transaction.

Representation agreements can be written, oral or implied. The key determinant is that the brokerage and the person have agreed that the brokerage will represent the person in respect of the trade. Although, the Act and its regulations do not define the term "*represent*" explicitly, it is meant to apply to situations when the registrant is acting as a fiduciary "*agent*" of the person from the perspective of the common law. In other words, the registrant has fiduciary obligations toward the person and is acting in their best interests in the transaction in terms of the advice and services that are provided. A customer is a person who has entered into a service agreement with a brokerage related to a real estate transaction, but who is not being represented by that brokerage as a client. This might apply to a situation in which a brokerage has entered into an agreement with a person to facilitate a real estate transaction, but the brokerage or its representatives are not providing any financial or fiduciary advice to the person as part of that agreement.

Although agreements with buyers and sellers can be written, oral or implied, registrants are required under the Act's regulations to reduce these agreements to writing and submit them to buyers and sellers for signature.

Sec. 10 of the Code of Ethics (Ont. Reg. 580/05) establishes minimum disclosures that must be made to buyers and sellers prior to entering into agreements with them. Registrants are required to describe the services that will be provided and the alternatives available to the potential client or customer. With respect to multiple representation, registrants are required to inform prospective buyers and sellers about the possibility of multiple representation, including a description of the services the brokerage would provide in those situations. Registrants also have to make it clear to buyers and sellers that they cannot represent multiple clients in a transaction unless all of the potential clients consent in writing to that representation.

Sec. 16 of the Code, requires further disclosures regarding multiple representation at the point in time where a registrant might enter into a multiple representation situation. Registrants are obligated to describe how the services provided to the client will differ from a single representation situation including any differences in the

REBBA 2002 (CONTINUED)

disclosure of information made to the client. Sec. 17 of the Code requires the registrant to make these disclosures at the earliest practical opportunity and in all cases before an offer to purchase in made.

Sec. 10, 16 and 17 of the Code operate in conjunction with Sec. 22 of Ont. Reg. 567/05 (GEN) which states:

MULTIPLE REPRESENTATION

22. A registrant shall not represent more than one client in respect of the same trade in real estate unless all of the clients represented by the registrant in respect of that trade consent in writing.

At the point that a registrant wishes to represent more than one client with respect to a real estate transaction, it must obtain the written consent of all of the parties it is representing. This written consent is required in situations where a single brokerage represents two parties to a trade even if different salespersons or brokers are representing the two parties to the trade. Given that the brokerage has a fiduciary relationship with more than one party to a trade, it must be clear to those parties about how information will be exchanged related to the transaction and how services will be provided in such a situation.

Consent to multiple representation is required not only when a brokerage is representing both the buyer and seller in a transaction, but in situations where the brokerage is representing multiple buyers in a single transaction. In the case of multiple buyers, it may not be clear that a single brokerage is representing multiple buyers until one or more buyers have expressed interest in the same property. In such situations, consent to the multiple representation would be required when the brokerage becomes aware that it is operating in a multiple representation situation.

In situations where a client or clients refuse to consent to a multiple representation, the brokerage must release one or more of its clients to seek alternate representation with respect to the transaction. The registrant cannot represent more than one party to a trade without the written consent of all parties it is representing.

With respect to services provided to customers, Sec. 10 of the Code requires registrants to disclose to buyers and sellers that they may represent more than one customer in a transaction. A brokerage does not require a customer's or client's written consent to provide services to an additional customer in a transaction. However, both Sec. 10 and 17 of the Code require registrants to clarify for all parties the nature of services they are providing to each party in situations where: a brokerage is providing services to more than one party in a transaction; or representing a client and providing services to a customer in the same transaction.

Sec. 11 of the Code also identifies minimum information that must be contained in agreements between registrants and buyers and sellers. Required information includes effective dates, amounts of remuneration or commission and a description of the services the brokerage is providing under the agreement. Sec. 12 of the Code requires brokerages to given copies of these agreements to buyers and sellers. Sec. 13, 14 and 15 of the Code require brokerages to reduce representation and service agreements to writing and submit them to buyers and sellers for signature.

Real Estate Council of Ontario
Tel: 416-207-4800 Toll Free: 1-800-245-6910 Fax: 416-207-4820
Office of the Registrar
AsktheRegistrar@reco.on.ca

For more information about RECO, visit: www.reco.on.ca

CASE LAW

Case Synopsis

MALPASS V. MORRISON AND NELSON — ONTARIO SUPERIOR COURT MAY, 2004

Buyer failed to complete a transaction after learning that a fourth bedroom in the home was illegal. The Sellers sued and the action was settled with the Buyers agreeing to pay the Sellers an amount exceeding $60,000. The Buyers then sued the real estate salesperson for negligence, breach of contract and breach of fiduciary duty arising from a real estate transaction.

The court accepted the Buyer's evidence that they made it very clear a fourth bedroom was an essential part of their requirements. They have four children and thirteen grandchildren. They began by looking at 2-storeys but ultimately bought a bungalow.

When they viewed the bungalow, they observed a basement room with a bed, a desk and a filing cabinet.

The evidence suggests there was no actual discussion of the fourth bedroom when the home was shown and no verification that the fourth bedroom was legal when the offer was made, even though the Buyers stated they emphasized the requirement for a fourth bedroom. While the home was not actually listed, there was a partially completed listing agreement and a *"Feature Sheet"* for the property that was provided to the Buyers. On the feature sheet, there was a blank opposite the fourth bedroom but the Buyers testified they thought it was a four bedroom home.

The court noted that the brokerage sold the property as a dual agent and that the Buyers stated they were not advised to consult their lawyer prior to making the offer. The court also noted that dual agency can lead to a conflict of interest and the agent must ensure that their fiduciary duties are not breached. The court refers to *Raso v. Dionisi* (1993), 12 O. R. (3rd) 580 in which the court cites Professor Foster as follows:

> *"an agent must be able to prove that the transaction was entered into by his principals after the agent has made full and fair disclosure of all material circumstances and of everything known to him respecting the subject matter of the contract which would be likely to influence the conduct of the principal."*

At trial, the Salesperson stated that the Buyers were business people, they were advised to discuss the offer with their lawyer, they were advised to include a home inspection condition, but declined, and they were informed it was a three bedroom home as evidenced by the feature sheet that did not indicate a fourth bedroom.

However, the Salesperson also testified that he knew the fourth bedroom may not be in compliance with municipal requirements and he did not inform the Buyers. He stated that he expected the information to come to light in a roundabout fashion, through the report of the building inspector that he states he recommended the Buyers to obtain.

The court noted he was aware the Buyers did not obtain the inspection report. The court also stated that it strains logic to imagine that a real estate agent would want to use such a circuitous route to advise a client of an important piece of information, one that would surely bear on whether or not they wanted to purchase the house. It puts the client to far more trouble and expense that is necessary, if it only results in them having a piece of information that the agent could have given them, and was obliged to give them, in the normal course of his doing business with the clients. No inspection took place and he clearly failed in his duty of care by failing to disclose the material information that he knew about the property and he was therefore negligent.

continued...

Case Synopsis | *MALPASS V. MORRISON AND NELSON* | ONTARIO SUPERIOR COURT MAY, 2004

CASE LAW

For Duty of Care, the court cited *Watson v. Holyoke, (1986) O. J. No. 541 (HJC)*:

> A term is normally implied in a contract of agency that the agent will carry out his part of the contract with reasonable diligence. *Bowstead on Agency, 13th ed., p.114.* An agent acting for reward is bound to exercise such skill, care and diligence in the performance of his undertaking as is usual or necessary, in or for the ordinary or proper conduct of the profession or business, in which he is employed, or is reasonably necessary for the proper performance of the duties undertaken by him. *Bowstead supra p. 115 and 116.* Whether an agent has exercised the required degree of care or skill is a question of fact. *Bowstead supra p. 126.* The remedy for an agent's breach of duty of care would be damages based on the loss sustained by the principal from the breach.
>
> The *Restatement of Agency* states at p. 381 that unless otherwise agreed, an agent is subject to a duty to use *reasonable efforts* to give his principal information which is relevant to affairs entrusted to him and which [...] the principal would desire to have [...]. *Bowstead on Agency* adds that to keep their principals informed of matters which are of their concern is an aspect of the agent's duty of care.
>
> The British Columbia Court of Appeal held in *Laycock v. Lee* (1912), 1 D.L.R. 91 (B.C.C.A.) that a broker has a duty to disclose to the principal all facts concerning the value of the property that the principal (in that case) was selling and anything about the state or the location of the property that could affect its value. The broker must also disclose anything that affects the property's "*suitability for the principal's purpose, the legality of the current use of the property, zoning or development plans being made by others for the property or the area in which it is situated, [...] and any potential problems which may arise with respect to a transaction.*"
>
> The court determined that the Salesperson either told the Buyers that it was a four bedroom home or at the very least, left them with the impression that it was, in spite of the listing. Since the fourth bedroom was crucial to the Buyers, it arguably makes the information about the fourth bedroom's legal use a material fact (since it would affect their decision about the property – indeed, finding out about the bedroom did affect their decision to purchase the home and they backed out of the deal). See *Ocean City Realty Ltd. v. A. M. Holdings LTD.* (1987), 44 R.P.R. 312 36 D.L.R. (4th) 94 which states the test of materiality "*is an objective one to be determined by what a reasonable man in the position of the agent would consider, in the circumstances, would be likely to influence the conduct of his principal.*" It is clear that the bedroom's non-compliance would qualify.

The court determined the Salesperson breached their fiduciary duties and their duty of care in exercising the fiduciary duties and awarded the Buyers the amount of their losses.

Case Questions

1. Is it likely that the outcome would have been different if it were not dual agency (multiple representation)?	**2.** In what key areas did the Buyer's testimony conflict with the testimony of the Salesperson?

CASE LAW

Case Synopsis

MONTOUR ET AL V. CENTURY 21 CARRIE REALTY LTD. ET AL
COURT OF QUEEN'S BENCH OF MANITOBA 2006

This is a claim by a Buyer to recover a local improvement levy of $337.50 per year for a further 10 years. The Buyers claimed they were quoted the estimated annual taxes without mention of the additional local improvement levy. After purchasing the property they became aware of the additional payment required to the municipality. The local improvement charge was levied over a 20 year period and 10 years was remaining.

The Buyers stated it was their understanding the defendant was their agent. The court noted the salesperson was also agent for the Seller, as the Seller was the salesperson's father.

This was a credibility case as the plaintiffs claimed they were not informed of the extra charge and the defendant denied keeping that information from the Buyers.

As there was no evidence that the amount of the extra charge was disclosed, and no written information on the property that included the local improvement charge, the court found in favour of the plaintiffs and ordered the salesperson to pay the Buyers the amount of the extra charge over the 10 year period, less $300, as the payment by the salesperson to the Buyers would be prior to the amounts due in subsequent years.

Case Questions

1. While this case is not entirely about agency, what can be learned by this case about agency?	2. How could the salesperson have avoided this situation?

Case Synopsis

ESBIN REALTY CORPORATION V. DAUSON PROPERTIES LTD. & THE NOIK GROUP OF COMPANIES
ONTARIO SUPERIOR COURT JUNE, 2006

CASE LAW

This case is an appeal of a Small Claims Court decision in which the real estate broker was awarded a commission for the leasing of a commercial unit. The commission agreement stated:

> I [the defendant] agree to pay you a commission equivalent to...$1.00 p.s.f. per year on any Lease or Agreement to Lease affected either during the currency of this agreement from any source whatsoever, or within 6 months thereafter with any party to whom you [the plaintiff], your representatives or Co-operating Brokers have introduced my said property during the currency of this Agreement provided you have given me written notice not later than seven (7) calendar days after the expiry of this Agreement of the names of such parties so introduced....
>
> All enquiries from any source whatsoever shall be referred to you and all offers submitted to me shall be brought to your attention before acceptance.......

The space at issue was a 1,724 square feet commercial unit and it was unoccupied. The unit was rented by the landlord to an existing commercial tenant of a smaller unit in the building.

In the initial trial the court found:

> That the Broker introduced the tenant to the unit during the currency of the listing agreement.
>
> That the Broker would have been able to conclude a leasing agreement with the tenant while the listing was in force if the Broker had known of the tenant's interest.
>
> That the Broker could not comply with the 7 day notice provision in the listing agreement as it was unaware of the tenant's interest.
>
> That the agreement entered into between landlord and tenant was a new lease rather than an amendment to their existing lease.

The appeal court agreed with all of these findings, as it gave considerable weight to the fact that the landlord failed to inform the Broker of the tenant's interest in leasing the unit. The court quoted the listing agreement which stated the landlord would inform the Broker of "*all enquiries from any source whatsoever*". The appeal court also stated the Broker "*notionally*" introduced the tenant to the unit, even though the tenant was an existing tenant in the building.

The appeal court determined that the landlord tried to avoid its obligation to the Broker. The court dismissed the appeal and upheld the award of the commission to the Broker.

Case Questions

1. Did the brokerage have any contact with the tenant during the listing period?	2. What if the tenant's initial contact with the landlord about the vacant space had taken place during the holdover period of the listing? Would the brokerage have had a claim for commission?

CHAPTER DISCUSSION

1. CREATION OF AGENCY

Provide an example, related to real estate brokerage, where an agency relationship is created by ratification.

2. DUTIES OF THE AGENT

List the common law duties of the agent to the principal and give three examples from the *Real Estate and Business Brokers Act* where the common law duties of the agent to the principal are codified more specifically in statute law.

CHAPTER DISCUSSION

3. DELEGATION

a. For many years it was standard practice for the duties of the agent to the principal to be delegated automatically to co-operating brokerages under the MLS® system. This practice has changed in recent years. Explain.

b. An agent can bring a principal into legal relations with third parties. Therefore, a principal can be held liable for the statements and conduct of the agent. Does the transition to buyer representation increase or decrease this potential for liability for the seller of a property? Explain.

CHAPTER DISCUSSION

4. DUTIES OF THE PRINCIPAL

Provide an example related to real estate brokerage that illustrates the meaning of "*indemnification*" of the agent by the principal.

5. THIRD PARTIES

Describe the duties of an agent to the third parties to a transaction.

CHAPTER DISCUSSION

6. TERMINATION OF AGENCY

From the examples below, list the term that best describes the method of termination of the agency relationship.

a. The sellers send the brokerage a registered letter stating they no longer want to sell the property and that the brokerage will not be permitted access to the property.	b. The brokerage requests a price reduction. The seller refuses. The brokerage suggests that the property should be taken off the market because it will not sell at the listed price. The seller agrees.
c. The property is sold for 99% of list price.	d. The first mortgagee obtains a Final Order of Foreclosure.

7. THE TYPICAL REAL ESTATE TRANSACTION

Seller Smith selects Salesperson Lee of ABC Realty Inc. to list his home. Lee places the property on the local MLS® listing service. Salesperson Martin of XYZ Real Estate Ltd. arranges an appointment to show the property to Mrs. Jones who has signed a buyer representation agreement with XYZ Real Estate Ltd. Seller Smith sells to Buyer Jones.

a. Provide a step-by-step description of the forms of agency disclosure that would be used for this typical transaction. Be specific as to the type of form, the nature of the disclosure and the timing for each step, from the beginning of the scenario to the final sale.

CHAPTER DISCUSSION

7. THE TYPICAL REAL ESTATE TRANSACTION (continued)

b. What duties are owed by Salesperson Martin and XYZ Real Estate Ltd. to Buyer Jones?

c. What duties are owed by Salesperson Martin and XYZ Real Estate Ltd. to Seller Smith?

KNOWLEDGE INTEGRATION

Notables

- Agency has evolved over time as a part of common law. The term *agency* is not used for regulatory purposes in REBBA 2002 which refers to *representation*.
- The principal-agent relationship is most commonly established by express agreement.
- Types of agency include buyer agency, dual agency, seller agency, single agency and sub-agency.
- An agent is authorized by a principal to represent that principal in business transactions with another party.
- For agency purposes, a principal is an individual who authorizes the agent (brokerage) to act on his/her behalf in an agency relationship.
- The primary duties owed to an agent by a principal are remuneration and indemnification.
- Authority is the legal power or right given by a principal and accepted by the agent to act on the principal's behalf in a business transaction with a third party.
- Authority is usually granted by express agreement (written or oral) but may also be created by estoppel (conduct) and ratification (conduct after the fact), by operation of law or by implied authority.
- The Listing Agreement and Buyer Agency Agreement (now referred to as a Buyer Representation Agreement) both establish appointment of an agent (authority) for differing objectives.
- REBBA 2002 uses the term *representation* making no reference to *agency* as described in common law.

Chapter Mini-Review

Solutions are located in the Appendix.

1. The relationship between employer and employee is a good example of agency.

   ○ True ○ False

2. Agency is created by ratification if the principal accepts the benefits of the agent's previously unauthorized act.

   ○ True ○ False

3. All registrants in Ontario must adhere to disclosure requirements set out in the Code of Ethics of the Canadian Real Estate Association (CREA).

   ○ True ○ False

4. An agency relationship established by way of a listing agreement would probably be terminated by impossibility if the structure being offered for sale was destroyed by fire.

   ○ True ○ False

Chapter Mini-Review (continued)

5. Unintended or implied dual agency (referred to in REBBA 2002 as *multiple representation*) can occur when a registrant unwittingly represents two parties in the same transaction.

   True False

6. An agent must obey the principal's lawful instructions and is subject to detailed and direct control or supervision by that principal when either marketing that principal's (seller's) property or locating suitable property for a buyer as the principal.

   True False

7. An agent can accept a finder's fee for referring the buyer to a mortgage broker without disclosing this fact to the seller client, provided that such fee is a minimal amount of money.

   True False

8. Under REBBA 2002, a buyer representation agreement must be in writing and signed by the buyer or seller client.

   True False

9. A brokerage cannot represent more than one client in the same transaction without receiving informed, written consent from the respective clients.

   True False

10. REBBA 2002 only contemplates two types of agreements: representation agreements and service agreements.

    True False

Active Learning Exercises

Solutions are located in the Appendix.

Exercise 1

As a buyer representative, you obtain an offer which is presented to the seller and accepted. According to the MLS® listing, as co-operating brokerage you are receiving 3% commission from the seller, through the listing brokerage. The Offer is conditional on the buyer arranging a first mortgage. You assist the buyer in completing the application, which you deliver to the mortgagee. You get letters confirming the buyer's income and deliver them to the mortgagee. The mortgagee asks your firm to give a letter of opinion of the value of the property and pays a fee of $100. The mortgage is approved and you deliver the commitment letter to the buyer, who signs it. You return the letter to the mortgagee and pick up the mortgage instructions for delivery to the buyer's lawyer.

After the sale closes, you receive a thank you letter from the mortgagee with a cheque for $500 payable to you as a "*finder's fee.*"

a. Do you see any potential problems here? Explain.

b. How would you handle the situation?

Exercise 2

You have a property listed at $169,900 and agree to co-operate with Broker Bill, who declares he is acting under sub-agency. Bill brings you an offer from the buyer for $155,000 and states: "We should have no problem putting this deal together. My client has already told me she would go as high as $165,000 if necessary."

a. Do you see any problems here? Explain.

b. What do you do when you see the seller?

Exercise 3

a. I have an uncertified cheque from a buyer who submitted the deposit at the time of signing the offer. The offer is open for acceptance for seven days. When do I deposit the cheque in my Trust Account?

b. My seller has told me to obtain certified cheques for all deposits before I present any offers. Comment.

Exercise 4

"*I sold a property and the deposit is in the listing brokerage's trust account. Before the deal closed the brokerage went bankrupt. The Trustee tells me that when the deal closes, the money will come out of trust into the general account and will then be split pro rata among all the creditors of the listing brokerage. I may get ten cents on the dollar.*" Discuss with specific reference to *Commission Trust Agreements*.

Exercise 5

Brokerage X, with an exclusive listing, permits Brokerage Y to co-operate as a declared sub-agent. Y brings an offer from Company A and it is accepted by the seller. Later the seller learns that Y has a substantial interest in Company A which was not disclosed. The seller refuses to pay commission. X sues.

a. What is the result?

b. Why?

c. Would your answer be different if co-operating brokerage Y had declared as a buyer brokerage, representing the buyer? Explain.

Exercise 6

A property is owned by Jones Manufacturing Limited. An offer to purchase is showing the seller as "Jones Manufacturing." It is accepted by Mr. Jones who signs on the line for the seller with his normal signature "J. Jones."

a. Is there a contract?

b. If not, can Mr. Jones be liable personally? If so, on what basis?

Exercise 7

The brokerage obtains a listing using the standard OREA listing authority. The property sells, but the buyer fails to close because the sale of the buyer's existing property fell through at the last minute.

The brokerage claims the commission indicated in the listing, based on the fact that it obtained an unconditional offer that was accepted.

a. Do you agree with the brokerage? Explain.

b. What if the scenario above is somewhat different and the buyer was ready and willing to close, but the sale did not close because the sellers decided at the last minute they did not want to sell the property? Would the brokerage then have a claim for commission? Explain.

c. In both scenarios, under what circumstances could the brokerage remove the deposit from the Trust Account?

Exercise 8

You act on behalf of a developer who agrees to pay your brokerage a 4% commission on the purchase of twenty residential properties. He intends to demolish the buildings and put up a commercial development. You have checked with the municipality and are told that this proposal meets all the requirements of the Official Plan and the Zoning by-laws, and that services are available. You are to prepare twenty Agreements of Purchase and Sale.

a. None of the properties are listed for sale at this time. How would you proceed, to best meet the objectives set out by the developer?

b. What special provisions would you include in the Agreement of Purchase and Sale (Form 100) to deal with this situation?

c. Given the circumstances, would there be a more appropriate way to calculate the commission in this situation? Explain.

Exercise 9

You listed a property and sold it to Penny Layne. Before the transaction closes, Penny approaches you to tell you she has someone who is interested in purchasing from her and Penny wants you to assist in selling to the second buyer. Penny will pay you a commission on the second sale.

What steps would have to be taken before you could represent Penny for the resale of the property?

CHAPTER 5

Contract Law

Introduction

The essential elements of a contract have been established and refined by common law hundreds of years ago. Real estate salespeople draft agreements, notices, waivers etc., and must apply these common law principles on a daily basis. A contract contains six essential elements that must be present during the contracting process in order to make the agreement enforceable: offer and acceptance (mutual agreement), capacity of the parties, lawful object, consideration and genuine intention.

If any one of these elements is missing, the contract may be deemed illegal, void or voidable. In particular, lack of genuine intention is a major factor in making a contract void or voidable. The issue of void and voidable contracts speaks to much larger issues. For example, has one or both parties misunderstood the intent of the agreement? Misunderstanding, in the broadest sense, can be common, mutual or unilateral. Misrepresentation can be innocent, fraudulent or negligent. A contract may be terminated by agreement, performance, impossibility of performance, operation of law or breach. If a contract is breached then the injured party may seek remedies in the form of damages, quantum meruit, specific performance or an injunction.

Learning Outcomes

At the conclusion of this chapter, students will be able to:

- Outline the essential elements of a contract.
- Differentiate between void and voidable contracts.
- Identify and discuss typical misrepresentations encountered in real estate contracts.
- Identify mistakes encountered in real estate contracts.
- Explain options available when a contract is breached and outline various ways in which agreements may be terminated.
- Discuss the role of power of attorney in the signing of various documents.
- Discuss regulatory requirements involving written agreements, offers to purchase, inducements, and inaccurate representations as set out in REBBA 2002.
- Apply concepts involving contract law to typical situations encountered by salespersons and brokers.

CONTRACT ESSENTIALS

The law of contracts covers a large sector of law in general, and basic familiarity with the legal requirements of a contract is necessary to understand real estate law. The following information deals only with the highlights and with particular situations affecting real estate transactions.

Definition of a Contract

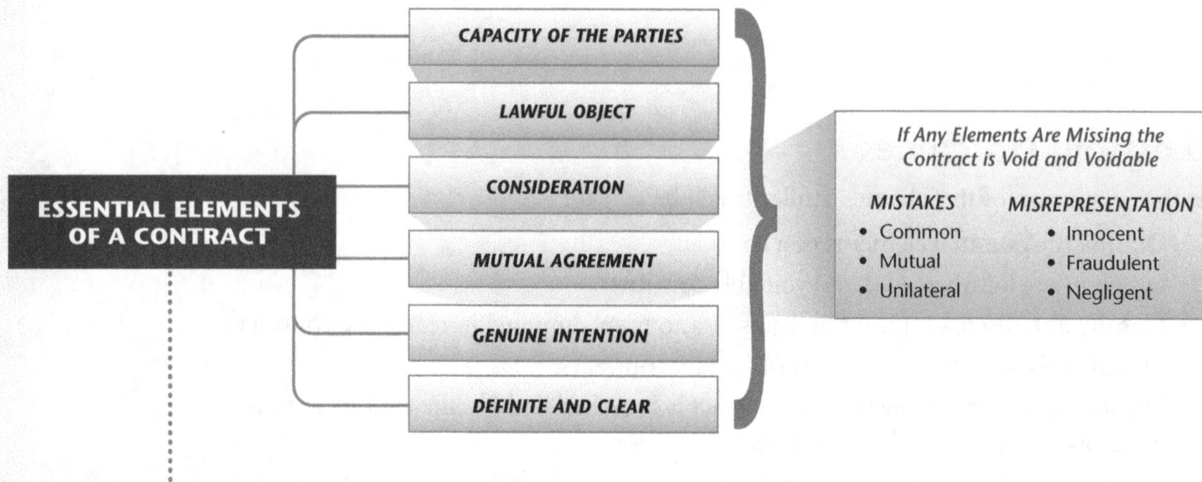

A contract is a legally binding agreement between two or more capable persons for consideration or value, to do or not to do some lawful and genuinely intended act.

In other words, a contract is a binding promise of one person made to another or others. It is more than a mere offer to do something, or a mere statement of intention, and requires a meeting of the minds of the parties whereby a legal rather than a moral obligation is created, imposing an enforceable duty to fulfil the promise on the one party and conferring a legal right on the other to claim its fulfilment. Very often for a typical contract, there will be promises given by each party to the other, in which case the promises are said to be mutual.

In reality, the contract is the agreement between the parties, not the document on which it may be written. The document is only a piece of paper purporting to give evidence of a contract between the parties. If any of the elements essential to the contracting process are absent, it will matter very little how well the document has been prepared. The document cannot give evidence of a contract that does not exist at law.

Statute of Frauds CURIOSITY 

The Statute of Frauds requires that contracts for the sale of any interest in land or for leases exceeding three years must be in writing to be enforceable. The statute does not require the use of a particular form.

Required Elements

Certain elements must be present to make the contract enforceable.

- The parties entering into a contract must be legally competent to contract (capacity of the parties).
- The contractual arrangement must be lawful (lawful object or *legality of object*).
- Each party must receive something (consideration).
- There must be offer and acceptance (mutual agreement).
- Both parties must consent to the terms of the contract (genuine intention).
- The agreement must be certain (*definite and clear*).

A contract, not fulfilling all requirements, may be either void or voidable:

- Void (*never came into existence*);
- Voidable (*originally valid but capable of being rejected by the offended parties at a later time*); or
- Illegal (*not enforceable by the courts*).

VOID

A contract that is void is said to be a nullity at law, with no force or legal effect. As far as the law is concerned, the agreement does not exist. Neither party can enforce it and neither party has any obligations under it.

The question of void and voidable contracts relates to much larger issues concerning avoidance of a contract. In other words, cases may arise where the elements of a valid contract are present (i.e., not void) but where the promise of one or both parties has been given on the basis of or affected by some misunderstanding, false inducement, force, or the like, so that the offended party has rights of redress. Usually the two types of redress for grievances of this kind are either to allow avoidance of the contract altogether or to obtain damages for the conduct of the other party. Such instances involve voidable contracts as opposed to void contracts; i.e., contracts that do not exist.

EXAMPLE *Void*

A void contract can occur when the agreement is impossible to perform. For example, Seller Smith and Buyer Jones enter into an agreement of purchase and sale for the acquisition of an isolated cottage owned by Smith. Unknown to either party, Smith's cottage was destroyed by fire during the winter. All of the elements of the contract are in existence, but the structure is not. Both buyer and seller are mistaken as to this essential fact and the contract is impossible to perform and would undoubtedly be judged void.

VOIDABLE

That which is enforceable, valid and binding until rendered void is voidable. A contract that is voidable is one where the offended party may make a choice. The person may choose to avoid the contract and treat it as being at an end, or to treat it as subsisting and enforce it against the offending party.

Practitioners might encounter the issue of voidable contracts in the case of minors. As a general statement, a minor (the age of majority will vary between provinces) cannot be held liable for contracts unless it can be said that the contract was for necessities, being generally food, clothing, medical services and lodging. Not only must the item be of a category recognized by the law as being a necessity, but it also must be necessary to that particular infant or minor at that particular time. The category of lodging would not likely be extended by the courts to the purchase of a house since there are many alternative ways to obtain shelter.

Contracts entered into by a minor for the purchase or sale of land are voidable by the minor. If the minor does nothing to avoid the contract within a reasonable time after he/she reaches the age of majority, then the contract becomes binding. However, the minor may repudiate the contract upon reaching the age of majority by notifying the other contracting party. The minor cannot recover what he/she may have paid during minority on account of the contract, but the other contracting party whose contract has been repudiated cannot compel performance of the balance of the contract following repudiation. In many instances, the matter of repudiation is finally resolved in the courts because of the fact that minors may be liable for their contracts where such contracts were for necessities. In making decisions, courts also look at such factors as the knowledge of the infant of his/her rights under the law of contract and whether the minor has acted in any way to indicate that he/she intends to carry out obligations under the contract. However, if the minor acts in any way to indicate that he/she intends to carry out his/her obligations under the contract, such as making payments after reaching the age of majority, then the courts will likely not allow the contract to be repudiated by the minor.

It is immaterial that the minor may have held himself/herself out to be over the age of majority (legal age). Even under such circumstances, the minor has the option of voiding the contract. Another important factor is that an adult representing the minor cannot approach the court to have the contract voided. Such a contract is binding until the minor brings the case to court. If an adult represents the minor by co-signing the contract, the contract cannot be voided even by the minor.

If a real estate salesperson suspects that a potential buyer is under age, it is advisable to request proof of age before proceeding. If in fact the potential buyer is under age, then the salesperson should advise the individual that a guardian or trustee, duly authorized, must sign the contract on his/her behalf so that it will be legally enforceable.

Contracts entered into by others with limited capacity, such as mentally incompetent persons or intoxicated persons, may also be voidable.

EXAMPLE *Voidable Contract*

An example of a voidable contract involving undue influence can include a situation where one party, by virtue of a special relationship to the other, is in a position of confidence and abuses that position. In cases such as relations between parent and child or solicitor and client, presumption of undue influence may arise that can be rebutted by showing that, in fact, the person susceptible to influence was able to form a decision free of any sort of control.

The fact that the person claiming undue influence received independent legal advice or independent valuations of the property are excellent ways of establishing that no undue influence occurred. Where undue influence is shown, the contract is voidable, not void. That is, the person claiming undue influence must go to court to have the contract adjudged void.

The issue of void and voidable contracts goes well beyond the normal scope of real estate activities. Legal advice is strongly recommended on such matters.

Capacity of the Parties

Parties to a contract must, at the time when the contract is made, have the legal capacity to make the contract.

PERSONS

While contractual promises are enforceable against anyone having legal capacity, some persons are deemed by law as either incapable of contracting or having only limited capacity to contract. In cases involving limited capacity, the contract is usually considered voidable; that is, the contract is valid until the individual goes to court to void it. As long as the person of limited capacity allows the contract to exist, it may not be voided. Some examples of those with limited capacity to enter a contract include:

- Minors (those under the age of majority),
- Mentally incompetent persons,
- Intoxicated persons or persons incapable of understanding the nature of a contract by virtue of excessive use of drugs or chemicals; and
- Illiterates.

Minor

A person who is under the age of legal competence is a minor. Simply put, all contracts with infants for the sale or purchase of land are generally voidable, sometimes void, and not usually considered valid and binding on the minor.

EXAMPLE ***Minor***

Broker/Owner Johnson, of ABC Realty Inc., is conducting a brief review session for salespeople on the fundamentals of contract law concerning agreements/contracts and, in particular, legal issues surrounding persons under the age of majority.

Apparently, one of the condominium site salespeople encountered an unusual situation at an open house. A young couple wanted to submit an offer on a one bedroom unit. The salesperson, on discovering that one of the two individuals was a minor, called Johnson for guidance. A brief conversation with the potential buyers confirmed the salesperson's suspicion. The offer was drafted in the non-minor's name (following confirmation of age), and the seller/developer was informed about the situation.

Following is a brief synopsis of Johnson's notes for the sales meeting regarding the status of a minor involved in the agreement/contract for real property:

- *All contracts of minors for the purchase or sale of land are voidable by the minor. It is immaterial whether or not the minor has purported to be over the age of majority. In rare circumstances the court could hold that a reasonable purchase of a home was a necessity and a contract for such was binding on the minor.*
- *A minor may avoid a contract made during the age of minority for a reasonable time after majority, providing that nothing occurs after majority that might be deemed to be ratification of the contract, such as making an additional deposit or payment.*
- *The contract is binding upon the other party until avoided by the minor, but it is doubtful if the minor can obtain specific performance unless the other party has received all the benefits given under the contract.*
- *Should the minor avoid the contract, any benefits obtained must be returned, but it is not clear whether this must be done at the time of avoidance.*
- *The minor, in the absence of any fraud by the other side, cannot recover any payment made upon the contract.*
- *If the contract contains a penalty or is otherwise to the disadvantage of the minor, it is probably void. In that case, the minor can always recover payments that have been made, at least if no consideration has been received under the contract.*

In the case of a voidable contract, the minor would be entitled to avoid the contract at any time until a reasonable time after age of majority. However, if the contract is ratified after majority, the right to avoid it generally disappears. Avoidance is the privilege of the minor and the other side is bound until the minor repudiates the contract.

The age of legal competence (age of majority) was traditionally 21 years of age, but in Ontario it is now 18 years.

Illiterate

Illiterate is defined as unable to read or write. In terms of a contract, the question about an illiterate person and whether the contract is binding rests on whether the person knew what was being signed (a rule known as non est factum).

EXAMPLE *Illiterate*

Buyer Jones, having practically no knowledge of reading or writing, inspected a property on Main Street with his wife and daughter. The salesperson was unaware of the buyer's limitations as he was able to converse freely on a wide range of topics, particularly concerning house construction and design.

The salesperson drafted an agreement/contract based on instructions from the buyer and delivered it for signature. Once signed by Jones (he was capable of affixing his signature only) the agreement/contract was accepted by the sellers. However, only two days before closing, Jones refused to close, arguing that he was unable to read or write and, therefore, the contract was not binding.

While the ultimate decision by a court concerning Jones' illiteracy would depend on circumstances, several arguments can be put forth against his claim. Jones displayed a working knowledge of houses and was capable of carrying on a full and complete discussion with the salesperson. His family was present to assist (assuming they were literate), and lastly, he provided the salesperson with details of how the offer was to be drafted.

Infant

An infant is defined as a person who is a minor, under the age of legal competence, and thus incapable of the independent judgement necessary to undertake a legal obligation. Practitioners should be particularly sensitive to situations involving potential minors transacting real property.

CAPACITY OF PARTIES BEYOND PERSONS

The capacity of parties extends beyond persons and the following is provided for descriptive purposes only.

Corporation	Usually has the rights, powers and privileges to enter into contracts concerning the purchase and sale of real property unless specific restrictions are located in the articles of incorporation or the corporation has not enacted empowering provisions in its by-laws. Two important cautions are required concerning corporations involved in acquisition or disposition of real estate. First, does the corporation exist and secondly, does it have the right to enter into such contracts?
Partnership	Normally provides under provincial legislation that any partner may bind the other partners in a transaction during the ordinary course of business.

Condominiums/ Co-operatives	Permitted to enter into contracts for the purchase and sale of real property in line with incorporation documents or statutory regulations limiting the scope of such organizations.
Non-Profit Organizations	Have the rights, powers and privileges to enter into contracts for the purchase and sale of real property. For example, incorporation documents of a real estate board often specifically mention the right to acquire and dispose of real estate.

Lawful Object

If the object of the contract is illegal by statute or common law, the contract will be void and unenforceable in the courts. For example, a contract would not be considered lawful if the acquisition involved criminal activity or was a direct violation of competition policy (*Competition Act*) or deliberate evasion of taxes (*Income Tax Act*). In such instances, the contract would be totally void. Examples of illegality or no lawful object would include contracts:

- Contrary to public policy or good morals;
- Injurious or prejudicial to the safety of the state or to the public service;
- Tending to pervert justice or abuse the legal process;
- In restraint of trade such as price fixing;
- In restraint of personal liberty or marriage; and
- For the commission of a criminal offence or civil wrong or relating to gambling or wagering (unless authorized by means of provincial statutes).

Often, buyers and sellers believe that a sale made on a Sunday is illegal and void. The Supreme Court of Canada held that the particular section of the *Lord's Day Act* relating to this issue was unconstitutional in view of the *Canadian Charter of Rights and Freedoms.*

The object in a real estate transaction is the transferral of ownership of the seller's property to a buyer. If this object is illegal according to a statutory provision or common law then the entire contract would be void and unenforceable.

EXAMPLE ***Lawful Object***

The showing on Smith's property was proceeding smoothly. Salesperson Ward had just completed touring the upper floors with Buyer Jones and was currently viewing the main floor rooms. Smith, while patiently following the salesperson and buyer, was frequently excusing himself to answer incoming telephone calls on a cellular phone. When reaching the basement, the salesperson discovered a flurry of activity. Instead of the traditional family room, the area was buzzing with activity. A full off-track betting operation unfolded before his eyes. The seller, noticing the salesperson's look of amazement, simply turned to the buyer and said:

> *Don't worry, we've had this operation going for two years. If you want to make some big money, why not join in. We'll continue to rent the basement. Just get Ward to put in an appropriate clause in the agreement.*

Ward is now contemplating an unlawful act that affects the lawful object of the contract.

Consideration

Consideration is what each party receives or is to receive in exchange for promises to act in a certain manner and is something that is given by a promisee to a promisor to make the promise binding. The essence of a valid, binding contract is the idea of a *bargain* between the parties. The bargain is the consideration of a contract and may consist of:

- An act in return for an act;
- A promise in return for a promise; or
- An act in return for a promise.

As a result, each side receives something from the other. In real estate transactions, consideration usually takes the form of a promise from the seller to sell in return for a sum of money to be received from the buyer. Consideration is best viewed in terms of the following four headings.

Value	What either party receives must have some value. Interestingly, the court does not assess the adequacy of this value, but only its existence. Sometimes, practitioners misunderstand the concept of valuable consideration. This does not mean that the consideration given has some extraordinary worth associated with it. The courts are only interested that it exists. Of course, if the consideration was so minimal as to make the contract one-sided, the courts might act based on the unconscionability of the agreement. Further, the court might review the adequacy of the consideration if undue influence, fraud, duress or misrepresentation exists.
Lawful	The best explanation is by example. If the buyer and seller knowingly agree to transact business based on stolen money or goods, the contract does not have lawful consideration.
Past Consideration	To quote an old phrase: *Old consideration is no consideration.* For example, the buyer of a cottage enters into an agreement to purchase a cottage for $85,000. Subsequent to that agreement, the seller mentions that he will include the boat. No documentation is prepared and no consideration is given. At closing, the boat has been removed by the seller. As consideration does not exist and past consideration ($85,000) did not include the boat, the buyer does not have an enforceable contract concerning the boat.
Seal	A contract can be made binding without consideration if a seal is used. Where a promise is made under seal, no consideration is required since the law presumes the act of sealing replaces consideration. Therefore, in the case of an agreement/contract, if legal seals are affixed at the time of signing, no consideration is required. This is only valid if the parties are clearly aware of the legal effect that a seal has on the contract.

The ancient method of sealing by wax and swearing a solemn oath has been replaced in modern legal practice by a variety of methods to indicate that the document has been signed under seal. Generally, the courts will now accept anything from red wafers to preprinted or hand written seals as long as it is clear the parties signing knew, or were directed to the fact, that they were signing under seal. Also, the legal seal of a corporation does not perform the same function, valuable consideration is still required, unless legal seals are also present.

While, in many instances, the corporate seal is unnecessary for signing documents, any document signed on behalf of a company under its corporate seal and indicating the authority of the person signing by inserting that person's position above the signature would be good business practice. If a corporate seal is not used, the following words should be used:

I have the authority to bind the corporation.

The act of placing a mark or symbol on a document is evidence and assurance of the intent to carry out promises contained therein. A sealed document provides added confirmation of intent of the parties to perform an agreement/contract. Under old conveyancing law, an official seal was often used as a substitute for consideration. Where a promise is made under seal, no consideration is required since the law presumes that the solemn act of sealing replaces consideration.

Following are selected rules relating to consideration.

- If a promise is not made under seal, consideration is necessary to make it binding.
- Must be of some value, but need not be equal to what is received in return. It has been held that a peppercorn is valuable consideration as long as the promisor accepts it as such.
- Must move from the promisee to the promisor. However, many ask what does the buyer (as promisee) receive as consideration for a promise not to revoke the offer? The answer in most instances is nothing, but the promise is usually made under seal.
- Must be lawful.
- The promisee cannot rely on past conduct or promises as consideration. It must be present or future consideration to be effective.

Valuable Consideration

If a person promises to do something, the law will not enforce that promise unless something is received or promised in exchange. Whatever is given or is to be given is referred to as valuable consideration, and is therefore anything to which a value can be attached, given by the promisee to the promisor, and may be:

- An act in return for an act;
- A promise in return for a promise; or
- An act in return for a promise.

EXAMPLE *Valuable Consideration*

Seller Smith and Buyer Jones have entered into an agreement/contract. Jones has agreed to pay $238,000 to Smith for his detached two-storey home at 123 Main Street. The valuable consideration is $238,000 in exchange for title to the property. Consideration received by the seller is $238,000, in the form of a $20,000 deposit and a promise of the balance on completion. Consideration received by the buyer is a promise of title to the property upon final payment.

Mutual Agreement (Offer and Acceptance)

A contract is formed when the offer (made by the offeror) is accepted by the other party (the offeree). The following items are general rules concerning basic requirements for an offer. The offer:

- Must be complete and definite in its terms.
- Must be made to one or more persons or corporations, or to the public at large.
- Must remain open for acceptance for a reasonable period of time.
- May be revoked or withdrawn prior to acceptance, subject to certain limitations.
- Must be communicated to the offeree.

The acceptance of the offer is based on four requirements. The acceptance must be:

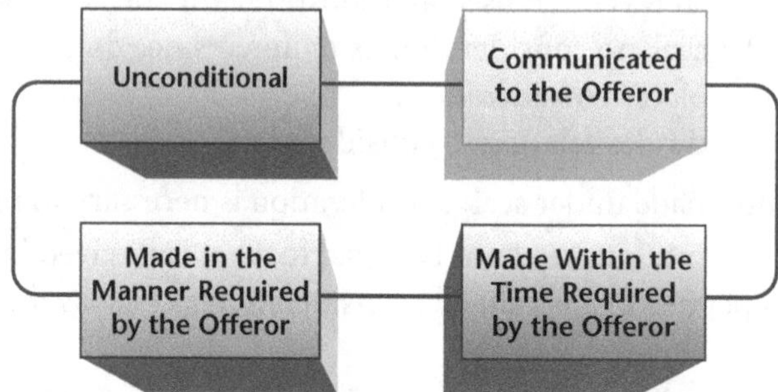

Where the communication of acceptance is permitted by mail, telegram or fax, such acceptance is deemed to be completed upon the letter having been mailed, the telegram sent or the fax transmitted. The contract is binding even if the letter, telegram or fax is not received. Further, if an offer is made in the form of a promise upon the performance of a future act, the process of carrying out that act can constitute acceptance.

Genuine Intention

The agreement must be genuine and give more than the outward appearance of a contract. In other words, one of the parties may have been induced to enter into the agreement by improper means and the document does not express what was intended.

Inducements by improper means are caused by four different circumstances.

Mistakes	The term mistake is narrowly defined for contract purposes. The courts will not declare a contract void simply because of a mistake of the parties. Three types of mistakes are normally considered: • A ***common*** mistake in which both parties make the same mistake: that is, each is mistaken about some underlying fundamental fact; • A ***mutual*** mistake in which the parties misunderstand each other and are at cross purposes; and • A ***unilateral*** mistake in which one of the parties is mistaken concerning a fundamental character of the contract.
Misrepresentation	A false statement or assertion made by one party to the other, before or at the time of contracting, with regard to some existing fact, matter or circumstance affecting the contract. Misrepresentations are viewed as innocent, fraudulent or negligent.

Duress or Undue Influence	Duress occurs when a person does not act with his/her free will, but instead through fear of personal suffering. Undue influence is the improper use of one person's power over another to induce that person into a contract. Following are selected examples that might fall under *undue influence.* • One party is knowledgeable and experienced while the other is ill-informed and inexperienced. • A gift is made by a child to an adult, guardian or ward; a beneficiary to a trustee; a patient to a doctor; a person to a spiritual advisor; or, a client to a solicitor. • A real estate salesperson purchases property from his/her client. The person appearing to have exerted undue influence must prove that the transaction was reasonable and fair and that no advantage was gained due to his/her position. The fact that the person claiming undue influence received independent legal advice or valuation of a property is valid to establish that a reasonable transaction occurred.
Failure to Disclose	The non-disclosure of latent defects might invalidate a contract. A latent defect is generally described as a defect that is unknown to the buyer but is material to the enjoyment of the property. The buyer might not have entered into the contract had he/she been aware of the defect. An example could be the presence of ground contamination because of a prior owner's use and spillage/seepage of a hazardous product.

Definite and Clear

The terms of an agreement must be definite and clear and if the essential terms have not been agreed upon, a binding contract does not exist. However, this does not mean that the terms have to be decided. A term of a contract can be established through arbitration by a third party.

Some terms of a contract will, if necessary, be implied by law. A contract in which no date was specified for possession might be held to be invalid for lack of certainty, particularly if the phrase *time is of the essence* is contained in the agreement. If the terms, conditions and other provisions of the agreement establish with reasonable certainty that the parties intended possession to occur within reasonable time limits, then the court might interpret the contract so as to give effect to the intent of the parties as determined from the additional circumstances.

A frequent cause of uncertainty is the agreement to negotiate some time in the future. A sale at a price to be fixed by arbitration through a third party is one thing, but a sale at a price to be fixed by subsequent negotiations between seller and buyer is not a concluded contract until these negotiations have resulted in an agreed price. This problem frequently arises with a right to renew a lease, or with a right given to a tenant to purchase property during or at the end of a lease. If the rent or price is simply left to be agreed upon, no agreement exists.

In summary, if a vital and material condition of the contract is undetermined, no contract exists, but merely an undertaking to seek a contract at a future time.

MISREPRESENTATION

A representation may be defined as a statement or assertion made by one party to the other, before or at the time of contracting, regarding some existing fact, matter or circumstance affecting the contract or its object. Simply put, misrepresentation is a false statement of fact.

Distinguishing between a representation and a mere exaggeration or statement of intention or opinion can be difficult. The statement '*This is the best deal in town*' may be treated as an exaggeration, not giving rise to legal rights, although it might be false or misleading pursuant to the *Competition Act*. If, however, a specific statement is made to the effect that a property can be put to a certain type of use, this statement is a representation. If proven false, a misrepresentation has been made.

Misrepresentation is a complicated area of law that is usually categorized as innocent, fraudulent or negligent. The following is provided as a general guideline only.

Innocent

An innocent misrepresentation is a statement by one party of a material fact that is untrue, but is honestly believed to be true. If the victim of misrepresentation is induced into a contract based on such a statement, he/she may refuse to complete the contract, attempt to have it set aside and attempt to recover anything paid or delivered under it. He/she can also defend any action brought against him/her under the contract, but as a general rule cannot recover damages if the misrepresentation was innocent.

EXAMPLE 1 *Misrepresentation—Innocent Misrepresentation*

Seller Smith is offering his home for sale through the local real estate board's MLS® service. A buyer, upon inspecting the property, asks if the nearby school offers grades K–8. The seller, unable to reach the school, calls a neighbour and confirms that fact. The buyer relies upon this statement and purchases the property only to discover that both his children could not attend this school, but would have to travel five miles by bus. The school now provides only junior grades K–4. He refuses to close the transaction arguing that a misrepresentation, no matter how innocent, has occurred.

EXAMPLE 2 *Misrepresentation—Innocent Misrepresentation*

Salesperson Lee, when asked if the basement had any leakage, informed the buyer that the seller had clearly stated to him at the time of listing that there were no leakage problems whatsoever in the basement area. The salesperson did, however, suggest to the buyer that he could place a condition in the offer or require a warranty from the seller regarding his concern. The buyer elected to place a warranty in the agreement. Following closing, water seepage occurred in the property. Salesperson Lee had innocently misrepresented this situation, based on what he believed were sincere, honest representations made by the seller.

Fraudulent

A fraudulent misrepresentation has three elements:

- The misrepresentation must be made with the knowledge of its falsity or with reckless disregard for its truth on the part of the person making it.
- The purpose must have been to induce the other party to enter a contract.
- The misrepresentation must have been acted on to the other party's prejudice.

Where such fraud exists, the party deceived may resist enforcement of the contract, and that party has the right to recover damages for deceit.

EXAMPLE 1 *Misrepresentation—Fraudulent Misrepresentation*

Salesperson Lee is listing Seller Smith's property. During casual conversation, Smith admits to a problem of basement leakage, but emphasizes that this only occurs in a heavy downpour. Smith insists that Lee not mention this fact and Lee agrees.

Buyer Jones purchases the property following assurances from Lee that no dampness problem exists in the basement. Jones closes the sale and discovers the leakage problem. A law suit ensues to recover damages on the basis of fraudulent misrepresentation.

A principal is liable for misrepresentations made by his agent, if made with express or implied authority. Authority will be implied where the misrepresentation is made in the course of, and within the scope of, duties of the agent; e.g., when showing the property.

The owner may be liable for representations about the property made by the broker or sales representative. With fraudulent misrepresentation made by an agent, both the person making it and the principal will be liable for damages. Salesperson Lee, in the preceding example, agrees with the seller and fails to disclose pertinent information about the leakage. Consequently, both the selling brokerage and sales representative could be liable for damages.

EXAMPLE 2 *Misrepresentation—Fraudulent Misrepresentation*

Salesperson Ward, when asked if the well provided an adequate water supply, told the buyer that there was more than ample water to meet all usual household requirements. The salesperson had already been told by the seller that gallonage tests performed last summer revealed less than two gallons per minute, although the flow revived somewhat during spring and fall periods. However, the seller asked that this information not be disclosed to any potential buyer. Salesperson Ward has made a fraudulent misrepresentation.

Negligent

If there is a special relationship between the parties and a misrepresentation is made negligently, then the person who is misled will have an action for damages. When it is clear that the statement was made with intention that it be relied on, and that the person did rely on it, then a claim for damages may arise. This could occur in situations where the buyer has relied on a real estate salesperson (who is agent for the seller), for example, the agent misrepresented the financial statements of the seller's business.

An agent has also been held liable for negligent misrepresentation as to the quantity of property included in a transaction; and for failing to confirm information in a listing and making wrongful representations of the property carrying costs, knowing that the buyer was relying on his/her expertise and advice. It is negligent to misrepresent that the property may be used for a specific purpose if, in fact, that use may be illegal under the zoning by-laws of that municipality. Appraisers have been held responsible for inaccuracies in their reports that were relied upon by lenders. In all these situations an assumption is made that care, as well as honesty, is demanded.

EXAMPLE 1 ***Misrepresentation—Negligent***

A mortgagee employed an appraiser to appraise a property for mortgage loan purposes. The appraiser relied on statements of the mortgagor and gave a high value based on the property having been approved for a subdivision. Such approval had not been given. A mortgage was subsequently registered, a default occurred and a deficiency also arose on a subsequent sale. The court held that the appraiser was liable to the mortgagee for the deficiency for failing to make enquiries that a reasonable, careful and prudent appraiser would have made.

EXAMPLE 2 ***Misrepresentation—Negligent***

Salesperson Lee listed a two-storey home backing onto a new housing development. When securing the listing, the seller admitted that he could not locate the rear boundary of the property. To complicate matters, no recent survey existed. Lee showed the property to a prospective buyer. When asked about the size of the property, Lee confidently pointed to two iron bars at the extreme rear left and right corners of the lot, then paced off the distance and informed the buyer that the depth was around 250 feet.

Based on this representation, the buyer bought the property, only to discover that the two survey pins related to the development area and not to the property. In fact, the lot had a depth of 150 feet. The buyer sued the brokerage and the seller for negligent misrepresentation arguing that the salesperson owed a duty of care in providing information that misled and injured the buyer.

MISTAKE

The word mistake, in legal terms as it applies to real estate contracts, has a narrow meaning. Not every mistake or simple error affects a contract and is considered a legal mistake of fact. The law does not simply declare a contract void simply because one or other of the parties makes a mistake. Only certain types of mistakes give rise to a remedy. Obviously, the determination of a mistake and its impact on a contract is a legal issue and appropriate advice should be obtained.

As a guideline for practitioners, mistakes can be grouped under three common headings.

COMMON MISTAKE	MUTUAL MISTAKE	UNILATERAL MISTAKE
Both parties to the contract know the intention of the other, accept it, but are somehow mistaken concerning some underlying material or fundamental fact. As an example, both seller and buyer believe that the property includes a right-of-way to the beach, but in fact nothing supports this belief. The buyer and seller enter into an agreement/contract that, among other terms, describes a specific right-of-way along with appropriate measurements. The error does not in fact create an easement or any beneficial interest and is viewed only as a common mistake between the parties.	The parties misunderstand each other and are at cross purposes. For example, the seller owns two lots on opposite sides of a lake. The buyer believes he/she is buying the south shore property, while the seller believes the north shore property is being sold. The parties would be agreeing based on a mutual mistake regarding location.	One party is mistaken and the other party knows of this mistake concerning a fundamental aspect of a contract. As an example, the buyer believes that the lot is approximately one acre in size, and the seller is clearly aware of this mistaken belief and does not make the buyer aware of the situation. The buyer then proceeds with the purchase based on the mistaken fact.

Mistakenly Signed Document

A mistakenly signed document can be described as the signing of a document that is fundamentally different from that which was contemplated.

As a general guideline for real estate practitioners, where a person is induced by the fraud of another to sign a written document, such as a listing agreement, agreement/ contract, amendment or notice, that is materially or fundamentally different from that which was expected, the person signing may successfully plead that the document is not valid. This is known as the doctrine of non est factum. Basically, the person never intended to sign the document and therefore in the eyes of the law never did sign the document. As with any mistake in legal documents and contracts, the exact circumstances are subject to close scrutiny and legal advice is recommended.

EXAMPLE *Mistakenly Signed Document*

Seller Smith is marketing a large tract of industrial land. All the signage, supporting documents and verbal information provided to Buyer Jones and his buyer representative indicate that the property has an area of approximately 90,000 square feet. This figure is also clearly stated in the agreement/contract and an old, barely readable survey is provided to Jones at the time of signing.

At the point of closing, Jones refuses to complete the sale, as the property only contains about 60,000 square feet. Smith argues that the old survey in Jones' possession has the correct square footage and, therefore, he must close. Jones argues that the document is not valid and had he known the material difference in size, he would never have signed the agreement/contract.

Non Est Factum

Non est factum is literally translated as *it is not his deed.* This terminology relates to the legal rule that a person who was induced innocently or fraudulently by another to sign a written document, which is fundamentally different from that which he/she contemplated, is not bound by that document. The document is invalid on the grounds that the mind of the signer did not accompany the signature. He/she never intended to sign and, therefore, in contemplation of the law, the individual never did sign the document to which his/her name is appended.

Non est factum cannot be pleaded where a person misunderstands something that he/she intended to sign. If a person believes that the contract says one thing, but does not read it and then finds out that the contract says something else, he/she has no defence. In this situation, the person has simply been negligent in not reading the contract. Similarly, a blind or illiterate person, who knows the general nature and effect of the contract, would be bound by it unless the contract was falsely read to the individual or it was not read when he/she requested that it be.

Pleading of non est factum in regards to a contract is not a simple matter and expert legal advice should be obtained.

EXAMPLE *Non Est Factum*

Buyer Jones signed an agreement to buy a lot on Main Street, owned by Smith, and intended to build a new home. At time of inspection and signing of the agreement, Smith was not involved, but rather another person representing Smith.

Smith ultimately confirmed that the individual representing his interests had done so fraudulently and without proper authority. As a result, Smith argued successfully that the agreement was non est factum and he was not bound in any way by that agreement.

CONTRACT DOCUMENTS

Contract documents typically refer to the preprinted agreement/contract forms along with necessary schedules and addenda relating to that specific agreement.

Contract documents apply to the agreement of purchase and sale as well as leases. In residential real estate, contract documents for the purchase of a new home might include drawings, specifications, plans, schedules, descriptions and warranties that substantiate the terms of the contract. In commercial real estate, contract documents normally consist of the agreement/contract along with drawings, specifications, survey, buyer and seller covenants, conditions, additional contract terms and assumption of mortgage. In the case of a lease, the documents would include the preprinted offer to lease together with the layout of the demised premises, landlord's and tenant's work, conditions and additional lease details.

Contract documents also include any modifications following agreement of the parties. Modifications are generally documented by way of amendments. Formats will vary by provincial jurisdiction. The following are typical documents which may be attached to an agreement/contract to purchase a newly constructed home.

EXAMPLE ***Contract—Contract Documents***

ABC Realty Inc. is selling new homes currently under construction. To provide a complete package for the buyer, the brokerage is including the following documents and schedules.

Agreement/Contract

Schedule A: *New Home Warranty Plan* (dependent on the provincial jurisdiction)
Schedule B: *New Home Warranty Program*
Schedule C: *Construction Specifications*
Schedule D: *Upgrades and Alterations*
Schedule E: *Other Terms and Conditions*

Interpretation

When a dispute arises as to a contract's meaning or the rights under it, the courts apply varied legal rules of evidence and interpretation to discover what the parties to the contract intended. One important rule is the *parol evidence rule* which provides that a completed written contract may not be altered, varied or amended except in writing and may not be explained or added to by verbal agreement or evidence as to the intention of the parties. Exceptions exist, but the general rule must be considered significant in the drafting of agreements so that every term, warranty, condition or representation on which one or other of the parties relies will be incorporated into the written document.

Privity

The general rule is that only parties to the contract can enforce it or be bound by it. If A employs B to do work on C's house in return for payment, A and B have certain rights against each other that can be enforced at law, but C has no legal rights against B for non-performance of the work because he/she is not a party to or *privy* to the contract between A and B. (C does have legal rights against A for non-performance of the work because of the contract between C and A.)

Similarly, a broker (or salesperson) is only a witness to the signing of a contract for a property sale. Therefore, if a breach of the contract occurs, the seller can only sue the buyer and vice versa. The brokerage, acting on the seller's behalf, cannot be sued by either of the contracting parties under the terms of the contract since he/she is not privy to the contract. However, the brokerage may be sued independent of the contract if he/she encouraged the seller or the buyer to enter into the contract by the provision of misleading information or as a consequence of negligence or error. Only the brokerage, not the salesperson, can sue the seller for a real estate commission as the salesperson is not a party to the contract—he/she is only representing the brokerage.

An assumed but invalid exception is the case of a contract entered into by a broker who makes it known to the other party that he/she was in fact acting on behalf of an undisclosed principal. The principal can step in and enforce the contract since, according to the law of agency, he/she was really a party to the contract and the broker (or agent) was a mere extension of the principal.

Electronic Contracts — FOCUS

The *Electronic Commerce Act, 2000* (ECA) allows contracts to be created and signed electronically. For real estate, these contracts have included seller and buyer representation agreements and, as of July 1, 2015, now include agreements of purchase and sale, and leases. The Act and its Regulations govern the creation, recording, transmission, and storage of contracts electronically.

Due to the critical nature of real estate contracts, registrants should seek guidance from their brokerage to ensure the proper procedures and appropriate software are used when using electronic agreements.

BREACH

A breach is a failure to fulfill an obligation under a contract. Breach of a contract by one of the parties results in the imposition of a new obligation in place of the broken one by conferring a right of legal action on the party injured by the breach. A breach may discharge the injured party from further obligations to perform his/her side of the bargain. Breach may occur through an express refusal to perform the contract, making it impossible to perform through one's own act, or through the failure to perform.

If a breach goes to the root of a contract, the injured party has the option to either accept the breach and treat himself/herself as relieved or discharged from performance, or to treat the contract as subsisting and, if available, seek other remedies such as specific performance. If the breach does not go to the root of the contract, it will give rise only to a right of the other party to sue for damages, not to an option to discharge the contract.

If there are several promises, only some of which are broken, or if there is only a partial failure to perform or complete the contract, a question may arise as to whether the other party can put an end to the contract or sue for damages. The answer will depend on the expressed or implied intention of the parties, and whether the breach was substantial enough to go to the root of the contract.

EXAMPLE *Contract—Breach*

Despite warnings from his real estate brokerage and lawyer, Buyer Jones insisted that the salesperson present an unconditional offer on a large home owned by Smith. Jones was confident that his present home would sell before the July closing of the new residence. By July, Jones was unable to sell his home and was declined interim financing to close the purchase. Smith sued for breach of contract and received damages to compensate for losses incurred in placing the property back on the market to secure another buyer.

Remedies

Five remedies are available in relation to a breach of contract involving real property.

RESCISSION

A rescission sets aside the contract; e.g., buyer requests the court to set aside a contract because the builder has encountered financial difficulties, has only begun renovation work and is apparently unable to complete the job.

DAMAGES

Damages represent compensation for losses incurred. The most common remedy is monetary damages awarded by a court to recompense an injured party for a loss suffered by reason of a breach. Every breach gives rise to a right to this remedy and the measure of damages recoverable is the amount that may fairly and reasonably be considered either:

- Arising naturally (i.e., according to the usual course of events occurring from such breach of contract itself); or
- As may reasonably be supposed to have been in the contemplation of the parties at the time the contract was made.

Damages are given as financial compensation and not as a punishment for the breach or for the motive or manner of the breach, and so the plaintiff in a damage action must prove the actual amount of the damages. The plaintiff also has a duty to mitigate those damages by taking any reasonable steps available following the breach in order to reduce the extent of the loss.

EXAMPLE 1 *Contract—Damages*

Seller Smith sells his property unconditionally and Buyer Jones refuses to close due to insufficient funds. Smith places the property back on the market to find a new buyer. The damages normally sought would include the cost of re-marketing and disposing of the property, incidental costs incurred by the seller (e.g., cost of borrowing funds if a subsequent purchase was affected), any loss incurred if the property sold at a lesser price than originally agreed to with Jones and a sum of money for inconvenience and related matters.

EXAMPLE 2 *Contract—Damages—Leases*

If Landlord Smith breaches any covenants, Tenant Jones may sue for provable loss resulting from the breach. In rare circumstances, a breach by a landlord will give the tenant rights other than to damages.

If Tenant Jones vacates possession, the rent must still be paid until proper termination of the lease occurs. The tenant agreed to pay a rental amount and is liable for that amount. The landlord can sue for damages for any loss resulting from the tenant's failure to pay rent as agreed. That loss may include the unpaid rent, any deficiency in monies received from a new tenant and the cost of re-renting, including legal fees and leasing agent commission.

EXAMPLE 3 *Contract—Damages—Agency Agreement*

ABC Realty Inc. may be liable to Seller Smith for damages involving negligence or breach of duty (e.g., incompetence). Seller Smith would have a claim against the brokerage who committed the wrongful act that caused damage to the principal. Since a loss can involve a reduction in property value, carrying costs, legal fees and interest, the amount can be substantial.

EXAMPLE 4 *Contract—Damages—Contract*

Seller Smith refuses to close a sale after a binding agreement was entered into with Buyer Jones. Assuming this situation proceeds to litigation, the court will probably assess the measure of damages as the amount that may fairly and reasonably be considered either arising naturally (according to the usual course of things) from the breach, or such as may be reasonably supposed to have been contemplated by the parties at the time they made the contract.

In other words, Jones may incur direct damages for expenses related to finding other accommodation. However, Jones may also have had unique plans for the property; e.g., partial use for a new business enterprise. His inability to establish the business, as a consequence of the breach, may factor into a final assessment of damages. As with all court cases, the awarding of damages or the extent of an award varies on the merits of the case.

QUANTUM MERUIT

Quantum meruit is a court determination of a reasonable sum of money for work or services performed. If a contract has been discharged by breach after the injured party has done part but not all of what was promised under the contract, that person is entitled to the reasonable value (quantum meruit) of what was done from the party committing the breach.

EXAMPLE *Contract—Quantum Meruit*

ABC Realty Inc. enters into an exclusive two-year agreement to manage a building with a contract where compensation is received semi-annually for units rented during the preceding six-month period. Owner Smith breaches the contract eight months into the contract period and refuses to pay for ten units rented during the first six-month period. ABC Realty Inc. is entitled to compensation for the work performed.

SPECIFIC PERFORMANCE

Specific performance is a court decree or order that the party in breach must do the specific thing that was promised. This is a discretionary remedy and not an absolute right. It will be awarded only where damages are not an adequate remedy, the contract is fair and just, and the injured party acts promptly and fairly in claiming a right to specific performance.

EXAMPLE *Contract—Specific Performance*

Buyer Jones has a binding contract to purchase adjacent lands to his property for the purpose of expanding his business enterprise. The acquisition of this property is vital to meet local zoning regulations and environmental requirements. Prior to closing, Jones has already started expansion/renovation work in anticipation of the closing. The owner of the land refuses to close and lacks any substantive reason for doing so. Jones sues for specific performance.

An agreement to sell land is an example of the sort of contract that may be specifically enforceable, given the character of the particular land or its importance to the buyer. It may be that damages would be insufficient compensation.

INJUNCTION

Where the broken promise was to refrain from doing something, the court may award an injunction to restrain the offending party from doing that act. More simply put, an injunction is a court order stopping a party from continuing a breach.

The court will not compel the performance of a contract for personal service or employment, but may award an injunction to prevent the offending party from serving or performing elsewhere. The granting of an injunction, also a discretionary remedy, will be subject to the same conditions as in the case of specific performance.

A common case involves the breach of a covenant not to use the premises in a particular manner. A case might involve the tenant in a shopping plaza who agrees under the lease not to offer a specific service within the plaza and then proceeds to breach the agreement by offering that service.

Another instance might involve a tenant in a large industrial building who has specifically agreed not to store, process or otherwise handle certain hazardous waste products on the premises and then breaches that agreement following occupancy.

In discussing remedies for breach of contract, the issues of costs and interest frequently arise. The successful litigant may be awarded interest on the amounts given. That interest may be calculated from the date of the breach and can vary depending on the prime rate. The court can also award costs that normally involve all disbursements paid to court officials and others involved in the litigation, and a proportion of the costs that are payable to the litigant's own lawyer. The award will vary with the amount of the claim and the particular court jurisdiction. In rare situations, the judge can order full compensation of all costs.

TERMINATION/DISCHARGE

There are five common methods to terminate a contract involving real property.

By Mutual Agreement	A contract may be discharged by mutual agreement of the parties that it shall no longer bind them, or that it shall be replaced by another contract in altered terms, which are substituted for discharge within itself.
By Performance	A contract may be discharged by performance or tender of performance of the contract, in which case the obligations of the performing party are fulfilled and the rights of the other party are satisfied.
By Impossibility of Performance	A contract may be discharged because of the impossibility of performance, or frustration, whereby supervening and unanticipated circumstances arising after the making of the contract are held to absolve the parties from their obligations.
By Operation of Law	A contract may be discharged by operation of law; e.g., discharge from bankruptcy, alteration by one party without consent of the other. Also, rights and obligations under a contract may merge into a subsequent higher contract; e.g., a warranty concerning some aspect of the property may merge or terminate at the closing unless there is some specific wording within the agreement/contract that clearly states that such warranty shall survive the closing. A contract may also be discharged by operation of law when one party alters the contract without the consent of the other.
By Breach	Breach or the breaking of the contract by one of the parties, results in the imposition of a new obligation by conferring a right of legal action on the party injured by the breach.

Mutual Release

This term commonly referring to a mutual release form signed by the appropriate parties acknowledging that an agreement no longer binds them.

The preprinted wording for a mutual release is published as a standard form by the Ontario Real Estate Association. The form provides for a full release of all liabilities, covenants, obligations, claims and sums of money arising from an agreement/contract. This form also releases both parties from any claim from the agent involved in the transaction except as otherwise provided for.

Null and Void

Null and void can be described as having no legal force or effect. This term is commonly found in an agreement/contract for the sale of real property that involves a condition and related waiver. A typical wording for the waiver follows:

> *Unless the buyer gives notice in writing delivered to the seller by _______ p.m. on the ______ day of _________________, 20xx, that this condition is fulfilled, this Offer shall be null and void and the deposit shall be returned to the buyer in full without deduction. This condition is included for the benefit of the buyer and may be waived at the buyer's sole option by notice in writing to the seller within the time period stated herein.*

EXAMPLE *Null and Void*

Seller Smith entered into an agreement with Buyer Jones for the sale of his home at 123 Main Street. The offer was conditional upon Jones securing a new first mortgage for not less than $140,000, with an interest rate of 7.5% and payments of about One Thousand and Twenty-four Dollars and Eighteen Cents ($1,024.18). Jones was unable to qualify, based on the lender's 32% GDS ratio. The offer had stated that if a notice confirming that the mortgage has been arranged was not provided by the time specified, then the agreement/contract would be null and void. Jones provided notice to Smith of his inability to secure mortgage financing within the stated time limit. The contract became null and void and the brokerage issued a cheque to Jones for the amount of the deposit after both parties signed a mutual release.

POWER OF ATTORNEY

Power of attorney is a delegated written authority granted to a person to act legally on behalf of another, including the signing of documents. More specifically, a power of attorney is an instrument in writing whereby one person (the donor) appoints another (the attorney) as his/her attorney and confers upon the attorney the authority to perform certain specified acts or kinds of acts on behalf of the donor.

- The donor is the person who grants the power of attorney.
- The attorney is the person who exercises the power of attorney.

Practitioners may encounter powers of attorney in signing various documents; e.g., listings and agreements of purchase and sale. Ontario recognizes three types of written authorization to sign and/or act on another's behalf:

A Power of Attorney For Personal Care	This power of attorney is pursuant to the *Substitute Decisions Act*, R.S.O. 1992 concerning medical/care decisions.
A Continuing Power of Attorney for Property	Also under the *Substitute Decisions Act*, this power of attorney continues in force even during a subsequent Donor incapacity.
A Power of Attorney	This older form of power of attorney (pursuant to the *Powers of Attorney Act*, R.S.O. 1990) was most commonly used prior to the enactment of the *Substitute Decisions Act*. This form deals with property and other matters, but is infrequently used as it does not continue in force during a subsequent donor incapacity.

Real Property

Powers of attorney are of a general nature, but can be given for a specific purpose and time; i.e., dealing with a particular property. The Continuing Power of Attorney for Property is commonly used, given its continuance despite a subsequent donor incapacity.

Statutory provisions govern the giving of such power, effective date, limitations, revocation, who may act as the attorney, obligations of the attorney and other significant legal issues. Accordingly, donors should seek legal advice.

A Continuing Power of Attorney for Property dealing with real estate must be registered in the registry office showing both the donor and the attorney. Any document that is signed by the attorney, on behalf of the donor, should be in the donor's name. When the attorney signs a document pursuant to the power of attorney, that document should state that the donor was of age when the power of attorney was signed and that the power of attorney is in effect.

EXAMPLE *Power of Attorney*

Susan Smith has been appointed the attorney for William Smith to sell William Smith's home. The listing agreement, agreement of purchase and sale, deed and supporting documentation show "William Smith" as the seller. Documents would be signed by Susan Smith as follows:

Susan Smith,
as Attorney for William Smith

The documents would also contain a recital such as:

Continuing Power of Attorney for Property (or Power of Attorney) registered January 1, 2006 as Instrument No. LT 123456. To the best of my knowledge and belief the Continuing Power of Attorney for Property [or Power of Attorney] is still in full force and effect and the principal was at least 18 years of age when it was executed.

An attorney can only sign for the donor who granted the power of attorney. The attorney cannot sign documents for other parties, such as the donor's spouse or the donor's co-owner. Separate powers of attorney for those other parties would be necessary.

Practitioners Acting Under a Power of Attorney CAUTION

The attorney has legal obligations, duties and liabilities and it is therefore recommended that salespersons and brokers not act as attorneys for their clients. One concern is whether the RECO errors and omissions insurance program would cover actions as an attorney under a power of attorney. Further, dual agency would be virtually impossible under a power of attorney. The attorney effectively steps into the shoes of the donor/client. Given these and other potential complications, legal advice should be sought.

REBBA 2002

The following pages focus on regulatory requirements involving inducements, offers to purchase, written agreements, and inaccurate representations.

Inducement

GEN, Sec. 25

INDUCEMENTS

25. (1) The definitions of "sell" and "seller" in section 1 and the definitions of "buy" and "buyer" in section 2 do not apply to this section. O. Reg. 567/05, s. 25 (1).

(2) A registrant shall not, as an inducement to purchase, lease or exchange real estate, make any representation or promise that the registrant or any other person will sell, lease or exchange the real estate. O. Reg. 567/05, s. 25 (2).

(3) A registrant shall not, as an inducement to purchase real estate, make any representation or promise that the registrant or any other person will,

(a) purchase or sell any of the purchaser's real estate;

(b) procure for the purchaser a mortgage or extension of a mortgage or a lease or extension of a lease; or

(c) purchase or sell a mortgage or procure a loan. O. Reg. 567/05, s. 25 (3).

(4) A registrant shall not, as an inducement to sell real estate, make any representation or promise that the registrant or any other person will,

(a) purchase any of the seller's real estate;

(b) procure a mortgage, extension of a mortgage, lease or extension of a lease; or

(c) purchase or sell a mortgage or procure a loan. O. Reg. 567/05, s. 25 (4).

(5) Subsections (2), (3) and (4) do not apply to a representation or promise if the registrant has entered into a written contract with the person to whom the representation or promise is made that obligates the registrant to ensure that the promise or representation is complied with. O. Reg. 567/05, s. 25 (5).

A registrant must not, as an inducement to purchase, lease or exchange real estate, make any representation or promise that the registrant or any other person will sell, lease or exchange the real estate. However, this provision does not apply if the registrant has entered into a written contract with the person to whom the promise was made that obligates the registrant to comply with that promise.

Offers to Purchase Real Estate

REBBA, Sec. 35.1

35.1 (1) *No registrant shall,*

(a) *while acting on behalf of a purchaser, present an offer to purchase real estate except if the offer is in writing;*

(b) *represent to any person that a written offer to purchase real estate exists except if the offer is in writing. 2013, c. 13, Sched. 3, s. 1.*

Records

(2) *A brokerage acting on behalf of a seller shall retain, for the period of time prescribed, copies of all written offers that it receives to purchase real estate or copies of all other prescribed documents related to those offers. 2013, c. 13, Sched. 3, s. 1.*

Request for inquiry by registrar

(3) *A person who has made a written offer to purchase real estate or a registrant acting on behalf of such a person may request that the registrar make an inquiry to determine the number of written offers that the brokerage acting for a seller has received to purchase the real estate. 2013, c. 13, Sched. 3, s. 1.*

Inquiry

(4) *On receiving a request under subsection (3), the registrar may make an inquiry of the brokerage and the brokerage shall,*

(a) *respond within a reasonable period of time, or within the time that is prescribed; and*

(b) *at the request o8f the registrar, provide the registrar with copies of the written offers or other documents that it is required to retain under subsection (2). 2013, c. 13, Sched. 3, s. 1.*

Disclosure by registrar

(5) *The registrar shall determine the number of written offers that the brokerage has received to purchase the real estate and shall disclose the number of the offers as soon as practicable, or within the period of time that is prescribed, to the person who requested the inquiry under subsection (3), but shall not disclose the substance of any of the offers or the identity of the person making any of the offers. 2013, c. 13, Sched. 3, s. 1.*

Other action by registrar

(6) *Nothing in this section limits the authority of the registrar to take any other action against a registrant that this Act authorizes the registrar to take. 2013, c. 13, Sched. 3, s. 1.*

Retention of Offers that are not Accepted

OTH, Sec. 19.1

19.1 (1) *Despite section 18, for the purposes of subsection 35.1 (2) of the Act, this section applies when a brokerage acting on behalf of a seller received a written offer to purchase real estate for the purposes of presenting it to the seller, but the offer did not result in the purchase of the real estate. O. Reg. 307/14, s. 1.*

(2) *If the written offer was made by a person who was a client or customer of a registrant, then the brokerage acting on behalf of the seller shall keep, for at least one year after the date the brokerage received the written offer for the purposes of presenting it to the seller, either a copy of the written offer or a copy of a document that includes the following information:*

1. *The name and signature of the person who made the offer to purchase the real estate.*
2. *The name and contact information of the seller of the real estate.*
3. *The name of the brokerage and of the broker or salesperson who acted for the seller.*
4. *The name of the brokerage and of the broker or salesperson who acted for the person who made the offer.*
5. *The address, legal description or other identifier of the real estate on which the offer was made.*
6. *The date and time the offer was made.*
7. *The date and time the offer was received by the brokerage for the purposes of presenting it to the seller, and the means by which the offer was received, such as in person or by fax.*
8. *If the brokerage presented the offer to the seller, the date of presentation.*
9. *The date and time, if any, until which the offer was irrevocable. O. Reg. 307/14, s. 1.*

continued...

19.1 (3) *If the written offer was made by a person who was not a client or customer of a registrant, then the brokerage acting on behalf of the seller shall keep a copy of the written offer for at least one year after the date the brokerage received the written offer for the purposes of presenting it to the seller. O. Reg. 307/14, s. 1.*

When a registrant is acting on behalf of a buyer, only written offers may be presented. For a written offer to be valid, the offer must be signed. A registrant cannot indicate that an offer has been received unless it is in writing.

The seller's brokerage must retain a copy of every written offer it receives from a buyer, including any counter offer and any unsuccessful offer. The brokerage may retain an equivalent summary document (e.g., the OREA Form 801, included later in this chapter for reference purposes only) for each offer rather than retaining a copy of the offer in its entirety providing:

- The seller's brokerage receives the offer on behalf of the seller;
- The offer is made through a brokerage on behalf of the buyer;
- The offer did not result in a transaction (i.e., the offer was unsuccessful/not accepted); and
- The summary contains all the required information.

The offer retention provisions in the Act enable the Registrar to determine the number of offers received by a seller's brokerage for a property in the event that the Registrar receives a request from a buyer who made a written offer on the property, or a registrant acting on behalf of such a buyer. When requested by the Registrar, the seller's brokerage must provide the Registrar with a copy of every written offer received for the property, or the equivalent summary documents, as applicable.

Example 1 *Retaining Unsuccessful Offers*

A listing salesperson receives an offer from a co-operating brokerage, which is presented to the sellers. The sellers then counter the offer, which is presented to the buyers. The buyers do not accept the counter offer and submit a counter offer of their own. The sellers decline the buyers' counter offer and there are no further negotiations. In this situation, the listing brokerage must retain a copy of each of the two offers from the buyers or an equivalent summary of those two offers (i.e., the original offer and the counter offer). If the buyers had not been customers or clients of either the listing or co-operating brokerage, then the listing brokerage would need to retain the copies of the two offers in their entirety.

Example 2 *Retaining Successful/ Unsuccessful Offers*

A listing salesperson receives an offer from a co-operating brokerage, which is presented to the sellers. The sellers then counter the offer, which is presented to the buyers. The buyers do not accept the counter offer and submit a counter offer of their own. The sellers accept the buyers' counter offer and the purchase closes two months later. In this situation, the listing brokerage must either retain a copy of the original offer from the buyers or an equivalent summary document of that original offer for at least one year from the date of receipt by the listing brokerage, and must also retain a copy of the accepted offer from the buyer in its entirety for at least six years.

Copies of Written Agreements

CODE, Sec. 12

> *12. If a brokerage and one or more other persons enter into a written agreement in connection with a trade in real estate, the brokerage shall ensure that each of the other persons is immediately given a copy of the agreement. O. Reg. 580/05, s. 12.*

This provision encompasses any written agreement between two or more parties including buyer and seller representation agreements, service agreements and amendments, notices and releases relating to such agreements. See Sec. 28 of the Code regarding agreement copies.

Example — *Seller Representation Agreement—Commercial Property*

The seller agrees to list her commercial property for an eight-month period. The longer time period is needed given the property's uniqueness and the need for adequate time to properly market the offering to foreign investors. The seller initials the appropriate provision on the first page of the listing (see Sec. 11 regarding the listing period extending beyond six months) and signs the listing agreement. The listing salesperson immediately provides the seller with a copy of the signed agreement.

Conveying Offers

CODE, Sec. 24

24. (1) A registrant shall convey any written offer received by the registrant to the registrant's client at the earliest practicable opportunity. O. Reg. 580/05, s. 24 (1).

(2) A broker or salesperson shall establish a method of ensuring that,

(a) written offers are received by someone on behalf of the broker or salesperson, if the broker or salesperson is not available at the time an offer is submitted; and

(b) written offers are conveyed to the client of the broker or salesperson at the earliest practicable opportunity, even if the broker or salesperson is not available at the time an offer is submitted. O. Reg. 580/05, s. 24 (2).

(3) Without limiting the generality of Subsections (1) and (2), those Subsections apply regardless of the identity of the person making the offer, the contents of the offer or the nature of any arrangements for commission or other remuneration. O. Reg. 580/05, s. 24 (3).

(4) Subsections (1) to (3) are subject to any written directions given by a client. O. Reg. 580/05, s. 24 (4).

(5) Subsections (1) to (4) also apply, with necessary modifications, to,

(a) written amendments to written offers and any other written document directly related to a written offer; and

(b) written assignments of agreements that relate to interests in real estate, written waivers of conditions in agreements that relate to interests in real estate, and any other written document directly related to a written agreement that relates to an interest in real estate. O. Reg. 580/05, s. 24 (5).

(6) Subsections (1) to (5) apply, with necessary modifications, if a brokerage and a customer have an agreement that provides for the brokerage to receive written offers. O. Reg. 580/05, s. 24 (6).

(7) Subsections (1) to (5) apply, with necessary modifications, to brokers and salespersons employed by a brokerage, if the brokerage and a customer have an agreement that provides for the brokerage to receive written offers. O. Reg. 580/05, s. 24 (7).

The fundamental obligation centres on offers being presented at the earliest practicable opportunity to the client (or a customer who has an agreement that provides for the brokerage to receive offers). This ethical obligation also requires the availability of another registrant should the broker or salesperson be unavailable.

The provision further requires the delivery of offers regardless of who makes the offer, the contents of the offer, the commission arrangements and to any related documents, e.g., waiver of conditions.

Example 1 *Multiple Offers*

The property at 10 Main Street is an 'in demand' property. The listing salesperson has received an offer, with co-operating brokerages notifying her of two additional offers. The listing salesperson notifies her buyer and the co-operating brokerages of the number of competing offers but does not reveal any of the contents of the offers. The listing salesperson calls the seller client to arrange an appointment for presentation of the offers. As per brokerage policy and in keeping with Sec. 24, the offers are presented in the order received by the listing brokerage regardless of price, terms or the source of the offer.

Example 2 *The Delayed Offer*

The listing salesperson has received notice of an offer from a co-operating brokerage, but delays calling the seller for one day in an attempt to obtain an offer from his prospective buyer client. Fortunately, the seller is only inconvenienced by the delay and suffers no financial hardship. However, the co-operating brokerage files a complaint with RECO and disciplinary action is taken pursuant to Sec. 24. The listing salesperson was protecting his own interests rather than holding the interests of the client above all else, except the law.

Example 3 *The Client's Instructions*

The listing salesperson receives a written note from the client stating that she will be on a European vacation for two weeks and will only consider offers upon her return. During her first week away, a co-operating brokerage obtains an offer with a 48-hour irrevocable clause. The listing salesperson informs the brokerage that the seller will not consider offers until her return. The co-operating brokerage has the buyer amend the offer accordingly and logs ahead for a presentation upon the seller's return. The listing salesperson and co-operating brokerage have acted in compliance with the Code. However, as a critical comment, the listing salesperson should have put an appropriate notation on the listing information to inform other salespeople of the circumstance; e.g., "no offers to be presented prior to _______."

Written and Legible Agreements

CODE, Sec. 27

27. (1) A registrant who represents a client in respect of a trade in real estate shall use the registrant's best efforts to ensure that,

(a) any agreement that deals with the conveyance of an interest in real estate is in writing; and

(b) any written agreement that deals with the conveyance of an interest in real estate is legible. O. Reg. 580/05, s. 27 (1).

(2) Subsection (1) applies, with necessary modifications, if a brokerage and a customer have an agreement that provides for the brokerage to provide services to the customer in respect of any agreement that deals with the conveyance of an interest in real estate. O. Reg. 580/05, s. 27 (2).

Sec. 27 requires agreements to be *in writing*, but also adds that such agreements must be legible. Additionally, this section applies both to a client and to a customer (who has an agreement with the brokerage that involves providing services in relation to an agreement involving a conveyance of an interest in real estate).

Example 1 *The Amendment*

The seller wants to advance the completion date by one week to align with the purchase of another home. The co-operating brokerage checks with the buyer, advises that there is no problem with the revision and states that the buyer has already called his lawyer, so no further action is required. The listing salesperson, in keeping with Sec. 27, does not want to rely on verbal communication, prepares an amendment to the agreement, has the seller sign and then forwards the document to the co-operating brokerage to obtain the buyer's signature.

Example 2 *A Legible Agreement*

The salesperson has an offer that has been counter-signed (initialled) twice with numerous changes and agreed to by the parties. Unfortunately, the number of revisions makes the agreement almost unreadable given strikeouts, additions and initials. To ensure legibility, the salesperson produces a new typed offer reflecting what he believes to be all agreed changes. The parties review and sign the new agreement.

Copies of Agreements

- CODE, Sec. 28

28. (1) *If a registrant represents a client who enters into a written agreement that deals with the conveyance of an interest in real estate, the registrant shall use the registrant's best efforts to ensure that all parties to the agreement receive a copy of the agreement at the earliest practicable opportunity. O. Reg. 580/05, s. 28 (1).*

(2) *Subsection (1) applies, with necessary modifications, if a brokerage and a customer have an agreement that provides for the brokerage to provide services to the customer in respect of any agreement that deals with the conveyance of an interest in real estate. O. Reg. 580/05, s. 28 (2).*

This provision applies both to a client and to a customer (who has an agreement that involves the brokerage providing services to that customer). While this ethical obligation does not specifically state that registrants should also forward a copy of any accepted agreement to the lawyer for the respective client or customer, this customary practice is assumed.

Example 1 *Distributing Copies*

The salesperson employed by the co-operating brokerage has successfully concluded negotiations following a presentation to the seller and his listing representative. The seller has signed the agreement, received a copy at time of acceptance and completed the acknowledgement. The salesperson immediately returns to the buyers, delivers their copies and obtains their written acknowledgement.

The salesperson retains a copy for the co-operating brokerage and the buyers' solicitor and delivers the remaining copies (including the original agreement containing acknowledgements from both seller and buyers) to the listing brokerage. The listing brokerage distributes a copy to the seller's solicitor. Note: Delivery procedures may vary by marketplace.

Example 2 *Copies of the Agreement, Schedules and Amendments*

Salespersons employed by the listing and the co-operating brokerage successfully conclude a new house agreement. The agreement contains several schedules (e.g., HST rebate, upgrades and warranty provisions). Further, two amendments are necessary following signing that relate to two changes: cost of a particular upgrade and a one-week adjustment to the completion date. Copies of all documents are immediately provided to the seller and the buyer. The brokerages, as is customary, send full copies as well to the respective lawyers.

Delivery of Deposits and Documents

CODE, Sec. 29

29. Except as otherwise provided by law, if a registrant is representing a client or providing services to a customer in connection with a trade in real estate, and the client or customer has entered into an agreement in connection with the trade that requires the registrant to deliver a deposit or documents, the registrant shall deliver the deposit or documents in accordance with the agreement. O. Reg. 580/05, s. 29.

This provision requires that registrants, while not a party to an agreement, are bound to deliver deposits and documents in accordance with that agreement. This provision applies to both clients and customers who have entered into agreements in connection with trades in real estate; e.g., agreements of purchase and sale.

Example *The Survey*

The salesperson has just concluded the sale of a commercial retail site. The deposit is to be placed in the trust account upon acceptance, an existing survey is to be located by the seller and given to the buyer within 10 days, and a financing condition must be fulfilled within 20 days failing which the offer becomes null and void. The salesperson ensures that the deposit is placed in trust in accordance with the Regulations (not to exceed five business days from receipt), receives the survey, delivers same to the buyer and obtains a written acknowledgement, and lastly completes a notice removing the condition, once the financing is obtained. As such, the salesperson has complied with Sec. 29 of the Code.

Inaccurate Representations

CODE, Sec. 37

37. (1) A registrant shall not knowingly make an inaccurate representation in respect of a trade in real estate. O. Reg. 580/05, s. 37 (1).

(2) A registrant shall not knowingly make an inaccurate representation about services provided by the registrant. O. Reg. 580/05, s. 37 (2).

This requirement regarding inaccurate representations provides that a registrant must not make incorrect statements regarding either a trade in real estate or services provided by that registrant.

Example 1 *The Cracked Tile Floor*

A salesperson, when showing a property, advises the buyer client that a minor crack in the main level family room floor is 'nothing to worry about' and is probably due to slight house movement in winter months. Following closing, the buyer discovers that the seller installed walls in the basement immediately below the family room when finishing a lower games area. In doing so, the floor was accidentally raised approximately ½" causing cracking in the tile floor. Total cost for repair/replacement was $4,500. A complaint was lodged based on an inaccurate representation with disciplinary action taken against the registrant.

Example 2 *The Incentive*

A salesperson, attempting to expand business opportunities, advertises that every seller who lists within the next 30 days will receive a free gift valued at $300.00. A seller lodged a complaint stating that the incentive was misleading. Apparently, the gift amounted to a comparative market evaluation readily offered by most registrants in that community at no charge. Disciplinary action was taken in accordance with Sec. 27 of the Code.

Error, Misrepresentation, Fraud, Etc.

CODE, Sec. 38

> *38. A registrant shall use the registrant's best efforts to prevent error, misrepresentation, fraud or any unethical practice in respect of a trade in real estate. O. Reg. 580/05, s. 38.*

This provision not only requires that the registrant avoid fraud, error or misrepresentation, but must also take steps to prevent it.

Example 1 *Avoiding Possible Error*

A salesperson, when asked by a buyer client about zoning requirements, broadly describes his current understanding of local restrictions, but then ensures that the client is directed to an appropriate authority and/or includes a condition in any offer to avoid any possible error or misrepresentation. In doing so, the salesperson has taken reasonable steps to avoid error and misrepresentation when advising the client.

Example 2 *Diligent Management*

A broker of record, when conducting her usual review of recent trades and related documentation, notes certain irregularities involving three recent commercial transactions completed by the same salesperson. All three involve the same buyer who is shown on the agreements as buying in trust for a company yet to be formed. Further, all three are conditional upon satisfactory financing with no specifics as to what particular financing is being sought.

The broker of record, suspicious of some impropriety, immediately speaks with the salesperson to investigate further. Apparently the buyer client being represented is an employee of a land development company. The company wants to assemble several abutting downtown parcels of land, hence the reason for the anonymity. The salesperson also explains that none of the sellers are clients of the brokerage and notes a condition was inserted in each agreement stating that the offer is conditional upon the seller's solicitor fully reviewing the agreement. As for the vague financing conditions, the broker of record informs the salesperson that brokerage policy dictates specifics in all financing conditions. The broker of record also requires the salesperson submit all offers, prior to signature, for review over the next six month period.

As at July 1, 2015, brokerages acting on behalf of sellers must meet new requirements for handling offers. Questions and answers related to written offers and the retention of unaccepted offers are provided on the pages that follow.

RECO Q&As—Bill 55: Changes for Handling of Offers, Page 1 of 4

Q&As

Q1: I received three unsuccessful offers, along with one successful offer. Only two of the unsuccessful offers included summary documents. What should I do?

A: For the unsuccessful offer that did not include a summary document, you have to retain the offer. For the two unsuccessful offers that included the summary, you could choose to retain the offer or the summary document. The successful offer must always be retained in its entirety (Agreement of Purchase and Sale) for at least six years.

Q2: What about counter offers that amend the original offer?

A: Every written offer to a seller, including changes in the course of negotiating, is considered a separate offer. The brokerage must retain a record for every offer, including those made in any negotiations. So, if a buyer puts in an offer, and later makes two more offers in negotiations, the seller's brokerage will need to retain a record for all three of the offers. You could retain summary documents, or the offers in their entirety.

Q3: Can one summary document be used to cover all counter offers from one buyer?

A: The summary document could be designed to accommodate several offers. OREA expects to have a form available by July 1, 2015. Alternately, your brokerage may create a form for you to use.

Q4: What about offers that come directly from a buyer, and not through a brokerage?

A: The summary document can only be used when the buyer is making an offer through a brokerage. For offers coming from a buyer directly, you must retain the offer in its entirety. Keeping the full offer is necessary in case RECO needs to contact the buyer that made the offer, since the summary document does not contain contact information.

Q5: If RECO asks for documentation for the offers on a property, how much time will I have to provide it?

A: Generally RECO will expect to receive the documentation upon request, but no later than two weeks, unless otherwise directed.

RECO Q&As—Bill 55: Changes for Handling of Offers, Page 2 of 4

Q6: How long will it take for RECO to determine the number of written offers that a brokerage received?

A: RECO will aim to determine the number of written offers as quickly as possible. Each situation is unique, so it is not possible to offer a typical timeline. The volume of requests we receive will also be a factor.

Q7: If a buyer or seller is delivering or receiving offers directly, or through a lawyer, do I still have to retain records for the offers?

A: Your brokerage has to retain the offers it receives on the seller's behalf. If the seller or some other party receives offers directly, you do not have to retain the offers.

Q8: How long do I have to retain the record of each offer?

A: For unsuccessful offers, you must retain either the offer in its entirety, or a suitable summary document, for at least one year from the day the offer is signed by the buyer. You must retain the successful offer in its entirety for six years.

Q9: Can I retain records for offers beyond one year?

A: You may retain records beyond the minimum one year. It is imperative that you ensure the confidentiality of those documents for as long as you retain them.

Q10: What happens to a failed offer presentation (no transaction occurs)?

A: All offers that a listing brokerage receives must be retained, whether the property in question was sold or not. If no transaction occurred, the brokerage may retain the summary document instead of the actual offer, if it was submitted through a brokerage.

Q11: What happens to collected paperwork/information when the transaction completes?

A: The offer that resulted in a successful transaction must be retained in its entirety for the required six years, a summary document cannot be used. The summary may be used only for unsuccessful offers.

RECO Q&As—Bill 55: Changes for Handling of Offers, Page 3 of 4

Q12: When can I retain a summary document instead of a full offer?

A: The seller's brokerage may retain a summary document if:

- The seller's brokerage receives the offer on behalf of the seller;
- The offer is made through a brokerage on behalf of the buyer;
- The offer did not result in a transaction; and
- The summary contains all the required information.

Q13: What information must be included in the summary document?

A: The summary document must include:

- The name and signature of the buyer.
- The name and contact information of the seller.
- The name of the buyer's brokerage and their representative.
- The name of the seller's brokerage and their representative.
- The address, legal description or other identifier of the property.
- The date and time the offer was made.
- The date and time the offer was received by the brokerage, and how the offer was received, such as in person or by fax.
- The date of presentation, if the brokerage presented the offer to the seller.
- The date and time, if any, until which the offer was irrevocable.

Q14: Will RECO return the written offers that it obtains from the brokerage?

A: When RECO requests that a brokerage provide offers, it will identify whether the brokerage should provide originals or copies, and upon request return any original documents after the process is complete.

Q15: Does this only apply to competing offer situations?

A: No, the regulations apply to *all* offers received through a brokerage.

Q16: If I have a letter of intent from a buyer, can I indicate that I have received an offer?

A: If the letter is binding on the part of the buyer, you would then indicate that you have received an offer.

Q17: Does this apply to offers to lease?

A: No, the regulations only apply to offers to purchase real estate.

RECO Q&As—Bill 55: Changes for Handling of Offers, Page 4 of 4

Q18: Can my brokerage start retaining records of offers any time, or do we have to wait for July 1?

A: You can begin retaining records at any time, but you must retain records as of July 1. However, RECO will only be able to determine the number of offers on a property for transactions that occurred as of July 1.

Form 801 Offer Summary Document, Page 1 of 1

Form 801
for use in the Province of Ontario

Offer Summary Document
For use with Agreement of Purchase and Sale

For Brokerage submitting the offer on behalf of the Buyer:
When sent to the Listing Brokerage this form can be used as evidence that you have a written signed offer from a Buyer to the Seller.

REAL PROPERTY ADDRESS: .... (the "property")
(municipal address and/or legal description)

for an Agreement of Purchase and Sale dated: the .... day of ...., 20.............. ("offer")

This offer was submitted by: **BROKERAGE:** ....

SALES REPRESENTATIVE/BROKER: ....

I/We, ..., have signed an offer for the property.
Name of Buyer(s)

....	....	....	....
Buyer signature	Dated	Buyer signature	Dated

This offer was submitted, ... to the Listing Brokerage at .... a.m./p.m. on the .... day of
(by fax, by email or in person)

...., 20........... Irrevocable until .... a.m./p.m. on the .... day of ...., 20............

(For Buyer counter offer - complete the following)

I/We, ..., have signed an offer for the property.
Name of Buyer(s)

....	....	....	....
Buyer signature	Date	Buyer signature	Date

An offer was submitted, ... to the Listing Brokerage at .... a.m./p.m. on the .... day of
(by fax, by email or in person)

...., 20........... Irrevocable until .... a.m./p.m. on the .... day of ...., 20............

For Listing Brokerage receiving the offer:

SELLER(S): ....

SELLER(S) CONTACT: ....
(ie. phone / email / fax)

LISTING BROKERAGE: ....

SALES REPRESENTATIVE/BROKER: ....

This offer was received, ... by the Listing Brokerage at .... a.m./p.m. on the .... day of ...., 20......
(by fax, by email or in person)

This offer was presented, ... to the Seller(s) at .... a.m./p.m. on the .... day of ...., 20......
(by fax, by email or in person)

Offer was: ❐ Accepted ❐ Signed Back/Countered ❐ Expired/Declined

Comments: ....

Form 801 Revised Sept 2015 **Page 1 of 1**

CASE LAW

Case Synopsis

RE/MAX GARDEN CITY REALTY INC. V. 828294 ONTARIO INC., LOURAS AND FLEMING
ONTARIO COURT MAY, 1992

An Agreement of Purchase and Sale was negotiated and the transaction was completed. As in most offers, the agreement contained an irrevocable direction for the lawyer to pay the listing brokerage the unpaid balance of the commission from the proceeds of the sale.

Prior to completion, the Seller gave the lawyer a new direction to pay the funds directly to the Seller. The lawyer requested and received an indemnification from the Seller for any actions that might arise from the non-payment of the balance of the commission to the brokerage. The indemnification stated that the Seller acknowledged and confirmed that the new direction was contrary to the irrevocable direction in the agreement and that the Seller made the new direction with the "*full knowledge of any and all consequences that may result thereto*". The brokerage was not paid by the lawyer.

The brokerage sued the Seller and the lawyer. The form used was the OREA Agreement of Purchase and Sale. The court pointed out that the direction to pay the brokerage was irrevocable and that there was a seal printed next to the Seller's signature and under the seal was the word (Seal). Above the Seller's signature was the statement "*In witness whereof I have hereunto set my hand and seal*" and next to the signature as witness, the words "*Signed, sealed and delivered in the presence of*".

The court stated "*By irrevocably instructing his solicitor to pay to the listing broker the unpaid balance, he was, indeed, carrying out his intention, as it then was.*" The court noted that there was no consideration in the agreement for the solicitor to be required to complete the direction and if there were no seal, the direction would not be enforceable. The court determined that the irrevocable direction, under seal, amounted to an equitable assignment of the funds, which was enforceable.

The court awarded the brokerage a judgment for $35,600, the balance of commission funds due on closing.

Case Questions

1. What did the court mean by stating the irrevocable direction lacked consideration?	2. What other irrevocable term of the agreement lacks consideration and requires a seal to give it force?

CASE LAW

Case Synopsis

3999581 CANADA INC. V. 1394734 ONTARIO INC.
ONTARIO COURT OF APPEAL APRIL, 2007

This is an appeal from a decision of the Superior Court of Ontario that rejected the Buyer's claim for specific performance with an abatement of the purchase price and awarded the Seller damages of over $58,000 due to the buyer refusing to complete the transaction when an abatement of the price was not agreed to by the sellers.

The parties entered into an Agreement of Purchase and Sale for $680,000 for a parcel of vacant land being approximately 98,950 square feet. After the Agreement was executed, but before closing, it was discovered that the land description was in error. The Seller did not have title to all of the Block of land described in the Agreement. The Sellers owned only part of the Block, measuring approximately 86,745 square feet, a difference of about .26 acres or 12%.

There was no dispute that the misrepresentation was an innocent mistake; there was no suggestion of any deceit on the part of the Seller.

While the physical boundaries of the land were readily identifiable on viewing the property, the Buyer testified at trial that he could not determine the square footage of the lands by standing in the field.

The Buyer discovered the discrepancy after engaging engineers to begin surveying and laying out a site plan. Instead of the 62 housing units the Buyer expected to erect, the engineers determined that only 54 units could be erected on the site. The Buyers sought to complete the transaction, subject to an abatement of the purchase price in the amount of $103,875.

The Seller refused to complete the transaction unless the full purchase price was paid.

The Buyer registered a caution against the land and sued for specific performance with an abatement of the price. The Seller made a counterclaim for damages.

The trial judge found that the land in question was immediately identifiable and quantifiable by a casual inspection because of its observable and obvious boundaries. The trial judge denied the request for specific performance and for an abatement in the purchase price and awarded the Seller damages for the Buyer's failure to close the transaction.

The appeal court did not agree with this conclusion. The court stated that while the Agreement of Purchase and Sale does not say specifically the purchase price was calculated on the basis of acreage or square footage, it clearly contemplates the land as being 98,590 square feet and there is uncontradicted evidence that the offered price by the Buyer was based on the square footage of the land and the intended use as a townhouse development.

The appeal court determined that specific performance with an abatement in the price was an equitable remedy and allowed the appeal. The Seller's award for damages was also denied.

Case Questions

1. On what basis did the original trial judge disallow the Buyer's claim?
2. If this were a case about a home in a residential neighbourhood with a similar percentage discrepancy in the size of the land, is the outcome of the case likely to be the same?

CASE LAW

Case Synopsis

GESNER V. ERNST SUPREME COURT OF NOVA SCOTIA MAY, 2007

This was a lengthy and involved case arising from the sale of a property in Lunenburg, Nova Scotia. After the Buyer completed the transaction, various problems with the property became evident and it resulted in lawsuits and counterclaims involving the Seller and Buyer, the former owner of the property, the real estate salesperson and the home inspector.

There was a substantial amount of money involved, as the Buyer ultimately moved out of the property and left it vacant and unheated for more than 5 years, resulting in considerable deterioration to the condition of the home. Prior to the Buyer moving out, the Buyer encountered a number of problems with the property including roof leakage, moisture problems, an infestation of carpenter ants, a fireplace that did not operate properly and the discovery of UFFI in an area around the fireplace. The legal fees would also have been substantial as there were lengthy court proceedings.

The Buyer sued for rescission of the purchase agreement with the Seller and also sued the home inspector for the full cost of tearing down the home and rebuilding at a cost of $328,581 plus additional damages in excess of $90,000. No damages were awarded for the claim against the former owner and the claim against the real estate salesperson for the sale was dismissed.

The court did not grant the Buyer the claim for rescission of the Agreement and the court further determined the Seller was not guilty of fraudulent or negligent misrepresentation.

The court did award the Buyer a claim against the home inspector for slightly less than $10,000, due to the presence of UFFI in a small area of the home around the fireplace.

Without going into the details of a complicated decision, the court did provide clarity with respect to the role of a Seller Property Disclosure Statement in a transaction. The court noted that the Seller completed an SPDS and agreed it would form a part of the contract of purchase and sale relating to the property. The Buyer testified that she read the Disclosure Statement prepared by the Seller prior to making an offer on the property and relied on the accuracy of the document. The Buyer signed the bottom of the Disclosure Statement the same day as she signed the Agreement of Purchase and Sale offering to purchase the property.

The court noted:

> A Property Condition Disclosure Statement is not a warranty provided by the vendor to the purchaser. Rather, it is a statement setting out the vendor's knowledge relating to the property in question. When completing this document the vendor has an obligation to truthfully disclose her knowledge on the state of the premises but does not warrant the condition of the property. Support for this conclusion may be found in the Disclosure Statement itself. While the top of the document indicates the Seller is responsible for the accuracy of the answers given, the document states "*the information contained in this statement has been provided by the Seller of the property and is believed to be accurate, however, it may be incorrect and it is the responsibility of the Buyer to verify the accuracy of this information...Buyers are urged to carefully examine the property and have it inspected by an independent party or parties to verify the above information.*"

The court also quoted *Davis v. Kelly, [2001] P.E.I.J. No. 123 DesRoches, C.J.T.D.* stated at 32: I take the law concerning Property Condition Disclosure Statements to be as stated by *Loo J.* of the British Columbia Supreme Court in *Lind v. MacLeod, [1977] B.C.J. no. 3134, 1997 Carswell B.C. 3046 (B.C.S.C.).* Madam Justice Loo held that such statements do not require vendors to warrant properties but rather to state problems of which they are aware. Upon sufficient disclosure, the maxim of buyer beware applies as the purpose of the Property Condition Disclosure Statement is to raise questions and concerns rather than to give detailed answers.

...continued

CASE LAW

Case Synopsis GESNER V. ERNST SUPREME COURT OF NOVA SCOTIA MAY, 2007

The court noted that as a general rule, absent fraud, mistake or misrepresentation, a buyer of existing real estate takes the property as he or she finds it unless the buyer protects him or herself by contracting terms. Caveat Emptor *(McGrath v. MacLean et al. (1979), 95 D.L.R. (3rd.) 144 (Ont. C.A.))*.

The law relating to the rule of caveat emptor has been stated and restated on many occasions. *Halsbury's Laws of England. 3rd ed., vol. 34, p. 211*, succinctly states the law as follows:

Defects of quality may be either patent or latent. Patent defects are such as are discoverable by inspection and ordinary vigilance on the part of a purchaser; latent defects are such as would not be revealed by any inquiry which a purchaser is in a position to make before entering into a contract for purchase.

As regards to patent defects, the vendor is not bound to call attention to them: the rule is caveat emptor; a purchaser should make inspection and inquiry as to that which he is proposing to buy. If he omits to ascertain whether the land is such as he desires to acquire, he can not complain afterwards on discovering defects of which he would have been aware if he had taken ordinary steps to ascertain its physical condition…".

In other words, patent defects are those readily discoverable by ordinary inspection. Vendor is under no duty to draw attention to patent defects which can readily be observed by the purchaser if he pays ordinary attention during inspection. If the purchaser fails to observe patent defects on inspection he cannot be heard to complain about such defects later and the rule of caveat emptor applies. On the other hand, latent defects are those not readily apparent to the purchaser during ordinary inspection of the property he proposes to buy. If latent defects are actively concealed by the vendor, the rule of caveat emptor does not apply and the purchaser can, at his option ask for rescission of the contract and/or compensation for damages resulting therefrom.

Halsbury, supra, p. 212, dealing with concealment by vendor, states:

Any active concealment by the vendor of defects which would otherwise be patent is treated as fraudulent, and the contract is voidable by the purchaser, if he has been deceived thereby. Any conduct calculated to mislead a purchaser or lull his suspicions with regard to a defect known to the vendor has the same effect.

On the topic of representation, the court quoted the Sixth Edition of Cheshire and Fifoot on the *Law of Contract at p. 226*:

A representation is a statement made by one party to the other, before or at the time of contracting, with regard to some existing fact or to some past event, which is one of the causes that induces the contract. Examples are a statement that certain cellars are dry, that premises are sanitary, or that the profits arising from a certain business have in the past amounted to so much a year.

In referring to fraudulent misrepresentation, the court quoted the text *Canadian Law of Vendor and Purchaser by DiCastri at p. 201*:

In order to succeed on the grounds that a contract was induced by false and fraudulent representations, a plaintiff must prove: (1) That the representations complained of were made to him by the defendant; (2) That they were false in fact; (3) That when made, they were known to be false or were recklessly made, without knowing whether they were false or true; (4) That by reason of the complained-of representations the plaintiff was induced to enter into the contract; (5) That within a reasonable time after the discovery of the falsity of the representations, the plaintiff elected to avoid the contract and accordingly repudiated it. The burden of proof is clearly on the plaintiffs.

The court noted: The Buyer submits there were problems with leaking in the house after the new roof was put on and that the Seller failed to disclose these problems to her. However, the Seller answered "*yes*" to question 6(c) of the Disclosure Statement, putting the Buyer on notice that repairs had been carried out over the past five years to correct leakage or dampness problems. Despite being put on notice, the Buyer did not make any inquiries of the Seller concerning the answer to question 6(c). In my view, sufficient notice was made to the Buyer and the Buyer has not satisfied me that the Seller deliberately or fraudulently misrepresented her knowledge of the property when completing this section of the Disclosure Statement.

Without going into detail, the court came to the same conclusion with respect to the Seller's disclosure (on the Disclosure Statement) of the other problems with the property and the court dismissed the Buyer's claims against the Seller.

CASE LAW

Case Synopsis | GESNER V. ERNST SUPREME COURT OF NOVA SCOTIA MAY, 2007

Case Questions

1. While the common law of contract makes a distinction between patent and latent defects, REBBA 2002 does not make this distinction. What does the REBBA Code require with respect to this issue?

2. If a Buyer wants the seller to provide a warranty concerning the property or a part of the property, what should be done by the salesperson?

CHAPTER DISCUSSION 

1. OFFER AND ACCEPTANCE

Describe in some detail the step-by-step requirements for an offer and acceptance to create a binding agreement.

2. CONSIDERATION

a. For consideration to be valid, certain characteristics must be present. Describe these requirements for consideration to be valid.

CHAPTER DISCUSSION

2. CONSIDERATION (continued)

b. For a typical Agreement of Purchase and Sale, describe the consideration being exchanged in the transaction.

3. IRREVOCABILITY

An offer is irrevocable until 10:00 p.m. on February 10, 20xx. Is it really irrevocable? Discuss.

CHAPTER DISCUSSION

4. CAPACITY

The law protects certain parties who are not considered capable of entering into a binding contract. Who is protected? Explain.

5. LAWFUL OBJECT

For a contract to be enforceable it must have a lawful object. Provide at least six examples where the terms of an agreement would be unenforceable due to illegality. The examples must relate to real estate transactions.

CHAPTER DISCUSSION

6. MISTAKE

If a mistake made in the contracting process is considered serious enough to have prevented a "*meeting of the minds*," no contract exists under law. Provide an example related to the sale of real estate.

7. MISREPRESENTATION

a. Explain the main differences between an opinion, an innocent misrepresentation, a negligent misrepresentation and a fraudulent misrepresentation.

CHAPTER DISCUSSION

7. MISREPRESENTATION (continued)

b. *"A real estate salesperson is considered to be a specialist in the marketing of real property and this makes it more difficult for the salesperson to claim that a misrepresentation made by the salesperson is innocent rather than negligent or fraudulent."* Discuss.

8. RISK REDUCTION

The majority of lawsuits and Errors and Omissions claims against real estate brokerages involve some form of misrepresentation about a property or the service being provided by the brokerage. There are a number of steps that the brokerage can take to minimize the risk. Build a list of standard business practices that salespersons (brokerages) should follow on a day-to-day basis to minimize the risk of lawsuits and E & O claims.

KNOWLEDGE INTEGRATION

Notables

- A contract is a binding promise of one person made to another or others.
- Contracts have six basic elements that must be present in order to make the contract enforceable.
- A void contract never came into existence and a voidable contract was originally valid but capable of being rejected.
- Some persons are deemed by law as either incapable of contracting or having only limited capacity to contract.
- If a contract is illegal by statute or common law, the contract will be void and unenforceable by the court.
- Consideration is fundamental to a binding contract, but a contract can be binding without consideration if a seal is used.
- Misrepresentation can be innocent, fraudulent or negligent.
- Only certain types of mistakes can give rise to a remedy for purposes of contract law.
- *Not Est Factum* is a legal rule which states that a person innocently or fraudulently induced into a contract is not bound to that contract.
- Privity refers to a general legal rule that only parties to a contract can enforce or be bound by it.
- A contract can be terminated through five common methods, one of which is a breach that can also give rise to damages.
- REBBA 2002 includes various regulatory requirements concerning both agreements and inaccurate representations that complement contract law specifically in regard to the trading of real estate.

Chapter Mini-Review

Solutions are located in the Appendix.

1. One of the essential elements of an enforceable contract is that the agreement must be definite and clear.

   ◯ True ◯ False

2. A voidable contract is one that is a nullity at law.

   ◯ True ◯ False

3. An infant's right to avoid a contract is extinguished at the moment of reaching the age of majority.

   ◯ True ◯ False

4. All contracts with infants for the purchase of land are generally voidable by the infant.

   ◯ True ◯ False

5. If a statement of opinion turns out to be false, it is either an innocent or fraudulent misrepresentation.

   ◯ True ◯ False

Chapter Mini-Review (continued)

6. Specific performance is a discretionary remedy for breach of contract and will not normally be granted if an award of damages would be adequate.

   ○ True ○ False

7. If a contract is breached and the injured party did part of what was promised to be undertaken, the injured party is entitled to quantum meruit as a remedy.

   ○ True ○ False

8. A buyer has a contract with a builder to construct a commercial structure. Following successful completion, the contract is effectively terminated by operation of law.

   ○ True ○ False

9. According to REBBA 2002, a copy of a written agreement regarding a trade in real estate must immediately be given to each of the other persons to that agreement upon signing.

   ○ True ○ False

10. A salesperson who asks the seller client to seek expert advice, rather than making a statement about a situation that could ultimately prove incorrect, is complying with intent of Sec. 38: Error, Misrepresentation, Fraud, Etc. in the Code of Ethics.

    ○ True ○ False

11. When a seller's brokerage receives a written offer from a buyer and during the course of negotiations, receives a counter offer from the same buyer that is not accepted, the brokerage may retain the unsuccessful counter offer as record of both offers.

    ○ True ○ False

Active Learning Exercises

Solutions are located in the Appendix.

Exercise 1

An Offer is presented to the seller, John Smith, who owns the house which is rented. Smith and his wife, Mary, have never lived there, and Smith signs acceptance of the offer, adding these words: "*I accept the above offer subject to the approval of my wife.*" A copy is given to the buyer.

His wife, Mary, does not agree to the price and the buyer is so notified. The buyer claims a valid contract exists because Mary was not an owner, and not required to consent under the *Family Law Act*, and has nothing to do with the property. Is the buyer right? Explain.

Exercise 2

An offer is presented for $145,000 to Velma Seller. She tells the salesperson, "*That is not enough. Go back and get a higher offer.*" The salesperson leaves with the offer and goes back to the buyers, who refuse to budge. The salesperson calls Velma and tells her there is no deal. Velma instructs the salesperson to come back with the offer as she still has time to sign and accept it as originally offered.

a. Is Velma Seller correct? Explain.

b. Would it make any difference if Velma had said, "Leave this with me, I want to think about it. While I'm thinking, ask the buyers whether they are prepared to increase the purchase price?"

Exercise 3

You take an offer of $145,000 to a seller who refuses the price but agrees to a sign back for $150,000, changes the sale price and initials it. No other change is made to the terms of the offer, which expires at 11:59 p.m. tonight. You return to the buyer, who agrees after a long discussion that this is a good buy, and initials the change at 11:45 p.m. Is there a contract? Explain.

Exercise 4

Putting a seal on a document is a solemn act that indicates that an individual agrees to be bound to a promise.

a. Why is the seal particularly important in deciding whether or not the buyer's offer is irrevocable?

b. Is the black mark on the Agreement of Purchase and Sale a seal?

c. What should you normally explain to the buyer and seller about the seal?

Exercise 5

Buyer A and Seller B enter into a written Agreement of Purchase and Sale in which there is no deposit and the agreement was not signed under seal. On the date set for completion, A refuses to go through with the transaction claiming that since there was no deposit, there was never a contract due to lack of consideration. Comment.

Exercise 6

You show your prospective buyers several homes. They decide to make an offer on one property and ask you to prepare the offer. The property is on MLS® and the information is at your office, so you go there to prepare the offer. While you are gone, the buyers celebrate their proposed purchase with two bottles of champagne. When you return, they are very happy and obviously drunk. You know that the offer is exactly what they wanted, so you have it signed anyway. You then get the seller to sign it without telling him anything about the condition of the buyers. Naturally, the next day the buyers feel that they paid too much for the property and want to get out of the deal.

a. Can the seller force them to complete the deal? Explain.

b. What if you presented the offer to the listing salesperson who didn't know anything was wrong, and the listing salesperson presented it to the seller?

Exercise 7

You present an offer for a property that is shown on the listing to be owned by "*John Ward Properties*" and that is how you describe the seller. When Mr. Ward signs the offer he does so in the signature area as "*John Ward Properties Limited, John Ward.*"

a. Who is the seller?

b. Is there a contract?

Exercise 8

The brokerages in Anycity, Ontario have a meeting and everyone decides to charge 7% commission on every listing. Two months later, one of the brokerages lists a property for 5% and the others threaten to sue that brokerage for damages for breach of contract. What will happen, and why?

Exercise 9

Some contracts are said to be illegal because they breach a provision of the law. Does every breach of the law make the contract void? Discuss.

Exercise 10

A seller lists a property with you and shortly after the listing is signed, the building burns to the ground. Is the listing valid? Discuss.

Exercise 11

"*I thought that the commission in the Listing was 6% but in fact it was 8%. I didn't notice it and I didn't read all of the terms of the listing. I knew it was a listing and the brokerage didn't mislead me. I just wasn't paying attention.*" Is the listing valid?

Exercise 12

A buyer signs an offer to purchase for $100,000 which the seller accepts. The buyer decides to sell this contract to another buyer before the sale closes. The buyer assigns the agreement and makes a profit of $10,000.

a. Can the buyer do that?

b. What if there was a mortgage back to the seller for $95,000?

Exercise 13

A buyer wants to be certain that everything in the property is in order. The buyer is returning to Mexico, and will not be back until the day of closing and will not be able to do a personal inspection until after closing. What can be included in an offer to cover these concerns?

Exercise 14

When showing one of his listings and trying to obtain an offer, Salesperson Bert tells the buyer all of the following. Check all statements that could prove to be misrepresentations.

- ☐ *This is a nice area for a young family.*
- ☐ *This home has a dry basement.*
- ☐ *I have never seen any water or dampness in the basement.*
- ☐ *This home has a new furnace.*
- ☐ *You can put an inground pool here, no problem.*
- ☐ *I think this is the best deal on the market today in this price range.*

SECTION II

AGENCY REPRESENTATION, CONTRACT LAW AND THE AGREEMENT OF PURCHASE AND SALE

CHAPTER 6

The Agreement of Purchase and Sale

Introduction

Whether or not an agreement between buyer and seller is enforceable depends upon the accuracy and care with which the Agreement of Purchase and Sale has been completed. There are a number of pre-printed terms that are considered essential to the agreement. A real estate practitioner must be totally familiar with these terms and have the knowledge required to properly complete the form and explain each of the terms to the buyer and seller.

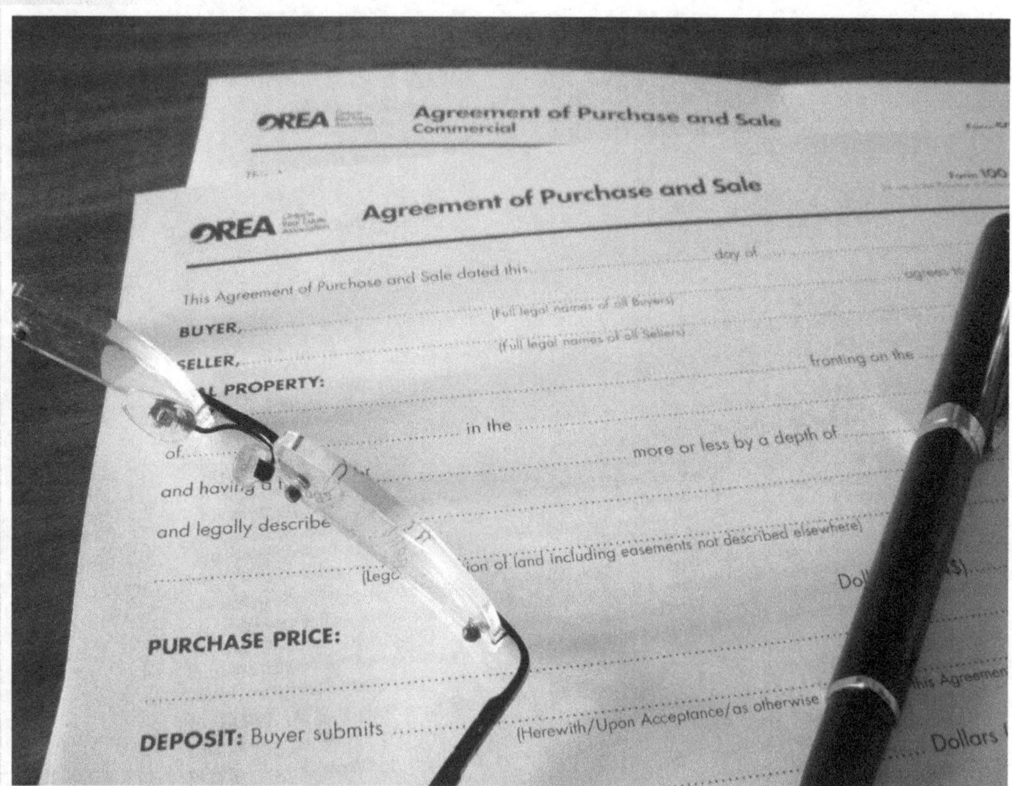

NOTE:
This chapter highlights clauses and terms in the residential *Agreement of Purchase and Sale* (OREA Form 100). The *Agreement of Purchase and Sale—Condominium Resale* (OREA Form 101) and the *Agreement of Purchase and Sale—Commercial* (OREA Form 500) are also included for comparative purposes.

Learning Outcomes

At the conclusion of this chapter, students will be able to:

- Identify and explain the importance of selected clauses and terms in the Agreement of Purchase and Sale (OREA Form 100).
- Explain requirements regarding the proper completion of the Agreement of Purchase and Sale (OREA Form 100).
- Outline various requirements regarding irrevocability, witnessing, signing-sealing and delivery of signed copies of the agreement.
- Compare terms provided in the residential agreement with those found in the Agreement of Purchase and Sale—Condominium Resale (OREA Form 101) and the Agreement of Purchase and Sale—Commercial (OREA Form 500).

THE AGREEMENT OF PURCHASE AND SALE

This agreement is a written document by which one party agrees to sell and another agrees to purchase and title passes upon the payment of an agreed purchase price.

The Statute of Frauds requires an agreement for the sale of land to be put in writing. In Ontario, the form most commonly used for the sale of real property is the Agreement of Purchase and Sale. The top portion of the form identifies the buyer, seller and property. The purchase price is then spelled out, followed by the deposit. Fixtures excluded from the purchase price and chattels included in the purchase price are defined. Time limits are set out for offer irrevocability, completion date and time to search title. This is followed by a series of printed clauses outlining the obligations of the parties to the transaction and space for signing and witnessing. Balance due on completion, a description of any financing and any special terms and conditions will appear on Schedule A.

Various agreements are used for different types of properties and circumstances including the In addition to the residential agreement, the *Agreement of Purchase and Sale – Condominium Resale* and the *Agreement of Purchase and Sale – Commercial* are included later in this chapter for reference and comparison purposes.

AGREEMENT SUMMARY

Deposit

A deposit is a payment of money or other valuable consideration as a pledge for fulfillment of a contract. If failure of performance occurs, the deposit is usually forfeited. If performance is undertaken, the deposit usually acts as a part payment toward the purchase price.

The deposit in real estate transactions, which may be paid by cheque, certified cheque or cash, forms two functions. First, it is a sign of good faith and sincerity by the person making the deposit; secondly, it represents part of the purchase price. Five to ten percent of the offered price appears sufficient to illustrate good faith in the transaction.

REBBA 2002 REQUIREMENTS

Under previous legislation, brokerages were allowed two days to deposit funds received in trust into the real estate trust account. This time limit has been increased to five business days (GEN, Subsec. 17(1)). Business days, for purposes of REBBA 2002, excludes Saturdays, Sundays and statutory holidays as defined in the *Interpretations Act* (Subsection 29(1)).

The time limit provided in the legislation is a maximum limit *or* the maximum number of days. Registrants are reminded that time is of the essence in all matters concerning deposits and agreements for the conveyance of an interest in real estate.

The Code also addresses deposits (as well as other documents). If a registrant is representing a client through a representation agreement or providing services to a customer by way of a service agreement in connection with a trade in real estate, the registrant must deliver the deposit (or other documents) in accordance with the agreement (REBBA, Sec. 29).

Failed agreements of purchase and sale return of deposits

An Agreement of Purchase and Sale ("Agreement") may not be completed for a number of reasons, including unsatisfied conditions relating to matters such as financing, rezoning approval, a home inspection or the sale of a buyer's current home. This failure to satisfy a condition may raise an issue about the return of the deposit held in a brokerage's real estate trust account.

The wording of a condition clause in an Agreement, for example, "*This offer is conditional upon the buyer obtaining satisfactory financing within five banking days, failing which the deposit shall be returned to the buyer in full without deduction*" may appear to be clear in terms of the return of the deposit if the condition isn't waived.

However, in some cases the courts, in reviewing a condition clause in an Agreement, have imposed obligations on the party who is to satisfy the condition. For this reason, a party to the Agreement may dispute the return of the deposit and the issue of entitlement to the deposit may have to be resolved by the courts.

Sec. 27(1) of the *Real Estate and Business Brokers Act, 2002* (the "Act") requires a brokerage to maintain a properly designated trust account at a recognized financial institution. All trust funds must be deposited in the account of the brokerage named in the Agreement to hold the deposit. Sec. 17(1) of Regulation 567/05 (GEN) made under the Act requires that a deposit received by the brokerage who under the Agreement is to hold the deposit must be deposited in that brokerage's real estate trust account within five business days of receipt.

A brokerage may only disburse the funds held in the real estate trust account in accordance with the terms of the trust. This is important to the purposes of the Act – consumer protection and regulation of trading in real estate. Breach of trust is an offence contrary to Sec. 27(1) of the Act; a criminal offence under the Criminal Code of Canada; and may create a civil cause of action against the trustee, i.e. the brokerage.

Brokerages as trustees of a consumer's money have important responsibilities, including a legal duty to observe a high standard of care and to act impartially when dealing with potential beneficiaries of a trust. The proper course of action in the case of a failed Agreement is to disburse the trust money in accordance with a release or direction signed by the parties to the Agreement or pursuant to a court order. The parties to the Agreement are the seller and buyer. If the parties to the Agreement are or become involved in a court action it may be possible to arrange to have the deposit money held in trust paid into court. The advice of a lawyer may be advisable in any of these situations.

In summary, in the case of a failed transaction, a brokerage should only disburse the deposit in two circumstances:

1. In accordance with a release or direction signed by all parties to the Agreement (Mutual Release) or;
2. Upon receipt of a direction from the Court (Court Order).

TRUST ACCOUNT
Section 27(1) of the Act

27. (1) Every brokerage shall,

(a) maintain in Ontario an account designated as a trust account, in,

(i) a bank, or an authorized foreign bank, within the meaning of section 2 of the Bank Act (Canada),

(ii) a loan or trust corporation, or

(iii) a credit union, as defined in the Credit Unions and Caisses Populaires Act, 1994;

(b) deposit into the account all money that comes into the brokerage's hands in trust for other persons in connection with the brokerage's business;

(c) at all times keep the money separate and apart from money belonging to the brokerage; and

(d) disburse the money only in accordance with the terms of the trust. 2004, c. 19, s. 18 (18).

TRUST FUNDS
Section 17 of Regulation 567/05

17. (1) If an amount of money comes into a brokerage's hands in trust for another person in connection with the brokerage's business, the brokerage shall deposit the amount in the trust account maintained under section 27 of the Act within the five business days.

(2) In Subsection (1), "business day" means a day that is not,

(a) Saturday, or

(b) a holiday within the meaning of Subsection 29(1) of the Interpretation Act.

Real Estate Council of Ontario
Tel: 416-207-4800 Toll Free: 1-800-245-6910 Fax: 416-207-4820
Office of the Registrar
AsktheRegistrar@reco.on.ca

REBBA 2002
Real Estate & Business Brokers Act, 2002

For more information about RECO, visit: www.reco.on.ca

Irrevocable

Irrevocable refers to the incapability of being recalled or revoked, unchangeable or unalterable. Agreements for the purchase and sale of real estate typically provide for an irrevocable date by either the buyer or seller until a specific time on a specified date, after which time, if the offer is not accepted, it becomes null and void and the deposit is returned to the buyer in full without deduction. Irrevocable dates also apply in the case of counter offers.

A person making an offer to purchase real estate may withdraw that offer at any time prior to the communication of acceptance of the offer back to the offeror (unless otherwise provided for in the agreement). Therefore, once communication has taken place the offer becomes a legally binding contract and thus is irrevocable.

A question always arises as to whether a prospective buyer is actually bound by the word *irrevocable*, as there is no contract until the seller accepts the offer and the buyers generally receive no consideration for their promise not to withdraw the offer. However a promise made under seal is generally binding on the person making the promise, even in the absence of consideration. This is one of the main reasons for having the seals on agreements.

However, no unanimous agreement exists among members of the legal profession as to the effectiveness of the seal in binding the buyers to the irrevocable date. Sales representatives must do everything possible to make sure the offers they present are free of legal loopholes. Prudent sales representatives should always have the offer signed under seal, and if a dispute arises, advise sellers to refer the matter to their solicitor.

The person making the offer has the right to specify the length of the irrevocable time. The irrevocable period is undoubtedly one of the most potent pressuring devices available in making an offer or a counter offer. Some buyers and sellers will attempt to keep the irrevocable time extremely short to swing negotiations in their favour. The prudent salesperson should negotiate a reasonable time period so that the parties can make an informed decision and complete the agreement within the required time period.

More or Less

This term, often found in a property description, is intended to cover slight, unimportant or unsubstantial inaccuracies of which both parties are willing to assume the risk.

Notice

A notice is either information about, or warning of, something. Notice may be by personal observation or by written or oral message from another person.

Legally, various types of notice exist, including notice by publication (e.g., publishing a notice in the newspaper to bring a lawsuit, estate probate or bankruptcy to the attention of the public) and a constructive notice (notice presumed to have been received; e.g., as in the mailing of a notice in lieu of delivery). The most frequent form of notice for real estate purposes is a personal notice that represents direct written or oral communication with the parties to a transaction. Real estate practitioners encounter notices most frequently concerning conditions being fulfilled in the agreement; e.g., conditional upon financing and sale of the buyer's home and the associated notice removing the condition.

EXAMPLE ***Notice Concerning Change of Ownership***

Salesperson Garcia has just sold a rental property with 12 units. Both the current owner and the new buyer want to ensure a smooth transition. One issue involves personal notice to the tenants concerning the change of ownership and related matters. Garcia, in addition to various other clauses in the agreement, inserts the following:

> *Upon completion of this sale, the seller shall provide the buyer confirmation of a notice to all tenants advising them of the new owner and requiring all future rents to be paid as the buyer directs. The seller will pay to the buyer any rent paid to the seller in error or in violation of the direction for a period of six months following completion, after which the seller may refuse to accept rent from tenants or return it to them.*

EXAMPLE ***Notice Concerning Condition***

Salesperson Ward is drafting an agreement that includes a condition concerning financing. She wants to ensure that all financial arrangements are concluded within fifteen days and that proper notice is given when the arrangements are concluded.

> *This offer is conditional upon the buyer arranging, at the buyer's own expense, a new first mortgage for not less than Eighty Thousand Dollars ($80,000.00), bearing interest at a rate of not more than 7.5% per annum, calculated semi-annually not in advance, repayable in blended monthly payments of about Five Hundred and Eighty-five Dollars and Twenty-five Cents ($585.25) including both principal and interest, and to run for a term of not less than 5 years. Unless the buyer gives notice in writing delivered to the seller personally or in accordance with any other provisions for the delivery of notice in this Agreement of Purchase and Sale or any Schedule thereto by 5 p.m. on the 25th day of February, 20xx that this condition is fulfilled, this offer shall be null and void and the deposit shall be returned to the buyer in full without deduction. This condition is included for the benefit of the buyer and may be waived at the buyer's sole option by notice in writing to the seller as aforesaid within the time period stated herein.*

Representations/Warranties

Real estate practitioners encounter situations where buyers wish to have certain matters confirmed regarding the property and improvements related thereto. For example, the buyer may express concern about the condition of the swimming pool and the salesperson may be required to insert a clause to cover potential problems. While many variations exist, one particular wording is provided for illustration purposes.

> *The seller represents and warrants to the best of the seller's knowledge and belief that the swimming pool and equipment are now, and on the completion date shall be, in good working order. The parties agree that this representation and warranty shall survive and not merge on completion of this transaction, but apply only to the state of the property existing at completion of this transaction.*

In specialized areas of real estate, such warranties and representations can be very detailed. For example, in the case of a dock, boathouse or pier involving a recreational property, the seller may have to represent and warrant to the best of his/her knowledge that the dock has received all necessary approvals and permits from the appropriate municipal, provincial and/or federal departments/ministries as well as other required authorities.

Recommended warranty clauses usually state *the party* (buyer or seller) *represents and warrants*. These two terms should be clearly differentiated. A representation is a statement made by one party to the other, before or at the time of contracting, regarding some existing fact or to some past event. The representation typically involves some fact regarding the property that is of importance in the negotiations. As such, a representation can be one of the causes that induces a contract and, therefore, could be the basis for rescinding the agreement.

A warranty is a statement or covenant that is subsidiary or collateral to the contract. It is an assurance by one party, typically but not necessarily reduced to writing within an agreement, that verifies, confirms or otherwise attests to a specific circumstance. As a consequence, the party receiving such warranty may rely upon such warranty and not investigate the issue further. A breach of warranty entitles the buyer to damages only and does not permit the buyer to rescind the contract.

These terms, in turn, should be differentiated from a condition. Whether or not a specific statement is a warranty or a condition is a question of contract and precise wording. The decision to use a condition, warranty or other representation will depend largely on circumstances. Following are two warranty clauses that might be found in an agreement to address specific situations; e.g., well and sewage systems. These clauses are inserted for information purposes only.

The seller represents and warrants, to the best of the seller's knowledge and belief, that during the seller's occupancy of the property, the pump and all related equipment serving the said property have performed adequately, and that the well is capable of supplying adequate water volume of not less than ___ gallons per minute at standing level and that the water is potable. The parties agree that this representation and warranty shall survive and not merge on completion of this transaction, but apply only to the state of the property at completion of this transaction.

The seller represents and warrants, to the best of the seller's knowledge and belief, that all sewage systems serving the property are wholly within the limits of the said property, and have been constructed according to the proper regulations and have received all required certificates of installation and approval pursuant to the [appropriate environmental legislation].

To illustrate the difference between a warranty and a condition, the first clause has been worded as a condition precedent and includes a time limit for the performance of the condition and also a waiver provision.

This offer is conditional upon the buyer determining at the buyer's own expense that:

1. *The pump and all related equipment serving the property are in proper operating condition.*
2. *There is an adequate supply of water of not less than ___ gallons per minute at standing level and that the water is potable.*

Unless the buyer gives notice in writing delivered to the seller personally or in accordance with any other provisions for the delivery of notice in this Agreement of Purchase and Sale or any Schedule thereto by 12 p.m. on the 1st day of May, 20xx, that these conditions have been fulfilled, this offer shall become null and void and the deposit shall be returned to the buyer in full without deduction. These conditions are included for the sole benefit of the buyer and may be waived at the buyer's option by notice in writing to the seller as aforesaid within the time period stated herein.

EXAMPLE *Representations/Warranties*

Owner Smith has provided various representations and warranties about the property to Buyer Jones. In particular, two representations concern any problems with electrical, plumbing and heating systems, and structural aspects of the building. Jones and Smith have agreed that the warranties shall survive and not merge on completion of the transaction. Following is the clause drafted by the selling salesperson that follows various warranties set out in the agreement.

> *The Parties agree that the representations and warranties stated herein shall survive and not merge on completion of this transaction, but apply only to the state of the property at completion of this transaction.*

Successors and Assigns

This clause regarding heirs, executors and administrators of the deceased, commonly referred to in preprinted agreements, states that the agreement is binding upon and shall ensure to the benefit of the buyers and sellers and each of their successors, assigns and personal representatives.

EXAMPLE *Successors and Assigns*

Seller Smith sold his property unconditionally using the standard preprinted agreement and subsequently purchased another home to align with the scheduled sale date. Prior to closing, the buyer passed away; however, based on the 'successors and assigns clause' within the agreement, the estate of the buyer may be obligated to continue with the purchase.

Time Is Of The Essence

This term is normally found in an agreement for the sale of real property, requiring punctual performance of the contract terms.

EXAMPLE *Time is of the Essence*

A typical wording found in a preprinted clause of an agreement is provided for illustration purposes.

> *Time shall in all respects be of the essence hereof provided that the time for doing or completing of any matter provided for herein may be extended or abridged by an agreement in writing signed by Vendor and Purchaser or by their respective lawyers who may be specifically authorized in that regard.*

Urea Formaldehyde Foam Insulation

Acronym: UFFI Urea formaldehyde is a colourless, chemical compound found in certain resins, glues and bonding agents and, for real estate practitioners, is most commonly associated with insulation. UFFI is a low density foam made from plastic resins, a foaming agent and compressed air. At time of installation, UFFI has the appearance and consistency of shaving cream. While normally identified as a white or cream-coloured substance, at least one product contained blue dye.

A controversy arose from the curing process when the product was injected into walls and other areas in residential property, and formaldehyde gas was released. A product ban appeared in 1980 because of potential health concerns, after an estimated 100,000 Canadian homes were insulated, mostly between 1975 and 1979 under government incentive programs for homeowners.

A general consensus now minimizes UFFI as a health concern. However, The Canadian Real Estate Association has strongly urged its members to stay informed, not to treat UFFI as a finalized issue and maintain UFFI references in listing and sales documents, and more particularly, the agreement.

EXAMPLE ***Urea Formaldehyde Foam Insulation—Clause in Agreement***

A wording similar to the following may be found in recommended or mandated preprinted agreements.

> *Seller represents and warrants to the buyer that during the time the seller has owned the property, the seller has not caused any building on the property to be insulated with insulation containing urea formaldehyde, and that to the best of the seller's knowledge no building on the property contains or has ever contained insulation that contains urea formaldehyde. This warranty shall survive and not merge on the completion of this transaction, and if the building is part of a multiple unit building, this warranty shall only apply to that part of the building which is the subject of this transaction.*

Note that the above clause relates to continuing concerns regarding urea formaldehyde foam insulation. The seller is warranting that there is no such insulation. Replacing this wording with an appropriate clause concerning testing and an inspection may be necessary. This circumstance could arise when the seller has refused to provide the warranty; i.e., a mortgagee selling under power of sale.

EXAMPLE ***Urea Formaldehyde Foam Insulation— Property Condition Disclosure Statement***

A typical question that might be found in a Property Condition Disclosure Statement relating to both UFFI and asbestos is illustrated.

> *To your knowledge, do the buildings or other improvements on the property now contain either one or both of urea formaldehyde foam insulation (UFFI) and asbestos, or do you remember ever receiving any information which led you to believe that the buildings or other improvements on the property previously contained either one or both of UFFI and asbestos?*

COMMISSION—ENTITLEMENT

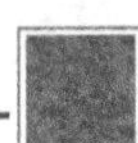

A registrant is not entitled to a commission or other remuneration unless a written agreement is signed by the party paying the commission or the registrant has shown the property to a buyer (or introduced buyer and seller to one another in relation to the buying or selling of an interest in real estate).

COMMISSIONS

23. (1) Subject to subsection 33 (3) of the Act and subsection (2), a registrant shall not charge or collect a commission or other remuneration in respect of a trade in real estate unless,

(a) the entitlement to the commission or other remuneration arises under a written agreement that is signed by or on behalf of the person who is required to pay the commission or other remuneration; or

(b) the entitlement to the commission or other remuneration arises under an agreement that is not referred to in clause (a) and,

(i) the registrant has conveyed an offer in writing that is accepted, or

(ii) the registrant,

(A) shows the property to the buyer, or

(B) introduces the buyer and the seller to one another for the purpose of discussing the proposed acquisition or disposition of an interest in real estate. O. Reg. 567/05, s. 23 (1).

STATUTE OF FRAUDS

The statute of frauds is a statutory law providing that certain contracts, including real estate contracts, must be in writing to be enforceable at law.

The Statute of Frauds, although requiring written evidence of a contract for the sale of an interest in land, does not require that any particular form be used. More specifically, this statute prohibits the bringing of any actions under certain circumstances, including any contract or sale of lands, unless some memorandum or note thereof is in writing and signed by the party to be charged.

The Courts of Equity, however, have modified the strict reliance on this statute by the Doctrine of Part Performance. This doctrine applies to contracts of land that are not in writing, where one party has actually performed part of the bargain, so as to suggest very clearly the existence of a contract for land. In such instances, where the person will suffer a loss if the contract is not performed, the courts will enforce the agreement. However, this part performance must be very clear (e.g., the building of a house on the land or renovating the property) and the plaintiff must clearly suffer loss if no contract exists. If the contract is ambiguous as to whether a sale or leasing of the land occurred under which the party renovated the premises, then the agreement may be unenforceable depending on the interpretation of the court given the evidence presented. Organized real estate uses standard preprinted agreements in the interest of accuracy and consistency.

Electronic Signatures and the Agreement of Purchase and Sale — MARKET MEMO

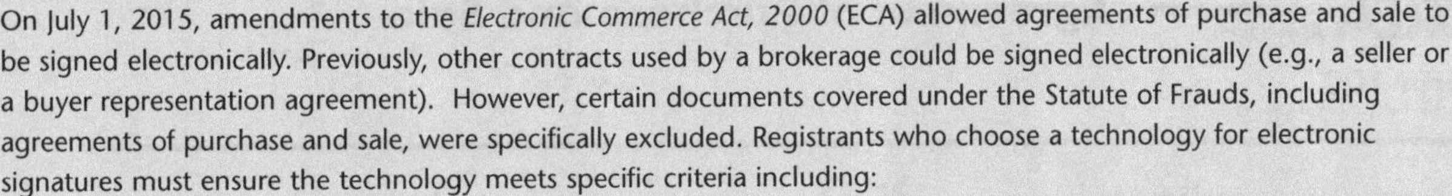

On July 1, 2015, amendments to the *Electronic Commerce Act, 2000* (ECA) allowed agreements of purchase and sale to be signed electronically. Previously, other contracts used by a brokerage could be signed electronically (e.g., a seller or a buyer representation agreement). However, certain documents covered under the Statute of Frauds, including agreements of purchase and sale, were specifically excluded. Registrants who choose a technology for electronic signatures must ensure the technology meets specific criteria including:

- ***Authentication:*** the ability to confirm the signature is from the person from whom it is supposed to be
- ***Unauthorized use:*** the signature must be permanent and tamper-proof to prevent fraudulent use of the signature

All parties to an agreement must consent to the use of electronic signatures. While consent can be implied, it is recommended that the consent be in writing to avoid future disputes. If any party to an agreement insists on using written signatures, registrants must oblige. Mortgage providers and financial institutions may also insist on paper documents with written signatures.

Due to the critical nature of the agreement of purchase and sale, brokers of record should ensure extra caution is taken when using electronic signatures because of specific procedures and audit trails that must take place. Working electronically does not change any obligation registrants have under REBBA 2002.

Form 100 Agreement of Purchase and Sale, Page 1 of 6

OREA Ontario Real Estate Association

Agreement of Purchase and Sale

Form 100
for use in the Province of Ontario

This Agreement of Purchase and Sale dated this .... day of .... 20...........

BUYER, ..., agrees to purchase from
(Full legal names of all Buyers)

SELLER, ..., the following
(Full legal names of all Sellers)

REAL PROPERTY:

Address ....

fronting on the .... side of ....

in the ....

and having a frontage of .... more or less by a depth of .... more or less

and legally described as ....

.... (the "property")
(Legal description of land including easements not described elsewhere)

PURCHASE PRICE: Dollars (CDN$) ....

.... Dollars

DEPOSIT: Buyer submits ....
(Herewith/Upon Acceptance/as otherwise described in this Agreement)

.... Dollars (CDN$) ....

by negotiable cheque payable to .... "Deposit Holder" to be held in trust pending completion or other termination of this Agreement and to be credited toward the Purchase Price on completion. For the purposes of this Agreement, "Upon Acceptance" shall mean that the Buyer is required to deliver the deposit to the Deposit Holder within 24 hours of the acceptance of this Agreement. The parties to this Agreement hereby acknowledge that, unless otherwise provided for in this Agreement, the Deposit Holder shall place the deposit in trust in the Deposit Holder's non-interest bearing Real Estate Trust Account and no interest shall be earned, received or paid on the deposit.

Buyer agrees to pay the balance as more particularly set out in Schedule A attached.

SCHEDULE(S) A..**attached hereto form(s) part of this Agreement.**

1. **IRREVOCABILITY:** This offer shall be irrevocable by .... until .... a.m./p.m. on the ....
(Seller/Buyer)

   day of .... 20 ...., after which time, if not accepted, this offer shall be null and void and the deposit shall be returned to the Buyer in full without interest.

2. **COMPLETION DATE:** This Agreement shall be completed by no later than 6:00 p.m. on the .... day of ....

   20 .... Upon completion, vacant possession of the property shall be given to the Buyer unless otherwise provided for in this Agreement.

INITIALS OF BUYER(S): ( ) **INITIALS OF SELLER(S):** ( )

Form 100 Revised 2015 **Page 1 of 6**

Form 100 Agreement of Purchase and Sale, Page 2 of 6

3. **NOTICES:** The Seller hereby appoints the Listing Brokerage as agent for the Seller for the purpose of giving and receiving notices pursuant to this Agreement. Where a Brokerage (Buyer's Brokerage) has entered into a representation agreement with the Buyer, the Buyer hereby appoints the Buyer's Brokerage as agent for the purpose of giving and receiving notices pursuant to this Agreement. **Where a Brokerage represents both the Seller and the Buyer (multiple representation), the Brokerage shall not be appointed or authorized to be agent for either the Buyer or the Seller for the purpose of giving and receiving notices.** Any notice relating hereto or provided for herein shall be in writing. In addition to any provision contained herein and in any Schedule hereto, this offer, any counter-offer, notice of acceptance thereof or any notice to be given or received pursuant to this Agreement or any Schedule hereto (any of them, "Document") shall be deemed given and received when delivered personally or hand delivered to the Address for Service provided in the Acknowledgement below, or where a facsimile number or email address is provided herein, when transmitted electronically to that facsimile number or email address, respectively, in which case, the signature(s) of the party (parties) shall be deemed to be original.

FAX No.: .... (For delivery of Documents to Seller)   FAX No.: .... (For delivery of Documents to Buyer)

Email Address: .... (For delivery of Documents to Seller)   Email Address: .... (For delivery of Documents to Buyer)

4. **CHATTELS INCLUDED:**..

....

....

....

....

Unless otherwise stated in this Agreement or any Schedule hereto, Seller agrees to convey all fixtures and chattels included in the Purchase Price free from all liens, encumbrances or claims affecting the said fixtures and chattels.

5. **FIXTURES EXCLUDED:**..

....

....

....

....

6. **RENTAL ITEMS (Including Lease, Lease to Own):** The following equipment is rented and **not** included in the Purchase Price. The Buyer agrees to assume the rental contract(s), if assumable:

....

....

....

The Buyer agrees to co-operate and execute such documentation as may be required to facilitate such assumption.

7. **HST:** If the sale of the Property (Real Property as described above) is subject to Harmonized Sales Tax (HST), then such tax shall be .... (included in/in addition to) the Purchase Price. If the sale of the Property is not subject to HST, Seller agrees to certify on or before closing, that the sale of the Property is not subject to HST. Any HST on chattels, if applicable, is not included in the Purchase Price.

INITIALS OF BUYER(S): ( )   **INITIALS OF SELLER(S):** ( )

Form 100 Revised 2015 **Page 2 of 6**

Form 100 Agreement of Purchase and Sale, Page 3 of 6

8. **TITLE SEARCH:** Buyer shall be allowed until 6:00 p.m. on the .... day of ...., 20..........., (Requisition Date) to examine the title to the Property at Buyer's own expense and until the earlier of: (i) thirty days from the later of the Requisition Date or the date on which the conditions in this Agreement are fulfilled or otherwise waived or; (ii) five days prior to completion, to satisfy Buyer that there are no outstanding work orders or deficiency notices affecting the Property, and that its present use (..) may be lawfully continued and that the principal building may be insured against risk of fire. Seller hereby consents to the municipality or other governmental agencies releasing to Buyer details of all outstanding work orders and deficiency notices affecting the property, and Seller agrees to execute and deliver such further authorizations in this regard as Buyer may reasonably require.

9. **FUTURE USE:** Seller and Buyer agree that there is no representation or warranty of any kind that the future intended use of the property by Buyer is or will be lawful except as may be specifically provided for in this Agreement.

10. **TITLE:** Provided that the title to the property is good and free from all registered restrictions, charges, liens, and encumbrances except as otherwise specifically provided in this Agreement and save and except for (a) any registered restrictions or covenants that run with the land providing that such are complied with; (b) any registered municipal agreements and registered agreements with publicly regulated utilities providing such have been complied with, or security has been posted to ensure compliance and completion, as evidenced by a letter from the relevant municipality or regulated utility; (c) any minor easements for the supply of domestic utility or telephone services to the property or adjacent properties; and (d) any easements for drainage, storm or sanitary sewers, public utility lines, telephone lines, cable television lines or other services which do not materially affect the use of the property. If within the specified times referred to in paragraph 8 any valid objection to title or to any outstanding work order or deficiency notice, or to the fact the said present use may not lawfully be continued, or that the principal building may not be insured against risk of fire is made in writing to Seller and which Seller is unable or unwilling to remove, remedy or satisfy or obtain insurance save and except against risk of fire (Title Insurance) in favour of the Buyer and any mortgagee, (with all related costs at the expense of the Seller), and which Buyer will not waive, this Agreement notwithstanding any intermediate acts or negotiations in respect of such objections, shall be at an end and all monies paid shall be returned without interest or deduction and Seller, Listing Brokerage and Co-operating Brokerage shall not be liable for any costs or damages. Save as to any valid objection so made by such day and except for any objection going to the root of the title, Buyer shall be conclusively deemed to have accepted Seller's title to the property.

11. **CLOSING ARRANGEMENTS:** Where each of the Seller and Buyer retain a lawyer to complete the Agreement of Purchase and Sale of the property, and where the transaction will be completed by electronic registration pursuant to Part III of the Land Registration Reform Act, R.S.O. 1990, Chapter L4 and the Electronic Registration Act, S.O. 1991, Chapter 44, and any amendments thereto, the Seller and Buyer acknowledge and agree that the exchange of closing funds, non-registrable documents and other items (the "Requisite Deliveries") and the release thereof to the Seller and Buyer will (a) not occur at the same time as the registration of the transfer/deed (and any other documents intended to be registered in connection with the completion of this transaction) and (b) be subject to conditions whereby the lawyer(s) receiving any of the Requisite Deliveries will be required to hold same in trust and not release same except in accordance with the terms of a document registration agreement between the said lawyers. The Seller and Buyer irrevocably instruct the said lawyers to be bound by the document registration agreement which is recommended from time to time by the Law Society of Upper Canada. Unless otherwise agreed to by the lawyers, such exchange of the Requisite Deliveries will occur in the applicable Land Titles Office or such other location agreeable to both lawyers.

12. **DOCUMENTS AND DISCHARGE:** Buyer shall not call for the production of any title deed, abstract, survey or other evidence of title to the property except such as are in the possession or control of Seller. If requested by Buyer, Seller will deliver any sketch or survey of the property within Seller's control to Buyer as soon as possible and prior to the Requisition Date. If a discharge of any Charge/Mortgage held by a corporation incorporated pursuant to the Trust And Loan Companies Act (Canada), Chartered Bank, Trust Company, Credit Union, Caisse Populaire or Insurance Company and which is not to be assumed by Buyer on completion, is not available in registrable form on completion, Buyer agrees to accept Seller's lawyer's personal undertaking to obtain, out of the closing funds, a discharge in registrable form and to register same, or cause same to be registered, on title within a reasonable period of time after completion, provided that on or before completion Seller shall provide to Buyer a mortgage statement prepared by the mortgagee setting out the balance required to obtain the discharge, and, where a real-time electronic cleared funds transfer system is not being used, a direction executed by Seller directing payment to the mortgagee of the amount required to obtain the discharge out of the balance due on completion.

13. **INSPECTION:** Buyer acknowledges having had the opportunity to inspect the Property and understands that upon acceptance of this offer there shall be a binding agreement of purchase and sale between Buyer and Seller. **The Buyer acknowledges having the opportunity to include a requirement for a property inspection report in this Agreement and agrees that except as may be specifically provided for in this Agreement, the Buyer will not be obtaining a property inspection or property inspection report regarding the Property.**

14. **INSURANCE:** All buildings on the property and all other things being purchased shall be and remain until completion at the risk of Seller. Pending completion, Seller shall hold all insurance policies, if any, and the proceeds thereof in trust for the parties as their interests may appear and in the event of substantial damage, Buyer may either terminate this Agreement and have all monies paid returned without interest or deduction or else take the proceeds of any insurance and complete the purchase. No insurance shall be transferred on completion. If Seller is taking back a Charge/Mortgage, or Buyer is assuming a Charge/Mortgage, Buyer shall supply Seller with reasonable evidence of adequate insurance to protect Seller's or other mortgagee's interest on completion.

INITIALS OF BUYER(S): ( ) **INITIALS OF SELLER(S):** ( )

Form 100 Revised 2015 **Page 3 of 6**

Form 100 Agreement of Purchase and Sale, Page 4 of 6

15. **PLANNING ACT:** This Agreement shall be effective to create an interest in the property only if Seller complies with the subdivision control provisions of the Planning Act by completion and Seller covenants to proceed diligently at Seller's expense to obtain any necessary consent by completion.

16. **DOCUMENT PREPARATION:** The Transfer/Deed shall, save for the Land Transfer Tax Affidavit, be prepared in registrable form at the expense of Seller, and any Charge/Mortgage to be given back by the Buyer to Seller at the expense of the Buyer. If requested by Buyer, Seller covenants that the Transfer/Deed to be delivered on completion shall contain the statements contemplated by Section 50(22) of the Planning Act, R.S.O.1990.

17. **RESIDENCY:** (a) Subject to (b) below, the Seller represents and warrants that the Seller is not and on completion will not be a non-resident under the non-residency provisions of the Income Tax Act which representation and warranty shall survive and not merge upon the completion of this transaction and the Seller shall deliver to the Buyer a statutory declaration that Seller is not then a non-resident of Canada; (b) provided that if the Seller is a non-resident under the non-residency provisions of the Income Tax Act, the Buyer shall be credited towards the Purchase Price with the amount, if any, necessary for Buyer to pay to the Minister of National Revenue to satisfy Buyer's liability in respect of tax payable by Seller under the non-residency provisions of the Income Tax Act by reason of this sale. Buyer shall not claim such credit if Seller delivers on completion the prescribed certificate.

18. **ADJUSTMENTS:** Any rents, mortgage interest, realty taxes including local improvement rates and unmetered public or private utility charges and unmetered cost of fuel, as applicable, shall be apportioned and allowed to the day of completion, the day of completion itself to be apportioned to Buyer.

19. **PROPERTY ASSESSMENT:** The Buyer and Seller hereby acknowledge that the Province of Ontario has implemented current value assessment and properties may be re-assessed on an annual basis. The Buyer and Seller agree that no claim will be made against the Buyer or Seller, or any Brokerage, Broker or Salesperson, for any changes in property tax as a result of a re-assessment of the property, save and except any property taxes that accrued prior to the completion of this transaction.

20. **TIME LIMITS:** Time shall in all respects be of the essence hereof provided that the time for doing or completing of any matter provided for herein may be extended or abridged by an agreement in writing signed by Seller and Buyer or by their respective lawyers who may be specifically authorized in that regard.

21. **TENDER:** Any tender of documents or money hereunder may be made upon Seller or Buyer or their respective lawyers on the day set for completion. Money shall be tendered with funds drawn on a lawyer's trust account in the form of a bank draft, certified cheque or wire transfer using the Large Value Transfer System.

22. **FAMILY LAW ACT:** Seller warrants that spousal consent is not necessary to this transaction under the provisions of the Family Law Act, R.S.O.1990 unless Seller's spouse has executed the consent hereinafter provided.

23. **UFFI:** Seller represents and warrants to Buyer that during the time Seller has owned the property, Seller has not caused any building on the property to be insulated with insulation containing ureaformaldehyde, and that to the best of Seller's knowledge no building on the property contains or has ever contained insulation that contains ureaformaldehyde. This warranty shall survive and not merge on the completion of this transaction, and if the building is part of a multiple unit building, this warranty shall only apply to that part of the building which is the subject of this transaction.

24. **LEGAL, ACCOUNTING AND ENVIRONMENTAL ADVICE:** The parties acknowledge that any information provided by the brokerage is not legal, tax or environmental advice.

25. **CONSUMER REPORTS: The Buyer is hereby notified that a consumer report containing credit and/or personal information may be referred to in connection with this transaction.**

26. **AGREEMENT IN WRITING:** If there is conflict or discrepancy between any provision added to this Agreement (including any Schedule attached hereto) and any provision in the standard pre-set portion hereof, the added provision shall supersede the standard pre-set provision to the extent of such conflict or discrepancy. This Agreement including any Schedule attached hereto, shall constitute the entire Agreement between Buyer and Seller. There is no representation, warranty, collateral agreement or condition, which affects this Agreement other than as expressed herein. For the purposes of this Agreement, Seller means vendor and Buyer means purchaser. This Agreement shall be read with all changes of gender or number required by the context.

27. **TIME AND DATE:** Any reference to a time and date in this Agreement shall mean the time and date where the property is located.

INITIALS OF BUYER(S): ◯ **INITIALS OF SELLER(S):** ◯

Form 100 Revised 2015 **Page 4 of 6**

28. SUCCESSORS AND ASSIGNS: The heirs, executors, administrators, successors and assigns of the undersigned are bound by the terms herein.

SIGNED, SEALED AND DELIVERED in the presence of: IN WITNESS whereof I have hereunto set my hand and seal:

.... (Witness) .... (Buyer) (Seal) DATE ....

.... (Witness) .... (Buyer) (Seal) DATE ....

I, the Undersigned Seller, agree to the above offer. I hereby irrevocably instruct my lawyer to pay directly to the brokerage(s) with whom I have agreed to pay commission, the unpaid balance of the commission together with applicable Harmonized Sales Tax (and any other taxes as may hereafter be applicable), from the proceeds of the sale prior to any payment to the undersigned on completion, as advised by the brokerage(s) to my lawyer.

SIGNED, SEALED AND DELIVERED in the presence of: IN WITNESS whereof I have hereunto set my hand and seal:

.... (Witness) .... (Seller) (Seal) DATE ....

.... (Witness) .... (Seller) (Seal) DATE ....

SPOUSAL CONSENT: The Undersigned Spouse of the Seller hereby consents to the disposition evidenced herein pursuant to the provisions of the Family Law Act, R.S.O.1990, and hereby agrees with the Buyer that he/she will execute all necessary or incidental documents to give full force and effect to the sale evidenced herein.

.... (Witness) .... (Spouse) (Seal) DATE ....

CONFIRMATION OF ACCEPTANCE: Notwithstanding anything contained herein to the contrary, I confirm this Agreement with all changes both typed and written was finally accepted by all parties at .... a.m./p.m. this .... day of..............................., 20..........

.... (Signature of Seller or Buyer)

INFORMATION ON BROKERAGE(S)

Listing Brokerage .... Tel.No.(................) ....

.... (Salesperson / Broker Name)

Co-op/Buyer Brokerage .... Tel.No.(................) ....

.... (Salesperson / Broker Name)

ACKNOWLEDGEMENT

I acknowledge receipt of my signed copy of this accepted Agreement of Purchase and Sale and I authorize the Brokerage to forward a copy to my lawyer.

.... DATE .... (Seller)

.... DATE .... (Seller)

Address for Service ....

.... Tel.No.(...........)....................

Seller's Lawyer ....

Address ....

Email ....

(...........).................... (...........).................... Tel.No. FAX No.

I acknowledge receipt of my signed copy of this accepted Agreement of Purchase and Sale and I authorize the Brokerage to forward a copy to my lawyer.

.... DATE .... (Buyer)

.... DATE .... (Buyer)

Address for Service ....

.... Tel.No.(...........)....................

Buyer's Lawyer ....

Address ....

Email ....

(...........).................... (...........).................... Tel.No. FAX No.

FOR OFFICE USE ONLY **COMMISSION TRUST AGREEMENT**

To: Co-operating Brokerage shown on the foregoing Agreement of Purchase and Sale:
In consideration for the Co-operating Brokerage procuring the foregoing Agreement of Purchase and Sale, I hereby declare that all moneys received or receivable by me in connection with the Transaction as contemplated in the MLS® Rules and Regulations of my Real Estate Board shall be receivable and held in trust. This agreement shall constitute a Commission Trust Agreement as defined in the MLS® Rules and shall be subject to and governed by the MLS® Rules pertaining to Commission Trust.

DATED as of the date and time of the acceptance of the foregoing Agreement of Purchase and Sale. Acknowledged by:

.... (Authorized to bind the Listing Brokerage) .... (Authorized to bind the Co-operating Brokerage)

Form 100 Revised 2015 **Page 5 of 6**

Form 100 Agreement of Purchase and Sale, Page 6 of 6

Form 100
for use in the Province of Ontario

Schedule A
Agreement of Purchase and Sale

This Schedule is attached to and forms part of the Agreement of Purchase and Sale between:

BUYER, ..., and

SELLER, ...

for the purchase and sale of ....

.... dated the .... day of ...., 20................

Buyer agrees to pay the balance as follows:

This form must be initialed by all parties to the Agreement of Purchase and Sale.

INITIALS OF BUYER(S): **INITIALS OF SELLER(S):**

Form 100 Revised 2015 **Page 6 of 6**

Form 101 Agreement of Purchase and Sale—Condominium Resale, Page 1 of 6

OREA Ontario Real Estate Association

Agreement of Purchase and Sale
Condominium Resale

Form 101
for use in the Province of Ontario

This Agreement of Purchase and Sale dated this .... day of .... 20...........

BUYER, ..., agrees to purchase from
(Full legal names of all Buyers)

SELLER, ..., the following
(Full legal names of all Sellers)

PROPERTY:
a unit in the condominium property known as .... No..........................
(Apartment/Townhouse/Suite/Unit)

located at ....

in the ....

being .... Condominium Plan No ....
(Legal Name of Condominium Corporation)

Unit Number .... Level No. .... Building No. .... together with ownership

or exclusive use of Parking Space(s) ...., together with ownership or exclusive use of
(Number(s), Level(s))

Locker(s) ...., together with Seller's proportionate undivided tenancy-in-common interest
(Number(s), Level(s))
in the common elements appurtenant to the Unit as described in the Declaration and Description including the exclusive right to use such other parts of the common elements appurtenant to the Unit as may be specified in the Declaration and Description: the Unit, the proportionate interest in the common elements appurtenant thereto, and the exclusive use portions of the common elements, being herein called the "Property".

PURCHASE PRICE: Dollars (CDN$) ....

.... Dollars

DEPOSIT: Buyer submits ....
(Herewith/Upon Acceptance/as otherwise described in this Agreement)

.... Dollars (CDN$) ....

by negotiable cheque payable to .... "Deposit Holder" to be held in trust pending completion or other termination of this Agreement and to be credited toward the Purchase Price on completion. For the purposes of this Agreement, "Upon Acceptance" shall mean that the Buyer is required to deliver the deposit to the Deposit Holder within 24 hours of the acceptance of this Agreement. The parties to this Agreement hereby acknowledge that, unless otherwise provided for in this Agreement, the Deposit Holder shall place the deposit in trust in the Deposit Holder's non-interest bearing Real Estate Trust Account and no interest shall be earned, received or paid on the deposit.

Buyer agrees to pay the balance as more particularly set out in Schedule A attached.

SCHEDULE(S) A..**attached hereto form(s) part of this Agreement.**

1. **IRREVOCABILITY:** This offer shall be irrevocable by .... until .... a.m./p.m. on the ....
(Seller/Buyer)

   day of .... 20 ...., after which time, if not accepted, this offer shall be null and void and the deposit shall be returned to the Buyer in full without interest.

2. **COMPLETION DATE:** This Agreement shall be completed by no later than 6:00 p.m. on the .... day of ....,

   20 .... Upon completion, vacant possession of the property shall be given to the Buyer unless otherwise provided for in this Agreement.

INITIALS OF BUYER(S): ( ) **INITIALS OF SELLER(S):** ( )

Form 101 Agreement of Purchase and Sale—Condominium Resale, Page 2 of 6

3. **NOTICES:** The Seller hereby appoints the Listing Brokerage as agent for the Seller for the purpose of giving and receiving notices pursuant to this Agreement. Where a Brokerage (Buyer's Brokerage) has entered into a representation agreement with the Buyer, the Buyer hereby appoints the Buyer's Brokerage as agent for the purpose of giving and receiving notices pursuant to this Agreement. **Where a Brokerage represents both the Seller and the Buyer (multiple representation), the Brokerage shall not be appointed or authorized to be agent for either the Buyer or the Seller for the purpose of giving and receiving notices.** Any notice relating hereto or provided for herein shall be in writing. In addition to any provision contained herein and in any Schedule hereto, this offer, any counter-offer, notice of acceptance thereof or any notice to be given or received pursuant to this Agreement or any Schedule hereto (any of them, "Document") shall be deemed given and received when delivered personally or hand delivered to the Address for Service provided in the Acknowledgement below, or where a facsimile number or email address is provided herein, when transmitted electronically to that facsimile number or email address, respectively, in which case, the signature(s) of the party (parties) shall be deemed to be original.

FAX No.: .... (For delivery of Documents to Seller) FAX No.: .... (For delivery of Documents to Buyer)

Email Address: .... (For delivery of Documents to Seller) Email Address: .... (For delivery of Documents to Buyer)

4. **CHATTELS INCLUDED:**..

....

....

....

....

Unless otherwise stated in this Agreement or any Schedule hereto, Seller agrees to convey all fixtures and chattels included in the Purchase Price free from all liens, encumbrances or claims affecting the said fixtures and chattels.

5. **FIXTURES EXCLUDED:**..

....

....

....

6. **RENTAL ITEMS (Including Lease, Lease to Own):** The following equipment is rented and **not** included in the Purchase Price. The Buyer ` agrees to assume the rental contract(s), if assumable:

....

....

....

The Buyer agrees to co-operate and execute such documentation as may be required to facilitate such assumption.

7. **COMMON EXPENSES:** Seller warrants to Buyer that the common expenses presently payable to the Condominium Corporation in respect of the Property are approximately $ .... per month, which amount includes the following: ....

....

....

8. **PARKING AND LOCKERS:** Parking and Lockers are as described above or assigned as follows: ....

.... at an additional cost of: ....

INITIALS OF BUYER(S): ( ) **INITIALS OF SELLER(S):** ( )

Form 101 Revised 2015 **Page 2 of 6**

Form 101 Agreement of Purchase and Sale—Condominium Resale, Page 3 of 6

9. HST: If the sale of the Property (Real Property as described above) is subject to Harmonized Sales Tax (HST), then such tax shall be .... the Purchase Price. If the sale of the Property is not subject to HST, Seller agrees to certify on or before
(included in/in addition to)
closing, that the sale of the Property is not subject to HST. Any HST on chattels, if applicable, is not included in the Purchase Price.

10. TITLE SEARCH: Buyer shall be allowed until 6:00 p.m. on the .... day of ...., 20......., (Requisition Date) to examine the title to the Property at Buyer's own expense and until the earlier of: (i) thirty days from the later of the Requisition Date or the date on which the conditions in this Agreement are fulfilled or otherwise waived or; (ii) five days prior to completion, to satisfy Buyer that there are no outstanding work orders or deficiency notices affecting the Property, and that its present use (..) may be lawfully continued. If within that time any valid objection to title or to any outstanding work order or deficiency notice, or to the fact the said present use may not lawfully be continued, is made in writing to Seller and which Seller is unable or unwilling to remove, remedy or satisfy or obtain insurance save and except against risk of fire (Title Insurance) in favour of the Buyer and any mortgagee, (with all related costs at the expense of the Seller), and which Buyer will not waive, this Agreement notwithstanding any intermediate acts or negotiations in respect of such objections, shall be at an end and all monies paid shall be returned without interest or deduction and Seller, Listing Brokerage and Co-operating Brokerage shall not be liable for any costs or damages. Save as to any valid objection so made by such day and except for any objection going to the root of the title, Buyer shall be conclusively deemed to have accepted Seller's title to the Property. Seller hereby consents to the municipality or other governmental agencies releasing to Buyer details of all outstanding work orders and deficiency notices affecting the Property, and Seller agrees to execute and deliver such further authorizations in this regard as Buyer may reasonably require.

11. TITLE: Buyer agrees to accept title to the Property subject to all rights and easements registered against title for the supply and installation of telephone services, electricity, gas, sewers, water, television cable facilities and other related services; provided that title to the Property is otherwise good and free from all encumbrances except: (a) as herein expressly provided; (b) any registered restrictions, conditions or covenants that run with the land provided such have been complied with; (c) the provisions of the Condominium Act and its Regulations and the terms, conditions and provisions of the Declaration, Description and By-laws, Occupancy Standards By-laws, including the Common Element Rules and other Rules and Regulations; and (d) any existing municipal agreements, zoning by-laws and/or regulations and utilities or service contracts.

12. CLOSING ARRANGEMENTS: Where each of the Seller and Buyer retain a lawyer to complete the Agreement of Purchase and Sale of the Property, and where the transaction will be completed by electronic registration pursuant to Part III of the Land Registration Reform Act, R.S.O. 1990, Chapter L4 and the Electronic Registration Act, S.O. 1991, Chapter 44, and any amendments thereto, the Seller and Buyer acknowledge and agree that the exchange of closing funds, nonregistrable documents and other items (the "Requisite Deliveries") and the release thereof to the Seller and Buyer will (a) not occur at the same time as the registration of the transfer/deed (and any other documents intended to be registered in connection with the completion of this transaction) and (b) be subject to conditions whereby the lawyer(s) receiving any of the Requisite Deliveries will be required to hold same in trust and not release same except in accordance with the terms of a document registration agreement between the said lawyers. The Seller and Buyer irrevocably instruct the said lawyers to be bound by the document registration agreement which is recommended from time to time by the Law Society of Upper Canada. Unless otherwise agreed to by the lawyers, such exchange of the Requisite Deliveries will occur in the applicable Land Titles Office or such other location agreeable to both lawyers.

13. STATUS CERTIFICATE AND MANAGEMENT OF CONDOMINIUM: Seller represents and warrants to Buyer that there are no special assessments contemplated by the Condominium Corporation, and there are no legal actions pending by or against or contemplated by the Condominium Corporation. The Seller consents to a request by the Buyer or the Buyer's authorized representative for a Status Certificate from the Condominium Corporation. Buyer acknowledges that the Condominium Corporation may have entered into a Management Agreement for the management of the condominium property.

14. DOCUMENTS AND DISCHARGE: Buyer shall not call for the production of any title deed, abstract, survey or other evidence of title to the Property except such as are in the possession or control of Seller. Seller agrees to deliver to Buyer, if it is possible without incurring any costs in so doing, copies of all current condominium documentation of the Condominium Corporation, including the Declaration, Description, By-laws, Common Element Rules and Regulations and the most recent financial statements of the Condominium Corporation. If a discharge of any Charge/Mortgage held by a corporation incorporated pursuant to the Trust And Loan Companies Act (Canada), Chartered Bank, Trust Company, Credit Union, Caisse Populaire or Insurance Company and which is not to be assumed by Buyer on completion, is not available in registrable form on completion, Buyer agrees to accept Seller's lawyer's personal undertaking to obtain, out of the closing funds, a discharge in registrable form and to register same, or cause same to be registered, on title within a reasonableperiod of time after completion, provided that on or before completion Seller shall provide to Buyer a mortgage statement prepared by the mortgagee setting out the balance required to obtain the discharge, and, where a real-time electronic cleared funds transfer system is not being used, a direction executed by Seller directing payment to the mortgagee of the amount required to obtain the discharge out of the balance due on completion.

15. MEETINGS: Seller represents and warrants to Buyer that at the time of the acceptance of this Offer the Seller has not received a notice convening a special or general meeting of the Condominium Corporation respecting; (a) the termination of the government of the condominium property; (b) any substantial alteration in or substantial addition to the common elements or the renovation thereof; OR (c) any substantial change in the assets or liabilities of the Condominium Corporation; and Seller covenants that if Seller receives any such notice prior to the date of completion Seller shall forthwith notify Buyer in writing and Buyer may thereupon at Buyer's option declare this Agreement to be null and void and all monies paid by Buyer shall be refunded without interest or deduction.

INITIALS OF BUYER(S): ( ) **INITIALS OF SELLER(S):** ( )

Form 101 Revised 2015 **Page 3 of 6**

Form 101 Agreement of Purchase and Sale—Condominium Resale, Page 4 of 6

16. INSPECTION: Buyer acknowledges having had the opportunity to inspect the Property and understands that upon acceptance of this offer there shall be a binding agreement of purchase and sale between Buyer and Seller. **The Buyer acknowledges having the opportunity to include a requirement for a property inspection report in this Agreement and agrees that except as may be specifically provided for in this Agreement, the Buyer will not be obtaining a property inspection or property inspection report regarding the Property.**

17. APPROVAL OF THE AGREEMENT: In the event that consent to this sale is required to be given by the Condominium Corporation or the Board of Directors, the Seller will apply forthwith for the requisite consent, and if such consent is refused, then this Agreement shall be null and void and the deposit monies paid hereunder shall be refunded without interest or other penalty to the Buyer.

18. INSURANCE: The Unit and all other things being purchased shall be and remain at the risk of the Seller until completion. In the event of substantial damage to the Property Buyer may at Buyer's option either permit the proceeds of insurance to be used for repair of such damage in accordance with the provisions of the Insurance Trust Agreement, or terminate this Agreement and all deposit monies paid by Buyer hereunder shall be refunded without interest or deduction. If Seller is taking back a Charge/Mortgage, or Buyer is assuming a Charge/Mortgage, Buyer shall supply Seller with reasonable evidence of adequate insurance to protect Seller's or other mortgagee's interest on completion.

19. DOCUMENT PREPARATION: The Transfer/Deed shall, save for the Land Transfer Tax Affidavit, be prepared in registrable form at the expense of Seller, and any Charge/Mortgage to be given back by the Buyer to Seller at the expense of the Buyer.

20. RESIDENCY: (a) Subject to (b) below, the Seller represents and warrants that the Seller is not and on completion will not be a non-resident under the non-residency provisions of the Income Tax Act which representation and warranty shall survive and not merge upon the completion of this transaction and the Seller shall deliver to the Buyer a statutory declaration that Seller is not then a non-resident of Canada; (b) provided that if the Seller is a non-resident under the non-residency provisions of the Income Tax Act, the Buyer shall be credited towards the Purchase Price with the amount, if any, necessary for Buyer to pay to the Minister of National Revenue to satisfy Buyer's liability in respect of tax payable by Seller under the non-residency provisions of the Income Tax Act by reason of this sale. Buyer shall not claim such credit if Seller delivers on completion the prescribed certificate.

21. ADJUSTMENTS: Common Expenses; realty taxes, including local improvement rates; mortgage interest; rentals; unmetered public or private utilities and fuel where billed to the Unit and not the Condominium Corporation; are to be apportioned and allowed to the day of completion, the day of completion itself to be apportioned to the Buyer. There shall be no adjustment for the Seller's share of any assets or liabilities of the Condominium Corporation including any reserve or contingency fund to which Seller may have contributed prior to the date of completion.

22. PROPERTY ASSESSMENT: The Buyer and Seller hereby acknowledge that the Province of Ontario has implemented current value assessment and properties may be re-assessed on an annual basis. The Buyer and Seller agree that no claim will be made against the Buyer or Seller, or any Brokerage, Broker or Salesperson, for any changes in property tax as a result of a re-assessment of the Property, save and except any property taxes that accrued prior to the completion of this transaction.

23. TIME LIMITS: Time shall in all respects be of the essence hereof provided that the time for doing or completing of any matter provided for herein may be extended or abridged by an agreement in writing signed by Seller and Buyer or by their respective lawyers who may be specifically authorized in that regard.

24. TENDER: Any tender of documents or money hereunder may be made upon Seller or Buyer or their respective lawyers on the day set for completion. Money shall be tendered with funds drawn on a lawyer's trust account in the form of a bank draft, certified cheque or wire transfer using the Large Value Transfer System.

25. FAMILY LAW ACT: Seller warrants that spousal consent is not necessary to this transaction under the provisions of the Family Law Act, R.S.O. 1990 unless Seller's spouse has executed the consent hereinafter provided.

26. UFFI: Seller represents and warrants to Buyer that during the time Seller has owned the Property, Seller has not caused any building on the Property to be insulated with insulation containing ureaformaldehyde, and that to the best of Seller's knowledge no building on the Property contains or has ever contained insulation that contains ureaformaldehyde. This warranty shall survive and not merge on the completion of this transaction, and if the building is part of a multiple unit building, this warranty shall only apply to that part of the building which is the subject of this transaction.

27. LEGAL, ACCOUNTING AND ENVIRONMENTAL ADVICE: The parties acknowledge that any information provided by the brokerage is not legal, tax or environmental advice.

28. CONSUMER REPORTS: The Buyer is hereby notified that a consumer report containing credit and/or personal information may be referred to in connection with this transaction.

29. AGREEMENT IN WRITING: If there is conflict or discrepancy between any provision added to this Agreement (including any Schedule attached hereto) and any provision in the standard pre-set portion hereof, the added provision shall supersede the standard pre-set provision to the extent of such conflict or discrepancy. This Agreement including any Schedule attached hereto, shall constitute the entire Agreement between Buyer and Seller. There is no representation, warranty, collateral agreement or condition, which affects this Agreement other than as expressed herein. For the purposes of this Agreement, Seller means vendor and Buyer means purchaser. This Agreement shall be read with all changes of gender or number required by the context.

30. TIME AND DATE: Any reference to a time and date in this Agreement shall mean the time and date where the Property is located.

INITIALS OF BUYER(S): ( ) **INITIALS OF SELLER(S):** ( )

Form 101 Revised 2015 **Page 4 of 6**

Form 101 Agreement of Purchase and Sale—Condominium Resale, Page 5 of 6

31. SUCCESSORS AND ASSIGNS: The heirs, executors, administrators, successors and assigns of the undersigned are bound by the terms herein.

SIGNED, SEALED AND DELIVERED in the presence of: IN WITNESS whereof I have hereunto set my hand and seal:

.... (Witness) .... (Buyer) (Seal) DATE ....

.... (Witness) .... (Buyer) (Seal) DATE ....

I, the Undersigned Seller, agree to the above offer. I hereby irrevocably instruct my lawyer to pay directly to the brokerage(s) with whom I have agreed to pay commission, the unpaid balance of the commission together with applicable Harmonized Sales Tax (and any other taxes as may hereafter be applicable), from the proceeds of the sale prior to any payment to the undersigned on completion, as advised by the brokerage(s) to my lawyer.

SIGNED, SEALED AND DELIVERED in the presence of: IN WITNESS whereof I have hereunto set my hand and seal:

.... (Witness) .... (Seller) (Seal) DATE ....

.... (Witness) .... (Seller) (Seal) DATE ....

SPOUSAL CONSENT: The Undersigned Spouse of the Seller hereby consents to the disposition evidenced herein pursuant to the provisions of the Family Law Act, R.S.O.1990, and hereby agrees with the Buyer that he/she will execute all necessary or incidental documents to give full force and effect to the sale evidenced herein.

.... (Witness) .... (Spouse) (Seal) DATE ....

CONFIRMATION OF ACCEPTANCE: Notwithstanding anything contained herein to the contrary, I confirm this Agreement with all changes both typed and written was finally accepted by all parties at .... a.m./p.m. this .... day of......................................., 20..........

.... (Signature of Seller or Buyer)

INFORMATION ON BROKERAGE(S)

Listing Brokerage .... Tel.No.(...............)....................

.... (Salesperson / Broker Name)

Co-op/Buyer Brokerage .... Tel.No.(...............)....................

.... (Salesperson / Broker Name)

ACKNOWLEDGEMENT

I acknowledge receipt of my signed copy of this accepted Agreement of Purchase and Sale and I authorize the Brokerage to forward a copy to my lawyer.

.... DATE .... (Seller)

.... DATE .... (Seller)

Address for Service ....

.... Tel.No.(...........)....................

Seller's Lawyer ....

Address ....

Email ....

(...........).................... (...........).................... Tel.No. FAX No.

I acknowledge receipt of my signed copy of this accepted Agreement of Purchase and Sale and I authorize the Brokerage to forward a copy to my lawyer.

.... DATE .... (Buyer)

.... DATE .... (Buyer)

Address for Service ....

.... Tel.No.(...........)....................

Buyer's Lawyer ....

Address ....

Email ....

(...........).................... (...........).................... Tel.No. FAX No.

Property Manager: .... (Name) (Address) (Tel No.,FAX No)

FOR OFFICE USE ONLY **COMMISSION TRUST AGREEMENT**

To: Co-operating Brokerage shown on the foregoing Agreement of Purchase and Sale:
In consideration for the Co-operating Brokerage procuring the foregoing Agreement of Purchase and Sale, I hereby declare that all moneys received or receivable by me in connection with the Transaction as contemplated in the MLS® Rules and Regulations of my Real Estate Board shall be receivable and held in trust. This agreement shall constitute a Commission Trust Agreement as defined in the MLS® Rules and shall be subject to and governed by the MLS® Rules pertaining to Commission Trust.

DATED as of the date and time of the acceptance of the foregoing Agreement of Purchase and Sale. Acknowledged by:

.... (Authorized to bind the Listing Brokerage) .... (Authorized to bind the Co-operating Brokerage)

Form 101 Revised 2015 **Page 5 of 6**

Form 101 Agreement of Purchase and Sale—Condominium Resale, Page 6 of 6

Form 101
for use in the Province of Ontario

Schedule A
Agreement of Purchase and Sale – Condominium Resale

This Schedule is attached to and forms part of the Agreement of Purchase and Sale between:

BUYER, ..., and

SELLER, ...

for the purchase and sale of ....

.... dated the .... day of ...., 20 ....

Buyer agrees to pay the balance as follows:

This form must be initialed by all parties to the Agreement of Purchase and Sale.

INITIALS OF BUYER(S):  **INITIALS OF SELLER(S):** 

Form 101 Revised 2015 **Page 6 of 6**

OREA Ontario Real Estate Association

Form 500
for use in the Province of Ontario

Agreement of Purchase and Sale
Commercial

This Agreement of Purchase and Sale dated this .... day of ...., 20....................

BUYER, ..., agrees to purchase from
(Full legal names of all Buyers)

SELLER, ..., the following
(Full legal names of all Sellers)

REAL PROPERTY:

Address ....

fronting on the .... side of ....

in the ....

and having a frontage of .... more or less by a depth of .... more or less

and legally described as ....

.... (the "property")
(Legal description of land including easements not described elsewhere)

PURCHASE PRICE: Dollars (CDN$) ....

.... Dollars

DEPOSIT: Buyer submits ....
(Herewith/Upon Acceptance/as otherwise described in this Agreement)

.... Dollars (CDN$) ....

by negotiable cheque payable to.. .... "Deposit Holder" to be held in trust pending completion or other termination of this Agreement and to be credited toward the Purchase Price on completion. For the purposes of this Agreement, "Upon Acceptance" shall mean that the Buyer is required to deliver the deposit to the Deposit Holder within 24 hours of the acceptance of this Agreement. The parties to this Agreement hereby acknowledge that, unless otherwise provided for in this Agreement, the Deposit Holder shall place the deposit in trust in the Deposit Holder's non-interest bearing Real Estate Trust Account and no interest shall be earned, received or paid on the deposit.

Buyer agrees to pay the balance as more particularly set out in Schedule A attached.

SCHEDULE(S) A ....**attached hereto form(s) part of this Agreement.**

1. **IRREVOCABILITY:** This offer shall be irrevocable by .... until .... a.m./p.m. on
(Seller/Buyer)

   the .... day of ...., 20....................., after which time, if not accepted, this offer shall be null and void and the deposit shall be returned to the Buyer in full without interest.

2. **COMPLETION DATE:** This Agreement shall be completed by no later than 6:00 p.m. on the .... day of ....

   ...., 20............................... Upon completion, vacant possession of the property shall be given to the Buyer unless otherwise provided for in this Agreement.

INITIALS OF BUYER(S): ◯ **INITIALS OF SELLERS(S):** ◯

The trademarks REALTOR®, REALTORS® and the REALTOR® logo are controlled by The Canadian Real Estate Association (CREA) and identify real estate professionals who are members of CREA. Used under license.

Form 500 Revised 2015 **Page 1 of 6**

Form 500 Agreement of Purchase and Sale—Commercial, Page 2 of 6

3. **NOTICES:** The Seller hereby appoints the Listing Brokerage as agent for the Seller for the purpose of giving and receiving notices pursuant to this Agreement. Where a Brokerage (Buyer's Brokerage) has entered into a representation agreement with the Buyer, the Buyer hereby appoints the Buyer's Brokerage as agent for the purpose of giving and receiving notices pursuant to this Agreement. **Where a Brokerage represents both the Seller and the Buyer (multiple representation), the Brokerage shall not be appointed or authorized to be agent for either the Buyer or the Seller for the purpose of giving and receiving notices.** Any notice relating hereto or provided for herein shall be in writing. In addition to any provision contained herein and in any Schedule hereto, this offer, any counter-offer, notice of acceptance thereof or any notice to be given or received pursuant to this Agreement or any Schedule hereto (any of them, "Document") shall be deemed given and received when delivered personally or hand delivered to the Address for Service provided in the Acknowledgement below, or where a facsimile number or email address is provided herein, when transmitted electronically to that facsimile number or email address, respectively, in which case, the signature(s) of the party (parties) shall be deemed to be original.

FAX No.: .... (For delivery of Documents to Seller)

FAX No.: .... (For delivery of Documents to Buyer)

Email Address: .... (For delivery of Documents to Seller)

Email Address: .... (For delivery of Documents to Buyer)

4. **CHATTELS INCLUDED:** ....

....

....

....

....

Unless otherwise stated in this Agreement or any Schedule hereto, Seller agrees to convey all fixtures and chattels included in the Purchase Price free from all liens, encumbrances or claims affecting the said fixtures and chattels.

5. **FIXTURES EXCLUDED:** ....

....

....

....

....

6. **RENTAL ITEMS (Including Lease, Lease to Own):** The following equipment is rented and **not** included in the Purchase Price. The Buyer agrees to assume the rental contract(s), if assumable:

....

....

....

....

The Buyer agrees to co-operate and execute such documentation as may be required to facilitate such assumption.

7. **HST: If the sale of the property (Real Property as described above) is subject to Harmonized Sales Tax (HST), then such tax shall be in addition to the Purchase Price.** The Seller will not collect HST if the Buyer provides to the Seller a warranty that the Buyer is registered under the Excise Tax Act ("ETA"), together with a copy of the Buyer's ETA registration, a warranty that the Buyer shall self-assess and remit the HST payable and file the prescribed form and shall indemnify the Seller in respect of any HST payable. The foregoing warranties shall not merge but shall survive the completion of the transaction. If the sale of the property is not subject to HST, Seller agrees to certify on or before closing, that the transaction is not subject to HST. Any HST on chattels, If applicable, is not included in the Purchase Price.

INITIALS OF BUYER(S): ( ) **INITIALS OF SELLERS(S):** ( )

Form 500 Revised 2015 **Page 2 of 6**

Form 500 Agreement of Purchase and Sale—Commercial, Page 3 of 6

8. **TITLE SEARCH:** Buyer shall be allowed until 6:00 p.m. on the .... day of..., 20................, (Requisition Date) to examine the title to the property at his own expense and until the earlier of: (i) thirty days from the later of the Requisition Date or the date on which the conditions in this Agreement are fulfilled or otherwise waived or; (ii) five days prior to completion, to satisfy himself that there

   are no outstanding work orders or deficiency notices affecting the property, that its present use (..) may be lawfully continued and that the principal building may be insured against risk of fire. Seller hereby consents to the municipality or other governmental agencies releasing to Buyer details of all outstanding work orders and deficiency notices affecting the property, and Seller agrees to execute and deliver such further authorizations in this regard as Buyer may reasonably require.

9. **FUTURE USE:** Seller and Buyer agree that there is no representation or warranty of any kind that the future intended use of the property by Buyer is or will be lawful except as may be specifically provided for in this Agreement.

10. **TITLE:** Provided that the title to the property is good and free from all registered restrictions, charges, liens, and encumbrances except as otherwise specifically provided in this Agreement and save and except for (a) any registered restrictions or covenants that run with the land providing that such are complied with; (b) any registered municipal agreements and registered agreements with publicly regulated utilities providing such have been complied with, or security has been posted to ensure compliance and completion, as evidenced by a letter from the relevant municipality or regulated utility; (c) any minor easements for the supply of domestic utility or telephone services to the property or adjacent properties; and (d) any easements for drainage, storm or sanitary sewers, public utility lines, telephone lines, cable television lines or other services which do not materially affect the use of the property. If within the specified times referred to in paragraph 8 any valid objection to title or to any outstanding work order or deficiency notice, or to the fact the said present use may not lawfully be continued, or that the principal building may not be insured against risk of fire is made in writing to Seller and which Seller is unable or unwilling to remove, remedy or satisfy or obtain insurance save and except against risk of fire (Title Insurance) in favour of the Buyer and any mortgagee, (with all related costs at the expense of the Seller), and which Buyer will not waive, this Agreement notwithstanding any intermediate acts or negotiations in respect of such objections, shall be at an end and all monies paid shall be returned without interest or deduction and Seller, Listing Brokerage and Co-operating Brokerage shall not be liable for any costs or damages. Save as to any valid objection so made by such day and except for any objection going to the root of the title, Buyer shall be conclusively deemed to have accepted Seller's title to the property.

11. **CLOSING ARRANGEMENTS:** Where each of the Seller and Buyer retain a lawyer to complete the Agreement of Purchase and Sale of the property, and where the transaction will be completed by electronic registration pursuant to Part III of the Land Registration Reform Act, R.S.O. 1990, Chapter L4 and the Electronic Registration Act, S.O. 1991, Chapter 44, and any amendments thereto, the Seller and Buyer acknowledge and agree that the exchange of closing funds, non-registrable documents and other items (the "Requisite Deliveries") and the release thereof to the Seller and Buyer will (a) not occur at the same time as the registration of the transfer/deed (and any other documents intended to be registered in connection with the completion of this transaction) and (b) be subject to conditions whereby the lawyer(s) receiving any of the Requisite Deliveries will be required to hold same in trust and not release same except in accordance with the terms of a document registration agreement between the said lawyers. The Seller and Buyer irrevocably instruct the said lawyers to be bound by the document registration agreement which is recommended from time to time by the Law Society of Upper Canada. Unless otherwise agreed to by the lawyers, such exchange of the Requisite Deliveries will occur in the applicable Land Titles Office or such other location agreeable to both lawyers.

12. **DOCUMENTS AND DISCHARGE:** Buyer shall not call for the production of any title deed, abstract, survey or other evidence of title to the property except such as are in the possession or control of Seller. If requested by Buyer, Seller will deliver any sketch or survey of the property within Seller's control to Buyer as soon as possible and prior to the Requisition Date. If a discharge of any Charge/Mortgage held by a corporation incorporated pursuant to the Trust And Loan Companies Act (Canada), Chartered Bank, Trust Company, Credit Union, Caisse Populaire or Insurance Company and which is not to be assumed by Buyer on completion, is not available in registrable form on completion, Buyer agrees to accept Seller's lawyer's personal undertaking to obtain, out of the closing funds, a discharge in registrable form and to register same, or cause same to be registered, on title within a reasonable period of time after completion, provided that on or before completion Seller shall provide to Buyer a mortgage statement prepared by the mortgagee setting out the balance required to obtain the discharge, and, where a real-time electronic cleared funds transfer system is not being used, a direction executed by Seller directing payment to the mortgagee of the amount required to obtain the discharge out of the balance due on completion.

13. **INSPECTION:** Buyer acknowledges having had the opportunity to inspect the property and understands that upon acceptance of this offer there shall be a binding agreement of purchase and sale between Buyer and Seller.

14. **INSURANCE:** All buildings on the property and all other things being purchased shall be and remain until completion at the risk of Seller. Pending completion, Seller shall hold all insurance policies, if any, and the proceeds thereof in trust for the parties as their interests may appear and in the event of substantial damage, Buyer may either terminate this Agreement and have all monies paid returned without interest or deduction or else take the proceeds of any insurance and complete the purchase. No insurance shall be transferred on completion. If Seller is taking back a Charge/Mortgage, or Buyer is assuming a Charge/Mortgage, Buyer shall supply Seller with reasonable evidence of adequate insurance to protect Seller's or other mortgagee's interest on completion.

INITIALS OF BUYER(S): ( ) **INITIALS OF SELLERS(S):** ( )

Form 500 Revised 2015 **Page 3 of 6**

Form 500 Agreement of Purchase and Sale—Commercial, Page 4 of 6

15. **PLANNING ACT:** This Agreement shall be effective to create an interest in the property only if Seller complies with the subdivision control provisions of the Planning Act by completion and Seller covenants to proceed diligently at his expense to obtain any necessary consent by completion.

16. **DOCUMENT PREPARATION:** The Transfer/Deed shall, save for the Land Transfer Tax Affidavit, be prepared in registrable form at the expense of Seller, and any Charge/Mortgage to be given back by the Buyer to Seller at the expense of the Buyer. If requested by Buyer, Seller covenants that the Transfer/Deed to be delivered on completion shall contain the statements contemplated by Section 50(22) of the Planning Act, R.S.O.1990.

17. **RESIDENCY:** (a) Subject to (b) below, the Seller represents and warrants that the Seller is not and on completion will not be a non-resident under the non-residency provisions of the Income Tax Act which representation and warranty shall survive and not merge upon the completion of this transaction and the Seller shall deliver to the Buyer a statutory declaration that Seller is not then a non-resident of Canada;
(b) provided that if the Seller is a non-resident under the non-residency provisions of the Income Tax Act, the Buyer shall be credited towards the Purchase Price with the amount, if any, necessary for Buyer to pay to the Minister of National Revenue to satisfy Buyer's liability in respect of tax payable by Seller under the non-residency provisions of the Income Tax Act by reason of this sale. Buyer shall not claim such credit if Seller delivers on completion the prescribed certificate.

18. **ADJUSTMENTS:** Any rents, mortgage interest, realty taxes including local improvement rates and unmetered public or private utility charges and unmetered cost of fuel, as applicable, shall be apportioned and allowed to the day of completion, the day of completion itself to be apportioned to Buyer.

19. **TIME LIMITS:** Time shall in all respects be of the essence hereof provided that the time for doing or completing of any matter provided for herein may be extended or abridged by an agreement in writing signed by Seller and Buyer or by their respective lawyers who may be specifically authorized in that regard.

20. **PROPERTY ASSESSMENT:** The Buyer and Seller hereby acknowledge that the Province of Ontario has implemented current value assessment and properties may be re-assessed on an annual basis. The Buyer and Seller agree that no claim will be made against the Buyer or Seller, or any Brokerage, Broker or Salesperson, for any changes in property tax as a result of a re-assessment of the property, save and except any property taxes that accrued prior to the completion of this transaction.

21. **TENDER:** Any tender of documents or money hereunder may be made upon Seller or Buyer or their respective lawyers on the day set for completion. Money shall be tendered with funds drawn on a lawyer's trust account in the form of a bank draft, certified cheque or wire transfer using the Large Value Transfer System.

22. **FAMILY LAW ACT:** Seller warrants that spousal consent is not necessary to this transaction under the provisions of the Family Law Act, R.S.O.1990 unless Seller's spouse has executed the consent hereinafter provided.

23. **UFFI:** Seller represents and warrants to Buyer that during the time Seller has owned the property, Seller has not caused any building on the property to be insulated with insulation containing ureaformaldehyde, and that to the best of Seller's knowledge no building on the property contains or has ever contained insulation that contains ureaformaldehyde. This warranty shall survive and not merge on the completion of this transaction, and if the building is part of a multiple unit building, this warranty shall only apply to that part of the building which is the subject of this transaction.

24. **LEGAL, ACCOUNTING AND ENVIRONMENTAL ADVICE:** The parties acknowledge that any information provided by the brokerage is not legal, tax or environmental advice, and that it has been recommended that the parties obtain independent professional advice prior to signing this document.

25. **CONSUMER REPORTS: The Buyer is hereby notified that a consumer report containing credit and/or personal information may be referred to in connection with this transaction.**

26. **AGREEMENT IN WRITING:** If there is conflict or discrepancy between any provision added to this Agreement (including any Schedule attached hereto) and any provision in the standard pre-set portion hereof, the added provision shall supersede the standard pre-set provision to the extent of such conflict or discrepancy. This Agreement including any Schedule attached hereto, shall constitute the entire Agreement between Buyer and Seller. There is no representation, warranty, collateral agreement or condition, which affects this Agreement other than as expressed herein. For the purposes of this Agreement, Seller means vendor and Buyer means purchaser. This Agreement shall be read with all changes of gender or number required by the context.

27. **TIME AND DATE:** Any reference to a time and date in this Agreement shall mean the time and date where the property is located.

INITIALS OF BUYER(S): **INITIALS OF SELLERS(S):**

Form 500 Revised 2015 **Page 4 of 6**

28. SUCCESSORS AND ASSIGNS: The heirs, executors, administrators, successors and assigns of the undersigned are bound by the terms herein.

SIGNED, SEALED AND DELIVERED in the presence of: IN WITNESS whereof I have hereunto set my hand and seal:

....

.... (Witness) .... (Buyer/Authorized Signing Officer) (Seal) DATE ....

.... (Witness) .... (Buyer/Authorized Signing Officer) (Seal) DATE ....

I, the Undersigned Seller, agree to the above offer. I hereby irrevocably instruct my lawyer to pay directly to the brokerage(s) with whom I have agreed to pay commission, the unpaid balance of the commission together with applicable Harmonized Sales Tax (and any other taxes as may hereafter be applicable), from the proceeds of the sale prior to any payment to the undersigned on completion, as advised by the brokerage(s) to my lawyer.

SIGNED, SEALED AND DELIVERED in the presence of: IN WITNESS whereof I have hereunto set my hand and seal:

....

.... (Witness) .... (Seller/Authorized Signing Officer) (Seal) DATE ....

.... (Witness) .... (Seller/Authorized Signing Officer) (Seal) DATE ....

SPOUSAL CONSENT: The Undersigned Spouse of the Seller hereby consents to the disposition evidenced herein pursuant to the provisions of the Family Law Act, R.S.O.1990, and hereby agrees with the Buyer that he/she will execute all necessary or incidental documents to give full force and effect to the sale evidenced herein.

.... (Witness) .... (Spouse) (Seal) DATE ....

CONFIRMATION OF ACCEPTANCE: Notwithstanding anything contained herein to the contrary, I confirm this Agreement with all changes both typed and written was finally accepted by all parties at .... a.m./p.m. this .... day of.., 20..........

.... (Signature of Seller or Buyer)

INFORMATION ON BROKERAGE(S)

Listing Brokerage .... Tel.No.(................)..................................

.... (Salesperson / Broker Name)

Co-op/Buyer Brokerage .... Tel.No.(................)..................................

.... (Salesperson / Broker Name)

ACKNOWLEDGEMENT

I acknowledge receipt of my signed copy of this accepted Agreement of Purchase and Sale and I authorize the Brokerage to forward a copy to my lawyer.

.... DATE .... (Seller)

.... DATE .... (Seller)

Address for Service ....

.... Tel.No.(...........)........................

Seller's Lawyer ....

Address ....

Email ....

(...........)...................................... (...........)..................................
Tel.No. FAX No.

I acknowledge receipt of my signed copy of this accepted Agreement of Purchase and Sale and I authorize the Brokerage to forward a copy to my lawyer.

.... DATE .... (Buyer)

.... DATE .... (Buyer)

Address for Service ....

.... Tel.No.(...........)........................

Buyer's Lawyer ....

Address ....

Email ....

(...........)...................................... (...........)..................................
Tel.No. FAX No.

FOR OFFICE USE ONLY **COMMISSION TRUST AGREEMENT**

To: Co-operating Brokerage shown on the foregoing Agreement of Purchase and Sale:
In consideration for the Co-operating Brokerage procuring the foregoing Agreement of Purchase and Sale, I hereby declare that all moneys received or receivable by me in connection with the Transaction as contemplated in the MLS® Rules and Regulations of my Real Estate Board shall be receivable and held in trust. This agreement shall constitute a Commission Trust Agreement as defined in the MLS® Rules and shall be subject to and governed by the MLS® Rules pertaining to Commission Trust.

DATED as of the date and time of the acceptance of the foregoing Agreement of Purchase and Sale. Acknowledged by:

.... (Authorized to bind the Listing Brokerage) .... (Authorized to bind the Co-operating Brokerage)

Form 500 Revised 2015 **Page 5 of 6**

Form 500 Agreement of Purchase and Sale—Commercial, Page 6 of 6

OREA Ontario Real Estate Association

Form 500
for use in the Province of Ontario

Schedule A
Agreement of Purchase and Sale – Commercial

This Schedule is attached to and forms part of the Agreement of Purchase and Sale between:

BUYER, ..., and

SELLER, ...

for the purchase and sale of ....

.... dated the .... day of ...., 20..................

Buyer agrees to pay the balance as follows:

This form must be initialed by all parties to the Agreement of Purchase and Sale.

INITIALS OF BUYER(S):  **INITIALS OF SELLERS(S):** 

Form 500 Revised 2015 **Page 6 of 6**

CASE LAW

Case Synopsis

DOL V. MARLENE MUSCLOW INSURANCE AGENCY LTD.
ONTARIO SUPERIOR COURT APRIL, 2006

This case is all about an uncompleted transaction. In October of 2003 an Agreement of Purchase and Sale was entered into for a commercial property in Bancroft, Ontario. The sale was not completed and the Buyer sued for breach of contract. The Seller made a counterclaim for damages resulting from being unable to sell or rent the property for a period of time.

The facts with respect to how the Agreement of Purchase and Sale was drawn up by the real estate salespeople are nothing less than shocking. According to the evidence, the salesperson for the Buyer obtained a blank offer to purchase signed by the Buyer. After viewing the property with the husband of the Buyer, the salesperson filled in the offer for the Buyer. The Buyer's husband was authorized to some degree in a note to enter into an agreement or to act on the Buyer's behalf. The Seller's husband accepted the offer by virtue of a power of Attorney, on behalf of the Seller who was out of town.

The court noted that "*the offer is very strange, to say the least. It was clear that it was either done in a great hurry or that absolutely no thought whatsoever was put into the exact terms.*" Bancroft is described as the "*City of Bank*". The sums of money in figures do not correspond to the amounts expressed in writing (evidently due to the fact that an offer of $175,000 was countered at $190,000 and only the price in words was changed). The error that caused the biggest problem was the fact that the property as shown to the Buyer and described in the Agreement of Purchase and Sale had a frontage of 165 feet and a depth of 54 feet. In reality, these numbers were reversed and the Reference Plan mentioned in the Agreement of Purchase and Sale as 21 R-10455, but not attached to the agreement, clearly indicated the frontage to be 54 feet with a depth of 165 feet. (*It is interesting that both the Buyer and the Seller were not actually present for the offer negotiations and despite the fact that they were both represented by real estate salespeople, the Agreement of Purchase and Sale contained such careless errors*).

The very next day after the offer was accepted, the mistake in the lot dimensions was discovered and the Buyer was informed.

The Seller tried to rectify the agreement while the Buyer tried to renegotiate the price, and the transaction did not close. Evidence was presented at the trial that the Buyer was willing to complete the transaction at a price in the range of $145,000 to 150,000.

The court concluded that the Buyer attempted to gain maximum advantage from the defendant's mistake and made no effort to mitigate her damages. The court dismissed the Buyer's claim for an abatement in price and for specific performance.

When the Buyer was informed of the error in the description of the lot, the Buyer registered both the Agreement of Purchase and Sale and a Certificate of Pending Litigation on title. This formed the basis of the Seller's counter-claim, as the Seller could not sell or rent the property until the legal issues were settled, and the expenses for the property over that period of time were substantial.

The court found in favour of the counter-claim and awarded the Seller approximately $40,000, plus legal costs.

The court dismissed all claims against both real estate salespeople named in the action.

Case Questions

1. How did the conduct of the Buyer compared to the conduct of the Seller play a part in the court's decision?
2. Comment on the conduct of the real estate salespeople in this case in relation to the decision of the court.

Case Synopsis

SELLATHURAI V. SRISKANDA ONTARIO SUPERIOR COURT JUNE, 2007

CASE LAW

The buyer of a property sued the Seller of the property because the municipality issued an order to cease the operation of a "*Banquet Hall*" as the use was contrary to the zoning bylaw. When the Buyer purchased the property in the year 2000, the Agreement of Purchase and Sale contained the clause:

> *The Vendor warrants that the property is presently zoned for a Party Hall and that the property can be used as a Party Hall providing accommodation to 300 people.*

The Notice of Violation from the municipality was served in April 2002. The Buyer spent considerable time applying to the municipal Committee of Adjustments and then appealing to the OMB to obtain a variance to permit a Banquet Hall under the existing zoning. The Buyer was not successful, mainly because of concerns over the need for parking for the Banquet Hall use and the other users on the multi-unit property.

The Seller of the property argued that only a Party Hall use was warranted and not a Banquet Hall. Ultimately, this distinction was not an issue in the resolution of this case.

The court cited 3 issues in the decision. As the property was purchased in the year 2000 and there was evidence the municipality advised the Buyer prior to closing to verify that the property complied with the zoning requirements, the court determined the Buyer's claim could not succeed under the *Limitations Act*, as more than 6 years had passed since the purchase.

Secondly, after purchasing the property, the Buyer transferred the title of the property to a corporation late in 2000, thus creating an issue of privity of contract. The corporation was not a party to the original agreement in which the Party Hall warranty was made, and therefore the corporation could not rely on the warranty.

The court also identified a problem with the warranty itself. The warranty failed to state the warranty would not merge and would survive completion of the transaction. The court quoted Fraser-Reid et al. v. Droumtsekas et al. (1979) Supreme Court of Canada at paragraph 8: *Although it is the general rule that acceptance of a deed is prima facie full execution of the agreement to convey and preliminary agreements and understandings relating to the sale of land become merged in a conveyance, such rule is not applicable to independent covenants or collateral situations in an agreement of sale not intended by the parties to be incorporated in the conveyance.*

The wording of the warranty in the Agreement dealing with Urea Formaldehyde Foam Insulation states it will not merge on closing and this indicates the parties "*turned their minds to the fact of possible merger upon closing of the transaction. Their failure to provide that the warranty for zoning of the premises was not to merge on closing establishes that this provision did merge when the transaction was completed and the deed transferred. Thus, it cannot now be relied on.*"

For these reasons, the court rejected the Buyer's claim.

Case Questions

1. If the warranty merged, what effect did that have for the Buyer?

2. Even if the decision of the court may have been based mainly on the issues of privity of contract and the *Limitations Act*, what lesson does this case illustrate for real estate salespeople?

CHAPTER DISCUSSION

1. IDENTIFICATION OF THE PARTIES

You receive an offer on one of your listings with the buyers identified as "*Mr. and Mrs. Jim Jones.*" Do you have any concerns? Explain.

2. PROPERTY DESCRIPTION

For a lot with a 48 foot frontage, in your opinion, how much of a discrepancy would the words "*more or less*" cover? Explain.

Do the following legal descriptions look okay to you? Explain.

a. 15 Maple Street, Toronto.

b. Part of Lot 23, Plan 249, more particularly described as Part of 2 on 15R2657.

c. Part of Lot 19, Concession XII, being approximately 40 acres.

CHAPTER DISCUSSION

3. DEPOSIT

a. You receive an offer on one of your listings from a co-operating brokerage. A $10,000 deposit cheque is submitted with the offer and there is a clause in the offer stating the deposit cheque will be deposited in the bank "*after acceptance of the offer.*" The offer is irrevocable for ten days. Comment.

b. During a listing presentation, the seller, an experienced investor, insists that the buyer's deposit be given directly to the seller rather than placed in the brokerage's Trust Account. Comment.

4. FIXTURES AND CHATTELS

The "*Chattels Included*" section of an offer describes *refrigerator, stove and fireplace screen.* Comment.

CHAPTER DISCUSSION

5. DATES AND TIME LIMITS

What basic guidelines would you follow in choosing a time for the title search to expire? Explain.

6. PRESENT USE

The property has a basement apartment rented at $425 per month. You have verified that this use is illegal. How would you deal with this issue in the buyer's offer? Explain.

7. APPORTIONMENTS

In the Condominium—Resale Agreement, on what basis is the seller's contribution to the reserve fund adjusted? Explain.

CHAPTER DISCUSSION

8. SIGNATURES

What does the *Real Estate and Business Brokers Act* require with respect to the dating of signatures?

9. ACKNOWLEDGEMENT

Salesperson Lee obtains an offer on one of his listings that is open for acceptance until 11:59 p.m. tonight. At a quarter to midnight the sellers sign their acceptance. It is late and Lee decides to call the buyers in the morning to give them the good news. Comment.

KNOWLEDGE INTEGRATION

Notables

- The Statute of Frauds requires that an agreement for the sale of land be put in writing.
- REBBA 2002 has set a five business day limit on depositing funds, but this is minimum requirement. Deposits should be made as soon as possible. Time is of the essence in all such matters.
- A brokerage should only disburse a deposit under two circumstances: in accordance with a mutual release by all parties or a direction from the Court.
- Harmonized sales tax rules and calculations are complex. Carefully review the detailed discussion provided. Contact the Canada Revenue Agency for current information (**www.cra.gc.ca**).
- The issue of whether an offer is irrevocable by a buyer remains a matter of legal debate. A signature under seal is generally binding, but expert advice is needed should a dispute arise.
- The term more or less is intended to cover slight, unimportant inaccuracies only.
- Be fully aware of the role of listing and co-operating brokerages regarding notices, as outlined in the agreement of purchase and sale.
- A representation typically involves some fact of importance regarding a property. A warranty is an assurance, usually put in writing that verifies, confirms or attests to a specific circumstance.
- While UFFI has been minimized as a health concern, the topic is not a finalized issue.
- Commission entitlement is subject to requirements set out in REBBA 2002.

Chapter Mini-Review

Solutions are located in the Appendix.

1. A deposit relating to an agreement of purchase and sale is usually forfeited if failure of performance occurs.

   ○ True ○ False

2. A brokerage can only disburse the deposit in the case of a failed agreement if a mutual release is signed by all parties to the agreement.

   ○ True ○ False

3. A representation is essentially the same as a warranty for purposes of real estate trading.

   ○ True ○ False

4. A warranty might involve the seller confirming to the buyer in writing that the pool is fully operational and has no leaks, given that the agreement is being negotiated in the winter months.

   ○ True ○ False

5. In the Agreement of Purchase and Sale (OREA Form 100) the heirs, executors, administrators, successors and assigns are bound by the agreement.

   ○ True ○ False

Chapter Mini-Review (continued)

6. According to REBBA 2002, a registrant is only entitled to a commission or other remuneration if a written agreement is signed by the party paying the commission.

   ○ True ○ False

7. A registrant is obligated to use electronic signatures if either the buyer or seller makes a request that the agreement of purchase and sale be created and transmitted electronically.

   ○ True ○ False

Active Learning Exercises

Solutions are located in the Appendix.

Exercise 1

The postal designation for a property is 100 Main Street, Newton. The tax office shows a frontage of 86 feet. The Owner claims that the assessment is under appeal as the property is not that large. It is Saturday morning and you are anxious to prepare an offer. How would you deal with this situation?

Exercise 2

In a normal transaction, the deposit is made payable to the ______________________

____

On the sale of your client's house for $100,000 cash in a falling market you should get a deposit of $______________________.

Exercise 3

The offer provides for fifteen days from acceptance to search the title. The offer is conditional for a sixty-day period on the buyer's property being sold. Describe any problems.

Exercise 4

Your Seller has accepted an offer and has moved to Newfoundland. The closing is in five weeks. The weeds are growing almost as fast as the grass. The pool water is dirty and green with algae. A window has been broken by some playful neighbours. The buyer refuses to close until the property is in the same condition as it was on the day the offer was signed.

What should you do?

Exercise 5

The seller's employer, a small computer manufacturer, holds a small second mortgage that cannot be assumed by the buyer. It is not shown in the listing and neither the listing brokerage nor the selling brokerage are aware of the mortgage.

a. How does this affect the transaction?

b. The seller wants to be certain the deal will close. What steps should the seller undertake and when?

Exercise 6

The seller has a survey plan that shows a problem with the fence line. In fact, the reason for the sale is because of disputes with the neighbours. You want to be certain the deal will close.

What do you do in preparing the offer?

Exercise 7

While you are showing a property to a buyer, he/she indicates that it would suit him/her perfectly because it backs onto a park and therefore there will be no interference for his/her ham radio antenna.

a. Is there anything in OREA Form 100 that might give you cause for concern?

b. How do you deal with this situation?

■ Exercise 8

You have sold a property to your client buyers and one week before closing they call to ask you to arrange a pre-closing inspection so that they can take some measurements. When you contact the listing office to set a time for the inspection, to your dismay, you are informed that the sellers say "*Not possible*".

a. Do the sellers have the right to deny this request? Explain.

b. How could this situation have been avoided?

SECTION III

SALE OF A BUSINESS

A business can be broadly defined as any undertaking for the purpose of profit, including any interest in any such undertaking. The sale of a business is a specialized field and various statutory requirements must be addressed that a real estate practitioner would not encounter in a typical residential transaction. This section outlines specific requirements for the sale of a business as set out in the *Bulk Sales Act* and the *Real Estate and Business Brokers Act, 2002*. Because of additional tax and legal issues related to the sale of a business, real estate practitioners should encourage buyers and sellers to seek independent professional advice on these matters.

The main purpose of the *Bulk Sales Act* is to protect the trade creditors of a business. Steps will be taken by the lawyers for the buyers and sellers to protect all parties. However, a registrant involved in the sale of a business must be aware of the requirements of the *Bulk Sales Act* when communicating with the buyers and sellers and when drafting the agreement. The *Real Estate and Business Brokers Act, 2002* requires the brokerage to comply with certain requirements when involved in the sale of a business. A registrant who ignores or is unaware of these basic requirements would not only be violating the statute, but also be risking RECO disciplinary action and possible legal action for failure to act in a conscientious and diligent manner.

CHAPTER 7

Bulk Sales Act and REBBA 2002

Introduction

The *Bulk Sales Act* and REBBA 2002 both have specific requirements that must be adhered to when selling a business. By way of introduction to these regulatory matters, key factors to consider when listing a business are highlighted. Registrants must address whether business shares or assets are being sold, determine the existence of financial statements, establish what is and is not included in the sale, obtain details of any leases, franchise agreements and licences, and collect various supporting documents. A number of tips are also provided regarding the selling of businesses.

The OREA *Agreement of Purchase and Sale—Business in Leased Premises Under the Bulk Sales Act (Ontario)* is illustrated, followed by a detailed discussion of procedures for trade creditor protection under the *Bulk Sales Act* and associated stipulations required within an agreement. The matter of collecting and paying taxes is also addressed before addressing specific requirements set out under REBBA 2002 and the use of a *Sale of Business—Affidavit* (OREA Form 503) to assist in complying with those regulatory requirements.

Learning Outcomes

At the conclusion of this chapter, students will be able to:

- Outline various special considerations and necessary documents when listing a business for sale.
- Briefly identify key issues to consider in the sale of a business, particularly concerning financing.
- Discuss key provisions within the *Agreement of Purchase and Sale—Business in a Leased Premises Under the Bulk Sales Act (Ontario).*
- Identify and describe requirements of the *Bulk Sales Act* concerning trade creditor protection and procedures that must be followed.
- Describe selected taxation issues that arise in the sale of a business that warrant independent professional advice.
- Detail requirements set out in REBBA 2002 including the use of a *Sale of Business—Affidavit* in complying with those requirements.

LISTING OF A BUSINESS

As with any specialty area, real estate practitioners must understand unique requirements regarding the type of property being marketed. With businesses, various documents and special considerations also arise. The sum of all documents available to a potential buyer is normally referred to as the *documentation package.*

Business Shares or Assets A vital factor in listing a business is establishing whether the shares of the business, or its assets, are to be sold. If shares in a corporation are being sold, the buyer assumes all assets and liabilities. He/she will have the use and benefit of such items as the company name, copyrights, leases and real estate, unless otherwise agreed. If only assets are being sold, the seller normally assumes responsibility for any existing debt; e.g., accounts payable, but retains all accounts receivables. The buyer acquires the remaining assets, such as equipment, inventory and goodwill. Tax implications arise from either approach and the tax position of seller and buyer can be complex. The listing salesperson is strongly advised to confirm that the buyer and seller have consulted accountants regarding such matters.

Financial Statements The balance sheet (statement of assets and liabilities), as of the last day of the fiscal year of the business, should be obtained for at least three (and preferably five or more) years of operation. Ideally, balance sheets are obtained from the seller's accountant and will be prepared for small businesses as unaudited statements used in the preparation of income tax returns.

The profit or loss statements (statement of revenue and expenses) should also be obtained for the same period, or as many years as available. The extent of historical financial documentation often translates directly into more accurate analysis of business trends and a more saleable listing.

In Ontario the *Real Estate and Business Brokers Act, 2002* (REBBA) requires that financial statements be delivered to the buyer or that the buyer waive compliance with this requirement. Standard forms have been developed for use by brokerages.

Fixtures and Chattels Detailed lists of fixtures and chattels are needed:

- A list of items included in the sale; and
- A list of items not included in the sale.

The *Real Estate and Business Brokers Act, 2002* (REBBA) does not specifically require a list of *included* fixtures and chattels, but only those items *excluded.* If various fixtures and chattels are not excluded, REBBA states that all such items are deemed to be included. As a point of prudence, conscientious salespeople obtain both lists to avoid any confusion. REBBA wording is specific regarding the scope of the list: '*...a list of all fixtures, goods, chattels, rights and other assets...*' Make certain that lists are complete.

Lease If the business premise is leased and not owned by the seller, a copy of the lease is required. The contents of the lease can directly affect both the value of the business and its marketability. Buyers will be particularly concerned with:

- Whether the lease can be assigned;
- Under what conditions the assignment can occur;

- The remaining term of the lease including any provisions for renewal; and
- The terms, benefits and restrictions contained in the lease.

Where a relatively short possession period remains, the buyer may require assurances that a satisfactory extension of the lease agreement can be arranged and require a condition to that effect in the agreement.

Franchise Agreements If the business operates under a franchise arrangement, a copy of relevant agreement(s) must be included in the documentation package. Conditions can exist within such documents that affect, or possibly nullify, the sale. For example, the franchisor normally charges an ongoing royalty fee for benefits accruing from the franchise affiliation. In most retail franchises, an advertising fee is also levied for regional and/or national promotional programs. The franchisor may further require approval of any new franchisee along with an appropriate condition inserted in any offer and may also require that a new owner undertake specific product training.

Licences Details of any operating licence(s) must be obtained from the seller and inserted in the documentation package. Depending on circumstances, information about how the buyer should obtain or have the licence(s) transferred is also necessary. A prime example would involve a licensed restaurant under the Liquor Licence Board of Ontario. The licence is awarded to the owner (as an individual) who operates the restaurant, and not to the premises. Any transfer of business ownership must be accompanied by the transfer of that liquor licence, subject to approval, to the new proprietor.

Financing Options Buyers rarely pay all cash for a business and, consequently, seller financing is commonly encountered as well as additional outside financing. In either or both instances, details should be clearly set out concerning the range of financing options available, as these can translate directly into an improved marketing position. For example, the buyer may have a 30% downpayment based on the purchase price, but unable to secure funds elsewhere. The balance of the purchase price can then be financed by a seller take back mortgage with the assets of the business as security.

An earnout can be used to pay off the mortgage. The terms of the earnout are established to suit the parties. The buyer is able to pay the balance of the purchase price from cash flow, while the seller concludes a sale by offering a favourable and manageable financing option. The buyer may also ask the seller to remain as a consultant for a pre-determined salary or fee. The buyer benefits from the seller's experience and knowledge, while the seller can ensure the continued success of the business and the payment of the outstanding balance.

Additional Documents The range of documents is dictated by the type of sale (assets vs. shares), the specific business involved and the creativity of the salesperson in providing a detailed offering to the marketplace. As with all commercial offerings, the better the documentation package, the more effective the overall marketing program, the better the prospects of a sale. Additional documents might include:

- Details of any equipment leases along with relevant terms and conditions;
- Copies of any notes, business contracts or unique agreements that affect the business and will be assigned to the buyer; e.g., franchise agreements, employment contracts, licensing agreements and client contracts;

- Demographic, economic or other statistical information in support of the business; e.g., trends in retailing and traffic counts;
- Photographs of the business (both exterior and interior) including trade fixtures;
- Copies of any appraisals completed on chattels and fixtures included in the sale; and
- Selected tax return information relating to the business.

SALE OF A BUSINESS

The sale of a business requires specialized knowledge particularly about provincial legislative requirements that may impact the sale, including the use of applicable forms.

Prospects must be properly qualified concerning financial matters, particularly given the challenges of securing business financing.

- Establish precisely how much actual cash or liquid assets can be applied to the purchase price.
- Ascertain whether the buyer intends to work on a full-time basis in the business being acquired, or simply purchase the enterprise as an investment as this will have considerable bearing on selecting the appropriate type of business.
- Determine if the buyer has any practical skills in the business under consideration. Experience is frequently a determining factor in whether a seller will accept or reject an offer, particularly when providing financing.
- Obtain permission to conduct a credit check.
- A buyer's net worth statement can be advantageous in assisting the seller in making a decision about a particular offer.
- Since many businesses involve seller financing, the buyer's willingness to enter into a personal guarantee should be established at the outset.
- Lastly, evaluate the buyer's attitudes, temperament, experience and aspirations. Often, businesses look attractive from an investment perspective but are not suited to a particular buyer; e.g., amount of manual labour needed, number of hours required, range of hours demanded (e.g., early or late) and necessity of specific skills.

By narrowing the field, both buyer and salesperson can work more productively in finding the right *fit*.

Agreement of Purchase and Sale

The *Agreement of Purchase and Sale—Business in Leased Premises Under the Bulk Sales Act (Ontario)* is illustrated. The form, in addition to standardized provisions usual to most agreements, addresses unique items relating to a business such as non-competition issues, representations/warranties by the seller concerning assets, residency, covenants and inventory.

Form 502 Agreement of Purchase and Sale—Business in Leased Premises, Page 1 of 5

Form 502
for use in the Province of Ontario

Agreement of Purchase and Sale
Business in Leased Premises Under the Bulk Sales Act (Ontario)

This Agreement of Purchase and Sale dated this.. day of .... 20....................

BUYER,.., agrees to purchase from
(Full legal names of all Buyers)

SELLER,.., the following
(Full legal names of all Sellers)

all the assets of the Business known as..(including the chattels, fixtures and inventory of the Business set out in schedule "A" as are now located upon the premises and inspected and approved by Buyer)

situated at the property known as ....(the "Business") together with the lease of the premises, and the trade name and goodwill of the Business (the "Assets").

PURCHASE PRICE: Dollars (CDN$)...

....Dollars

which total Purchase Price includes the amount of $...in respect of inventory of the Business.

DEPOSIT: Buyer submits ....
(Herewith/Upon Acceptance/as otherwise described in this Agreement)

.... Dollars (CDN$)..

by negotiable cheque payable to.. .... "Deposit Holder" to be held in trust pending completion or other termination of this Agreement and to be credited toward the Purchase Price on completion. For the purposes of this Agreement, "Upon Acceptance" shall mean that the Buyer is required to deliver the deposit to the Deposit Holder within 24 hours of the acceptance of this Agreement. The parties to this Agreement hereby acknowledge that, unless otherwise provided for in this Agreement, the Deposit Holder shall place the deposit in trust in the Deposit Holder's non-interest bearing Real Estate Trust Account and no interest shall be earned, received or paid on the deposit.

Buyer agrees to pay the balance as more particularly set out in Schedule A attached.

SCHEDULE(S) A...**attached hereto form(s) part of this Agreement.**

1. **IRREVOCABILITY:** This offer shall be irrevocable by .... until .... a.m./p.m. on the ....
(Seller/Buyer)
day of .... 20......................, after which time, if not accepted, this offer shall be null and void and the deposit shall be returned to the Buyer in full without interest.

2. **COMPLETION DATE:** This Agreement shall be completed by no later than 6:00 p.m. on the ....day of ....,
20....................... . Upon completion, vacant possession of the premises shall be given to the Buyer unless otherwise provided for in this Agreement.

3. **HST:** The parties hereto agree that this transaction shall be a taxable supply in accordance with the provisions of the Excise Tax Act (Canada), R.S.C. 1985, e-15, as amended. The Seller and Buyer agree to file the necessary Form electing not to have the Harmonized Sales Tax (HST) apply. The Buyer agrees to file the requisite election Form containing the prescribed information, together with a return for the Buyer's reporting period in which the transaction occurs, under the Excise Tax Act (Canada), as amended, on or prior to the date prescribed by such Act for making such election.

INITIALS OF BUYER(S): ◯ **INITIALS OF SELLER(S):** ◯

Form 502 Revised 2016 **Page 1 of 5**

Form 502 Agreement of Purchase and Sale—Business in Leased Premises, Page 2 of 5

4. **NOTICES:** The Seller hereby appoints the Listing Brokerage as agent for the Seller for the purpose of giving and receiving notices pursuant to this Agreement. Where a Brokerage (Buyer's Brokerage) has entered into a representation agreement with the Buyer, the Buyer hereby appoints the Buyer's Brokerage as agent for the purpose of giving and receiving notices pursuant to this Agreement. **Where a Brokerage represents both the Seller and the Buyer (multiple representation), the Brokerage shall not be appointed or authorized to be agent for either the Buyer or the Seller for the purpose of giving and receiving notices.** Any notice relating hereto or provided for herein shall be in writing. In addition to any provision contained herein and in any Schedule hereto, this offer, any counter-offer, notice of acceptance thereof or any notice to be given or received pursuant to this Agreement or any Schedule hereto (any of them, "Document") shall be deemed given and received when delivered personally or hand delivered to the Address for Service provided in the Acknowledgement below, or where a facsimile number or email address is provided herein, when transmitted electronically to that facsimile number or email address, respectively, in which case, the signature(s) of the party (parties) shall be deemed to be original.

FAX No.: .... (For delivery of Documents to Seller)

FAX No.: .... (For delivery of Documents to Buyer)

Email Address: .... (For delivery of Documents to Seller)

Email Address: .... (For delivery of Documents to Buyer)

5. **NON-COMPETITION:** Seller and the undersigned...jointly and severally covenant not to carry on or be engaged in or concerned with (either directly or indirectly in any manner whatsoever including without limitation as a principal, agent, partner or shareholder) any business competitive with or similar to the Business as presently carried on, within

   a radius of.................................kilometers of the premises for.......................................months after completion. The aforesaid covenant shall survive the completion of the transaction provided for herein.

6. **SEARCHES:** Buyer shall be allowed until 6:00 p.m. on the .... day of... 20.......... (Requisition Date) to satisfy the

   Buyer that there are no outstanding work orders or deficiency notices affecting the property, and that its present use (..) may be lawfully continued. If within that time any valid obligation to any outstanding work order or deficiency notice, or to the fact the said present use may not lawfully be continued, is made in writing to Seller and which Seller is unable or unwilling to remove, remedy or satisfy and which Buyer will not waive, this Agreement notwithstanding any intermediate acts or negotiations in respect of such obligations, shall be at an end and all monies paid shall be returned without interest or deduction and Seller, Listing Brokerage and Co-operating Brokerage shall not be liable for any costs or damages. Seller hereby consents to the municipality or other governmental agencies releasing to the Buyer details of all outstanding work orders and deficiency notices affecting the property, and Seller agrees to execute such further authorizations in this regard as Buyer may reasonably require.

7. **COVENANTS BY SELLER:** The Seller covenants;

   (a) the Assets are now and shall at the time of completion be owned by Seller free and clear of all encumbrances, liens or charges and no other person has now or shall at the time of closing have any interest in the assets except

   ....

   ....

   ....

   ....

   (b) Seller is not now and shall not at the time of completion be a non-resident person within the meaning of Section 116 of the Income Tax Act (Canada);

   (c) Seller is not in default of any agreements related to the Business and there are no actions, suits or proceedings against or on behalf of the Seller, pending or threatened, which may affect the Business, and the Seller is not aware of any existing grounds on which any such action, suit or proceeding might be commenced;

   (d) there is a good, valid and subsisting lease of the premises for a term of..years at a monthly rental of

   $... expiring

   on the .... day of.., 20........................ (a copy of which lease is attached hereto);

INITIALS OF BUYER(S): ( ) **INITIALS OF SELLER(S):** ( )

Form 502 Revised 2016 **Page 2 of 5**

Form 502 Agreement of Purchase and Sale—Business in Leased Premises, Page 3 of 5

(e) there are not now and shall not at the time of completion be any employees of the Business except the following, all of whom can be dismissed on the minimum applicable statutory notice period without further liability:

....

....

....

....

(f) the Business has been carried on in the ordinary course and all financial statements and other information provided to Buyer are true, accurate and correct in all material respects and have been prepared in accordance with generally accepted accounting principles applied on a consistent basis and Seller shall, at the time of completion, have no liabilities, contingent or otherwise, except as reflected therein or in the statement to be delivered pursuant to the Bulk Sales Act (none of which shall be inconsistent with past practice or materially adverse);
(g) no expenditures shall be made out of the ordinary course of business prior to closing and the Business shall be carried on up to the time of completion in the ordinary course and in a commercially reasonable manner with a view to preserving the goodwill of the Business; and
(h) the tangible Assets are now and shall at the time of completion be in good condition, subject only in the case of equipment to reasonable wear and tear.

8. FURTHER COVENANTS BY THE SELLER: The Seller covenants;
(a) to comply with Section 6 of the Retail Sales Tax Act;
(b) to comply with the Bulk Sales Act;
(c) to deliver to Buyer at or before the time of completion the written consent of the lessor to the assignment of the lease of the premises to Buyer; and
(d) to indemnify and save harmless the Buyer from and against all liabilities, claims and demands in connection with the purchased business existing or incurred as at the time of completion and not shown on the financial statements provided to the Buyer or in the statement delivered pursuant to the Bulk Sales Act or expressly agreed to be assumed by the Buyer in this Agreement.

9. BUYER REPRESENTATION AND WARRANTY: The Buyer represents and warrants that the Buyer is not now and shall not at the time of completion be a non-eligible person within the meaning of the Investment Canada Act.

10. COVENANTS BY BUYER: The Buyer covenants to pay all applicable retail sales tax and federal sales tax on completion (or furnish appropriate exemption certificates) eligible in respect to this transaction.

11. BUYER CONDITIONS: The Buyer's obligation to complete this transaction shall be subject to satisfaction of the following conditions (which may be waived in whole or in part by Buyer without prejudice to any claim for breach of covenant, representation or warranty):
(a) the representations and warranties of Seller shall be true at and as of completion as if given at that time;
(b) Seller shall have performed all covenants to be performed by Seller at or prior to the time of completion.

12. INVENTORY: Prior to completion, either party may elect by written notice to the other that the inventory shall be physically counted after the close of business on the day prior to completion and valued at Seller's cost thereof in which case the total Purchase Price shall be increased or decreased to the extent that the valuation so obtained is greater than or less than the amount set for inventory stated above. Failing such an election, neither Seller nor Buyer may dispute the amount of valuation of inventory.

13. ADJUSTMENTS: Any business taxes, insurance, rent, hydro, water, fuel, employee's wages and vacation pay and usual prepaid items being transferred to Buyer, as applicable, shall be apportioned and allowed to the day of completion, the day of completion itself to be apportioned to the Buyer.

14. DOCUMENT PREPARATION: The Bill of Sale and other transfer documents are to be prepared at Seller's expense and any security documents are to be prepared at the expense of Buyer, and each party is to pay the costs of registration of their own documents.

15. RISK: All the assets of the Business shall be and remain at risk of Seller until the completion of the transaction provided for herein.

16. TENDER: Any tender of documents or money hereunder may be made upon Seller or Buyer or their respective lawyers on the day set for completion. Money shall be tendered with funds drawn on a lawyer's trust account in the form of a bank draft, certified cheque or wire transfer using the Large Value Transfer System.

17. AGREEMENT IN WRITING: This offer when accepted shall constitute a binding agreement of purchase and sale, and time shall in all respects be of the essence of this Agreement. There is no representation, warranty, collateral agreement or condition affecting this Agreement other than as expressed herein. If there is conflict or discrepancy between any provision added to this Agreement (including any Schedule attached hereto) and any provision in the standard pre-set portion hereof, the added provision shall supersede the standard pre-set provision to the extent of such conflict. For the purposes of this Agreement, Seller means vendor and Buyer means purchaser. This Agreement shall be read with all changes of gender or number required by the context.

18. TIME AND DATE: Any reference to a time and date in this Agreement shall mean the time and date where the Business is located.

INITIALS OF BUYER(S): ( ) **INITIALS OF SELLER(S):** ( )

Form 502 Revised 2016 **Page 3 of 5**

Form 502 Agreement of Purchase and Sale—Business in Leased Premises, Page 4 of 5

19. SUCCESSORS AND ASSIGNS: The heirs, executors, administrators, successors and assigns of the undersigned are bound by the terms herein.

SIGNED, SEALED AND DELIVERED in the presence of: IN WITNESS whereof I have hereunto set my hand and seal:

(Witness) (Buyer/Authorized Signing Officer) (Seal) DATE

(Witness) (Buyer/Authorized Signing Officer) (Seal) DATE

I, the Undersigned Seller, agree to the above offer. I hereby irrevocably instruct my lawyer to pay directly to the brokerage(s) with whom I have agreed to pay commission, the unpaid balance of the commission together with applicable Harmonized Sales Tax (and any other taxes as may hereafter be applicable), from the proceeds of the sale prior to any payment to the undersigned on completion, as advised by the brokerage(s) to my lawyer.

(Witness) (Seller/Authorized Signing Officer) (Seal) DATE

(Witness) (Seller/Authorized Signing Officer) (Seal) DATE

THE UNDERSIGNED .... in consideration of Buyer entering into this Agreement, hereby executes this Agreement for the purpose of Clause 5.

SIGNED, SEALED AND DELIVERED in the presence of: IN WITNESS whereof I have hereunto set my hand and seal:

(Witness) (Seal) DATE

CONFIRMATION OF ACCEPTANCE: Notwithstanding anything contained herein to the contrary, I confirm this Agreement with all changes both typed and written was finally accepted by all parties at .... a.m./p.m. this .... day of ...., 20............ .

(Signature of Seller or Buyer)

INFORMATION ON BROKERAGE(S)

Listing Brokerage .... Tel.No.(............) ....

(Salesperson / Broker Name)

Co-op/Buyer Brokerage .... Tel.No.(............) ....

(Salesperson / Broker Name)

ACKNOWLEDGEMENT

I acknowledge receipt of my signed copy of this accepted Agreement of Purchase and Sale and I authorize the Brokerage to forward a copy to my lawyer.

(Seller) DATE

(Seller) DATE

Address for Service ....

Tel.No.(............)

Seller's Lawyer ....

Address ....

Email ....

(............) Tel.No. (............) FAX No.

I acknowledge receipt of my signed copy of this accepted Agreement of Purchase and Sale and I authorize the Brokerage to forward a copy to my lawyer.

(Buyer) DATE

(Buyer) DATE

Address for Service ....

Tel.No.(............)

Buyer's Lawyer ....

Address ....

Email ....

(............) Tel.No. (............) FAX No.

FOR OFFICE USE ONLY **COMMISSION TRUST AGREEMENT**

To: Co-operating Brokerage shown on the foregoing Agreement of Purchase and Sale:
In consideration for the Co-operating Brokerage procuring the foregoing Agreement of Purchase and Sale, I hereby declare that all moneys received or receivable by me in connection with the Transaction as contemplated in the MLS® Rules and Regulations of my Real Estate Board shall be receivable and held in trust. This agreement shall constitute a Commission Trust Agreement as defined in the MLS® Rules and shall be subject to and governed by the MLS® Rules pertaining to Commission Trust.

DATED as of the date and time of the acceptance of the foregoing Agreement of Purchase and Sale. Acknowledged by:

(Authorized to bind the Listing Brokerage) (Authorized to bind the Co-operating Brokerage)

Form 502 Revised 2016 **Page 4 of 5**

Form 502 Agreement of Purchase and Sale—Business in Leased Premises, Page 5 of 5

OREA Ontario Real Estate Association

Form 502
for use in the Province of Ontario

Schedule A
Agreement of Purchase and Sale – Business in Leased Premises

This Schedule is attached to and forms part of the Agreement of Purchase and Sale between:

BUYER,..

SELLER,..

for the purchase and sale of ....

.... dated the .... day of ...., 20....................

Buyer agrees to pay the balance as follows:

This form must be initialed by all parties to the Agreement of Purchase and Sale.

INITIALS OF BUYER(S): 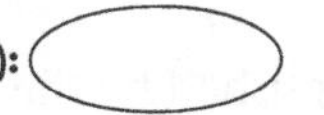 **INITIALS OF SELLER(S):** 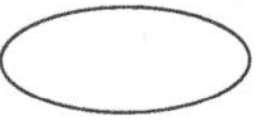

Form 502 Revised 2016 **Page 5 of 5**

THE BULK SALES ACT

The *Bulk Sales Act,* a provincial statute, is designed to protect the trade creditors of the seller when a sale of stock in bulk is occurring out of the ordinary course of the seller's business. The buyer must demand and receive from the seller a sworn statement of the seller's creditors. If the buyer does not comply with this Act, the sale of the bulk is voidable by an action started by a creditor.

The *Bulk Sales Act* can apply, not only where a business is being sold, but also to any sale where stock is being sold in bulk. This legislation sets out a number of requirements including, but not limited to, giving of notices to creditors, duties of the buyer, risks to the buyer if procedures are not followed, requirements concerning trade creditors' claims and amounts concerning such claims. Requirements of this Act should be reviewed in conjunction with those in the *Real Estate and Business Brokers Act,* 2002 (see subsequent discussion).

The parties to the transaction should also be aware of the tax implications of the sale of a business. Independent professional advice is required for both buyer and seller.

Trade Creditor Protection

A seller, generally, can sell whatever is owned without concern for personal or trade creditors. However, to protect trade creditors of the seller, the *Bulk Sales Act* requires that buyers follow certain procedures. If they fail to comply, the sale of the bulk may be voidable and buyers may be accountable to the creditors. Not every transaction is covered by the Act. This statute only affects a sale of stock in bulk outside of the ordinary course of the seller's business. Stock includes real or personal property, goods, chattels, fixtures and other defined items with which a person carries on trade or business.

Some sales are exempted including those by an estate, a trustee in bankruptcy or a creditor realizing upon a security. A judge may make an order exempting a transaction from this Act if the sale is advantageous to the seller and if it does not limit the ability to pay creditors.

Procedures

Procedures pursuant to the *Bulk Sales Act* are best described by way of example. A buyer may pay up to 10% of the purchase price to the seller who holds the monies in trust. The buyer must demand and receive from the seller, a sworn statement of the seller's creditors in a form prescribed by the Act. This form shows the names and addresses of the creditors, the amount owing and any security given. The buyer can complete the transaction directly with the seller if the statement shows that:

- the secured trade creditors' claims do not exceed \$2,500 and the unsecured trade creditors' claims do not exceed \$2,500; or
- the trade creditors' claims have been paid in full; or
- adequate provision is made for payment in full to the trade creditors out of the sale proceeds.

This may be accomplished by the purchaser making cheques payable directly to all of the creditors, or by the undertaking of the seller's solicitor to pay all trade creditors except those who may have signed a prescribed waiver.

A trustee may be appointed by the seller with the approval of unsecured trade creditors accounting for at least 60% of the number and value of claims that exceed $50. If such consent is not obtained, a judge can appoint a trustee. The trustee receives the proceeds of the sale and distributes them to all creditors as if the seller were bankrupt. A schedule of fees to the trustee is set out in the Act.

Within five days of the completion of the sale, an affidavit of the particulars of the transaction and the required forms must be filed with the Ontario Court (General Division) where the property is located. The buyer can obtain a court order for late filing if the time period is missed. After one year, if all the trade creditors are paid and no legal proceedings against the transaction have been commenced, the judge can make an order that the buyer need not file the documents. If the buyer does not comply with this Act, the sale of the bulk is voidable by an action started by a creditor of the seller.

If the sale is set aside and the buyer has taken possession of the stock in bulk, the buyer is personally liable to account to the creditors for its value. To put it simply, the buyer may pay for the stock twice, first when the seller is paid and second when held accountable by the creditors. The Ministry of the Attorney General is responsible for the *Bulk Sales Act.*

Stipulation in Agreement

As mentioned, the *Bulk Sales Act* applies if inventory is involved in the sale of a business and is designed to protect creditors, while imposing certain obligations on the buyer. Practitioners should be aware that this legislation relates only to situations where a sale of stock in bulk occurs outside the usual course of business or trade of the seller, and would therefore likely apply in the sale of a business. As a matter of note, the Act applies, not only where a business is being sold, but also to any sale where stock is being sold in bulk.

Under normal circumstances, a registrant will not have any direct participation in the actual processing of the sale after acceptance of the offer, as this normally falls to the lawyers for the seller and the buyer. However, the agreement must stipulate that the sale is made under the *Bulk Sales Act.* A ten percent limit on the amount of deposit applies and these funds must be taken subject to conditions set out in Section 6 of the Act:

> *The buyer may, before he receives a statement, pay to the seller on account of the purchase price a sum not exceeding 10% of the purchase price which shall form part of the proceeds of the sale which the seller shall hold in trust:*
>
> *(a) For the buyer until completion of the sale; or if the sale is not completed and the buyer becomes entitled to repayment of it; or until it is repaid to the buyer.*
>
> *(b) Where the sale is completed and a trustee has been appointed for the creditors; until the seller complies with the provisions under the Bulk Sales Act.*

REBBA 2002 (THE REAL ESTATE AND BUSINESS BROKERS ACT, 2002)

A business, for purposes of the Act, is an undertaking carried out for gain or profit and includes any interest in such undertaking. Provisions concerning the purchase of a business have not changed significantly from the previous Act, but all practitioners should carefully review legislative requirements (REBBA, Subsec. 1(1)). The buyer must receive, prior to a binding agreement:

- A profit and loss statement for the past 12 months or since the business was acquired by the person disposing of it;
- A statement of assets and liabilities; and
- A list of items (e.g., fixtures, chattels and other goods) that are not included.

The first and second requirements do not apply if the buyer signs a statement attesting to having received and read a statement from the person disposing of the business as to various matters relating to that business:

- Terms and conditions under which the person selling the business possesses the business premises;
- Terms and conditions relating to any sublet of the premises; and
- A statement that the person selling the business has provided all books of account in his/her possession, or has refused to do so, or has no books (GEN, Sec. 21).

PURCHASE OF BUSINESS: STATEMENTS TO BE DELIVERED

21. (1) The definitions of "buy" and "buyer" in section 2 do not apply to this section. O. Reg. 567/05, s. 21 (1).

(2) If the purchase of a business is negotiated by a brokerage on behalf of the person disposing of the business, the brokerage shall provide to the purchaser, before a binding agreement of purchase and sale is entered into, the following statements signed by or on behalf of the person disposing of the business:

1. A profit and loss statement for the business for the preceding 12 months or since the acquisition of the business by the person disposing of it.
2. A statement of the assets and liabilities of the business.
3. A statement containing a list of all fixtures, goods, chattels, other assets and rights relating to or connected with the business that are not included in the trade. O. Reg. 567/05, s. 21 (2).

(3) If the brokerage fails to provide the statement mentioned in paragraph 3 of subsection (2) in accordance with that subsection and the agreement of purchase and sale does not expressly deal with whether a fixture, good, chattel, other asset or right relating to or connected with the business is included in the trade, the fixture, good, chattel, other asset or right shall be deemed to be included in the trade. O. Reg. 567/05, s. 21 (3).

continued...

PURCHASE OF BUSINESS: STATEMENTS TO BE DELIVERED (CONTINUED)

(4) Paragraphs 1 and 2 of subsection (2) do not apply if a statement is signed by or on behalf of the purchaser and is delivered to the brokerage indicating that the purchaser has received and read a statement under oath or affirmation of the person disposing of the business that sets out the following:

1. The terms and conditions under which the person disposing of the business holds possession of the premises in which the business is being carried on.
2. The terms and conditions under which the person disposing of the business has sublet a part of the premises in which the business is being carried on.
3. All liabilities of the business.
4. A statement that the person disposing of the business has made available the books of account of the business that the person possesses for inspection by the purchaser, or that the person disposing of the business has refused to do so or has no books of account of the business, as the case may be. O. Reg. 567/05, s. 21 (4).

Affidavit: Sale of a Business

The Sale of Business Affidavit (OREA Standard Form 503) was developed to assist the listing brokerage and seller of business in complying with requirements prescribed under General Section 21 of the *Real Estate and Business Brokers Act, 2002.* In situations where the financial statements for the business are not delivered to the buyer as described in Subsection 21(2), the Sale of Business Affidavit is completed by the seller and delivered to the person acquiring the business before a binding agreement of purchase and sale is signed by the parties. The form requires a declaration under oath concerning:

- who is the owner of the business;
- whether the business premises are leased or owned;
- what portion of the business premise, if any, is sublet;
- liabilities, if any; and
- if there are, or are not, books of account for the business and an explanation of why the financial statements are not being delivered to the buyer.

The bottom portion of the form contains a waiver to be completed by the buyer, if he/she does not require the seller to comply with clauses (1) and (2) of Subsection 21(2).

Form 503 Sale of Business—Affidavit, Page 1 of 1

OREA Ontario Real Estate Association

Sale of Business

Affidavit

Form 503
for use in the Province of Ontario

I, ...
(Print Name)

of the .... of ....
(City, Town, Township, etc.) (Name of Municipality)

in the .... of ....
(Region, County or District) (Name of County or District)

to Wit: Make oath and say:

1. ☐ I am owner of a business situated at ....
or
☐ I am Director of .... which owns a business situated at
(Company)
....

2. Possession of the premises in which the business is being conducted is held:
☐ by virtue of ownership of the premises;
or
☐ by virtue of a lease (recite terms of lease or attach copy) ....
....

3. ☐ The .... of the premises in which the business is carried on
(Describe Area Sublet)
has been sublet to .... on the following terms:
....
or
☐ No part of the premises in which the business is being carried on has been sublet.

4. ☐ The liabilities of the business are comprised of current day-to-day accounts payable, a bank loan of $ ....,
a mortgage of $ .... and (list other liabilities) ....
....
or
☐ There are no liabilities other than current day-to-day accounts and the contingent liability in the lease.

5. ☐ Such books of account of the business as are in my/the company's possession have been made available to the person wishing to acquire the business;
or
☐ No books of account will be made available;
or
☐ There are no books of account of the business.

SWORN before me at the .... of..

in the .... of ....

this .... day of ...., 20.................. ....
(Signature)

Commissioner:..

WAIVER: Re: ....

I, ..., having received and read the statement under oath of the person disposing of the above business, hereby waive compliance with Sub-section (2), Paragraphs 1 and 2, of Section 21 of the General Regulations of the Real Estate and Business Brokers Act RSO, 2002.

.... DATE ....
(Buyer)

.... DATE ....
(Buyer)

Form 503 Revised 2010 **Page 1 of 1**

CASE LAW

Case Synopsis

MOHN V. DREISER ESTATE SUPERIOR COURT OF JUSTICE
COURT FILE # 1912/00 & 1935/00

This legal dispute focused on damages for negligent misrepresentation arising from the purchase of a lodge (motel/restaurant) facility. The buyer relied on seller representations that the business had operated profitably, as shown on income statements provided prior to signing the agreement of purchase and sale. The net operating income, according to the records for two previous successive years, was $68,328 and $64,054 respectively. The asking price of $399,900 appeared reasonable based on those figures. The real estate broker involved had, according to the buyer, prepared the financial information including a confidential memorandum containing selected property details. In defence, the broker claimed to have obtained the relevant facts from the owners and was innocently conveying the information.

As background, the agreement was signed in July with the new owner taking over the business in November. After closing, the buyer realized that the financial statements were incorrect and took legal action. An appraiser was engaged to establish market value as of the closing date. His analysis using the direct comparison approach indicated a value of $225,000. The appraiser could not use the income approach, as the business generated a negative cash flow.

An accounting expert was also retained. The resulting report outlined both represented and actual results of the business operation. According to documented evidence, the lodge had consistently sustained losses over the past several years. Further, the statements provided to the buyer were '*incomplete, inaccurate and not helpful to the purchaser.*'

The sellers argued that, since buying the property under power of sale four years earlier, they had built a growing, viable business. In fact, prior to the contract now under dispute, two other potential purchasers had signed agreements for $469,000 to buy the business, but neither was completed. Lastly, the sellers submitted that any subsequent loss in value was due to the new owner's neglect, particularly concerning cleanliness.

The legal dispute ultimately focused on two issues:

- Was the buyer mislead by negligent misrepresentations and what damages arise?
- Was the broker in breach of his duty of care, as well as statutory provisions imposed under Sec. 33 of the *Real Estate and Business Brokers Act*?

The Court, based on evidence presented, found the previous owners negligent in making representations both to the buyer and also to their agent. The Court also found that the broker owed the buyer a duty of care because of the special relationship that existed; i.e., the broker was a professional who possessed skills and knowledge, and provided information which the buyer relied upon to his detriment. The broker also owed a statutory duty pursuant to REBBA, Sec. 33 regarding provision of certain business records.

The Court found that the broker's conduct did not meet a reasonable standard of care, that he did not diligently pursue sufficient accurate information about the business and that he relied on the owners' representations rather than taking steps to satisfy himself of material facts.

The sellers and broker were found jointly and severally liable for damages of $195,959.48 plus costs. This sum included the difference between the purchase price and actual property value at closing. Also, this amount included necessary adjustments concerning the seller take back. The mortgage taken back was $249,000 based on the original selling price, but the adjusted mortgage when applying the appraiser's market value of $225,000 with the same down-payment would have been $75,000.

CASE LAW

Case Synopsis

MOHN V. DREISER ESTATE SUPERIOR COURT OF JUSTICE
COURT FILE # 1912/00 & 1935/00

Case Questions

1. The Court addressed the statutory duty imposed by Sec. 33 (now Section 21 of the General Regulation) of the *Real Estate and Business Brokers Act* regarding sale of a business. Outline basic requirements for financial and related documents that must be provided including any waiver provision.	**2.** What steps should a prudent salesperson or broker take regarding financial information when listing a commercial property?

CHAPTER DISCUSSION

1. SALE OF STOCK IN BULK PROCEDURES

a. What is a "*sale of stock in bulk*"?

b. Who does the *Bulk Sales Act* protect and what is the reason for this protection?

c. Briefly describe the requirements of the *Bulk Sales Act* when a "*sale of stock in bulk*" occurs.

CHAPTER DISCUSSION

2. TAX CONSIDERATIONS

What other issues related to provincial and federal tax must be addressed in the sale of a business? Explain.

3. REAL ESTATE AND BUSINESS BROKERS ACT, 2002 REQUIREMENTS

You have just listed a business and the seller is reluctant to allow prospective buyers to have access to the financial statements of the business. Explain how you would deal with this.

KNOWLEDGE INTEGRATION

Notables

- The sale of a business involves unique requirements that must be addressed.
- Registrants need to prepare a proper documentation package with all information necessary for a potential buyer.
- Make certain that the documentation package includes particulars of all leases, franchise agreements and licences.
- Business financing can be challenging. Take the time to set the stage properly with both buyer and seller.
- No standardized agreement form is used in Ontario for the sale of a business. The OREA Form 502 is used for illustration and instructional purposes.
- Carefully review all agreement provisions particularly concerning seller representations, warranties and covenants.
- The *Bulk Sales Act* is designed to protect trade creditors and procedures under that statute should be fully understood.
- Be aware of taxation issues, particularly concerning harmonized sales tax.
- REBBA 2002 sets out specific requirements regarding the provision of financial statements or, in the alternative, a required affidavit setting out certain particulars about the business.
- REBBA 2002 also requires that a list of items not included with the sale be provided to the buyer.
- A *Sale of Business–Affidavit* (OREA Form 503) is designed to meet requirements set out in REBBA 2002.

Chapter Mini-Review

Solutions are located in the Appendix.

1. The *Real Estate and Business Brokers Act, 2002* requires that a list of items included in the sale be provided to the buyer.

   ○ True ○ False

2. An earnout arrangement when acquiring a business allows the buyer to pay the balance of the purchase price from cash flow generated by that business.

   ○ True ○ False

3. The *Agreement of Purchase and Sale – Business in Leased Premises Under the Bulk Sales Act* includes a provision that the seller covenants to deliver to buyer at or before the time of completion the written consent of the lessor to the assignment of the lease of the premises to buyer.

   ○ True ○ False

4. A buyer acquiring a business and complying with the *Bulk Sales Act* remains responsible for debts owed under the business to trade creditors.

   ○ True ○ False

Chapter Mini-Review (continued)

5. The buyer of bulk inventory must demand and receive a sworn statement setting out the seller's creditors.

   ○ True ○ False

6. Under REBBA 2002, a buyer must receive a statement of assets and liabilities, a profit and loss statement and a list of items not included in the sale prior to a binding agreement.

   ○ True ○ False

7. The *Real Estate and Business Brokers Act* requires the seller to provide financial statements for the business to the buyer.

   ○ True ○ False

8. A profit and loss statement provided to a buyer by the seller of a business must cover the past 12-month period.

   ○ True ○ False

9. The waiver provisions allows the buyer to waive receipt of items and assets excluded from the sale.

   ○ True ○ False

Active Learning Exercises

Solutions are located in the Appendix.

Exercise 1

You are acting on behalf of a buyer who is purchasing a clothing store located in a local mall. The offer indicates an amount of $120,000 for inventory at cost. Before signing the offer, the buyer asks "What happens if the actual inventory on closing has a value more or less than this $120,000 indicated?"

a. How would you reply to this question? Base your answer on the pre-printed wording in the *Agreement of Purchase and Sale – Business in Leased Premises Under the Bulk Sales Act (Ontario)*

b. The buyer then states: "*I wonder if the Seller has any debts outstanding on the inventory. Could this be a problem?*" How would you respond?

Exercise 2

A client calls you to list a business for sale and tells you to sell it quickly for cash, as the client's creditors are pressing for payment. What concerns do you have, and describe how these concerns can be overcome.

Exercise 3

Your client runs a small business and has total accounts payable of $2,400 at the time of a proposed sale. Does the buyer have to worry about the creditors? If you are not certain, what should you do?

Exercise 4

a. In a typical transaction involving the "*sale of stock in bulk*," it may not be necessary for a trustee to be appointed. Explain.

b. A creditor may be willing to sign a "*waiver*" of the provisions of the *Bulk Sales Act*. Why might a creditor do this?

Exercise 5

Normally, in the sale of a business, the buyer receives a list of items and assets included in the transaction. Does this comply with the requirements of the *Real Estate and Business Brokers Act, 2002* with respect to the sale of a business? Explain.

Exercise 6

a. Describe the three statements to be delivered to a prospective buyer of a business before an offer to purchase is signed.

b. If these statements are not available, what alternative steps can be taken?

SECTION IV

SELECTED STATUTES

This section deals with various statutes that impact the real estate profession and the trading of real estate. The *Consumer Protection Act* applies to the selling of services and the *Competition Act* applies to advertising and competition issues. Real estate practitioners regularly seek permission to access credit and personal information from prospective buyers and tenants. This section outlines the requirements of the *Consumer Reporting Act*. The *Land Transfer Tax Act* is also included, as this tax is a cost of closing for a real estate transaction. There is an unusual section of the *Income Tax Act* which makes the buyer liable in certain circumstances for tax owed by the seller of a property. While rights of ownership to property have become recognized in law over time, the crown has retained the right of eminent domain, subject to the provisions of the *Expropriations Act*.

Salespersons require knowledge of relevant statutes when communicating with buyers and sellers regarding the responsibilities, rights, risks and rewards that accompany the ownership of real estate. There are a myriad of statutory requirements that must be addressed in marketing real estate and drafting agreements. This section provides important information that allows the real estate practitioner to provide a professional service to the consumer.

CHAPTER 8

The Consumer Protection Act and The Competition Act

Introduction

This chapter outlines the types of representations that would be considered false, misleading or unconscionable under the *Consumer Protection Act*. This Act does not impact the sale of real property, but does relate to the offering of goods and services such as when discussing matters with buyers and sellers concerning a representation (listing) agreement or a service agreement.

The *Competition Act* is also discussed with regard to both competition issues as well as advertising guidelines. In the case of advertising guidelines, emphasis is placed on false and misleading advertising including helpful parameters when dealing with specific topics such as abbreviations, advertised price, contests, fine print/disclaimers and so forth.

Learning Outcomes

At the conclusion of this chapter, students will be able to:

- Recognize the areas in which the *Consumer Protection Act* applies to the activities of real estate brokerages.
- Identify representations that could be a violation of the *Consumer Protection Act.*
- Explain the various remedies for consumers under the *Consumer Protection Act* and the consequences of violations of the Act.
- Demonstrate a knowledge of how brokerages must conduct their business in compliance with prohibitions against unfair competition and price fixing.
- Identify and discuss specific provisions in the *Competition Act* that directly relate to false and misleading advertising.
- Describe the requirements of Canada's Anti-Spam Legislation as it relates to a registrant's advertising and marketing.

THE CONSUMER PROTECTION ACT

The *Consumer Protection Act* (CPA) came into force on July 30, 2005 with expanded rights and remedies for consumers and businesses. The Act consolidated six existing consumer protection laws including the *Business Practices Act*, the *Consumer Protection Act*, the *Consumer Protection Bureau Act*, the *Loan Brokers Act*, the *Motor Vehicle Repair Act* and the *Prepaid Services Act*.

The *Consumer Protection Act* is designed to prohibit unfair practices in sales to consumers. Although the Act does not affect representations made during the course of selling "*real property*," it does apply to real estate brokerages when representations are made during the course of selling "*goods and services*" to consumers. A seller or buyer who complains, under this Act, that there has been an unfair practice in the selling of the registrant's services, may cancel the contract, sue for damages and/or file a complaint with the Consumer Protection Branch of the Ministry of Government Services.

As stated above, this act does not apply to representations about "*real property*." The type of contract that may be cancelled would therefore be a "*service*" or "*representation*" agreement. Sec. 2(2) of the Act sets out important exceptions relating to real estate transactions:

Exceptions
(Relevant Exceptions Bolded for Emphasis)

(2) This Act does not apply in respect of,

- *(a) consumer transactions regulated under the Securities Act;*
- *(b) financial services related to investment products or income securities;*
- *(c) financial products or services regulated under the Insurance Act, the Credit Unions and Caisses Populaires Act, 1994, the Mortgage Brokers Act or the Loan and Trust Corporations Act;*
- *(d) consumer transactions regulated under the Commodity Futures Act;*
- *(e) prescribed professional services that are regulated under a statute of Ontario;*
- ***(f) consumer transactions for the purchase, sale or lease of real property, except transactions with respect to time share agreements as defined in section 20; and***
- ***(g) consumer transactions regulated under the Residential Tenancies Act, 2006. 2002, c. 30, Sched. A, s. 2 (2); 2006, c. 17, s. 249.***

Further, other general provisions are also limited in their relevance to real estate, most notably those concerning future performance contracts (Sec. 22, 23 and 26), as well as Internet, direct and remote agreements.

Agreements Subject to Other Acts
(Relevant Exemption Bolded for Emphasis)

9.(1) *The supply of goods or services pursuant to an agreement that is subject to any of the following Acts is exempt from the application of sections 22, 23, 26 and 37 to 47 of the Act:*

1. *The Motor Vehicle Dealers Act or the Motor Vehicle Dealers Act, 2002.*
2. ***The Real Estate and Business Brokers Act or the Real Estate and Business Brokers Act, 2002.***
3. *The Travel Industry Act or the Travel Industry Act, 2002.*
4. *The Cemeteries Act (Revised), the Funeral Directors and Establishments Act or the Funeral, Burial and Cremation Services Act, 2002. O. Reg. 17/05, s. 9 (1).*

(2) *The exemption from the application of sections 22, 23 and 26 of the Act is effective even if section 21 of the Act states that sections 22 to 26 of the Act do apply in the circumstances. O. Reg. 17/05, s. 9 (2).*

Real property, as such, is not included in the definition of goods, but chattels (and chattels that become fixtures) are included. Real estate practitioners are affected when providing services; e.g., listing, representing buyers, appraising and arranging financing. For example, if a listing or buyer representation agreement is obtained through the use of an unfair practice as defined by the Act, the seller is entitled to rescind the contract.

UNFAIR PRACTICES

Unfair practices are grouped under false and unconscionable consumer representations. A false, misleading or deceptive consumer representation includes, but is not limited to, a representation:

- that the goods or services have sponsorship, approval, performance characteristics, and benefits or quantities that they do not have;
- that the person who is to supply the goods or services has sponsorship, approval, status, affiliation or connection that he/she does not have;
- that a specific price advantage exists, if it does not;
- that misrepresents the authority of a salesperson, representative, employee or agent to negotiate the final terms of the proposed transaction;
- that the proposed transaction involves or does not involve rights, remedies or obligations if the indication is false or misleading;
- that uses exaggeration, innuendo or ambiguity as to a material fact or fails to state a material fact if such use or failure deceives or tends to deceive; or
- that misrepresents the purpose or intent of any solicitation of or any communication with a consumer.

An unconscionable consumer representation made in respect of a particular transaction is determined by various considerations. An unconscionable consumer representation occurs if the person making the representation or the employer knows or ought to know:

- that the consumer is not reasonably able to protect his/her interests because of his/her physical infirmity, ignorance, illiteracy, inability to understand the language of an agreement or similar factors;
- that the price grossly exceeds that at which similar goods or services are readily available to like customers;
- that the consumer is unable to receive a substantial benefit for the subject matter of the consumer representation;
- that there is no reasonable probability of payment of the obligation in full by the consumer;
- that the proposed transaction is excessively one-sided in favour of someone other than the consumer;
- that the terms and conditions of the proposed transaction are so adverse to the consumer as to be inequitable;
- that he/she is making a misleading statement of opinion that the consumer is likely to rely upon to his/her detriment; or
- that he/she is subjecting the consumer to undue pressure to enter into the transaction.

COMPLAINT PROCEDURES

The consumer may complain of unfair practices, for example, in the case of a seller who claims to have signed a listing because of undue pressure.

Several alternatives are available in such cases:

- The seller may rescind or cancel the contract, which would terminate the listing upon giving a written notice to the agent, personally or by registered mail, within six months after the agreement was signed.
- The seller is also entitled to any remedy available at law including damages that may be ordered by a court for fraudulent or negligent misrepresentation or for breach of the duties of an agent.
- If rescission is not possible (property is sold and a selling agent may be entitled to payment under the agreement), the seller can recover the amount of commission paid that exceeds the fair value of the service, or damages, or both. The court can also award exemplary or punitive damages.

The seller has another avenue that involves filing a complaint with the Consumer Protection Branch of the Ministry of Government Services. An investigation, search of business premises, removal of records for copying and other administrative procedures may follow. Such a complaint may include the issuance of an order by the Director of the Consumer Protection Branch requiring compliance. A breach of the Act or failure to comply with the Director's order may result in prosecution.

Reference Consumer complaints arising from the representations and actions of real estate practitioners now largely fall under the jurisdiction of the Real Estate Council of Ontario (RECO). RECO assumed responsibility for the administration of the *Real Estate and Business Brokers Act* in 1997. The Council's mandate focuses primarily on consumer protection and administration of regulators requirements.

WEB LINKS

Consumer Protection Act Practitioners seeking additional information about this Act should contact the Ministry of Government Services at ***www.mgs.gov.on.ca***.

THE COMPETITION ACT

The *Competition Act* (formerly the *Combines Investigation Act*) is a federal statute addressing many forms of competition. The Act is intended to promote fair competition and efficiency in the Canadian marketplace. The legislation provides a framework for selected basic principles involving the conduct of businesses throughout Canada and applies, with few exceptions, to all business enterprises. The Act covers criminal as well as civil law matters. Criminal offences relate to price-fixing, bid-rigging and misleading advertising. Civil law issues include mergers, abuse of dominant position (activities to substantially lessen competition in the marketplace), exclusive dealing (hindering or preventing consumers from dealing with other suppliers) and refusal to deal (obstructing adequate supply of products to persons carrying on a business).

The Director of Investigation and Research, head of the Competition Bureau, is responsible for administration and enforcement of the Act. The Bureau falls under the responsibility of Industry Canada.

Prohibition Order/Compliance Guideline

During 1988, the *Competition Act* gained prominence in organized real estate relating to the operation of real estate boards and associations. Upon the application of the Attorney General of Canada, an Order of Prohibition relating to the *Competition Act* was issued on December 20, 1988. The Order was issued between the Federal Court and ten real estate boards named as respondents. The Canadian Real Estate Association (CREA), wishing to enter into the Prohibition Order, signed agreements with provincial associations and local boards in advance of the Order being issued. All members of CREA were required to undertake certain activities such as:

- Provide new members until 1995 with a copy of the compliance guideline;
- Comply with the *Competition Act* and specific paragraphs;
- Publish a copy of the Order in or with the MLS® listings once a year (local Board or Association); and
- Provide to CREA the names of any members whose membership in a board or association is terminated or refused, along with particulars.

A Compliance Guideline was developed by CREA to assist real estate boards and their members in recognizing competition problems that can result in serious criminal and civil penalties.

Bill C-20

In March 1999, Bill C-20 was proclaimed into law. This bill represented a significant overhaul of the *Competition Act* with amendments concerning deceptive telemarketing, disclosure by telemarketers, Competition Bureau interception of private communication in serious situations with judicial authority and protection of individual identities for persons reporting offences. In addition, Bill C-20 provided a maximum statutory limit of ten years for prohibition orders issued after proclamation of the bill. The Federal Court subsequently ruled that the Prohibition Order involving real estate ended on March 18, 1999, the day amendments to the *Competition Act* were proclaimed.

Principles of Competition

The General Assembly of The Canadian Real Estate Association adopted a *Principles of Competition* document to ensure that the overall message of competition law remains in the forefront of real estate board decision-making. The document, according to CREA Dispatch 99-42 (November 2, 1999) is designed as both a compliance and an education vehicle. The *Principles of Competition* is designed to assist boards and does not apply to individual practitioners as members of real estate boards. By-law and rule amendments were required for individual boards to adopt these principles.

The Board of Directors of The Canadian Real Estate Association also approved a second associated document titled the *Pledge of Competition*. This pledge broadly encompasses the scope of principles and interpretations and is reprinted below.

PLEDGE OF COMPETITION

Member Boards and Associations of The Canadian Real Estate Association support free and open competition. We believe in the principles embodied in the *Competition Act of Canada*. Therefore we adhere to a Code of Conduct which includes the following standards:

- Commission rates or fees members charge for services offered to the public, and the division of those fees among cooperating members, are solely the choice of those providing the services.
- A brokerage may offer any variety of services; e.g., exclusive, open, MLS® listings etc. Boards and real estate Associations accept MLS® listings regardless of the price, commission rates or fees, or the division thereof.
- Advertising by members and non-members is subject to the discretion of the individual, as long as it is honest and lawful. We encourage creative, competitive choice in the services advertised to the public.
- The business relationships between Broker members, their salespersons and non-members is theirs to determine. With regard to Board and Association membership, members may choose for themselves to work full or part time, as long as they remain available to serve the public on a regular basis and provided provincial enabling legislation does not otherwise authorize a limitation of such choice.
- All members are required to meet uniform and reasonable financial and educational standards. They are required to demonstrate integrity and character necessary to protect the public.

By using the MLS® and REALTOR® trademarks, all member Boards and Associations of The Canadian Real Estate Association proclaim adherence to these principles, designed to preserve free and open competition.

WEB LINKS

Competition Act For complaints or enquiries regarding the *Competition Act* contact the Competition Bureau at Industry Canada (***www.strategis.ic.ca***).

Advertising Guidelines

The *Competition Act*, while enforcing various matters, prohibits misleading advertising and deceptive business practices in the promotion of a service or the supply/use of a product. Industry Canada is responsible for the Act with enforcement and administration undertaken by the Competition Bureau. An excerpt of the *Competition Act* is provided.

False and Misleading Advertising—*Competition Act*

The *Competition Act*, although dictating procedures on a number of trading activities, is particularly broad in its approach to false or deceptive advertising practices. In particular, Section 52 of the *Competition Act* should be noted:

52 (1) No person shall, for the purpose of promoting, directly or indirectly, the supply or use of a product or for the purpose of promoting, directly or indirectly, any business interest, by any means whatever, knowingly or recklessly make a representation to the public that is false or misleading in a material respect.

The following are three important factors involving offences under this statute.

- The term material refers to any information which could affect a purchasing decision. In other words, any representation that might influence a consumer in the marketplace can fall under the Act. Consequently, the *Competition Act* touches upon practically every activity involving the day-to-day trading of real estate and related purchasing decisions.
- Proof of intention to deceive is not necessarily a prerequisite for charges under this statute. In fact, it is not a proper defence to argue that the misrepresentation was never intended. However, Subsection 60 (2) does state that a proper defence can be due diligence to correct the error.
- The definition of "misleading" is deliberately expanded to include non-literal impressions given by the advertisements. This is commonly referred to as the general impression test.

52 (4) In any prosecution for a contravention of this section, the general impression conveyed by the representation as well as the literal meaning thereof shall be taken into account in determining whether or not the representation is false or misleading in a material respect.

The actual wording of an advertisement may be technically correct, but the general impression can still be false.

Canadian Real Estate Association (CREA)

The Canadian Real Estate Association publishes an informative booklet with particular emphasis on false and misleading advertising, deceptive marketing practices and enforcement of applicable portions of the *Competition Act* by the Marketing Practices Branch of the Bureau of Competition Policy. The publication titled *Misleading Advertising Guide—Complying With The Competition Act* (CREA, 2008) also provides useful guidance for advertising by CREA for the purpose of trading in real estate.

An excerpt from this publication has been reprinted on the following page for information purposes only. This material was developed based upon publications, interpretations and opinions current at time of publication and is subject to change. Individuals are advised to access current information from appropriate authorities, the broker and/or legal counsel, prior to the development of any marketing materials.

GENERAL PARAMETERS

The issues of accuracy and clarity are fundamental to all advertising. Selected topics are discussed for guidance.

Abbreviations

The cost of classified advertising is a primary rationale for the use of abbreviations. Also, a host of codes and contractions are used when completing MLS® listing forms. Consequently, abbreviations are becoming more widespread in advertising. As a general rule, those found in local trading areas are acceptable provided that they do not confuse or mislead.

EXAMPLE *Advertising Guidelines—General Parameters—Abbreviations*

A reader in Toronto would understand the DVP as the Don Valley Parkway, and a buyer would correctly decipher 3 BR TH as a three-bedroom townhouse. However, ASSUME 1ST, 2ND, MIN DN, QUALF. could present problems. Abbreviations should be avoided whenever uninformed or innocent parties could misunderstand. This is particularly true when describing property uses, zoning, mortgaging or other specific attributes of a property.

Advertised Price

Subsection 58(3) of the *Competition Act* does permit *sales above the advertised price* in the case of private real estate transactions. Specifically, the actual reference in the Act excludes *the sale of a product by or on behalf of the person who is not engaged in the business of dealing in that product (e.g., private real estate sales).*

However, other representations concerning price come under scrutiny. Any reduction or other alteration of price should be clearly identified and not be materially misleading. Further, the suggestion of a *bargain* that is not substantiated can have legal ramifications. Consider the following case involving a property listed below market value.

EXAMPLE *Advertising Guidelines—General Parameters—Advertised Price (Hypothetical)*

The accused (a house builder in Anycity), promoting the sale of new homes in a brochure, stated that his homes were priced $10,000 below market value, and published the prices of homes recently sold in the market area for comparison purposes. An investigation revealed that the builder's homes were not priced below market value and that the comparison homes differed from those of the accused in several respects. The accused pleaded guilty to one charge under Subsection 52(1) of the *Competition Act*, was convicted and fined $10,000.

Human Rights Code

A salesperson, in advertising a property, cannot set out preferences for a specific class or group of individuals that are specifically forbidden under the Ontario Human Rights Code; e.g., colour, race, ethnic origin or religion. The issue of preferences also extends into the area of commercial and residential tenancies.

Contests

The *Competition Act* outlines basic rules for the operation of contests. Section 59 focuses primarily on adequate and fair disclosure of certain key facts:

- Approximate number and value of prizes included in the contest.
- Allocation of prizes by region, if applicable.
- Chances of winning (if it is within the knowledge of the advertiser).
- Whether or not a skill testing question is required to win the contest.
- Place where the contest rules may be obtained.
- The closing date of the contest.
- Any unusual restrictions or conditions relating to the promotional contest.

Practitioners are strongly encouraged to seek expert advice in the development of contests, particularly those involving games of chance, to ensure compliance with the lottery provisions of the *Criminal Code*, and other applicable provincial and federal statutes.

Coupons/Market Evaluation Certificates

Certificates and coupons, must clearly identify the service being provided. Disclaimers and limiting conditions should be consistent with the overall impression conveyed.

Fine Print/Disclaimers

Classified advertising and other types of promotional material often contain additional information in small print that either qualifies or otherwise expands the message being conveyed. Real estate practitioners, in order to save space, may relegate certain information to the *fine print*. Generally, this text will not arouse concern if it is additive and complementary to the main message. However, if the fine print in any way contradicts or otherwise limits the general impression conveyed by the main message, then a violation under the *Competition Act* may arise.

Disclaimers are frequently found in fine print. As a rule, such disclaimers should not contain information that materially limits or contradicts the main text or have any significant effect on the general impression being conveyed in the ad. The *Canadian Code of Advertising Standards*, Clause 1(d) provides guidance on the issues of disclaimers and asterisked *fine print* information.

> *Disclaimers or asterisked information must not contradict more prominent aspects of the message and should be located and presented in such a manner as to be clearly visible.*
>
> *Source:* November, 1990, revision to The Canadian Code of Advertising Standards as quoted in *Misleading Advertising Bulletin*, Issue 4, 1990 published by Industry Canada.

The size of the fine print has also come under scrutiny by the Director of Investigation and Research of the Competition Bureau. Fine print should be clearly visible, readable and relative to the print size used throughout other portions of the advertisement, and take into account the needs of the targeted audience (e.g., age of reader and ability to read). While *general impression* remains the ultimate test, the Director has indicated the acceptability of *7 point print size* as a minimum.

This sentence is printed in 7 point Arial.

However, such a minimum measurement is subject to the qualifiers mentioned above.

Free Offerings

If a product or service is advertised as *free*, then such an offering shall not include any condition or other requirement that the prospective customer would be unable to comply with. The Director of Investigation and Research also addresses the *two for one* offerings by citing the following example as a false representation: *Buy one real estate lot receive your next choice absolutely free*, where the price of the first lot is inflated to cover the cost of the *free* lot.

Multiple Listing Agreements

All MLS® listings are viewed as advertisements and consequently fall under the *Competition Act*. All members must ensure that listing information is accurate and correct.

As a rule, real estate practitioners are advised to include nothing on a listing agreement that cannot be verified by source documentation. Information concerning items such as

MISLEADING LEADLINES AND SIMILAR CLAIMS

Appraisal at No Obligation, Professional Estimate and Similar Terms
Some members advertise their services using such terms as above. Caution should be used in offering this service if the true intention of the member is merely to provide an estimate of value for the purpose of inducing the owner to decide whether or not to offer the property for sale. If a property owner mistakenly assumes that the member's estimate of value is, in fact, a valid property appraisal and relies on it for another purpose, and as a result of such reliance suffers loss, then the person supplying the information may be guilty of misleading advertising and may also be liable for damages. Members are advised to specify the purpose for which evaluations of property are provided.

Cash Buyers Waiting
This phrase and variations of it could be grossly misleading if it cannot be substantiated that cash buyers are, in fact, available to the advertiser and are ready to purchase at current market values.

Single Family Area
Care should be taken in the use of this phrase to determine that, in fact, multiple family development is not liable to take place in the area concerned.

Near School, Close to Transportation
These phrases beg the question of interpretation as to the meaning of near and close. To avoid misunderstanding, it would be more desirable to include the actual number of blocks or miles to the facility, and certainly some indication, in the case of a school, as to the type of school.

Bargain
If this term is used, it should only be used if the property clearly is a bargain when compared with similar properties in the relevant market which are available for purchase or have recently been sold.

Building Lot
A lot should only be described in this manner if it is a lot which either has been or will be approved for the erection of a house. (In some areas, checker-board development has led to the establishment of certain lots on which the municipality will not issue a building permit in the foreseeable future).

Future Investment
Future Investment is a highly vague and potentially misleading term which could cause a possible purchaser to believe financial gain was likely to be realized when, in fact, it might well not be. Especially in the residential market, use of this phrase should probably be avoided.

Future Subdivision Land, Future Development Land
Avoid reference to the possibilities for the future use which may not be realized, unless you can clearly identify specific plans and the conditions under which they might come to fruition.

Private
This word should not be used by a real estate agent because it indicates a sale by the vendor direct to the purchaser. This would include the home of a licensed agent.

New
New is an absolute term and therefore should not be used unless the facts support its use. A roof that is one and a half years old may be new, in as much as it replaces the original roof on the house, but it is not new. It is better to describe it as a roof, one and a half years old.

This same practice applies to major appliances, basic plumbing and wiring and other features which you might otherwise be tempted to describe as new, if they have been recently installed or renovated.

Estate Sale
The implication of this term is that the property is being sold by a trustee liquidating an estate and therefore might be obtained somewhat more cheaply. This can be seriously misleading if the property is being sold as a normal sale having no connection with the settling of an estate.

Easy Terms
Care must be taken with the use of the phrase easy terms. The phrase is relative and, if the meaning is not fully explained, could well be misleading. For example, easy terms for a family with moderate to high annual household income are certainly not easy terms for a family with low annual household income.

Stop Renting
Although a leadline like *Stop Renting* is unobjectionable where the cost of buying the home (including mortgage obligations) is generally within the reach of renters in the relevant market, the phrase can be misleading where the price or purchase terms do not support its use.

lot size, legal description, mortgage financing, taxes, chattels and fixtures, current zoning, and rentals, to mention a few, come under scrutiny. In fact, inaccurate representations are normally not only actionable under the federal statute but also under common law as either innocent or fraudulent misrepresentation.

The importance of accurate listing information and representations relating thereto is obviously a major factor in broker liability in the marketplace. Although lacking definitive Canadian research at this time, statistical information from the United States underscores the legal entanglements between buyers and brokers that undoubtedly arise from matters pertaining to the accuracy and adequacy of listing information. In fact, the majority of claims involve the buyer as claimant.

Personal Identification

Guidelines, procedures and specific wordings regarding identification of brokerages, brokers and salespersons in relation to promotional materials are addressed in REBBA 2002.

Pictures/Illustrations

No erroneous impression can be conveyed when a picture or illustration accompanies and forms part of an overall advertisement. For example, if homes are being sold in the $100,000–$150,000 price range, and the house pictured in the advertisement is a model other than that offered, an offence could arise under the *Competition Act.* Further, the fine print in such advertisements requires careful wording.

In the case of illustrations, it is common to see various *asterisked statements* in new home sales such as:

Illustrations are artist's concept only, prices and specifications subject to change without notice.

Limited quantities available in some price ranges.

Illustration only. Prices and specifications subject to change without notice, E. & O. E.

If a complaint is lodged under provisions of the *Competition Act*, the content of such statements including the respective sizes, and locations in relation to other advertised information would all be taken into consideration by the Director of Investigation and Research.

Promotional Claims

Real estate practitioners must be careful to correctly represent any claims concerning personal performance levels. As with many other areas of advertising, the general impression of the marketing piece and the actual text must agree, and the statement must be accurate and not misleading.

Caution is strongly advised when contemplating claim statements such as:

The best....in the area,
The first....in production,
The most popular choice for...,
The most...respected.......,
The largest..., etc.

While such claims may be substantiated, the Director of Investigation and Research will regard each case on its own merits. Ensure that performance claims are correct and accurate. Consider the following decision under the *Competition Act*:

The accused, in promoting a real estate service, made the following representation in newspaper advertisements: *For maximum exposure and results...over 90% of* [Name of Broker (Agent)] *Realty team listings have sold in 12 days or less.* Investigation revealed that the representation was untrue. Fine: $500.

If testimonials are utilized in promotional material, ensure that any statements printed are accurate, not taken out of context from a larger statement and that the person providing such statement has in fact received the services outlined in the testimonial. As a matter of policy, the signed statements of individuals should be kept on file in case their authenticity is ever questioned.

Summary

Advertising has become an increasingly complicated facet of real estate trading. Salespeople must consider legal issues and statutory regulations that surround the presentation of property and the provision of services in the marketplace. In the future, the industry will undoubtedly develop additional guidelines and utilize more complex disclosure forms to address the needs of an expanding, sophisticated consumer market.

A conscious move toward more definition in all stages of real estate negotiations has also appeared, be it the listing process, promotion of property, representations made to both buyer and seller during negotiations, and the drafting of complete terms to fully document agreements between parties. This demand for accuracy is neither isolated to real estate sales nor solely directed to salespersons' activities. Many brokerages have introduced seller disclosure forms to ensure accurate information when obtaining listing information from a principal. Listing forms, once a half-page document, now consume two pages or more. Proper disclaimers and qualifiers, once the exception, are now commonplace in all types of print advertising.

The future undoubtedly will demand even clearer delineation of facts, responsibilities and representations in the interest of fair marketing practices and consumer protection. Regulatory bodies are already confronting new issues surrounding private versus public information, direct mail and telephone canvassing procedures, increasingly detailed disclosure forms, and precise statements of agency responsibilities and duties. Ironically, for all the complexities of modern laws, be they decreed by parliament or declared in courts, the practitioner looking to the future will be best served by following the simple, unencumbered guidelines already established in codes of ethics designed by organized real estate and provincial regulatory bodies.

Canada's Anti-Spam Legislation (CASL)

Please note that the content provided below is for information purposes only. It is intended purely as an overview of Canada's anti-spam legislation (known as CASL) and how it may impact registrants. It is neither comprehensive nor intended to form legal opinion or advice. Registrants are advised to seek independent legal advice.

Canada's anti-spam legislation received Royal Assent on December 15, 2010, and became law on July 1, 2014. The full title of CASL is "*an Act to promote the efficiency and adaptability of the Canadian economy by regulating certain activities that discourage reliance on electronic means of carrying out commercial activities, and to amend the Canadian Radio-television and Telecommunications Commission Act, the Competition Act, the Personal Information Protection and Electronic Documents Act and the Telecommunications Act*" (S.C. 2010, c. 23).

PURPOSE OF THE ACT

Section 3 of the legislation sets out the purpose of the Act.

3. The purpose of this Act is to promote the efficiency and adaptability of the Canadian economy by regulating commercial conduct that discourages the use of electronic means to carry out commercial activities, because that conduct

   (a) impairs the availability, reliability, efficiency and optimal use of electronic means to carry out commercial activities;

   (b) imposes additional costs on businesses and consumers;

   (c) compromises privacy and the security of confidential information; and

   (d) undermines the confidence of Canadians in the use of electronic means of communication to carry out their commercial activities in Canada and abroad.

DEFINING AND UNDERSTANDING TERMS WITHIN THE ACT

Section 1 of the Act defines commercial activity, electronic message, and commercial electronic message (CEM) as follows:

"commercial activity" means any particular transaction, act or conduct or any regular course of conduct that is of a commercial character, whether or not the person who carries it out does so in the expectation of profit, other than any transaction, act or conduct that is carried out for the purposes of law enforcement, public safety, the protection of Canada, the conduct of international affairs or the defence of Canada.

"electronic message" means a message sent by any means of telecommunication, including a text, sound, voice or image message.

"commercial electronic message" is an electronic message that, having regard to the content of the message, the hyperlinks in the message to content on a website or other database, or the contact information contained in the message, it would be reasonable to conclude has as its purpose, or one of its purposes, to encourage participation in a commercial activity, including an electronic message that

(a) offers to purchase, sell, barter or lease a product, goods, a service, land or an interest or right in land;

(b) offers to provide a business, investment or gaming opportunity;

(c) advertises or promotes anything referred to in paragraph (a) or (b); or

(d) promotes a person, including the public image of a person, as being a person who does anything referred to in any of paragraphs (a) to (c), or who intends to do so.

A CEM may be described as any electronic message that encourages participation in a commercial activity regardless of whether there is an expectation of profit. As noted, a commercial activity is broadly defined and includes, among other things, activities such as offering properties for sale, and advertising/promoting goods, a service, or a person.

An electronic address is an email account, a telephone account, an instant message account, and any other similar form. Messages sent to other users on a social media platform, such as Facebook or LinkedIn, would also qualify as sending messages to electronic addresses. CASL does not apply to:

- Twitter posts
- Facebook wall posts
- websites
- blogs
- two-way voice communication between individuals
- faxes and voice recordings sent to a telephone account (however, registrants should be mindful of the requirements of the National Do Not Call List)

PROHIBITIONS AND REQUIREMENTS

Section 6 (1) of the Act prohibits the sending of CEMs unless the person to whom the message is sent has consented (either express consent or implied consent) to receiving it. Before sending a CEM to an electronic address, the sender must:

- obtain consent from the recipient
- identify himself/herself
- provide a means for the recipient to withdraw consent (i.e., an unsubscribe mechanism)

OBTAINING CONSENT

Consent can be written or implied. However, if challenged, the onus is on the sender to prove he/she has obtained consent to send the message. When requesting express consent, silence or inaction on the part of the intended recipient cannot be construed as providing consent.

Express consent must be obtained through an opt-in mechanism rather than opt-out. A pre-checked box for consent is not permitted as this would assume consent where it was not intended.

When requesting express consent, among other things, the following information must be included:

- the specific purpose must be clearly identified
- the name of the person requesting consent or, if a person is requesting consent on behalf of another person, both persons have to be identified
- contact information of the person(s) requesting consent, including a physical address and either a telephone number, email address, or website

In the case of a referral, consent from the recipient is not required provided that certain conditions are met.

- The referral must have been made by an individual who has an existing business relationship, an existing non-business relationship, a family relationship, or a personal relationship with both the sender and the recipient.
- The full name of the person making the referral and a statement that the CEM is being sent as a result of the referral must be included in the CEM.
- The CEM must contain the sender's identification information and an unsubscribe mechanism.

For more information about obtaining consent, go to the Canadian Radio-television and Telecommunications Commission (CRTC) website at **http://www.crtc.gc.ca/eng/archive/2012/2012-549.htm**.

Consent can be implied in situations such as:

- where there has been an existing business or non-business relationship in the last two years
- the recipient of a CEM has conspicuously published his/her electronic address (e.g., on a website) or has disclosed his/her electronic address (e.g., distribution of a business card)

However, where the recipient has conspicuously published or disclosed his/her electronic address, a CEM can only be sent if:

- the content of the message relates to the recipient's role, functions, or duties in an official or business capacity, and
- the recipient, when providing a business card or publishing his/her electronic address on a website, did not state that he/she did not wish to receive CEMs at that address

EXISTING BUSINESS/NON-BUSINESS RELATIONSHIPS

The legislation includes a transitional provision that relates to consent. Where there is an existing business or non-business relationship that includes the sending of CEMs, consent is implied for a period of 36 months commencing July 1, 2014. An existing business relationship exists where two people have been doing business together within the past two years. For registrants, this could include the purchase of a property, a listing agreement, or a buyer representation agreement. In the case of an inquiry about a registrant's services, the time limit for sending a CEM without express consent is six months from the inquiry.

Consent can be implied in non-business relationships (e.g., fellow members of an association, club, or voluntary organization). The requirement for identification information of the sender and an unsubscribe mechanism still exists.

In all cases, CEMs must contain an unsubscribe mechanism that is easy for the recipient to use. Furthermore, a recipient can terminate the consent if he/she indicates that he/she no longer wishes to receive CEMs. The transitional period can be used to obtain express consent for the receipt of CEMs where consent is currently implied. Express consent does not expire until the recipient withdraws his/her consent.

INSTALLING COMPUTER PROGRAMS

Section 8 of CASL applies when a computer program or application is installed on another person's computer system. A person must provide express consent before software or apps are installed on his/her electronic device. The following information must be provided to obtain express consent:

- the purpose for which the consent is being sought
- identification information of the person seeking consent
- the function and purpose of the computer program

Further disclosure of information may be required if the computer program performs additional functions, such as collecting personal information or interferes with the user's control of the computer system. For more information, go to **http://fightspam.gc.ca/eic/site/030.nsf/eng/h_00050.html.**

PENALTIES FOR VIOLATIONS

Violations of any of Sections 6 to 9 of CASL could result in an administrative monetary penalty of up to $1 million for an individual and up to $10 million for a business.

Directors, officers, agents, and mandataries (i.e., people who have been given the authority to act on behalf) of a corporation can be liable if they directly authorized, assented to, acquiesced in (e.g., allowed), or participated in the commission of the violation.

The legislation is available on the Government of Canada website at **http://fightspam.gc.ca.**

CHAPTER DISCUSSION

1. CONSUMER PROTECTION ACT

a. There are two major categories of representations that are prohibited under the *Consumer Protection Act.* Describe these two main types of representations and give at least two examples for each category (examples must relate to real estate).

b. A buyer learns that a number of statements made by a registrant at the time of the signing of the Buyer Representation Agreement were totally false. The buyer is convinced he would not have signed the agreement if his questions would have been answered truthfully. What can the buyer do? Explain.

CHAPTER DISCUSSION

2. THE COMPETITION ACT

You mention to another real estate salesperson in your office that the "*low downpayment*" advertisement he has been running in the newspaper for the last couple of weeks is an ad for a listing that has been sold for several days. He replies "*No problem. I am still getting lots of calls on that ad, so I am going to let it run for a while longer.*" Comment.

KNOWLEDGE INTEGRATION

Notables

- The *Consumer Protection Act* is designed to prohibit unfair practices in sales to consumers.
- This Act does not relate to representations when selling real property, but does apply to the selling of goods and services; e.g., approaching a consumer regarding a representation (listing) agreement.
- If a representation agreement is obtained through the use of an unfair practice, the seller is entitled to rescind the contract.
- A seller who claims that he has been the victim of an unfair practice (e.g., undue pressure when signing a listing agreement) has certain remedies under the Act.
- The *Competition Act* covers criminal as well as civil matters.
- Various guidelines are provided to assist registrants in ensuring compliance with the Act in regard to false and misleading advertising.
- Sec. 52 of the Act is focal to real estate brokerages, as it sets out important provisions concerning false and misleading advertising.
- A multiple listing agreement is viewed as an advertisement for purposes of the *Competition Act.*
- Section 6 (1) of Canada's Anti-Spam Legislation prohibits the sending of commercial electronic messages (CEMs) unless the person to whom the message is sent has consented (either express consent or implied consent) to receiving it.

Web Links

Web links are included for general interest regarding selected chapter topics.

Consumer Protection Act	Practitioners seeking additional information about this Act should contact the Ministry of Government Services at ***www.mgs.gov.on.ca***.
Competition Act	For complaints or enquiries regarding the *Competition Act* contact the Competition Bureau at Industry Canada (***www.strategis.ic.ca***).

Chapter Mini-Review

Solutions are located in the Appendix.

1. "You told them there was hardwood under the carpet on the main floor. You know that is not true, so you have violated the *Consumer Protection Act*."

   ○ True ○ False

2. A consumer complaining about an unfair practice in relation to the *Consumer Protection Act* may rescind or cancel the contract.

   ○ True ○ False

3. "It doesn't matter what they thought the ad meant. It is literally true and I am off the hook!"

   ○ True ○ False

4. An abbreviation widely used and understood in a local trading area would probably be acceptable and not misleading from a Competition Bureau perspective.

   ○ True ○ False

Chapter Mini-Review (continued)

5. An acceptable print size for disclaimers is 7 point, according to guidelines addressed in this chapter.

   True False

6. An advertisement stating that new homes are available from as low as $300,000 within a particular subdivision is misleading if, in fact, all homes in that price range have all been sold.

   True False

7. If a brokerage offers a contest, Section 59 of the *Competition Act* requires that two disclosures must be made regarding the approximate number and value of prices and the closing date of the contest.

   True False

8. Certificates and coupons distributed by real estate brokerages may include disclaimers, but these must be consistent with the overall message being conveyed.

   True False

Active Learning Exercises

Solutions are located in the Appendix.

Exercise 1

A salesperson cannot be guilty under the *Consumer Protection Act* by telling the buyer how easy it will be to obtain financing because this Act does not apply to the Agreement of Purchase and Sale. Comment.

Exercise 2

Give examples of several situations or statements made by real estate salespersons that could be unfair practices under the *Consumer Protection Act.*

Exercise 3

"*If a seller complains, I will just cancel the listing. That will be the end of the matter.*" Discuss.

Exercise 4

Salesperson Sharp tells the seller that the listing must be for ninety days because "*that is what the law requires. But you don't have to worry because I have priced your home right and it will sell within the month.*" Forty-five days later, the house remains unsold, and Sharp tells the seller "*The market has slowed down.*" What will likely happen if the seller wants to cancel the listing? What if it is on MLS®?

■ Exercise 5

A broker advertises: "*a family with all cash for a three bedroom home near Parkview School*" is looking for a property through the brokerage. However, this prospect does not in fact exist, and the broker is looking for listing leads. Tom Seller reads the ad, lists for ninety days and discovers the deception within a week. What recourse does Seller have?

■ Exercise 6

A seller lists a property with a broker because the broker told her that the commission for an exclusive sale is 4%, and that amount is less than competitors charge in the area. Later the seller finds that in fact the statement was false. Can the seller cancel the listing? Explain.

Exercise 7

As office manager, you are reading the advertisements placed in the local newspaper by your salespersons. Do you have any concerns about the following ad? Explain.

HOTTEST PROPERTY IN TOWN

PRICED WELL BELOW MARKET.

THIS GEM HAS ALL NEW WIRING AND FURNACE.

CALL ALBERT AT ABC REALTY INC. 555-1313

SECTION IV

SELECTED STATUTES

CHAPTER 9

The Consumer Reporting Act and The Land Transfer Tax Act

Introduction

Any real estate transaction would fall under the guidelines of the *Consumer Reporting Act* and permit a real estate practitioner to obtain credit information on a consumer as a *direct business need.* A report on the consumer would be obtained as standard procedure, for example, when a rental application is being processed or an agreement of purchase and sale provides for the buyer to assume the obligation of a mortgage, a report on the consumer would be obtained as standard procedure. This chapter outlines the requirements of the *Consumer Reporting Act,* and brokerages must comply with these requirements when obtaining information on consumers.

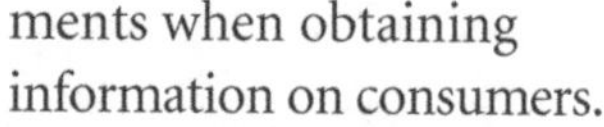

The second part of the chapter focuses on land transfer tax. Until recently, only provincial land transfer tax applied, but individuals buying property in Toronto are now faced with a second municipal tax. Registrants should be prepared to generally discuss land transfer tax calculations with buyers and sellers, along with basic details concerning first time buyer refunds on new and resale homes.

Learning Outcomes

At the conclusion of this chapter, students will be able to:

- Identify situations where the requirements of the *Consumer Reporting Act* apply.
- Explain the difference between credit and personal information.
- Apply the requirements of the *Consumer Reporting Act* when obtaining and using information on consumers.
- Describe procedures for calculating provincial land transfer tax and municipal land transfer tax (Toronto).
- Outline key provisions regarding first time buyer refunds for new and resale homes that apply to both provincial and municipal land transfer taxes.

THE CONSUMER REPORTING ACT

The *Consumer Reporting Act* is a provincial statute designed to protect consumers through specific rights:

- the right to revise incorrect information about personal credit history;
- the right to know what is being reported; and
- the right to ensure that information used by agencies is being correctly collected, stored and reported.

The *Consumer Reporting Act* also provides that the consumer must be given notice when information concerning an extension of credit or the obtaining of personal information is involved. When the consumer so requests, that person must also inform the consumer of the name and address of the consumer reporting agency being used.

The Act is written so that contracting out of its provisions is not possible and all salespeople and brokers should be fully aware of requirements.

Various OREA agreements (e.g., Agreement of Purchase and Sale (Form 100)) contain the following phrase:

> *The Buyer is hereby notified that a consumer report containing credit and/or personal information may be referred to in connection with this transaction.*

Access/Use of Reports

The Act permits a consumer reporting agency (i.e., a credit bureau) to provide reports to a person who the agency has reason to believe intends to use the information concerning the entering into or renewal of a tenancy agreement, in connection with credit, purchase or collection of a debt of a consumer, or for some other direct business need involving the consumer or intends to use the information for updating consumer report information already received.

Consumer Notification

A consumer, for purposes of the Act, includes a person engaging in any transaction other than in the course of carrying on a business, trade or profession. The Act provides a system whereby a consumer will always know whether credit was denied as a result of a bad consumer report. Specifically, the person making use of such information must give notice of this fact to the consumer. He/she must inform the consumer that within 60 days of receiving this notice, he/she can request the nature and source of the information where an agency is not involved, or the name and address of the consumer reporting agency.

Credit Information	Where a person proposes to extend credit to a consumer and a consumer report containing credit information only is being or may be referred to in connection with the transaction (e.g., a mortgage application involving a lender or a seller-take back arrangement), the person shall give written notice to the consumer at the time of application for credit or, if the application is made orally, then orally at the time of application. Credit information includes consumer details such as name, age, occupation, place of residence, previous places of employment, marital status, spouse's name and age, dependents, particulars of education/qualifications, place of employment, estimated income, paying habits, outstanding debt obligations, cost of living obligations and assets.
Personal Information	The Act also addresses personal information involving details other than credit information about a consumer's character, reputation, health, physical or personal characteristics, mode of living or any other matter concerning the consumer. Where a report concerning personal information is involved, advance written notice must be given to the consumer. The name and address of the consumer reporting agency must be supplied upon request.

Requesting Report

The Act states that every person shall, where requested by a consumer in writing or personally, inform the consumer whether or not a consumer report has been or is to be referred to in connection with a specified transaction or matter in which such person is engaged, and if so, provide the name and address of the consumer reporting agency supplying the report.

Credit Bureau

A credit bureau is a clearing house, also referred to as a *credit investigating agency*, for all types of credit related information. Essentially, companies involved in lending money provide the bureau with customer information and, in return, have access to the files established for each consumer. Credit reports are provided on request. The credit bureau receives information not only from lenders (credit grantors) but also from public record sources (judgments, bankruptcies). Most companies using credit cards within Canada, such as financial institutions, oil companies and department stores, use the service. Selected banks input information and the major Canadian-based automobile financing companies are also part of the system.

The credit bureau provides information that is usually updated on a 60-day basis. This varies depending on how information is transmitted between individual lenders and the bureau. Often, information is sent electronically which has improved both the accuracy and timeliness. Of course, the consumer has the ability not only to verify information being held on file but also to dispute or alter incorrect data.

Credit bureaus only compile information relating to credit. No data is collected relating to personal habits, affiliations, political or social connections. Further, not all credit information about an individual will be found in the records. The completeness of data is limited by the number of lenders that participate as members with the bureau in any particular locale. The report on an individual may be limited but still a useful indicator of the positive and negative aspects of a personal credit history.

Credit bureaus in Canada produce reports using a common or standardized language to ensure that reporting is consistent and that all credit grantors use the same terms to describe specific types of pay habits.

PROVINCIAL LAND TRANSFER TAX

Provincial land transfer tax is assessed on real property when a deed is registered transferring ownership of the property from one party to another. The tax uses a sliding scale of percentages based on property value.

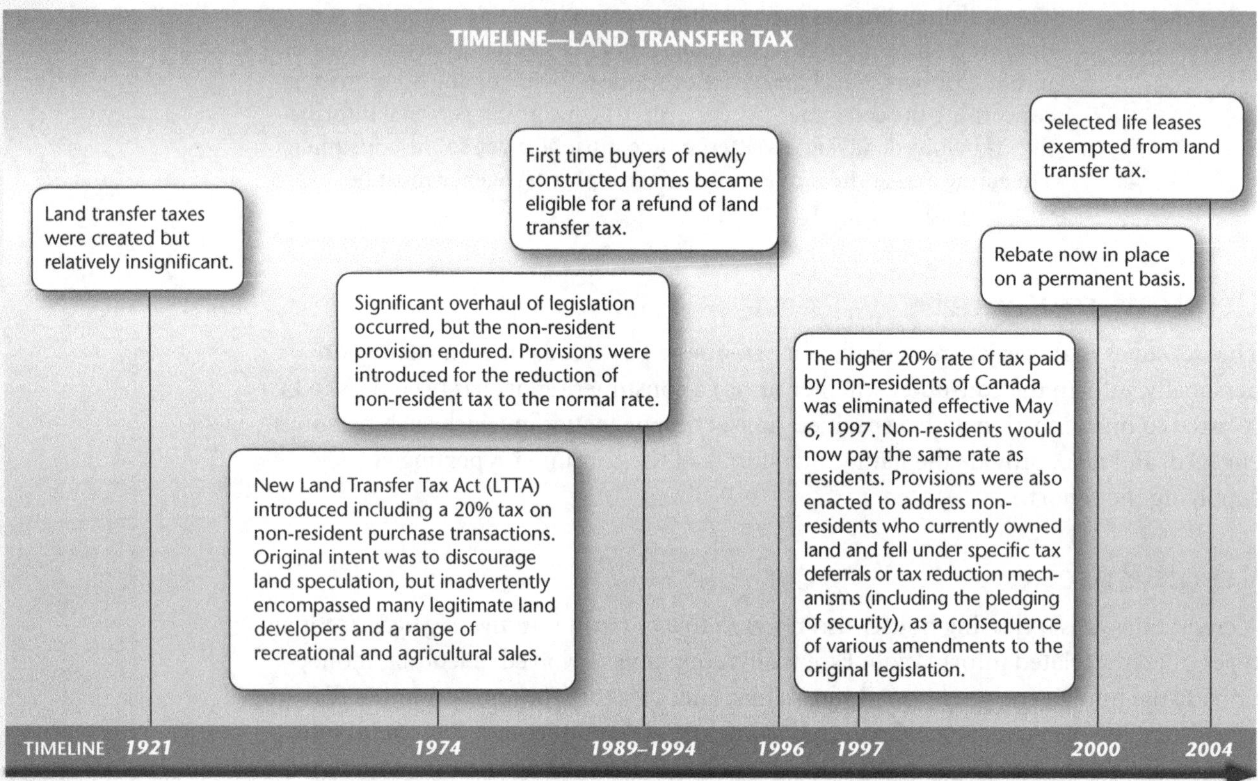

Real Property Registration

Real estate practitioners most commonly encounter the imposition of land transfer tax at the point of registration of real property. A purchaser, when entering into an agreement of purchase and sale, is obtaining an interest in land. A taxable event occurs, pursuant to the *Land Transfer Tax Act* (LTTA), when an interest in land is conveyed. More specifically, tax is payable based on three conditions: a registration is made under either the *Registry Act* or the *Land Titles Act*, the document being registered is a conveyance and the conveyance involves land.

The term *land* is precisely defined under the LTTA to include any estate, right or interest in lands including a leasehold interest, interest of an optionee and interest of a purchaser under an agreement to sell land. The definition encompasses a broad range of real estate transactions, but exceptions do exist; e.g., the transfer of a share in a company that owns real estate. As a general comment, the issue of whether or not land transfer tax applies to specific situations is best left to legal experts.

DISPOSITION OF UNREGISTERED INTERESTS

While practitioners most frequently associate land transfer tax with land registration, a second dimension of land transfer taxation was introduced in 1989 concerning dispositions. The LTTA, since 1989, has imposed land transfer tax on the disposition of a beneficial interest. The complexities of this system go beyond the current text, but a general understanding of the process is warranted. Essentially, the amendment encompasses the disposition of unregistered interests in which no registration of documents occurred; e.g., co-operatives and the use of trusts.

The legislative definition addresses any sale, transfer or assignment, however effected, involving any part of a beneficial interest. As with the registration provisions, the disposition definition includes a range of possibilities. The designers of the amendment excluded situations that were not intended to fall within the legislative scope; e.g., a transfer due to the death of an owner or the securing of a mortgage (including a discharge). Further, other dispositions of a beneficial interest were identified as attracting a nil tax rate; e.g., transfers to a spouse pursuant to a separation agreement and certain family transfers for natural love and affection.

The matter of taxing beneficial interests has caused some confusion. In 2002, the Ministry of Finance issued a notice pointing out specific rights to occupy that constitute a beneficial interest, including life lease, life tenure, equity lease or life tenancy. The Ministry views such rights as not being leasehold, but rather freehold interests and subject to the *Land Transfer Tax Act*. One exclusion is noteworthy, namely, a building built on leased land in which the unexpired term at point of disposition is less than 50 years, including any renewals or extensions.

EXEMPTION FOR LIFE LEASES

In April 2004, the government clarified matters concerning life leases by regulating an exemption concerning land transfer tax involving certain life lease developments. A life lease development is defined as land with self-contained units, organized as what is commonly known as a life lease project, where the right to occupy a unit is solely for the lifetime of an individual or for a term of at least 20 years.

Under the regulation, if the owner of the life lease development is a non-profit organization or a registered charity, and each individual who acquired the life lease interest in order to use the unit as his or her principal residence or as the principal residence of the individual's parent or spouse, they are exempt from the land transfer tax upon acquisition of the life lease interest. This regulation was passed retroactively and would entitle anyone who entered into a life lease arrangement under the above circumstances after July 18, 1989, but before March 28, 2003, to apply for a refund of land transfer tax paid.

WEB LINKS

Life Leases Those contemplating being involved with life leases should access ***www.e-laws.gov.on.ca***, go to Statutes and Associated Regulations and follow instructions to look up Regulations under the *Land Transfer Tax Act*. Expert advice is required on all matters involving land transfer tax and exemptions relating thereto.

Value of the Consideration

The value of the consideration is also a matter of legislative interpretation. Most land conveyances involving real estate practitioners are based on cash or its equivalent in an arm's length transaction. Accordingly, the tax is computed based on the sale price. However, the LTTA must address more complex situations, for example, the disposition of property for natural love and affection that also involves the assumption of debt. Special rules also apply in the case of a mortgage foreclosure. Further, determinations must be made when the value is not readily apparent; e.g., market value associated with a long-term (50 years+) lease or the contribution of land to the capital structure of a corporation in exchange for shares. Expert advice is required.

Tax Calculation

Currently, the land transfer tax in Ontario is as follows:

0.5%	on the first $55,000
1.0%	on portion between $55,000–$250,000
1.5%	on balance over $250,000.

If the land falls under the definition of single-family and duplex residences, an additional tax of 0.5% applies to consideration over $400,000.

EXAMPLE ***Land Transfer Tax***

A single-family home is purchased for $450,000. The following calculation applies:

LAND TRANSFER TAX RATE		EXAMPLE: Sale Price of $450,000	
VALUE ($'s)	TAX RATE	CALCULATION	TAX PAYABLE
0 – 55,000	.005 (0.5%)	$ 55,000 x .005	275
55,000 – 250,000	.01 (1.0%)	195,000 x .010	+1,950
250,000 – 400,000	.015 (1.5)	150,000 x .015	+2,250
400,000+	.015 + .005	50,000 x .020	+1,000
		$450,000	$5,475

- Above $400,000 surcharge applies to single-family and duplex residences only.
- Rebate applies to eligible new homes.
- Real property including beneficial interests (e.g., life lease, life tenure, equity lease or life tenancy) are subject to tax.

First Time Buyers Refund (New Houses)

Effective May 8, 1996, first time purchasers of newly-constructed homes became eligible for a refund of land transfer tax, until March 31, 1997. The deadline was subsequently extended through successive years and, as of the year 2000, was extended indefinitely.

Persons qualifying include individuals 18 years of age or older, who have not owned an interest in a home anywhere in the world and whose spouse (as defined in Section 29 of the *Family Law Act*) has not owned an interest in a home anywhere in the world while he/she was a spouse of the individual. (Home means an eligible home as defined in the *Ontario Home Ownership Savings Plan Act.*)

In order to qualify for a refund, the first time buyer must be purchasing a newly constructed home or an interest therein. A newly constructed home is one which the first time purchaser is entitled to a warranty under Section 13 of the *Ontario New Homes Warranties Plan Act* and which is sold to the first time purchaser by a vendor as defined in that Act. This newly constructed home must be occupied by the buyer as a principal residence within nine months of the conveyance.

If the individual owns less than 100% interest in the newly-built home, the amount will be calculated according to the amount of interest in the home. If the individual owns 100% of the new home and paid $250,000, the amount of land transfer tax payable is $2,225. The buyer will receive a refund based on the limit of $2,000. If however, the buyer owned 50% interest in the home, the amount will be 50% of $2,000.

The refund is not available if the first time purchaser has received an Ontario Home Ownership Savings Plan (OHOSP) based refund of land transfer tax under Section 9 of the *Land Transfer Tax Act* and vice versa. If an individual qualifies for this refund, as well as the OHOSP based refund, the first time buyer must decide which to claim. He or she can claim either but not both.

The applicant can receive a same-day refund of the land transfer tax by filing an affidavit for refund at the land registry office at the time of registration. If the applicant does not apply for a refund at the time of registration, he or she can apply for the refund by contacting the Ministry of Finance.

First Time Buyers Refund (Resale Homes)

The *Land Transfer Tax Act* was amended in late 2007 to include resale homes within the refund program, which was originally established for newly-constructed houses in 1996. Eligible first-time homebuyers of resale homes are now eligible for a refund up to $2,000 for agreements of purchase and sale entered into after December 13, 2007. Procedures and eligibility requirements generally parallel those established under the existing program. A resale home is referred to as an eligible home under the program. An eligible home includes a detached house, semi-detached house, townhouse, shares in a co-operative corporation, a mobile home meeting certain standards, a condominium unit, a residential dwelling that is a duplex, triplex or fourplex and a partial ownership interest as a tenant in common (subject to certain stipulations).

WEB LINKS

Provincial Land Transfer Tax First Time Buyers Refund For up-to-date information about this refund program including bulletins published by the Ministry of Revenue, go to ***www.rev.gov.on.ca.***

Harmonized Sales Tax For the very latest information on harmonized sales tax, go to ***www.rev.gov.on.ca*** and look up *Taxes and Charges* or go to ***www.cra-arc.gc.ca*** and look up *Goods and Services Tax/Harmonized Sales Tax (GST/HST)* under *Business* in the site map.

MUNICIPAL LAND TRANSFER TAX (TORONTO)

The Municipal Land Transfer Tax (MLTT) is charged on properties purchased in Toronto and on the disposition of all beneficial interests effective on closing dates on or after February 1, 2008. As with provincial land transfer tax, the MLTT is typically collected at time of registration. The tax payable is based on the following rates:

For property containing at least one, and not more than two, single family residences:

VALUE OF CONSIDERATION	MLTT RATE
Up to and including $55,000	0.5%
Over $55,000 to $400,000	1.0%
Over $400,000	2.0%

For all other property:

VALUE OF CONSIDERATION	MLTT RATE
Up to and including $55,000	0.5%
Over $55,000 to $400,000	1.0%
Over $400,000 to $40,000,000	1.5%
Over $40,000,000	1.0%

EXAMPLE *Municipal Land Transfer Tax (Toronto)*

The MLTT due and payable on a home with a $500,000 value of consideration is:

MLTT RATE		EXAMPLE: Sale Price of $500,000	
VALUE ($'s)	TAX RATE	CALCULATION	TAX PAYABLE
0 – 55,000	.005 (0.5%)	$ 55,000 x .005	275
55,000 – 400,000	.010 (1.0%)	345,000 x .010	+3,450
400,000 – 500,000	.020 (2.0%)	100,000 x .020	+2,000
		$500,000	$5,725

First time purchasers of newly constructed or resale residential property with two or less single-family residences are eligible for a rebate up to a maximum of $3,725.00.

WEB LINKS

Municipal Land Transfer Tax For additional details regarding tax calculations and rebates, go to the City of Toronto website at ***www.toronto.ca/taxes/mltt.htm***.

CHAPTER DISCUSSION 

1. CONSUMER REPORTS

Speedy Take-out Pizza is adding another location to their rapidly expanding business. You would like to do a credit check on the company before presenting their Offer to Lease to your client. Are there any requirements with which you must comply under the *Consumer Reporting Act*? Explain.

2. DISCLOSURES

Is it necessary to inform the consumer in every situation when a consumer report is being obtained? Explain.

CHAPTER DISCUSSION

3. PERSONAL INFORMATION

Using examples, explain the difference between credit information and personal information.

4. RENTAL APPLICATIONS

The rental application form that you are using requests the names of previous landlords for reference purposes. Does the *Consumer Reporting Act* apply to this situation? Explain.

CHAPTER DISCUSSION

5. LAND TRANSFER TAX

a. Everyone seems to have their own way of expressing the rate for provincial land transfer tax (and the municipal land transfer tax for Toronto). Set out the rate in the format that is the simplest and most understandable to you.

b. Is the provincial land transfer tax (and municipal land transfer tax for Toronto) something you should discuss with a prospective buyer-customer, and with a prospective buyer-client? Explain.

KNOWLEDGE INTEGRATION

Notables

- The *Consumer Reporting Act* provides that a consumer must be given notice when information concerning credit or personal information is involved.
- Credit information must be differentiated from personal information.
- A credit bureau receives information from lenders and other public sources, and provides credit reports upon request.
- Credit bureaus only compile information relating to credit.
- Provincial land transfer tax, as well as municipal land transfer tax (Toronto) is assessed on real property when property ownership is transferred.
- Seek legal advice on matters concerning provincial land transfer tax and the disposition of unregistered interests and exemptions concerning life leases.
- Provincial land transfer tax and municipal land transfer tax (Toronto) is normally based on the value of the consideration (i.e., sale price). Expert advice is required, as special rules apply concerning such things as disposition of property for natural love and affection.
- First time buyers can qualify for refunds relating to both the provincial land transfer tax and the municipal land transfer tax (Toronto) for new and resale homes.

Web Links

Web links are included for general interest regarding selected chapter topics.

Life Leases	Those contemplating being involved with life leases access ***www.e-laws.gov.on.ca***, go to *Statutes and Associated Regulations* and follow instructions to access Regulations under the *Land Transfer Tax Act*. Expert advice is required on all matters involving land transfer tax and exemptions relating thereto.
Provincial Land Transfer Tax First Time Buyers Refund	For up-to-date information about this refund program including bulletins published by the Ministry of Revenue, go to ***www.rev.gov.on.ca***.
Harmonized Sales Tax	For the very latest information on harmonized sales tax, go to ***www.rev.gov.on.ca*** and look up *Taxes and Charges* or go to ***www.cra-arc.gc.ca*** and look up *Goods and Services Tax/Harmonized Sales Tax (GST/HST)* under *Business* in the site map.
Municipal Land Transfer Tax	For additional details regarding tax calculations and rebates, go to the City of Toronto website at ***www.toronto.ca/taxes/mltt.htm***.

Chapter Mini-Review

Solutions are located in the Appendix.

1. The *Consumer Reporting Act* applies when obtaining financial information on a business operation.

   ○ True ○ False

2. You can obtain a consumer report to get information about your new neighbour.

   ○ True ○ False

3. If you deny a consumer a benefit because of information obtained in a credit report, you must give the consumer the name and address of the consumer reporting agency within 60 days of your refusal.

   ○ True ○ False

4. Credit bureaus compile various information about individuals beyond matters relating to credit, such as personal and political affiliations.

   ○ True ○ False

5. Consumers have the right to verify credit information being held on file.

   ○ True ○ False

6. Certain types of transfers attract a *nil* land transfer tax rate.

   ○ True ○ False

7. If a home located in Southwestern Ontario has a selling price of $325,000. The land transfer tax on this conveyance would be $3,350.

   ○ True ○ False

8. If the provincial land transfer tax paid is $4,500, the refund to the qualified first time buyer purchasing that home would be $2,250.

   ○ True ○ False

9. The municipal land transfer tax payable on a Toronto home selling for $380,000 would be $3,525.

   ○ True ○ False

10. The total land transfer tax payable on a Toronto home selling for $400,000 would be $7,100.

    ○ True ○ False

Active Learning Exercises

Solutions are located in the Appendix.

Exercise 1

What do you feel is the overall purpose of the *Consumer Reporting Act*?

Exercise 2

An application from a consumer is rejected due to information obtained in a consumer report. What protections are included in the *Consumer Reporting Act* to assist the consumer in dealing with this situation? Explain.

Exercise 3

a. You are acting for a prudent and cautious seller who is considering accepting an offer that contains a clause requiring the seller to take back a second mortgage. Describe in detail how you would handle this situation.

b. The buyer has a history of financial problems and the seller for a property you have listed increases the rate of interest on the second mortgage after receiving an unfavourable credit report. What is your responsibility to the buyer? Explain.

Exercise 4

In which of the following circumstances would a consumer have to be notified that a consumer report is being used?

a. When an employer is running a credit information report on a potential employee.
b. When a landlord is running a credit information report on a potential tenant.
c. When a lender is running a credit information report on a potential borrower.
d. All of the above.
e. None of the above.

Exercise 5

May is very excited about purchasing her first home. Her offer on a renovated detached 3 storey, 120 year old Victorian home currently being used as a legal duplex has been accepted. May paid $395,000 for the property. May knows that there will be significant closing costs including land transfer tax.

a. Is there any good news for May with respect to the land transfer tax she will have to pay?

b. Based on the above information, how much land transfer tax will May actually end up paying?

c. A year after closing the transaction on the duplex, May purchases a vacant cottage lot for $45,000. How much land transfer tax will May pay for the lot purchase?

Exercise 6

Calculate the provincial land transfer tax on a commercial property that sold for $2,565,000.

Exercise 7

Calculate the provincial land transfer tax on:

a. A parcel of vacant land selling for $385,000.

b. A parcel of vacant land selling for $850,000.

c. A single family home selling for $850,000.

CHAPTER 10

Income Tax Act (Canada) and the Expropriations Act

Introduction

A provision of the *Income Tax Act* makes the buyer liable for tax payable by the seller for a real estate transaction. Procedures can be followed to protect the buyer from this eventuality. These procedures, which are outlined in this chapter, are documented for the buyer's benefit in the standard Agreement of Purchase and Sale form. While a real estate practitioner is not directly involved in the application of these procedures, at the very least, the practitioner must be prepared to explain these provisions to the buyer or seller.

On occasion, a registrant may encounter an issue related to the expropriation of real property. Key provisions of the *Expropriations Act* are provided including a discussion of eminent domain, compensation and the role of the expropriating authority.

Learning Outcomes

At the conclusion of this chapter, students will be able to:

- Identify the risks under the *Income Tax Act* (Section 116) for a buyer, when the seller is a non-resident of Canada and is subject to special provisions regarding capital gains tax collection.
- Explain provisions with respect to the seller's income tax in the *Agreement of Purchase and Sale* (OREA Form 100) for the protection of the buyer.
- Discuss capital gains calculations including considerations in determining whether a gain is capital in nature or taxable income.
- Outline criteria in determining whether or not a home qualifies as a principal residence.
- Explain the expropriation process including provisions for the protection of property owners in the *Expropriations Act.*

THE INCOME TAX ACT (CANADA)

The *Income Tax Act*, a complex legislative document, affects a wide range of personal and corporate activities. On a personal basis, the Act sets requirements regarding capital cost allowances, independent contractor activities, allowable travel expenses, personal expenses and promotional activities, etc. Similarly, a host of corporate rules are in place concerning allowable corporate expenses, taxation of corporations and related matters.

In terms of real estate transactions, practitioners require selected knowledge of the Act concerning such items as capital gains on selected properties, capital gain versus business income, definition of principal residence, allowable rental expenses, capital cost allowance and collection of taxes from nonresidents. The Canada Revenue Agency (CRA) is responsible for the administration of this Act.

Disposition of Real Estate

Section 116 of the *Income Tax Act* sets out provisions for the collection of capital gains tax payable by non-resident sellers. The Act establishes a procedure requiring the non-resident seller to remit, in advance of the disposition, a calculated amount in order to obtain a certificate from the Minister of National Revenue, or alternatively to be remitted by the buyer on the seller's behalf within 10 days following sale completion. Essentially, the buyer or non-resident seller must pay a specified percentage of the amount by which the proceeds (or anticipated proceeds in the case of an advance payment) exceed the adjusted cost base of the property.

Practitioners should be aware that the disposition of depreciable property may complicate the situation as recapture is a consideration in establishing the amount to be withheld. The Agreement of Purchase and Sale (OREA Form 100) for example, addresses the issue of non-residency provisions of the *Income Tax Act.*

RESIDENCY: *Buyer shall be credited towards the Purchase Price with the amount, if any, necessary for Buyer to pay to the Minister of National Revenue to satisfy Buyer's liability in respect of tax payable by Seller under the non-residency provisions of the Income Tax Act by reason of this sale. Buyer shall not claim such credit if Seller delivers on completion the prescribed certificate or a statutory declaration that Seller is not then a non-resident of Canada.*

This clause requires that the necessary amount be credited to the buyer by the seller, to satisfy the non-residency provisions of the *Income Tax Act*, unless a certificate from the Minister is provided to the buyer. This carefully worded clause is important, as the buyer is liable under the Act for the tax owed by the non-resident seller.

Expert advice on such matters is strongly encouraged. As an added note, special rules apply to dispositions involving depreciable properties and sale of cottage properties (where the land only was purchased by the non-resident and a structure was subsequently built).

WEB LINKS

Income Tax Act For additional information visit the Canada Revenue Agency website at *www.cra.gc.ca*. Taxation topics are addressed under the appropriate heading.

CAPITAL GAIN

Capital gain refers to the gain from the disposition of capital property, a percentage of which must be added to taxable income on disposition of the asset. This section of the *Income Tax Act* was introduced on December 31, 1971, commonly referred to as valuation day. Capital property includes any item from which a capital gain or loss would be realized and includes depreciable property.

Capital Gain Calculations

A capital gain is a gain on the sale or exchange of capital assets that meets the criteria for a capital gain as set out in the *Income Tax Act*. Two real estate examples are provided. The first details a gain by a corporation (including calculation of taxable gain based on an assumed taxation level) and the second provides the calculation for a gain realized by an individual. Calculations can vary based on the type of property and the circumstances surrounding the investor/owner. Both examples assume that the gain realized meets the criteria for a capital gain.

The $134,926 taxable capital gain in *Example 1* does not constitute tax liability at the point of sale. Consideration must also be given to any recaptured capital cost allowance and unamortized expenses to arrive at a taxable income on sale. The applicable tax rate for the taxpayer is then applied to taxable income to arrive at the tax liability.

EXAMPLE 1

Anycity Investments Inc. acquired a commercial building several years ago and has recently sold the property for $1,329,684. The adjusted cost base was determined to be 1,000,000. The president of the company is estimating both the capital gain and taxable capital gain as follows:

Sale Price	$1,329,684
Adjusted Cost Base	–1,000,000
Cost of Sale	–59,832
Capital Gain Exemption	–0
Capital Gain	**$269,852**
Taxable Capital Gain (50%)	**$134,926**

EXAMPLE 2

In 1969, Mrs. Jones purchased a rental property containing four units at a cost of $38,000. On December 31, 1971, the value was established at $40,000. Throughout the ensuing years, the property was well maintained and produced above average rental income. Before selling it in 20xx, a new furnace was installed at a cost of $7,000. Later in the same year, the property was sold at market value for $500,000. Real estate commissions and other allowable selling expenses amounted to $30,000 with legal fees totalling $2,800. The capital gain calculation is:

Sale Price	$500,000
Adjusted Cost Base (40,000 + 7,000)	–47,000
Cost of Sale	–32,800
Capital Gain Exemption	–0
Capital Gain	**$420,200**

CAPITAL GAIN VS. TAXABLE INCOME

The *Income Tax Act* does not specifically set out whether or not a gain or loss is capital in nature. The taxpayer is responsible for reporting the gain as income or capital gain. This report may then be challenged by the CRA with the onus of proof on the taxpayer.

Over the years, the determination has been made based on a number of factors such as the intention of the taxpayer, relationship to the taxpayer's business, frequency of transactions, length of time held, nature of the transaction and objects of the corporation. Should a debate proceed to the Tax Court of Canada, the Court will consider relevant factors concerning taxpayer conduct before, during and after the period under appeal. Certain factors carry more weight in the process.

What was the taxpayer's intention at the time the property was purchased?

When a property is bought for investment, any resale profit could still be considered taxable as ordinary income if the apparent intent was to resell for a profit at a future date. The Tax Court will consider such things as reasons for the sale, compelling necessity, change in circumstance and external factors.

Relationship to the Taxpayer's Business

The Tax Court will undoubtedly classify profits as taxable under ordinary business income when a taxpayer uses expertise acquired in regular business activity to generate a profit on the purchase/sale of similar or related commodities. The Court also looks at the time and attention the taxpayer spent on the transaction. Real estate transactions of contractors, renovators, brokers (agents), salespeople and appraisers have typically fallen under close scrutiny.

Frequency of Transactions

Canada Revenue Agency will assess how often the taxpayer engages in the sale of capital property. Usually, frequency of such occurrences suggests the carrying on of a business for profit. Assessment as ordinary business income will be the result. However, even an isolated transaction can be so judged, given the right set of circumstances.

Nature of Transaction and Assets

Taxability as income may be indicated if the asset cannot normally be used either personally or for investment purposes. Mortgages are often judged under this test. If a mortgage is purchased at a substantial discount or has a short maturity date, the mortgagee may be viewed as being in a business that realizes profit from the transaction, thus invoking business income as opposed to capital gain.

Objects of the Corporation

The Tax Court will look at the articles of incorporation to determine if a transaction falls under the objects of the corporation, and if it is part of usual business. However, the absence of this provision may not be deemed conclusive by the Court. Proving that a specific sale fell beyond the normal course of affairs of the company is difficult and once again the burden of proof rests with the taxpayer.

SPECIAL NOTE: REAL ESTATE TRANSACTIONS

Profits would likely be taxed as regular business income if a taxpayer buys and sells real estate on a regular basis. However, if the taxpayer can prove that these dispositions were a planned and necessary part of a total investment program, then there may be a case for capital gains treatment of the profit. In the case of farmlands, if the taxpayer purchased or inherited the land and lived on it for a period of time, a disposition of the property will most likely be regarded as a capital gain.

Further, if a sale of real estate is not planned, that is brokerages are not employed, the property is not advertised, no sign or other visible evidence of active marketing is present, then the profit may be, but not always, treated as a capital gain. In some cases the profit from an eventual sale of the property might be deemed as a capital gain where the taxpayer purchased real estate for a third party to whom he/she expected to transfer it without profit, and was then left with the property when the third party backed out of the transaction.

Exemption: Principal Residence

Exemptions to the payment of capital gains have varied throughout the past decades. The major exemption for real estate practitioners to consider involves a principal residence. A principal residence is defined as a house, apartment in a duplex, apartment building or condominium, cottage, houseboat, trailer or mobile home, or a share in a co-operative housing corporation.

To qualify as a principal residence, certain criteria must be met:

- The taxpayer must own the housing unit, either jointly or solely;
- A family unit may only have one principal residence;
- The land upon which the housing unit sits cannot exceed one acre and any excess is not considered part of the principal residence unless the taxpayer can prove it is necessary for personal use and enjoyment;
- The unit must be ordinarily inhabited in the year (*ordinarily inhabited* is not defined in the *Income Tax Act*); and
- The unit must be designated as the taxpayer's principal residence for the year.

Appropriate expert advice should be sought in regard to capital gains issues and exemptions.

Capital Loss

Capital loss is a loss that is incurred from the disposition of capital property. Provisions in the *Income Tax Act* provide for the deduction of capital losses for both individuals and corporations.

EXAMPLE *Capital Loss*

In 1993, Mrs. Williams purchased a rental property containing four units at a cost of $488,000 and a few years later sold the property for $500,000. During the time of ownership, she made no significant improvements to the property. Real estate commissions and other allowable expenses amounted to $30,000 with legal fees totalling $2,800.

The capital loss calculation is as follows:

Sale Price	$500,000
Adjusted Cost Base	–488,000
Cost of Sale	–32,800
Capital Gain/Loss	**$(20,800)**

THE EXPROPRIATIONS ACT

Expropriation in Ontario means the taking of private property by the state for public use, with fair compensation to the owner, through the exercise of the right of eminent domain. In Ontario, according to the *Expropriations Act*, the legislative definition of expropriation is:

> *. . . the taking of land without the consent of the owner by an expropriating authority in the exercise of its statutory powers . . . (Expropriations Act, R.S.O. 1990, as amended, Sec. 1.).*

Eminent Domain

Eminent domain is the right of a government or municipal quasi-public body to acquire private property for public use. Eminent domain is acquired through a legal action called condemnation or expropriation in which the appropriate body determines the use is a public use and decides the price or compensation to be paid to the owner.

The expropriating authority is the Crown or any other agency empowered by provincial legislation, namely an expropriation act. Legislation typically sets out procedures for application to expropriate, appropriate hearings and methods of compensation.

EXAMPLE *Eminent Domain*

Smith's property is situated directly in the path of a new transportation route that will include highway and rail facilities, along with open space buffer zones, given rapid population expansion within the immediate area. The provincial government is acquiring property for this public use.

Accordingly, Smith's property falls under eminent domain and through condemnation is taken over by the government body. Smith is compensated based on prevailing market values within the immediate area.

Compensation

There are provisions for compensation to the owner and approval for the expropriation must be given by an "*approval authority.*" An owner who objects to the expropriation proposal can require a hearing. If the expropriation is approved, there are specific procedures to be followed to determine the compensation to be paid to the owner. The basis for the compensation is market value, with the possibility of additional payment for damages, disturbance, relocation difficulties and expenses. If an owner's rights are interfered with or reduced, the owner may be entitled to compensation for injurious affection.

As a form of appeal, the Ontario Municipal Board may be asked to determine the amount of compensation through an arbitration procedure.

Expropriating Authority

An expropriating authority is the Crown or any person empowered by statute to expropriate land, as defined in the Act. The *Ontario Expropriations Act* sets out procedures concerning the expropriation of lands within the province. This Act does not give the power to expropriate, as that power is found in the relevant statute. However, the Act makes the expropriation activity public by requiring the expropriating authority to obtain confirmation of the approving authority. Following the notice served by the expropriating authority, the owner may request a hearing (unless overridden by the Lieutenant Governor in Council). The Act then details the use of inquiry officers and the powers and duties of the approving authority (the appropriate Ministry).

If the expropriation is approved, the registration of a plan concerning the lands in question is then possible. The Act also sets out compensation methods involving special considerations; e.g., losses incurred by tenants, business loss, prepayment of a mortgage, injurious affection when the owner's rights are prejudiced or reduced in some way and special costs. Appeal procedures are also detailed, as well as the ability to issue a warrant concerning resistance to entry. A federal Act concerning expropriations exists that can affect land in Ontario, but such matters go beyond the scope of this text.

Real Estate practitioners are rarely involved in expropriation matters. However, an example is provided for illustration purposes outlining a fictitious scenario in which a government agency requires additional land from an adjacent owner.

EXAMPLE *Expropriation*

A government agency, adjacent to Smith's property, wishes to expropriate a small section of Smith's rear yard along with the land of adjoining neighbours to provide expanded area and buffer zones for a new, badly needed, building addition. The expropriation process is detailed below.

Application

- The expropriating authority serves a notice of application on each registered owner, including Smith.
- The notice is made by registered mail or personal delivery, or three consecutive publications of notice in local newspaper.
- Each property owner must be served, including all joint tenants.

Hearing

- If Smith wants a hearing, he must notify the expropriating authority within 30 days.
- The inquiry officer sets a time and place for a hearing and notifies the parties.
- The expropriating authority makes documents, plans and other relevant items available prior to the hearing.
- The hearing is held and the inquiry officer determines if the expropriation is fair, reasonable and sound in achieving objectives of the expropriating authority.
- The hearing report and opinion are filed with the approving authority.
- The inquiry officer must consider whether the taking of this specific land is reasonably defensible and not whether the expropriating authority's policy decision to expropriate is fair.
- The approving authority considers the report but is not bound by it, approves or does not approve the report, and subsequently delivers a decision including reasons within 90 days of the inquiry officer's report to Smith and other neighbouring residents affected.

Expropriation Plan

- Within three months of approval, a survey plan is registered against the lands by the expropriating authority.
- The expropriating authority becomes the owner by statutory vesting.

Compensation

- The expropriating authority attempts to come to an agreement with the owner(s) concerning compensation.
- If no agreement, the authority serves a notice of expropriation within 30 days of the registration of the expropriation plan.
- Compensation is assessed as of the date of plan registration unless Smith serves notice, within 30 days of receiving the notice of expropriation, and wants the value determined as of the notice of hearing or upon the service of the notice of expropriation. Given market volatility, Smith's choice can directly impact value.

Value of Expropriated Land

In expropriation, the common law market value approach applies; e.g., willing buyer and willing seller not under undue pressure.

Damages

Damages can be awarded under one or more of the following categories.

Disturbance

- Potential for claim owing to disturbance; e.g., business losses, cost of relocation, loss of profit or rent, loss of trees, loss of parking spaces, depreciation, loss through a forced sale of trade fixtures or other losses that can be proven.
- Usual to add five percent to the market value for damages;
- Value of other items; e.g., loss of personal amenities, relocation costs, legal/survey costs, business losses and goodwill may be considered.

Injurious Affection

- Claims such as loss of access to other land, road or dock retained by owner, loss of landscaping and parking areas, delay of construction, denial of access to business premises, damage to crops, dirt and noise from construction, and relocation of a creek bed or erosion caused by alterations by expropriating authority, less an added value contributed by those alterations.

Relocation Difficulties

- Claims for special problems facing the owner in relocation; e.g., additional costs of construction resulting from more stringent building codes or expenses incurred in complying with current zoning laws, and compensation to find a residence of equivalent accommodation to that expropriated.
- Special circumstances concerning financing; i.e., difference in interest rate as a result of relocation.

Payment to Others

- Tenant may be entitled to part of the disturbance cost.

Payment

- Payment made if no disagreement.
- If no settlement on compensation, authority serves notice within three months of registration of the survey plan.
- Notice includes amount offered for compensation and copy of the appraisal report.

Negotiations and Arbitration

- If unable to agree, either may serve notice of negotiations on the other.
- Board of negotiation meets with the parties to resolve.
- If not resolved or negotiations waived, parties can proceed to arbitration by service of a notice of arbitration.
- Appeal can be made to the Court of Appeal and from there to the Supreme Court of Canada.

Possession

- If no agreement on possession, the authority serves the owner with a notice of planned possession of at least three months in the future.
- A judge may adjust the date based on special circumstances; e.g., removing crops.

If the authority decides that the expropriated land is not necessary for its purposes and has not paid the owner, the authority can advise the owner of that fact. The owner then has the option of taking the property back or requiring the authority to pay for it. If expropriation is completed and monies paid and the authority wishes to sell, the owner may have a first right of refusal on the terms of the best offer received by the authority.

Jason Brooks
Guest Column

From the Financial Post August 26, 1998.
Reprinted with permission of the Financial Post and Jason Brooks.

A Tale Of Two Cities And How They Use Expropriation Law

John Mikrogianakis cannot understand why the government is doing this to him. He has spent 15 years building his Harvey's franchise in downtown Toronto. He owns the restaurant and the building. Now, the city of Toronto is taking it away from him and giving it to another private owner to build stores and a movie theatre.

"It's unfair," he says. "It's terrible, but that's the way it is."

Canadian laws give little protection to property rights. The shortcomings are clear when Mikrogianakis's case is compared to a recent similar case in the U.S.

Last month, in Atlantic City, N.J., a court decided entrepreneur Donald Trump and a state agency cannot take an elderly widow's house and turn it into limousine parking for the Trump Plaza. Just a week later, a panel of judges in Toronto decided the city of Toronto can take land from six property owners, including Mikrogianakis, and give it to a private company for redevelopment. Similar cases. Vastly different results.

When most people think about land expropriation, they think of highways, canals or hospitals. That's what Vera Coking in Atlantic City thought. That's what Mikrogianakis and others in Toronto thought. But in both cases, governments moved to seize property to hand it to other private owners for commercial use.

A U.S. judge relied on federal and state constitutions to tell Trump, '*no dice*'

In Atlantic City, Coking's problem began in 1994. Her home, where she has lived for 37 years, is next to Trump's casino. Trump wanted to raze her house for parking, so he turned to the New Jersey Casino Reinvestment & Development Authority, a state agency set up to help casino owners confiscate property. Trump picked out the property, and the Casino Authority moved to expropriate it. Its rationale: since casinos bring prosperity, transferring land to them is a public good.

The situation in Toronto is similar. A year and a half ago, property owners in downtown Toronto received notices resembling the one Coking got. The city wants 12 properties at the corner of Yonge and Dundas streets—a popular tourist area next to the Eaton Centre.

The plan is to resell six lots to PenEquity, a developer. Buildings will be torn down and an "urban entertainment centre" built, with retail stores, restaurants and Godzilla-sized movie theatres.

The city says the scheme will reinvigorate the downtown, therefore meeting the "public good" requirement for expropriation. It is relying on a provision of the law called "community improvement," which lets authorities expropriate because of age, dilapidation, or "any other reason."

The popular businesses at Yonge and Dundas fall into the "any other reason" category. Mikrogianakis's Harvey's isn't urban blight; nor are the other businesses being expropriated, such as KFC and Lick's.

Owners feel the prices they may be forced to accept are too low, though they will have the opportunity to seek higher prices through mediation or by going to the Ontario Municipal Board.

Mikrogianakis says the city offered him 50% of the value of his property.

"For the right price, everything's for sale," he says. "But they didn't offer a fair price."

Shoppers and moviegoers may rejoice at the entertainment complex, scheduled to be built next year, but the city's unusual use of expropriation law sets a terrifying precedent. If Toronto can take property from these people, what protects any of us from having our properties taken? Very little.

In Canada, property rights are not protected by the Constitution. That's why this property redistribution plan has met little resistance from provincial and local governments—and why the expropriation was upheld in Divisional Court in late July.

Which brings us back to Atlantic City, where the story has a happier ending. A judge on the New Jersey Superior Court was able to rely on both federal and state constitutions when he told Trump: no dice. The Fifth Amendment of the U.S. Constitution states private property can't "be taken for public use without just compensation," and most state constitutions, including New Jersey's, go even further to protect private property. The New Jersey judge decided the gains in handing Coking's house to Trump would have been "primarily private," therefore not meeting the criteria for expropriation.

It's time Canada and Ontario adopted similar protections of private property. Until then, owning property in Ontario is a crapshoot.

Jason Brooks is a fourth-year journalism and history student at Carleton University and a Koch summer fellow working at Reason magazine in Washington D.C.

CHAPTER DISCUSSION

1. CAPITAL GAINS

Build a list of factors that may be looked at in determining whether an individual has realized a capital gain or has earned business income.

2. BUYER LIABILITY

"*I am not paying legal fees. I am going to bring my certified cheque to the seller's lawyer and pick up the deed (and then put it in the freezer). There is nothing complicated about a real estate purchase.*" Comment.

CHAPTER DISCUSSION

3. THE AGREEMENT OF PURCHASE AND SALE

Within the pre-printed portion of the standard OREA Agreement of Purchase and Sale form, there are three alternatives for the buyer to be protected from having to pay income tax owed by the seller as a result of the sale. Explain the three alternatives.

4. EXPROPRIATION

Do you feel there is a fair balance within the *Expropriations Act* between the rights of the public-at-large and the rights of private property owners? Discuss.

CHAPTER DISCUSSION 

5. COMPENSATION

a. List the various forms of compensation available under the *Expropriations Act.*

b. Your city has decided to build an overpass for a railway in your neighbourhood. Unfortunately, the view from your living room in the future will be a concrete wall, you will no longer have access to the street from your driveway, and the noise and vibration from the trains will be significant. The project will not require the expropriation of any of your property. Can you expect any compensation? Explain.

KNOWLEDGE INTEGRATION

Notables

- Section 116 of the *Income Tax Act* provides that a non-resident seller must pay a specified percentage of the amount by which the sale proceeds exceed the adjusted cost base for the property.
- The buyer can be ultimately liable for tax remaining unpaid by a non-resident seller, if such amount is not credited to the buyer.
- The seller, as an option to crediting the amount payable, may provide an appropriate certificate from the Minister upon payment of the required amount.
- A capital gain is a gain on the sale or exchange of capital assets.
- The determination of whether or not a gain or loss is capital in nature involves various considerations, most notably the taxpayer's intention, relationship to the taxpayer's business and frequency of transactions.
- Various criteria must be met in order for a property to qualify as a principal residence and be exempt from the payment of capital gain.
- Eminent domain refers to the government right to acquire private property for public use.
- Compensation provisions for expropriation are based on market value for the expropriated property.
- Expropriation procedures are complex and expert advice is required on such matters.

Web Links

Web links are included for general interest regarding selected chapter topics.

Income Tax Act	For additional information visit the Canada Revenue Agency website at ***www.cra.gc.ca***. Taxation topics are addressed under the appropriate heading.

Chapter Mini-Review

Solutions are located in the Appendix.

1. Provisions of the *Income Tax Act* provide that a buyer of a property may be held responsible for paying income tax owed by a non-resident seller.

   ○ True ○ False

2. The non-resident seller may pay the applicable amount relating to the capital gain directly to the Minister of National Revenue.

   ○ True ○ False

3. The taxpayer's intention at time of purchase is irrelevant to the Tax Court in determining whether a gain is capital in nature or taxable income.

   ○ True ○ False

4. For purposes of qualifying as a principal residence, a family unit may only have one principal residence, which must be ordinarily inhabited in the year.

   ○ True ○ False

Chapter Mini-Review (continued)

5. A capital loss occurs when the sale price exceeds the adjusted cost base plus the cost of sale expenses.

   ○ True ○ False

6. The *Expropriations Act* is a federal statute, which enables an expropriating authority to terminate the rights of property owners in Ontario.

   ○ True ○ False

7. The government's right to expropriate can override the rights of property owners in Ontario.

   ○ True ○ False

8. An owner who has been served a Notice of Expropriation has the right to a hearing under the *Expropriations Act.*

   ○ True ○ False

Active Learning Exercises

Solutions are located in the Appendix.

Exercise 1

"*I am a real estate salesperson. I am not qualified to advise on income tax matters so I need not concern myself about it or even discuss it. Those are matters for the client and the client's tax advisor.*" Debate.

Exercise 2

In a normal real estate transaction in Ontario, who is responsible to pay any income tax on a sale when the seller is a resident of Canada? What if the seller is not a resident of Canada?

Exercise 3

A buyer buying real estate should make reasonable inquiries to determine the residency of the seller. How should that be done?

Exercise 4

The seller is shown in the Agreement of Purchase and Sale to be living in Florida. The offer is accepted by fax from Florida for a sale price of $200,000. The deal closes with no income tax paid by the seller.

a. If the seller is a non-resident, what affect does this have on the buyer?

b. What should the buyer have done to protect himself?

Exercise 5

You have acted as a sales representative for the sellers of a property in Ontario. Before the transaction closes, while talking to them on the telephone, they inform you that they are non-residents, a status which had not been declared to either their lawyer or the Income Tax authorities.

a. What do you do?

b. The sellers wish to avoid additional legal expenses and want to take care of the matter personally. They request your specific advice to be outlined in a short letter. How would you respond to their request?

Exercise 6

"*Our city council decides in a closed meeting that they are going to expropriate my home. I can have a hearing before an inquiry officer who will file a report. Whatever is said, they are going to take my home anyway. The whole thing is a waste of time.*" Discuss.

Exercise 7

The definition of market value in the case of expropriation should take into account that this owner does not want the land to be expropriated, does not agree that there should be a highway or airport in the area, and does not want a change in lifestyle. Discuss.

Exercise 8

Owners who have been served with a Notice of Expropriation have already made an offer on another property and are looking forward to moving. The Expropriating Authority then notifies them that it is no longer necessary to expropriate their existing home. What can they do? Explain.

SECTION V

SHARED OWNERSHIP AND RESIDENTIAL TENANCY

Chapter 11 outlines fundamentals of condominium ownership including highlighted provisions from the *Condominium Act.* Information regarding co-operatives and timesharing projects are also included, although these are not encountered as frequently by real estate practitioners.

Shared ownership requires specialized knowledge both when marketing such properties and drafting agreements. Most real estate practitioners become involved in the listing and marketing of condominium units and must be familiar with their unique characteristics.

Chapter 12 addresses residential tenancies. The relationship between landlord and tenant is examined, along with various statutory provisions set out in the *Residential Tenancies Act.* Registrants must be knowledgeable concerning basic regulatory requirements, as residential rentals are subject to various rules that directly affect day-to-day broker and salesperson access to rental units for showings. Particular emphasis is placed on rent regulations, notice required when an owner wants to take possession of a rental unit and other termination provisions.

CHAPTER 11

Shared Ownership

Introduction

Shared ownership spans many different types of ownership options that have appeared in the marketplace to address changing needs, particularly in large urban centres. Condominiums now represent a significant portion of all property within Ontario and fundamentals of how condominiums are created, managed and marketed is essential for registrants.

Emphasis is placed on provisions in the *Condominium Act* that impact the sale or lease of condominium units. Registrants need to be aware of such key topics such as the legal structure of condominiums including the declaration and description, the delineation of common elements vs. units, types of condominiums, disclosure requirements for new units, leasing provisions, reserve funds, status certificates, termination procedures and common use restrictions.

Co-operatives are discussed in terms of a unique agreement of purchase and sale that must be used, along with challenges regarding financing and background information concerning the *Co-operative Corporations Act*. Lastly, time share is addressed highlighting fee ownership vs. right to use interests.

Learning Outcomes

At the conclusion of this chapter, students will be able to:

- Outline the legal structure of a condominium established by way of a declaration and description.
- Differentiate between common elements and units, and calculate common expenses relating to those common elements.
- Identify and discuss different types of condominiums available in the Ontario marketplace.
- Identify various provisions in the *Condominium Act* relating to leasing and sale of units.
- Discuss information contained in a status certificate and the role of reserve funds in condominiums.
- Differentiate between equity and non-profit co-operatives and detail financing challenges associated with this form of ownership.
- Briefly discuss timeshare arrangements and differentiate between fee ownership and right-to-use interests.

OVERVIEW

Statutory provisions have been enacted to deal with some shared ownership concepts. These concepts include condominium, timesharing and co-operative housing.

The concept of condominium is an ancient device to permit separate ownership of individual parts of a property and shared ownership of common areas. In Ontario, condominium ownership was created by statute. The owner in fee simple creates a condominium by registering documents called a Declaration and Description. Upon registration of these documents, a corporation, without share capital, is formed. The objects and duties of the corporation are to manage the property and administer the common elements and corporate assets. The corporation is financed by common expenses paid by the unit owners.

The revised *Condominium Act (1998)* uses the term Status Certificate, rather than Estoppel Certificate. The legislation also provides for the creation of four new types of condominium corporations; common elements, phased, vacant land and leasehold.

Timesharing is a variation of the condominium concept in which a condominium is registered with all the normal provisions for units, but with an additional provision for a buyer's interest in the unit and common elements to be restricted to a particular time period.

With a co-operative, there is a corporation formed to own the real property. Buyers buy shares of the company and acquire rights to occupancy through a tenancy agreement with the corporation.

CONDOMINIUM

Condominium involves the freehold or leasehold ownership of a specified amount of space (the unit) in a multiple dwelling environment with tenancy in common ownership of the portions used jointly with other owners (the common elements). A condominium enables a person or other entity to share in the ownership and operation of a residential or commercial complex, while having negotiable title to an individual unit.

Condominium is not a new concept. The term condominium originated in Roman law referring to joint dominion or co-ownership. This form of ownership was introduced in Ontario approximately 40 years ago.

Provincial Legislation

The original *Condominium Act* in Ontario dates from 1967 and received only minor changes over three decades, despite well-documented shortcomings and deficiencies identified by successive governments. During the 1990s attempts were made to revise the legislation, but it was not until 2001 when a new statute came into existence.

This new Act introduced significant modification and additions that impacted developers, owners, managers, unit owners and other stakeholders including real estate practitioners. The *Condominium Act, 1998* was proclaimed on May 5, 2001, along with associated regulations; i.e., *Regulation 48/01* and *Regulation 49/01.*

The *Condominium Act, 1998*, a substantial document containing 189 sections, represents a compilation of proven procedures and concepts from previous legislation, combined with new and innovative approaches to the expanding world of condominium ownership.

For real estate practitioners, the most significant changes involved heightened consumer protection through increased disclosure requirements for new and resale condominium units. Further, the new Act introduced new condominium types to the marketplace; i.e., common elements, phased, vacant land and leasehold.

Legal Structure

Condominium legal structure is established through a declaration, aptly referred to as the condominium constitution, and the description (diagrammatic representations including surveys of the land and improvements).

A condominium is created in law when both the declaration and the description are registered. The owner of the land invokes the *Condominium Act* through this registration process. Registered encumbrancers, such as mortgagees and lien holders, must consent in the declaration to the invocation of the Act.

A corporation without share capital is automatically formed upon incorporation in which members are the unit owners. The land registrar for the applicable land registry office gives the corporation a name and sequential number; e.g., Waterloo South Condominium Corporation 986. The objects of the corporation centre on management of the property and corporation assets. These functions are paid for by unit owners through common expenses, in proportions specified in the declaration.

The corporation has a duty to effect unit owner compliance under the Act, the declaration and the by-laws and has the power to own, acquire, encumber and dispose of real and personal property according to the by-laws. The corporation does not provide limited liability. The unit owners are personally liable for all the debts and obligations of the condominium corporation.

THE CONDOMINIUM ACT

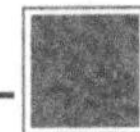

Real estate practitioners involved with new and/or resale condominium units should carefully review both the Act and Regulations, as well as pursue advanced education courses on condominium. Topics included are excerpts (or modifications thereof) from a condominium reference text, reprinted with permission of the author.

Summaries provided are general descriptions only. In particular, topics focus on areas of interest to practising salespersons and brokers. Limited details are included concerning governance matters (e.g., voting procedures, proxies and meeting notice protocols) and administrative concerns (e.g., internal audit procedures). Such topics go beyond the scope of this text, but are valid subjects for those specializing in condominium sales.

Board of Directors

A board of directors, elected pursuant to the Act and by-laws, consists of at least three persons or a greater number as specified in the by-laws. Directors are required to be a minimum age of 18 years and cannot be undischarged bankrupts or mentally incompetent persons.

A director ceases to be a director if either of the two latter events occur, or the individual concerned does not obtain a discharge for a lien (relating to the payment of common expenses) within 90 days of the registration of that lien. Directors are appointed for three years or such lesser period as specified in the by-laws. All business of the corporation is conducted at meetings of the board of directors.

Directors must adhere to a standard of care in their role by acting honestly and in good faith while exercising care, diligence and skill of a reasonable person in carrying out their function. Directors can rely in good faith on financial statements, reports or opinions of relevant experts (e.g., accountants, lawyers or engineers) and not be liable should a breach of duty occur. Directors may be indemnified and saved harmless by the corporation and the corporation may acquire appropriate insurance. However, such protections do not apply if the director acts dishonestly and/or not in good faith.

See **First Board** in this topic concerning the initial board put in place by the declarant. The above description relates to subsequent boards of directors.

By-Laws

Standard rules regarding a condominium's internal operations that involve governance (e.g., establishing procedures for borrowing funds, setting director remuneration and other regulatory matters) are referred to as by-laws.

By-laws are made, amended or repealed by the board of directors and must be consistent with the Act and the declaration. By-laws are not effective unless the owners of the majority of units vote in favour. A copy must be registered in the land registry office. Registered by-laws made by the declarant (i.e., the owner/developer) are valid until replaced.

Common Elements

All property within the condominium corporation except the units are known as the common elements. The clear delineation of units vs. common elements is essential and practitioners must understand the scope of ownership when listing/selling condominiums. Common elements are held by the owners, as tenants in common (undivided interest) in proportions as set out in the declaration. One or more owners may have exclusive use of selected common elements, such as parking spaces and balconies.

A board of directors may make an addition, alteration or improvement to the common elements without owner approval unless the owners requisition a meeting and vote against the proposed work. Additions, alterations and improvements of a substantial nature require approval of the owners who own 66% of the units. Owners may make additions, alterations and improvements to the common elements (e.g., installing a patio area or fence on an exclusive use common area) but are subject to board approval, a formal agreement and other criteria set out in the Act.

Common Expenses

Common expenses are those costs relating to the performance of the objects and duties of the corporation, including all expenses specified as common expenses in the Act or in a declaration.

The payment of common expenses and the amount of such expenses is an important consideration when purchasing a condominium. Owners contribute common expenses in proportions outlined in the declaration. Any default can result in a lien against the owner's unit (including legal costs and other expenses) which can be enforced in the same manner as a mortgage. No owner is exempt from this requirement, even if he/she has waived or abandoned the right to use the common elements, is making a claim against the corporation or is restricted from using such common elements.

The right to register a lien for common expense arrears, previously limited to residential condominiums in prior legislation, now includes non-residential condominiums.

EXAMPLE *Condominium Act: Common Expenses*

Owner James purchases a resale condominium unit in a 230-suite complex. The corporation has just finalized budget estimates for the upcoming year and established a total budget of $2,137,216. James' unit represents 0.3467% (.003467) of the total area of all units. Accordingly, James will be responsible to pay the following:

$2,137,216 x .003467 = $7,409.73 annually or $617.48 per month

If James' 3-bedroom unit consisted of 1,850 square feet, his common expenses (commonly quoted by real estate practitioners on a per square foot basis) would be $0.33 per square foot ($617.48 ÷ 1,850). Condominium common expenses can range significantly based on amenities offered.

Note: If James held title to a parking space (as opposed to having the exclusive right to occupy that parking space; i.e., an exclusive use common element), the proportionate share of the parking space would also be calculated. Assume that the parking space accounted for 0.0231% (.000231), then the added cost would be:

$2,137,216 x .000231 = $493.70 (annually) or $41.14 per month

Condominium Corporation

A condominium corporation is a corporation without share capital formed coincident with the registration of a declaration and description of a condominium.

A condominium corporation is unique in that it does not fall under the *Corporations Act*, but is subject to regulations under the *Condominium Act*. Owners share assets of the corporation in the same proportion as their interests in the common elements.

The corporation is managed by a board of directors consisting of at least three members. Primary objectives include the control, management and administration of the common elements and assets of the corporation, along with the compliance of owners, occupiers and lessees. The corporation is governed by five documents: objects, declaration, by-laws, rules and statutory provisions of the *Condominium Act*.

Condominium Corporations–Types

COMMON ELEMENT

This type of condominium corporation consists only of common interests held by owners in those common elements, but having no units. All references to unit or proposed unit in the Act are deemed to be references to a common interest in the corporation.

The common elements condominium corporation represents a significant advance in condominium legislation. Such corporations must be freehold, and not a vacant land or a phased condominium. Each owner of an interest in the common elements must own a freehold parcel of land to which their common interest attaches.

Upon registration of the declaration and description, the common interest of an owner attaches to that owner's parcel of land (e.g., a home located nearby) and remains attached even if that home is subsequently sold. A golf course, ski hill, park or road might be a *common elements condominium* in which owners are required to pay for maintenance, repair and modifications.

Common element condominiums represent a new concept in the Ontario marketplace. Detailed procedures, requirements and remedies for common element condominiums including important variations from other types of condominium go beyond the scope of this descriptive text.

LEASEHOLD

This form of condominium is a corporation in which all units and their appurtenant common interests are subject to leasehold interests by the owners. All leasehold interests in units, along with common interests, must be for the same term.

A leasehold interest in land can be divided into units and common elements and, subject to registration of a declaration and description, be described as a leasehold condominium. Each leasehold interest and its appurtenant common interest is valid even if the lessor is the owner of that interest. Leasehold interests and appurtenant common interests are for the same term. Leasehold terms cannot be less than 40 years (less a day) nor more than 99 years. Owners of units do not require consent to transfer, mortgage, lease or otherwise deal with their interest.

PHASED

A phased condominium corporation operates as a freehold corporation in which the declarant may create additional units or common elements within the corporation. The term phase refers to additional units and common elements that are created in accordance with the Act upon the registration of an amendment to both the original declaration and the description.

The phased condominium provides flexibility for declarants in the development process by permitting the registration of an initial development as a condominium and then being permitted to bring in successive units/common elements under that single condominium corporation. Under the previous Act, declarants involved with large developments had to register individual condominium corporations when involved with large projects involving several buildings and/or phases.

The ability to bring successive units/common elements under a single corporation produces economy of scale; e.g., avoids the need for several boards of directors within a larger development. Further, the grouping of several phases offers bulk buying advantages when purchasing services (e.g., utilities).

VACANT LAND

A vacant land condominium provides for the development and sale of units (i.e., land) without the necessity of immediately completing structures. Developers can market condominium ownership, complete services and related infrastructure, sell land to buyers subject to building requirements and register the condominium corporation—all prior to any construction occurring on individual land units.

Titles are transferred to buyers with homes and/or other structures to be built later. The declaration contains restrictions concerning future construction; e.g., building size, design, standards and commencement/ completion time frames. Ownership interests are based on land size. The unit owner must provide insurance for buildings and structures on the unit. By-laws can be passed regarding minimum maintenance requirements for units.

The declarant must build any buildings and structures on common elements prior to registration or provide a bond or other acceptable security for subsequent construction. The security is released once all buildings, structures, facilities and services are completed and approved.

STANDARD

A standard condominium is a freehold condominium that is not a common element or a vacant land condominium. Condominium corporations created prior to the new *Condominium Act* coming into force are classified as standard condominiums.

Declaration

The constitution of the condominium that effectively creates the condominium and sets out the responsibilities of the owners and the corporation.

The declaration, along with the description, is required for registration of a condominium corporation. The Act outlines both required and optional items. If any item in the declaration is inconsistent with the Act, the provisions of the Act prevail.

Declaration content varies according to condominium type; e.g., standard, phased, vacant land, common element and leasehold. Selected items are listed below.

- Statement that the *Condominium Act* governs the land and appurtenant interests.
- Consent of mortgagees.
- Proportionate interest of each unit in the common elements.
- Proportionate interest of each unit in allocating contribution to common expenses.
- Address for service, municipal address and mailing address (if different from service and/or municipal addresses).
- Parts of common elements used by one or more designated units and not by all owners.
- Common expenses of the condominium corporation.
- Conditions or restrictions concerning occupation or use of units and/or common elements.
- Responsibilities of the condominium corporation consistent with its objects and duties.
- Allocation of obligations to maintain units and common elements, including repairs after damage, in accordance with the Act.

Description

A diagrammatic presentation of the property and any structures within the condominium corporation. More specifically, this includes such items as the plan of survey, architectural plans, structural plans, boundaries of each unit, diagrams showing the shape and dimensions of each unit (in relation to other units), a surveyor's certificate and a description of any interests appurtenant to the land that are included with the property.

Disclosure Requirements—New Units

Stipulations are set out in the Act involving forthright disclosure concerning the purchase of a unit or proposed unit from a declarant. Every person who purchases a unit or proposed unit from a declarant must receive a copy of the current disclosure statement. Required contents for a disclosure statement are set out in the Act.

The buyer has certain rights associated with the delivery of disclosure documents. The buyer may rescind an agreement of purchase and sale and receive a refund of all monies given (including interest) if rescission is made by the purchaser within 10 days of receiving a disclosure statement, or receiving a copy of the agreement of purchase and sale executed by the declarant and the purchaser, whichever is the later.

If a material change occurs in a disclosure statement, a revised disclosure statement must be delivered to the purchaser within a reasonable time. Similarly, in the case of a material change, the buyer has certain rights regarding recission of the agreement of purchase and sale.

First Board

The board of directors, required within 10 days following registration, is appointed by the declarant. The first board consists of at least three persons, who hold office until the turn-over meeting. The first board must call a meeting before the later of:

- the 30th day after the declarant transfers 20% of the units; or
- the 90th day after the first unit is transferred.

At this meeting, the owners may elect two directors who hold office, in addition to those appointed by the declarant.

The first board must call a turn-over meeting to elect a new board not more than 21 days following the time when the declarant ceases to be the registered owner of the majority of units.

Interim Occupancy

Interim occupancy involves a circumstance in which a purchaser occupies a proposed unit prior to receiving a deed in registrable form.

Practitioners will encounter interim occupants in new condominium projects. A buyer has the right to pay any unpaid balance of the purchase price on assuming interim occupancy. The buyer can either elect to do so by paying such unpaid balance at the time the agreement is signed or within the time period statutorily permitted for rescinding the agreement; i.e., 10 days following the latter of receiving the duly executed agreement of purchase and sale or the disclosure statement.

A monthly occupancy fee is payable by the interim occupant and includes:

- monthly interest on any unpaid balance of the purchase price at the prescribed rate (as set out in Regulation 48/01);
- reasonable monthly estimate of municipal taxes; and
- the projected monthly common expense contribution.

If the purchaser is charged a monthly occupancy fee for more than six months, the reserve fund component of that fee following the six-month period must be held in trust by the declarant and remitted to the corporation upon registration of the declaration and description.

Lease of Units

Owners of leased units are required to notify the condominium corporation within 30 days of leasing or renewal of a lease and provide details regarding the lessee's name and the owner's name, along with a copy of the lease.

Practitioners should be aware that a prescribed form (Form 5, Regulation 49/01) is provided for this purpose. The owner must furnish the lessee with a copy of the declaration, by-laws and rules of the corporation.

The owner must also notify the corporation of lease termination, if not renewed. The corporation is required to maintain a record of all notices received. Practitioners should note that the term *lease*, for purposes of the *Condominium Act*, includes a sublease or assignment of lease.

Parking

The initial disclosure statement for new condominiums details whether or not parking is allowed in or on a unit, on the common elements or on an exclusive area within those common elements, along with any restrictions. Further, the disclosure must set out whether visitor parking is available, what costs, if any, apply and, if no visitor parking is available, what other facilities exist and where.

Practitioners most frequently encounter parking issues in resale units. Buyers need to carefully review all documentation provided with the status certificate to determine which type of parking is provided and what parking spaces, if any, are included with the unit. Also, restrictions may apply regarding the parking of recreational vehicles, commercial vehicles, small utility trailers and boats. Ceiling clearances may be a factor as well in underground garages, depending on the size of vehicle(s) driven.

Parking spaces can generally be grouped under the following four types.

Freehold	The unit owner owns the parking space, either within the unit description or separately titled. If the latter, the unit owner is typically permitted to sell the space(s) to another owner in the complex at fair market value, however, restrictions regarding such matters should be fully investigated.
Leasehold	The condominium corporation retains parking spaces and leases them to unit owners.
Exclusive Use Common Element	The condominium corporation owns the parking spaces, but grants the rights to use specific spaces as set out in the declaration.
Allocated/Assigned	The condominium corporation owns the parking spaces and assigns spaces to unit owners on a discretionary basis.

Performance Audit

A performance audit is a detailed examination and scrutiny of the common elements by an individual (with qualifications as set out in the Act). This audit includes inspecting major building components, reviewing condominium documentation and conducting a survey of owners concerning damage or defects. The individual then prepares/submits a written report to the board of directors.

Requirements concerning performance audits apply to condominium corporations with one or more units used for residential purposes and common elements condominium corporations. The person conducting the audit must hold a Certificate of Authorization (*Professional Engineers Act*) or Certificate of Practice (*Architects Act*).

The audit is designed to reveal deficiencies that might give rise to an Ontario New Home Warranty Program claim, whether or not the corporation falls under that program. The reader is reminded that ONHWP coverage is restricted to new residential condominiums and is further subject to other qualifying criteria.

The auditor may enter the property at reasonable times either alone or accompanied by appropriate experts, require the production of relevant documents and make examinations, tests or inquiries deemed reasonable. The performance audit must be completed no later than ten months following the registration of the declaration and description.

Reserve Fund

A reserve fund is used solely for major repair and replacement of common elements and corporation assets; e.g., roofs, building exterior finishes, roads, sidewalks, electrical, heating and plumbing systems and recreational/parking facilities.

Funds are collected from common expense and must be held in trust. Interest or other income from the reserve fund forms part of that fund. If repair costs to common elements exceeds monies in reserve, a special assessment may be required to meet such expenses. Repayment terms can vary considerably, but essentially the unit owners are required to contribute a specified sum in addition to normal monthly common expenses.

When a condominium is first registered and until a first reserve fund study and associated plan is completed, the reserve amount is the greater of money reasonably required for major repairs and replacements based on life expectancies and replacement costs, or 10% of the budgeted amount for contributions to the common expenses exclusive of the reserve fund.

Corporations are, thereafter, required to undertake reserve fund studies in accordance with prescribed time limits. Such ongoing studies, among other things, determine whether the existing funds in reserve and contributions collected are adequate. For new condominiums following proclamation of the *Condominium Act* in 2001, a reserve fund study must be completed in the year following registration. Within 120 days of receipt, the board must establish the plan for future funding; within 15 days provide owners (and the auditor) with a summary; and within 30 days following, implement the plan.

Rules

Rules involve directives and regulations developed by a condominium corporation that promote the safety, security and welfare of owners, property and assets of the corporation. Rules also prevent unreasonable interference with the use and enjoyment of common elements.

Practitioners should be aware of rules impacting condominiums being marketed, as they can directly impact the purchaser. The board of directors can make, amend or repeal rules that are reasonable concerning the common elements. The board must provide owners with a copy of the rules (made, amended or repealed), the effective date and notice that they may requisition a meeting. Rules are not effective until approved by the owners at a requisitioned meeting within 30 days. If no meeting is requisitioned within that period, the rules become effective.

Sale of New Units (Sale by Declarant)

The *Condominium Act* contains provisions regarding the sale of proposed and/or new condominium units. The owner/developer, referred to as the declarant (or proposed declarant) must fulfill various disclosure requirements as set out in the Act, most notably, the delivery of a disclosure statement.

The buyer may rescind the agreement with written notice within ten days of delivery of:

- the disclosure statement, or

- the receiving of a copy of the agreement of purchase and sale executed by the declarant and the purchaser, whichever is the later.

Any deposit concerning a right to enter into an agreement, on account of an agreement of purchase and sale, or on account of a sale concerning a proposed unit must be held in trust by the declarant's solicitor or a trustee of a prescribed class as set out in the Regulations. The first $20,000 of deposit, in the case of new residential condominiums, will also be covered by deposit protection under the *Ontario New Home Warranty Program.*

Practitioners are cautioned regarding the sale of new units as no universal pre-printed agreement of purchase and sale form is used in Ontario.

Sale of Resale Units

The Agreement of Purchase and Sale–Condominium Resale (OREA Form 101) is designed for resale condominium transactions. A copy of the OREA Form 101 is included in Chapter 6. In addition to pre-printed clauses unique to this form, real estate practitioners should clearly delineate what is included with the property; i.e., storage lockers and/or parking spaces. Further, any improvements or additions completed by the owner should be discussed and duly noted.

The status certificate, issued by the condominium corporation, sets out important details regarding the resale condominium unit and the condominium corporation.

Status Certificate

The Status Certificate is a document containing information regarding the operational, legal and financial dimensions of the condominium corporation. The corporation is required to give each person, so requesting, a status certificate with respect to a unit in the corporation.

Practitioners should be familiar with all aspects of the status certificate. The certificate must be provided within ten days by the corporation to anyone who requests this document. A prescribed fee, not to exceed $100 inclusive of all applicable taxes, can be charged.

The information contained within the status certificate and the accompanying documents are vital from a buyer's perspective in fully understanding both the status of an individual unit and the overall operation of the condominium corporation.

Certificate content includes, but is not limited to:

- Corporation's address for service; directors'/officers' names and addresses for service.
- Statement of common expenses (including default for the unit, if any).
- Amount payable by the unit for common expenses.
- Particulars of any increase in common expenses for the unit since the date of the current year budget. Reasons for the increase must also be provided.
- Statement concerning any assessments relating to the reserve fund since the date of the budget for the current year (including reasons for such assessments).
- Information concerning any applications regarding amendments to the declaration.
- Details of outstanding judgments.
- Status of any legal actions being taken against the condominium corporation.
- Current budget and most recent audited statement, including auditor's report.
- Copy of the current declaration, by-laws and rules.
- A listing of various current agreements; e.g., management and insurance.
- Statement that the person requesting the status certificate has the right to inspect agreements.
- Owner compliance with current agreements regarding modifications that relate to the unit; e.g., additions or changes to exclusive use common elements.
- Particulars concerning the most recent reserve fund study and the amount of the fund (no earlier than the end of the month within 90 days of the certificate) including any current plans to increase the fund.
- Number of units leased for the fiscal year preceding the status certificate date.
- Certificate or memorandum of current insurance policies.
- Any planned or proposed additions, alterations or improvements to the common elements, other assets of the corporation or services.
- A statement if a court has appointed an inspector pursuant to the Act.

Persons paying the fee for the certificate can, upon written request, also inspect certain agreements; e.g., management and insurance. Copies will be furnished for a fee. Upon written request, the name and address for service of the corporation, directors and officers, the person responsible for management and the individual delegated to provide status certificates can also be obtained.

The Act also sets out requirements in the event that information is omitted or a certificate is not provided, when requested. If any information is omitted, the statute provides that the certificate states there is no such information.

When a status certificate is requested and not provided within the required time limit (ten days), the Act states that a certificate is deemed to have been provided and:

- no default in common expenses has occurred;
- no increase in common expenses has occurred (since the date of the current year's budget); and
- no levies have been assessed against the unit.

Storage

Storage lockers, as with parking spaces, can be grouped under the following four categories:

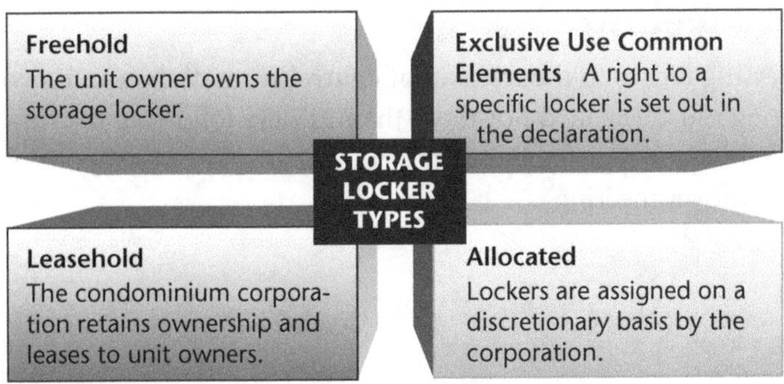

Termination

Condominium corporations can be terminated in four ways: consent, sale of property, substantial damage and court application.

Consent	Consent is required of owners of at least 80% of the units. Further, at least 80% of persons having registered claims against the property (created following registration of the declaration and description) must also give their consent.
Sale of Property	The Act ceases to govern the condominium if the property as a whole is sold. If a part is sold, the Act ceases to govern that part. An 80% majority vote is required; i.e., the owners of at least 80% of the units. If the common elements being sold are only for the use of owners of specific units, then those owners may consent to the sale, subject to other provisions in the Act. When the property is sold, the unit owners share net sale proceeds, as per their proportionate ownership share outlined in the declaration. Proceeds from common areas, designated as exclusive use elements for specific owners, are divided between the owners in proportion to their respective ownership.
Substantial Damage	If the condominium suffers damage, the board of directors will assess the scope of such damage and determine if it is substantial. Substantial, for purposes of the Act, is when the cost of repair equals or exceeds 25% of the replacement cost of all buildings and structures on the property. The owners are then notified accordingly. Upon receipt of such notice, a meeting of the owners can be requisitioned by the owners within 30 days. If the owners of at least 80% of the units consent, a notice of termination must be registered within 30 days. If no vote occurs in favour of termination, the corporation is obligated to make the necessary repairs.
Court Application	The Ontario Court (General Division), upon application by an owner, a mortgagee (or other encumbrancer) or the corporation, may terminate a condominium corporation according to criteria set out in the Act. When a court ordered termination occurs, the property ceases to be governed by the Act. The corporation's assets are then applied against all claims. The remaining funds are distributed among the owners in accordance with their proportionate interest in the common elements, as set out in the declaration.

Turn-Over Meeting

A turn-over meeting relates to the transfer of control from declarant to owners. The turn-over meeting must be called not more than 21 days following the time when the declarant ceases to be the registered owner of the majority of units. Four objectives are addressed in a turnover meeting.

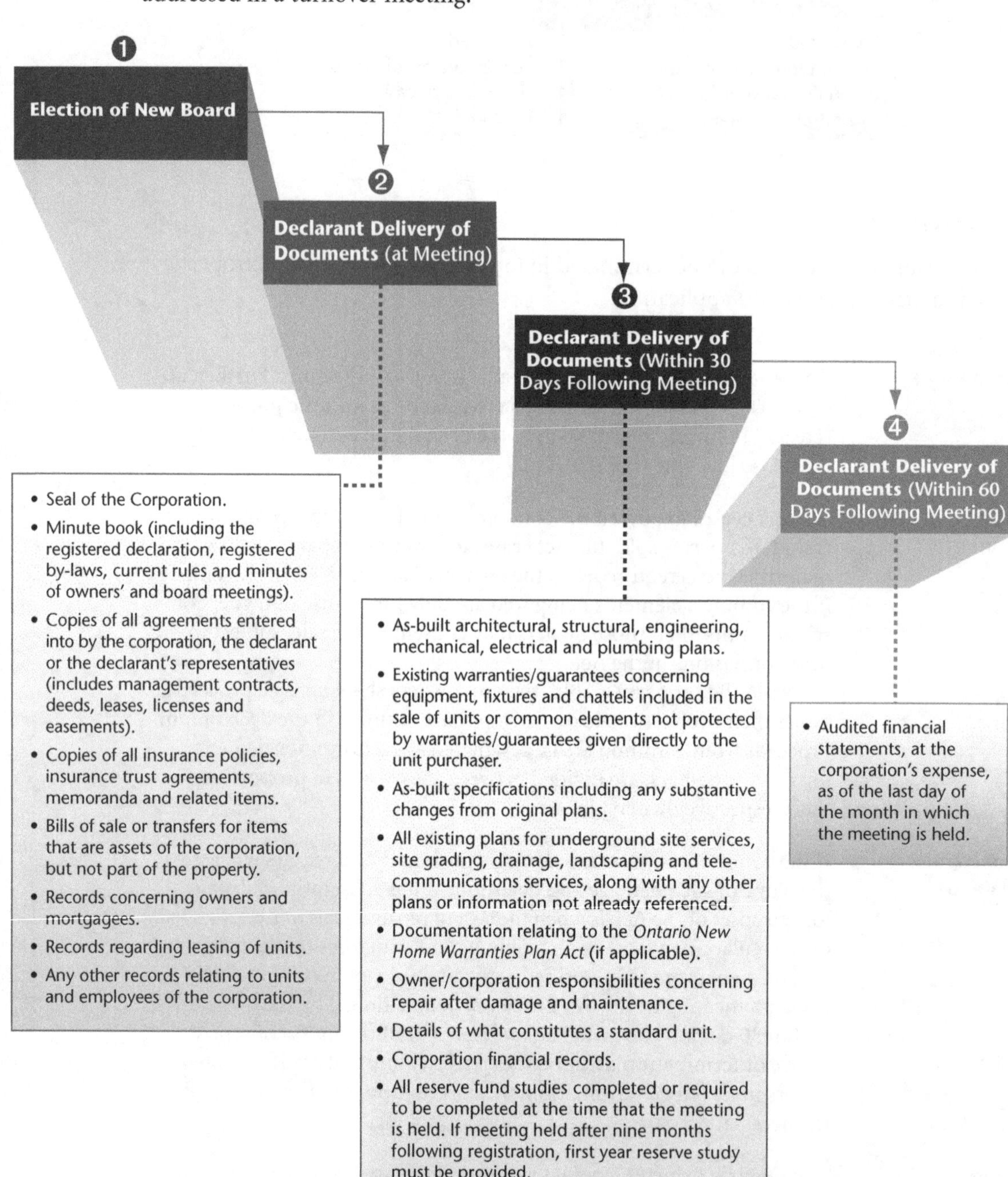

The corporation may make application to the Ontario Court (General Division) if materials are not supplied. Non-compliance by the declarant can result in an order by the Court to comply, along with the possibility of damages, court costs and fines.

Unit

A unit is that portion of the property so designated in the description and broadly described as the space defined by boundaries including all the land, structures and fixtures within that defined space. For purposes of the Act, all units are deemed to be property with each owner having exclusive ownership and use of his/her unit. Units are clearly differentiated from common elements held by the owners, as tenants in common (undivided interest), in proportions as set out in the declaration.

Units vs. Common Elements

The effect of condominium registration is to divide the property into units and common elements. Appurtenant to each unit is a proportionate ownership share of the common elements. The proportions of such shares are specified in the declaration. Each unit owner owns his/her unit separately, together with an undivided interest in the common elements.

Each unit owner is responsible for a proportionate share of common expenses, which is also set out in the declaration. As a general guideline, the allocation of ownership and responsibility for common expenses are in direct proportion to the unit size in relation to the total size of all units, but variations exist. Further, the allocations for ownership and common expenses can differ. Expert advice is required on such matters.

Use Restrictions

Use restrictions generally refer to limitations placed on unit owners as found in the declaration, by-laws and/or rules. Such restrictions are established initially by the declarant and modified by the condominium corporation as needed.

Use restrictions vary significantly in condominiums. The following examples have been taken from restrictions found in condominium documentation to represent the range of possibilities.

- No pets (or restrictions on pets; e.g., weight limit).
- White backing on exterior drapery materials with temporary draperies allowed during initial move-in period only.
- No outside installations; e.g., antennae, clotheslines, satellite dishes or other exterior telecommunication/radio devices.
- Parking restricted to private passenger vehicles only; i.e., no commercial vehicles in driveways.
- No signs permitted other than those approved by the corporation; e.g., name and/or address plate.
- No temporary structures or incidental permanent outside structures or improvements.
- No artificial vegetation, sculptures, weather vanes, birdbaths, flagpoles or fountains.
- No outside storage of garbage/trash/refuse containers.
- No awnings, canopies or shutters unless approved by the corporation.
- Garage doors shall be closed at all times (other than entering/exiting).

CO-OPERATIVE

Housing Co-operative

A housing co-operative is an incorporated business, pursuant to the *Co-operative Corporations Act* in Ontario, organized by individuals who join forces to acquire housing through joint ownership. Currently, Canada has more than 2,100 housing co-operatives with approximately 25% of those located in Ontario. Generally, the co-op provides a high level of security of tenure, not typically found in rental properties. Co-operative housing has proven attractive to individuals seeking to avoid the uncertainties of the rental market, while deriving the benefit of combined financial resources in the acquisition of affordable housing. Co-operatives originally gained popularity with university campuses, as they provided affordable accommodation for students.

Co-ops, as member-controlled organizations, are managed by a board of directors consisting of elected persons from the membership. Members pay a monthly housing charge to cover mortgage and operating costs. Housing charges rise with increases in operating costs, unlike rents that respond to market conditions, operating costs and provincial legislative controls in some instances; e.g., *Residential Tenancies Act.*

In Ontario, a housing co-operative is formed to own real property. Members may or may not hold shares in the co-operative depending on whether the property is an equity or non-profit co-operative. In both instances, members do not own specific units, however, they are protected by means of rights as set out in occupancy agreements (or similarly worded documents).

Equity Co-operative (with share capital)

An equity co-operative is a corporation that owns the land and buildings with members as shareholders in the corporation. Ownership is by way of a share certificate in combination with an occupancy agreement relating to a specific unit. The occupancy agreement may also provide for exclusive use of parking or locker spaces, as would be the case in a condominium. Co-operatives and condominiums must be clearly differentiated. In the former, an individual holds shares in a corporation; in the latter, ownership is by way of title to a specific unit.

Non-Profit Co-operative (without share capital)

Equity co-ops must be differentiated from non-profit co-operatives. A non-profit housing co-operative in Ontario (i.e., without share capital) has the primary objective of providing housing for its members without the purpose of gain for those members. At point of a dissolution, the co-operative will distribute any remaining property, after payment of debts and liabilities, in one or more non-profit housing co-operatives or charitable organizations.

Agreement of Purchase and Sale

The Agreement of Purchase and Sale (OREA Standard Form 100) cannot be used in the acquisition of an equity co-operative, as a suitable agreement must address a two-fold process: a share is sold and an occupancy agreement is created or assigned. The Agreement of Purchase and Sale—Co-operative Building Resale Agreement (OREA Standard Form 102) sets out the real property being granted by means of exclusive right to occupy and use, together with any parking spaces or lockers, and the appropriate shares being purchased in the corporation. The agreement also requires that the purchaser, on or before closing, enter into an occupancy agreement with the co-operative corporation and abide by the rules and regulations of that corporation.

Searches associated with the sale include a full search of title to the property, as well as the co-operative corporation. As no interest in land is being transferred, the new owner is provided documents in support of the new ownership, namely:

- new share certificate,
- assumption of occupancy agreement,
- other particulars concerning rights being acquired (e.g., the specific suite and other exclusive use areas),
- amount of the mortgage,
- rules/regulations, and
- by-laws (including a statement that the seller has complied with same).

The *Business Corporations Act* permits corporations (including co-operative corporations) to place restrictions on the transfer of shares. Consequently, anyone contemplating the purchase or sale of a unit should be aware of what restrictions exist, the process required to obtain approval if such do exist and associated time lines and costs.

Land transfer tax applies to the purchase of co-ops, despite the fact that a share is being sold, not an interest in land. The government refers to such a disposition as a beneficial interest in land for taxation purposes.

Financing

Equity co-ops present special financing challenges because the entire property must be mortgaged, as opposed to condominium units with distinct ownership. The co-op mortgage is effectively a blanket mortgage over the entire property with joint liability of owners in relation to their proportionate share of ownership. This poses several complications:

- When acquiring a suite in an equity co-op, the buyer must assume the applicable liability for the proportionate share of the mortgage and then secure secondary financing. Often lenders are reluctant to advance funds based on the pledge of security (the share) and assignment of collateral security (the occupancy agreement). In addition, the mortgagee will often require a personal guarantee.
- Cash purchases pose another challenge. The buyer must be assured that any obligation of the previous shareholder relating to the share is paid.
- A co-op typically provides for approval by the board of directors for any pledge of a share or assignment of an occupancy agreement, thereby introducing another element into the transaction process.
- Co-op owners are responsible for the proportionate share of any blanket mortgage and also potentially for obligations of other owners should these individuals fail to meet their financial commitments to the co-operative.

Form 102 Agreement of Purchase and Sale—Co-operative Building Resale Agreement, Page 1 of 6

Form 102
for use in the Province of Ontario

Agreement of Purchase and Sale
Co-operative Building Resale Agreement

This Agreement of Purchase and Sale dated this .... day of .... 20.............

BUYER, ..., agrees to purchase from
(Full legal names of all Buyers)

SELLER, ..., the following
(Full legal names of all Sellers)

REAL PROPERTY AND SHARES:

The exclusive right to occupy and use .... (the "Unit")

in the Co-operative Apartment Building located at: ....

in the ....

Parking Space(s) .... Locker ....(the "Property")

and .... shares (the "shares") in the Capital of .... (the "Corporation")

PURCHASE PRICE: Dollars (CDN$) ....

.... Dollars

DEPOSIT: Buyer submits ....
(Herewith/Upon Acceptance/as otherwise described in this Agreement)

.... Dollars (CDN$) ....

by negotiable cheque payable to .... "Deposit Holder" to be held in trust pending completion or other termination of this Agreement and to be credited toward the Purchase Price on completion. For the purposes of this Agreement, "Upon Acceptance" shall mean that the Buyer is required to deliver the deposit to the Deposit Holder within 24 hours of the acceptance of this Agreement. The parties to this Agreement hereby acknowledge that, unless otherwise provided for in this Agreement, the Deposit Holder shall place the deposit in trust in the Deposit Holder's non-interest bearing Real Estate Trust Account and no interest shall be earned, received or paid on the deposit

Buyer agrees to pay the balance as more particularly set out in Schedule A attached.

SCHEDULE(S) A..**attached hereto form(s) part of this Agreement.**

1. **IRREVOCABILITY:** This offer shall be irrevocable by .... until .... a.m./p.m. on the
(Seller/Buyer)
.... day of .... 20 ...., after which time, if not accepted, this offer shall be null and void and the deposit shall be returned to the Buyer in full without interest.

2. **COMPLETION DATE:** This Agreement shall be completed by no later than 6:00 p.m. on the .... day of ....
20 .... Upon completion, vacant possession of the property shall be given to the Buyer unless otherwise provided for in this Agreement.

INITIALS OF BUYER(S): ( ) **INITIALS OF SELLER(S):** ( )

Form 102 Revised 2015 **Page 1 of 6**

Form 102 Agreement of Purchase and Sale—Co-operative Building Resale Agreement, Page 2 of 6

3. **NOTICES:** The Seller hereby appoints the Listing Brokerage as agent for the Seller for the purpose of giving and receiving notices pursuant to this Agreement. Where a Brokerage (Buyer's Brokerage) has entered into a representation agreement with the Buyer, the Buyer hereby appoints the Buyer's Brokerage as agent for the purpose of giving and receiving notices pursuant to this Agreement. **Where a Brokerage represents both the Seller and the Buyer (multiple representation), the Brokerage shall not be appointed or authorized to be agent for either the Buyer or the Seller for the purpose of giving and receiving notices.** Any notice relating hereto or provided for herein shall be in writing. In addition to any provision contained herein and in any Schedule hereto, this offer, any counter-offer, notice of acceptance thereof or any notice to be given or received pursuant to this Agreement or any Schedule hereto (any of them, "Document") shall be deemed given and received when delivered personally or hand delivered to the Address for Service provided in the Acknowledgement below, or where a facsimile number or email address is provided herein, when transmitted electronically to that facsimile number or email address, respectively, in which case, the signature(s) of the party (parties) shall be deemed to be original.

FAX No.: .... (For delivery of Documents to Seller)   FAX No.: .... (For delivery of Documents to Buyer)

Email Address: .... (For delivery of Documents to Seller)   Email Address: .... (For delivery of Documents to Buyer)

4. **CHATTELS INCLUDED:**..

....

....

....

....

Unless otherwise stated in this Agreement or any Schedule hereto, Seller agrees to convey all fixtures and chattels included in the Purchase Price free from all liens, encumbrances or claims affecting the said fixtures and chattels.

5. **FIXTURES EXCLUDED:**..

....

....

....

6. **RENTAL ITEMS (Including Lease, Lease to Own):** The following equipment is rented and **not** included in the Purchase Price. The Buyer agrees to assume the rental contract(s), if assumable:

....

....

....

The Buyer agrees to co-operate and execute such documentation as may be required to facilitate such assumption.

7. **MAINTENANCE EXPENSES:** Seller warrants that the maintenance expenses presently payable to the Corporation in respect of the property are

approximately $ .... per month and include: ....

....

....

....

INITIALS OF BUYER(S): ( )   **INITIALS OF SELLER(S):** ( )

Form 102 Revised 2015 **Page 2 of 6**

Form 102 Agreement of Purchase and Sale—Co-operative Building Resale Agreement, Page 3 of 6

8. PARKING AND LOCKERS: Parking and Lockers are as described above or assigned as follows: ....

.... at an additional cost of: ....

9. HST: If the sale of the Property (Real Property as described above) is subject to Harmonized Sales Tax (HST), then such tax shall be

.... the Purchase Price. If the sale of the Property is not subject to HST, Seller agrees to certify on or before
(included in/in addition to)
closing, that the sale of the Property is not subject to HST. Any HST on chattels, if applicable, is not included in the Purchase Price.

10. APPROVAL: This Agreement is subject to Seller, at the Seller's own expense, obtaining approval of the Board of Directors of the Corporation to the sale and transfer of the Seller's shares in the capital of the Corporation to the Buyer and approval of the Buyer as shareholder and occupant of the

Unit, and if such approval is not obtained by 11:59 p.m. on the .... day of ...., 20............. this agreement shall become null and void and the Buyer's deposit shall be returned to the Buyer in full without deduction. The buyer agrees to cooperate and provide such information and documentation as may be within control of the Buyer in order to obtain said approval.

11. TITLE SEARCH: Buyer shall be allowed until 6:00 p.m. on the .... day of ...., 20......., (Requisition Date) to examine the Corporation's title to the Property at the Buyer's expense and until the earlier of: (i) thirty days from the later of the Requisition Date or the date on which the conditions in this Agreement are fulfilled or otherwise waived or; (ii) five days prior to completion, to satisfy the Buyer that there are

no outstanding work orders or deficiency notices affecting the Property, and that its present use (..) may be lawfully continued. If within that time any valid objection to title or to any outstanding work order or deficiency notice, or to the fact the said present use may not lawfully be continued, is made in writing to Seller and which Seller is unable or unwilling to remove, remedy or satisfy and which Buyer will not waive, this Agreement notwithstanding any intermediate acts or negotiations in respect of such objections, shall be at an end and all monies paid shall be returned without interest or deduction and Seller, Listing Brokerage and Co-operating Brokerage shall not be liable for any costs or damages. Save as to any valid objection so made by such day and except for any objection going to the root of the title, Buyer shall be conclusively deemed to have accepted Seller's title to the Property. Seller hereby consents to the municipality or other governmental agencies releasing to Buyer details of all outstanding work orders affecting the Property, and Seller agrees to execute and deliver such further authorizations in this regard as Buyer may reasonably require.

12. CORPORATION DOCUMENTATION: The Seller shall deliver to the Buyer on or before closing:
(a) a certified copy of the Resolution of the Board of Directors of the Corporation approving the Buyer as a shareholder and as an occupant of the Unit;
(b) a share certificate for the Seller's shares in the capital of the Corporation endorsed in favour of the Buyer;
(c) a certificate or letter from the Corporation confirming:
(i) with respect to the Property, that all charges and obligations have been paid or discharged as of the date of closing;
(ii) with respect to the Corporation that the affairs of the Corporation are in order and that there are no legal actions pending against the Corporation or contemplated by the Corporation, that there are no special assessments contemplated by the Corporation, that there are no orders or complaints against the real property by the Building, Health or Fire Departments, that no sale of real property is contemplated, and the Building is not and never has been insulated with Urea-Formaldehyde Foam Insulation.

13. OCCUPANCY AGREEMENT: The Buyer agrees on or before closing to enter into an Occupancy Agreement with the Corporation and to abide by the rules and regulations of the Corporation.

14. TITLE: Buyer agrees to accept the Corporation's title to the Property subject to all rights and easements registered against title for the supply and installation of telephone services, electricity, gas, sewers, water, television cable facilities and other related services; provided that title to the Property is otherwise good and free from all encumbrances except: (a) as herein expressly provided; (b) any registered restrictions, conditions or covenants that run with the land provided such have been complied with; and (c) any existing municipal agreements, zoning by-laws and/or regulations and utility or service contracts.

15. DOCUMENTS AND DISCHARGE: Buyer shall not call for the production of any title deed, abstract, survey or other evidence of title to the Property except such as are in the possession or control of Seller. If a discharge of any Charge/Mortgage, lien or other encumbrance held by a corporation incorporated pursuant to the Trust And Loan Companies Act (Canada), Chartered Bank, Trust Company, Credit Union, Caisse Populaire or Insurance Company and which is not to be assumed by Buyer on completion, is not available in registrable form on completion, Buyer agrees to accept Seller's lawyer's personal undertaking to obtain, out of the closing funds, a discharge in registrable form and to register same, or cause same to be registered, on title within a reasonable period of time after completion, provided that on or before completion Seller shall provide to Buyer a statement prepared by the mortgagee, lienholder or encumbrancer setting out the balance required to obtain the discharge, and, where a real-time electronic cleared funds transfer system is not being used, a direction executed by Seller directing payment to the mortgagee, lienholder or encumbrancer of the amount required to obtain the discharge out of the balance due on completion.

INITIALS OF BUYER(S): ( ) **INITIALS OF SELLER(S):** ( )

Form 102 Revised 2015 **Page 3 of 6**

Form 102 Agreement of Purchase and Sale—Co-operative Building Resale Agreement, Page 4 of 6

16. MEETINGS: Seller represents and warrants to Buyer that at the time of the acceptance of this Offer the Seller has not received a notice convening a special or general meeting of the Corporation respecting; (a) the termination of the government of the property; (b) the winding up or dissolution of the Corporation; (c) any substantial alteration in or substantial addition to the property or the renovation thereof; OR (d) any substantial change in the assets or liabilities of the Corporation; and Seller covenants that if the Seller receives any such notice prior to the date of completion the Seller shall forthwith notify Buyer in writing and the Buyer may thereupon at the Buyer's option declare this Agreement to be null and void and all monies paid by Buyer shall be refunded without interest or deduction.

17. INSPECTION: Buyer acknowledges having had the opportunity to inspect the Property and understands that upon acceptance of this offer there shall be a binding agreement of purchase and sale between Buyer and Seller. **The Buyer acknowledges having the opportunity to include a requirement for a property inspection report in this Agreement and agrees that except as may be specifically provided for in this Agreement, the Buyer will not be obtaining a property inspection or property inspection report regarding the Property.**

18. INSURANCE: The Unit and all other things being purchased shall be and remain at the risk of the Seller until completion. In the event of substantial damage to the real property Buyer may at the Buyer's option either permit the proceeds of insurance to be used for repair of such damage in accordance with the provisions of the Insurance Trust Agreement or other insurance arrangement, or terminate this Agreement and all deposit monies paid by Buyer hereunder shall be refunded without interest or deduction. If Seller is taking back a Charge/Mortgage, or Buyer is assuming a Charge/ Mortgage, Buyer shall supply Seller with reasonable evidence of adequate insurance to protect Seller's or other mortgagee's interest on completion.

19. RESIDENCY: (a) Subject to (b) below, the Seller represents and warrants that the Seller is not and on completion will not be a non-resident under the non-residency provisions of the Income Tax Act which representation and warranty shall survive and not merge upon the completion of this transaction and the Seller shall deliver to the Buyer a statutory declaration that Seller is not then a non-resident of Canada;
(b) provided that if the Seller is a non-resident under the non-residency provisions of the Income Tax Act, the Buyer shall be credited towards the Purchase Price with the amount, if any, necessary for Buyer to pay to the Minister of National Revenue to satisfy Buyer's liability in respect of tax payable by Seller under the non-residency provisions of the Income Tax Act by reason of this sale.Buyer shall not claim such credit if Seller delivers on completion the prescribed certificate.

20. ADJUSTMENTS: Maintenance expenses and, where billed to the Unit and not the Corporation, realty taxes, including local improvement rates; mortgage interest; rentals; unmetered public or private utilities and fuel; are to be apportioned and allowed to the day of completion, the day of completion itself to be apportioned to the Buyer. There shall be no adjustment for the Seller's share of any reserve or contingency fund to which the Seller may have contributed prior to the date of completion.

21. TIME LIMITS: Time shall in all respects be of the essence hereof provided that the time for doing or completing of any matter provided for herein may be extended or abridged by an agreement in writing signed by Seller and Buyer or by their respective lawyers who may be specifically authorized in that regard.

22. TENDER: Any tender of documents or money hereunder may be made upon Seller or Buyer or their respective lawyers on the day set for completion. Money shall be tendered with funds drawn on a lawyer's trust account in the form of a bank draft, certified cheque or wire transfer using the Large Value Transfer System

23. FAMILY LAW ACT: Seller warrants that spousal consent is not necessary to this transaction under the provisions of the Family Law Act, R.S.O.1990 unless Seller's spouse has executed the consent hereinafter provided.

24. LEGAL, ACCOUNTING AND ENVIRONMENTAL ADVICE: The parties acknowledge that any information provided by the brokerage is not legal, tax or environmental advice.

25. CONSUMER REPORTS: The Buyer is hereby notified that a consumer report containing credit and/or personal information may be referred to in connection with this transaction.

26. AGREEMENT IN WRITING: If there is conflict or discrepancy between any provision added to this Agreement (including any Schedule attached hereto) and any provision in the standard pre-set portion hereof, the added provision shall supersede the standard pre-set provision to the extent of such conflict or discrepancy. This Agreement including any Schedule attached hereto, shall constitute the entire Agreement between Buyer and Seller. There is no representation, warranty, collateral agreement or condition, which affects this Agreement other than as expressed herein. For the purposes of this Agreement, Seller means vendor and Buyer means purchaser. This Agreement shall be read with all changes of gender or number required by the context.

27. TIME AND DATE: Any reference to a time and date in this Agreement shall mean the time and date where the property is located.

INITIALS OF BUYER(S): ( ) **INITIALS OF SELLER(S):** ( )

Form 102 Revised 2015 **Page 4 of 6**

Form 102 Agreement of Purchase and Sale—Co-operative Building Resale Agreement, Page 5 of 6

28. SUCCESSORS AND ASSIGNS: The heirs, executors, administrators, successors and assigns of the undersigned are bound by the terms herein.

SIGNED, SEALED AND DELIVERED in the presence of: IN WITNESS whereof I have hereunto set my hand and seal:

.... (Witness) .... (Buyer) ● (Seal) DATE ....

.... (Witness) .... (Buyer) ● (Seal) DATE ....

I, the Undersigned Seller, agree to the above offer. I hereby irrevocably instruct my lawyer to pay directly to the brokerage(s) with whom I have agreed to pay commission, the unpaid balance of the commission together with applicable Harmonized Sales Tax (and any other taxes as may hereafter be applicable), from the proceeds of the sale prior to any payment to the undersigned on completion, as advised by the brokerage(s) to my lawyer.

SIGNED, SEALED AND DELIVERED in the presence of: IN WITNESS whereof I have hereunto set my hand and seal:

.... (Witness) .... (Seller) ● (Seal) DATE ....

.... (Witness) .... (Seller) ● (Seal) DATE ....

SPOUSAL CONSENT: The Undersigned Spouse of the Seller hereby consents to the disposition evidenced herein pursuant to the provisions of the Family Law Act, R.S.O.1990, and hereby agrees with the Buyer that he/she will execute all necessary or incidental documents to give full force and effect to the sale evidenced herein.

.... (Witness) .... (Spouse) ● (Seal) DATE ....

CONFIRMATION OF ACCEPTANCE: Notwithstanding anything contained herein to the contrary, I confirm this Agreement with all changes both typed and written was finally accepted by all parties at .... a.m./p.m. this .... day of ...., 20..........

....
(Signature of Seller or Buyer)

INFORMATION ON BROKERAGE(S)

Listing Brokerage .... Tel.No.(...............) ....

....
(Salesperson / Broker Name)

Co-op/Buyer Brokerage .... Tel.No.(...............) ....

....
(Salesperson / Broker Name)

ACKNOWLEDGEMENT

I acknowledge receipt of my signed copy of this accepted Agreement of Purchase and Sale and I authorize the Brokerage to forward a copy to my lawyer.

.... DATE ....
(Seller)

.... DATE ....
(Seller)

Address for Service ....

.... Tel.No.(..........)....................

Seller's Lawyer ....

Address ....

Email ....

(..........)................................ (..........)................................
Tel.No. FAX No.

I acknowledge receipt of my signed copy of this accepted Agreement of Purchase and Sale and I authorize the Brokerage to forward a copy to my lawyer.

.... DATE ....
(Buyer)

.... DATE ....
(Buyer)

Address for Service ....

.... Tel.No.(..........)....................

Buyer's Lawyer ....

Address ....

Email ....

(..........)................................ (..........)................................
Tel.No. FAX No.

Property Manager: ....
(Name) (Address) (Tel No.,FAX No.)

FOR OFFICE USE ONLY **COMMISSION TRUST AGREEMENT**

To: Co-operating Brokerage shown on the foregoing Agreement of Purchase and Sale:
In consideration for the Co-operating Brokerage procuring the foregoing Agreement of Purchase and Sale, I hereby declare that all moneys received or receivable by me in connection with the Transaction as contemplated in the MLS® Rules and Regulations of my Real Estate Board shall be receivable and held in trust. This agreement shall constitute a Commission Trust Agreement as defined in the MLS® Rules and shall be subject to and governed by the MLS® Rules pertaining to Commission Trust.

DATED as of the date and time of the acceptance of the foregoing Agreement of Purchase and Sale. Acknowledged by:

.... (Authorized to bind the Listing Brokerage) .... (Authorized to bind the Co-operating Brokerage)

Form 102 Revised 2015 **Page 5 of 6**

Form 102 Agreement of Purchase and Sale—Co-operative Building Resale Agreement, Page 6 of 6

OREA Ontario Real Estate Association

Form 102
for use in the Province of Ontario

Schedule A
Agreement of Purchase and Sale – Co-operative Building Resale

This Schedule is attached to and forms part of the Agreement of Purchase and Sale between:

BUYER, ..., and

SELLER, ...

for the purchase and sale of ....

.... dated the .... day of ...., 20..............

Buyer agrees to pay the balance as follows:

This form must be initialed by all parties to the Agreement of Purchase and Sale.

INITIALS OF BUYER(S): 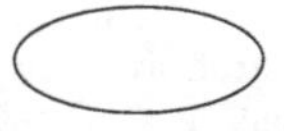 **INITIALS OF SELLER(S):** 

Form 102 Revised 2015 **Page 6 of 6**

CO-OPERATIVE CORPORATIONS ACT

The Financial Services Commission of Ontario (FSCO) regulates registration of organizations who conduct business as co-operatives under the *Co-operative Corporations Act*. The FSCO is an arm's length agency of the Ministry of Finance that became operational in July 1998 under the *Financial Services Commission of Ontario Act, 1997*.

Co-operatives are member-owned and controlled corporations. The Act does not regulate the day-to-day business of a co-operative, including the by-laws that are established for its operation. The legislation does require that one member equals one vote, regardless of the amount invested. The Act also sets out statutory requirements concerning offering statements and related disclosures; e.g., when securities are sold beyond basic membership shares and when surplus distribution occurs at point of termination.

Registration

Sections 4, 5 and 6 of the *Co-operative Corporations Act* detail registration requirements. The procedure for real estate co-operatives requires that a specific number of individuals (corporations or persons) file the articles of incorporation and other prescribed documents, and pay required fees to FSCO. FSCO then issues a certificate of incorporation. Detailed registration procedures, filing and record-keeping requirements and information concerning offering statements can be obtained from the Credit Union and Co-operatives Branch.

Types of Co-operatives

While housing co-operatives are discussed in this text, various other types of co-operatives exist. In total, the Financial Services Commission of Ontario lists 10 types:

Service Co-ops	Consumers Co-ops	Supply Co-ops
Marketing Co-ops	Producer Co-ops	Child Care Co-ops
Financing Co-ops	Farming and Supply Co-ops	Milk Transport Co-ops
Worker Co-ops	Housing and Housing Development Co-ops	

Some co-operatives issue securities to their members and, in certain instances, to restricted categories of non-members. Co-operatives can be incorporated with or without share capital. Individuals investing in a co-operative normally do so to realize certain personal goals, for example the availability of goods or jobs.

Co-operatives in Canada have various support organizations. In the case of housing co-ops, regional, provincial and national associations exist as well as various agencies providing development and management services. Practitioners are strongly advised to seek legal advice on all matters associated with housing co-operatives.

WEB LINKS

Co-operative Registration For additional information regarding how to register a co-operative, visit the Financial Services Commission of Ontario at ***www.fsco.gov.on.ca***.

CO-OWNERSHIP

The concept of co-ownership, a unique variation of condominiums and co-operatives, experienced some popularity in Ontario particularly during the mid-1980's. The buyer in a co-ownership building receives a deed in addition to an occupancy agreement. The deed represents the proportionate interest held in the building in relation to other tenant-in-common owners, but does not relate to a specific unit within that structure.

The issuance of a deed, however, does not alleviate most troublesome situations already identified under co-operatives, namely, the joint liability with other owners in regard to a blanket mortgage, the difficulty of securing secondary financing and other issues that go beyond the scope of this text. Legal advice is strongly encouraged.

TIMESHARE

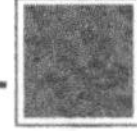

Timeshare involves the division of property rights into fractional interests based on time. Timeshare ownership has proven most popular in the sale of recreational properties, particularly in the case of southern vacation resorts. Timeshare is a relatively new concept in property ownership that generally falls under two broad categories.

FEE OWNERSHIP INTEREST	RIGHT-TO-USE OWNERSHIP
The right to encumber, convey or otherwise transfer the interest for all future time.	A non-fee interest in the designated property in which the buyer receives no registrable title. Instead, the owner of this interest has a contractual right to enjoy the use of the property for a specified period.

The concept of time as a divisible dimension of ownership was never contemplated in the original provincial statutes and regulations underlying either registry or land titles. Consequently, a certain degree of creativity was required to accommodate the intricacies of several owners occupying various time frames in one specific unit.

Most timeshare interests in this province are concentrated in recreational areas, namely, Collingwood and vicinity.

Fee Ownership Interest

Fee simple ownership is probably the most straight-forward method to acquire an interest in timeshare. Initially, a condominium corporation is created and registered in the condominium corporations index of the applicable land registration office with appropriate pages set up in a parcel register. Individual weeks are registered under the unit, with all 52 weeks being displayed with the percentage interest in each of the periods. The sum of interests must total 100%. A transfer number (document number for the transfer) is assigned when the week is conveyed to an owner.

The resale of this interest, either back to the declarant or another party, is recorded in chronological order under the unit register. The initial transfer from the declarant is typically accompanied by a notice of agreement. This agreement generally binds each owner to the restrictive covenants, rules, regulations and by-laws of the timeshare condominium project. When the fee simple ownership is conveyed, the new owner must also sign a notice of agreement ensuring continuance of such compliance.

Right-to-Use Interest

Various complications can arise in fee simple timeshare ownership, therefore, many timeshare ventures have moved toward right-to-use agreements. Essentially, the buyer of the right enters a contractual arrangement to enjoy the use of the property, while the title to the land and improvements rests with the developer, corporation or association. This type of ownership has become extremely attractive in many countries. It currently accounts for a significant portion of today's vacation timeshare industry.

Unlike fee simple arrangements, the creation of condominium is not required. Consequently, unit transactions remain within the parcel register pages, as opposed to individual unit register pages for each unit. Essentially, the owners obtain their interest through a notice of lease that designates the specific week being acquired. As with fee simple ownership, the right can be conveyed to others or encumbered subject to regulations included in the original timeshare documentation. The conveyance is accomplished through a notice of assignment of lease. Under land titles, any lease greater than three years must be registered on title to have validity. If the property is under registry, then the period is seven years. Right-to-use leases do not exceed 20 years. As with fee simple, the conveyance of interest is cross referenced to minimize confusion, given the large number of leases involving one specific unit.

Registration procedures are not precisely laid out in land registration statutes. The above information was summarized from information gained in one land registry office. Contact the Ministry of Government Services for current status of procedures.

Consumer Protection Act

Consumers have certain rights under the *Consumer Protection Act* when acquiring an interest in a timeshare. The Act reads as follows:

Requirements for time share agreements

27. Every time share agreement shall be in writing, shall be delivered to the consumer and shall be made in accordance with the prescribed requirements. 2002, c. 30, Sched. A, s. 27.

Cancellation: cooling-off period

28. (1) A consumer may, without any reason, cancel a time share agreement at any time from the date of entering into the agreement until 10 days after receiving the written copy of the agreement. 2002, c. 30, Sched. A, s. 28 (1).

Cancellation: failure to meet requirements

(2) In addition to the right under subsection (1), a consumer may cancel a time share agreement within one year after the date of entering into the agreement if the consumer does not receive a copy of the agreement that meets the requirements under section 27. 2002, c. 30, Sched. A, s. 28 (2).

Ref: Consumer Protection Act, Sec. 27 & 28.

This protection does not apply to Ontario residents when acquiring a timeshare interest outside of either the province or the country.

WEB LINKS

Consumer Protection Act See the Ministry of Government Services web site (***www.mgs.gov.on.ca***) for additional information regarding consumer rights relating to the *Consumer Protection Act.*

CASE LAW

Case Synopsis	*WATERLOO NORTH CONDOMINIUM CORPORATION V. WELDNER* ONTARIO SUPERIOR COURT OF JUSTICE COURT FILE #C-1011-02

In 2001, a condominium buyer was seeking a residential condominium complex that permitted dogs. Ultimately, that buyer entered into an agreement to purchase a unit through a real estate salesperson who was aware that the buyer had a dog. The condominium corporation clearly stated in its Declaration that no animals...including those usually considered pets could be kept or allowed in the units. The agreement made no reference to the pet prohibition, which had been passed by the condominium corporation approximately 10 months earlier in 2000. The offer also did not include a condition allowing the buyer time to satisfy herself that a dog would be permitted.

The sale closed approximately one month later on May 1st, 2001. Fifteen days following closing, the condominium corporation's solicitors wrote to the new owner stating that having a dog in the complex was contrary to the Declaration. In a subsequent letter, the corporation advised the owner that it would consider an amendment to the Declaration if other owners agreed. The new owner and other unit owners lobbied, but the resulting poll was insufficient to amend the Declaration. In March 2002, a follow-up letter once again warned that legal action would be taken if the dog was not removed. The action commenced approximately six months later.

The owner asked the Court to dismiss the action by exercising its discretion to exempt the dog from applicable provisions in the Declaration. Further, the owner argued that the condominium corporation did not take action quickly enough and, therefore, laches applies. Laches refers to negligent or unreasonable delay in pursuing a legal remedy. Lastly, the owner argued that the pet prohibition would be an act of discrimination pursuant to the Ontario Human Rights Code, as she suffered from an identified mental disorder involving depression.

The Court found in favour of the condominium corporation stating that the prohibition was reasonable, the buyer employed both a real estate representative and a lawyer to provide guidance, and the Estoppel Certificate (now referred to as a Status Certificate) highlighted the restriction. Interestingly, the Judge commented: ...perhaps her quarrel is with one of the professionals advising her.

On the matter of discrimination, the Court found that not having the dog did constitute a form of stress relating to her depression, but that such would not constitute a disability within the meaning of the Ontario Human Rights Code. The owner was ordered to permanently remove the dog from the unit and comply with the Declaration

Case Questions

1. What primary document provides buyers with information concerning significant restrictions relating to a particular condominium unit?

2. What information is readily available from condominium corporations that will assist a salesperson in providing better service to clients interested in specific projects?

CHAPTER DISCUSSION

1. CONDOMINIUM REGISTRATION

The buyer cannot obtain the deed to the unit until the condominium is registered. Explain.

2. CONDOMINIUM CORPORATION

a. A condominium corporation does not have limited liability. Explain.

CHAPTER DISCUSSION

2. CONDOMINIUM CORPORATION (continued)

b. A six year old condominium project has had virtually no problems and no unusual expenses. The seller of a unit complains he has contributed more than $3,000 to the reserve fund that is being held by the corporation. Comment.

3. CO-OPERATIVES

Compare and contrast the main features of condominium ownership and co-operatives.

KNOWLEDGE INTEGRATION

Notables

- Condominium is legally structured by way of a declaration and a description.
- Property within a condominium corporation, except the units, is referred to as the common elements.
- Owners contribute common expenses in proportions set out in the declaration.
- A condominium corporation is a corporation without share capital formed with the registration of the declaration and description.
- Condominium types include standard, common element, leasehold, phased and vacant land.
- Owners of leased premises in a condominium must notify the condominium corporation and provide certain details about the tenancy arrangements.
- Carefully review condominium documentation to assess what type of parking and locker space is being provided.
- The condominium corporation is required to give each person, so requesting, a status certificate with respect to a unit in the corporation.
- Use restrictions can vary significantly from one condominium to another.
- A housing co-operative (equity or non-profit) is an incorporated business, pursuant to the *Co-operative Corporations Act.*
- Timeshare involves the division of property rights into fractional interest based on time.
- Timeshare can be broadly grouped into fee ownership interest and right-to-use interest.

Web Links

Web links are included for general interest regarding selected chapter topics.

Co-operative Registration	For additional information regarding how to register a co-operative, visit the Financial Services Commission of Ontario at ***www.fsco.gov.on.ca***.
Consumer Protection Act	See the Ministry of Government Services web site (***www.mgs.gov.on.ca***) for additional information regarding consumer rights relating to the *Consumer Protection Act.*

Chapter Mini-Review

Solutions are located in the Appendix.

1. The owner of a condominium unit is personally responsible for the liabilities of the corporation.

   ○ True ○ False

2. A minimum of 10% of the monthly common expenses must be deposited in a reserve fund when a condominium is first registered and until a reserve fund study is completed.

   ○ True ○ False

3. A status certificate is only provided by a condominium corporation when an official request is received from either the buyer's or seller's lawyer prior to closing.

   ○ True ○ False

4. A buyer has forty-eight hours to cancel an offer to purchase for a new condominium unit.

   ○ True ○ False

5. A buyer has ten days to cancel an offer to purchase for a resale residential condominium unit.

   ○ True ○ False

6. The right to use an exclusive use common element parking space is granted by the condominium corporation.

   ○ True ○ False

7. An equity co-operative owns the land and buildings with members being shareholders in the corporation.

   ○ True ○ False

8. Land transfer tax does not apply to the sale of a co-operative, as the disposition involves a share and not real property.

   ○ True ○ False

9. Timeshare involves the division of property rights into fractional interests based on time.

   ○ True ○ False

10. The *Consumer Protection Act* provides certain rights to buyers of timeshare ownership located anywhere in Canada.

   ○ True ○ False

Active Learning Exercises

Solutions are located in the Appendix.

Exercise 1

"A condominium corporation is not the same as a normal company under the *Business Corporations Act*." Discuss.

Exercise 2

A condominium would likely have a higher value than a similar co-operative. Discuss.

■ Exercise 3

On your way to visit friends at their condominium, you slip and hurt yourself very badly on the sidewalk in front of their unit. You sue the Condominium Corporation and are awarded a large sum. The insurance and the reserve fund are not adequate to satisfy the court order. Do you have to forego the balance owing to you? Explain.

■ Exercise 4

You are approached by a potential seller to list her co-op apartment. List three matters that should concern you.

Exercise 5

Your uncle wants your advice as to whether it would be wise for him to purchase a ski chalet on a timesharing plan. In order to give competent advice, what more would you want to know?

SECTION V

SHARED OWNERSHIP AND RESIDENTIAL TENANCY

CHAPTER 12

Residential Tenancy

Introduction

This chapter deals with residential tenancies and associated statutory requirements. The relationship between landlord and tenant is outlined, including the duties of both the landlord and tenant. Specific requirements of landlord and tenant legislation are introduced to assist the practitioner with the marketing of tenanted properties and the drafting of agreements.

Practitioners involved with residential properties require detailed knowledge of the *Residential Tenancies Act, 2006* and associated Regulations, which took effect January 31, 2007 and replaced the *Tenant Protection Act, 1997*. A comparative table is provided illustrating major changes made with the introduction of the new Act in 2007.

The focus in this chapter is on specific regulatory requirements that most directly impact activities of brokerages, brokers and salespersons when dealing with tenanted properties. Topics include rights of entry, assignments, subletting, lawful rent and notice periods for termination (both before end of the rental period and at the end of the rental period). Mobile home parks and land lease communities are also discussed, particularly concerning rights to place for sale signs on these properties.

Learning Outcomes

At the conclusion of this chapter, students will be able to:

- Explain the legal relationship between landlord and tenant.
- Identify various changes in statutory requirements regarding residential tenancies with the *Residential Tenancies Act*, which was effective January 31, 2007.
- Identify and describe four types of tenancies.
- Discuss selected provisions contained in the *Residential Tenancies Act*, as well as key exemptions provided under that Act.
- Highlight selected provisions regarding mobile home parks and land lease communities that address selling of homes and signage.
- Summarize key points about key topics such as entry by the landlord (with and without notice), rent guidelines, tenant selection and termination by landlord and tenant.
- Apply the law related to landlord and tenant relations to situations that may be encountered by real estate practitioners.

RESIDENTIAL TENANCIES

The listing and sale of premises which are subject to residential tenancies presents some special challenges to real estate practitioners. Over the years, revisions to landlord and tenant legislation have provided a reasonable degree of security of tenure for residential tenants. Some areas of protection include the tenant's privacy, limitations on the right of the landlord to obtain vacant possession, rights/procedures concerning subletting, landlord provisions concerning entry and termination requirements.

The *Residential Tenancies Act* spells out procedures for termination of occupancy by landlord or by tenant. There are a limited number of circumstances under which a landlord is entitled to terminate the tenure of a tenant.

Rent Control

The original *Rent Control Act* imposed a form of rent review on residential tenancy units in the Province of Ontario. The concept of the Act was that, subject to certain exemptions, rent could not be increased by more than a certain percentage per year. Landlords could apply for increases above this amount if the increase could be justified and the proper procedures were followed. Originally, the rent control guidelines for a previous tenant applied to the new tenant after the previous tenant vacated. Current rent control guidelines, now embodied in other legislation, do not apply in this situation. Of course, the guidelines apply to any subsequent increases for the new tenant.

Recent Changes

Statutory law for residential tenancies in Ontario comes under the *Residential Tenancies Act (2006)*, replacing the *Tenant Protection Act*. This new statute became effective on January 31, 2007. While the new Act is said to replace the former Act, practitioners should be aware the bulk of the prior legislation regarding many provisions remains unchanged. Following are some of the more notable revisions:.

The Landlord and Tenant Board is responsible for all matters regulated under the *Residential Tenancies Act*.	Units are not subject to rent controls when first renting to a new tenant. Obviously, when they come up for renewal, rent control applies.
The landlord must give new tenants a pamphlet with information on the responsibilities of landlords and tenants, the role of the Landlord and Tenant Board and contact details. This pamphlet is available through the Landlord and Tenant Board.	The landlord can apply to the Landlord and Tenant Board for any justifiable increase in rent by more than the rent control guideline, if taxes, charges or utilities have increased. If utility costs or taxes go down, the rent must go down.

If the rent increase application is for capital expenditures or security services, there is a limit of three percent above the guideline for a maximum of three years. Once the capital expenditure is fully paid for, the rent must go down for any tenants who were living there at the time of the increase.	Like the previous legislation, a landlord may show a unit to a prospective tenant between 8:00 a.m. and 8:00 p.m. without written notice, if a notice of termination has been given and the landlord informs the tenant or makes a reasonable effort to inform the tenant of the intention to show the unit.
At a hearing for an above guideline rental increase application, the Board can decide to deny or delay the rent increase if there are serious outstanding maintenance issues or work orders.	The rate of interest that a landlord must pay to a tenant on a last month's rent deposit every year is the same as the annual rent increase guideline and landlords can use the interest to top up the last month's rent to keep it current.
The annual rent increase guideline is based on the Ontario Consumer Price Index (CPI), which is the rate of inflation.	A landlord has a statutory right to show a rental property to a potential buyer (8:00 a.m. to 8:00 p.m.) with written notice at least twenty-four hours in advance.
The tenant's flexibility to give as little as ten days' notice and move after receiving a notice of termination from the landlord for demolition or conversion also applies to situations where the landlord personally requires the unit.	A landlord has a statutory right to give notice on behalf of a buyer who personally requires the unit at the end of a term of tenancy. The ten day option applies for the tenant receiving such a notice.
The notice period for termination by a landlord for non-payment of rent is fourteen days (seven days for weekly tenancy). To avoid eviction, the tenant must pay the arrears by the termination date.	Except for a notice for non-payment of rent, when a notice of termination has been served on the tenant, the landlord must apply to the Board for an order terminating the tenancy not later than 30 days after the date specified in the notice of termination.
There is a shorter eviction process for tenants who cause wilful or excessive damage to a rental unit or building. This shorter process also applies to tenants who cause a disturbance in a small rental building where the landlord also resides. The notice period to the tenant is shortened to 10 days from 20 days. Landlords can apply to the Board for an eviction notice immediately after serving the notice.	

Commercial vs. Residential Statutory Rights — CURIOSITY

It should be noted that many of the protections for residential tenants under Ontario law do not apply to commercial tenancies, for example, security of tenure without a lease, distrain of tenant's possessions, security deposits and post-dated cheques.

TENANCY (TYPES)

The relationship of a landlord to a tenant arises from ancient feudal doctrines. Over the years, four major types of tenancy have developed.

Fixed Term

A fixed tenancy is one in which the tenant has exclusive possession for a specific term, which is normally agreed to in a written contract. In a fixed term lease, both the commencement and expiry dates must be determined before the lease takes effect. In a commercial fixed term tenancy, the tenancy ends on the expiry date and no notice is required, however, it is not unusual for the tenancy to continue on a periodic basis. In residential tenancies, if the tenant remains in possession of the property following the expiry date, the tenancy is deemed to continue on a month-to-month basis pursuant to the *Residential Tenancies Act.*

Periodic Tenancy

A periodic tenancy is a tenancy for a fixed period but indefinite length that can be made certain by notice of termination. In other words, the periodic tenancy automatically renews itself (usually on a weekly, monthly or yearly basis) unless notice is given to the contrary.

In residential tenancies, a periodic tenancy can be either in writing or oral and may simply state that the tenancy is on a month-to-month basis. If a residential tenant remains in a property following the expiration of a fixed term tenancy, the tenancy relationship normally converts into a periodic tenancy automatically.

EXAMPLE *Types of Tenancy—Periodic Tenancy*

Owner Smith enters into a commercial tenancy agreement with Jones whereby Jones has a monthly tenancy beginning on the first of each month. This tenancy will automatically renew itself for the same duration as the original period unless either Smith or Jones gives notice to terminate (a notice to quit) to the other.

Tenancy at Will

Tenancy at will arises when, after expiration of a lease, or when no lease exists, the tenant remains in possession with the consent of the landlord or the person entitled to possession.

Real estate practitioners should be aware that a tenancy agreement can occur by contract or by implication from the acts of the parties. An implied tenancy at will may arise when a tenant occupies premises without rent. An express tenancy at will may arise when a real estate transaction does not close on the scheduled date and possession is granted in anticipation of a future closing.

EXAMPLE *Types of Tenancy—Tenancy at Will*

Seller Smith sells his commercial property to Buyer Jones, but Jones has to wait for the closing of another property on the same day that is now delayed. The solicitors for Jones and Smith agree to allow Jones to take possession of the commercial property, provided that he agrees to vacate the premises without notice if the other transaction does not close in a short period of time.

While there are certain risks involved in such arrangements, the lawyers, as well as Jones and Smith, are confident that closing is a certainty. If this were not the case, Smith could well demand that Jones secure interim financing to close the sale. Further, the parties are comfortable with the arrangement as the property involves commercial usage and does not invoke legislative requirements that would normally be considered in a residential tenancy; e.g., specific notice periods and related requirements. Accordingly, the buyer and seller enter into a tenancy agreement to suit the circumstances.

Tenancy at Sufferance

This type of tenancy (also referred to as an *overholding tenancy*) could occur if a person has possession without the consent of the owner and without paying rent. It arises by implication of law in situations where the tenancy has been terminated but the tenant does not vacate. Tenancy at sufferance might typically arise if the tenant did not vacate after a proper notice to quit, or did not vacate after the fixed term tenancy expired. In certain circumstances, a tenant may be liable for damages or for double rent. Once again, residential overholding is subject to the *Residential Tenancies Act.*

EXAMPLE *Types of Tenancy—Tenancy at Sufferance*

Owner Smith, a commercial landlord, gives Tenant Jones a notice to vacate. Jones has occupied the property for several years. Smith, in giving notice, currently resides at a distant location and has no immediate use for the property, which is scheduled for redevelopment. Jones, while accepting the notice, remains on the property without paying any rent.

RESIDENTIAL TENANCIES ACT

Current Legislation

The *Residential Tenancies Act* is a complex piece of legislation spanning numerous provisions that not only impact residential premises, but also care homes and land lease properties. Selected, commonly encountered topics are outlined. Information provided has been excerpted (or modified) from a residential tenancy reference text, reprinted with permission of the author. Summaries are included for descriptive purposes only and the Act should be consulted directly on all tenancy matters.

WEB LINKS

Practitioners can obtain a copy of the Act and Regulations (go to ***www.e-laws.gov.on.ca***) and/or contact the Landlord and Tenant Board (***www.ltb.gov.on.ca***). Salespeople and brokers wishing to focus on residential tenancies are strongly encouraged to pursue advanced tenancy courses.

Rules and Guidelines CAUTION 

Practitioners must ensure that current guidelines are followed and correct forms used. The Landlord and Tenant Board (**www.ltb.gov.on.ca**) periodically amends policies and procedures, particularly concerning Rules of Practice, Interpretation Guidelines and Forms. Salespersons and brokers should also note that the *Residential Tenancies Act* is not the only legislation impacting landlords and tenants. Others include the Human Rights Code, *Condominium Act*, and the *Co-operative Corporations Act*.

Abandoned

The term abandoned is defined as the act of leaving a rental premises completely and finally. The *Residential Tenancies Act* sets out provisions concerning the abandonment of a rental unit and landlord rights concerning the disposal of tenant property. A unit is not considered abandoned if the tenant is still paying rent.

A landlord must proceed cautiously regarding a seemingly abandoned unit. A unit is not abandoned when the rent is paid. However, confusion can arise when the unit appears vacated and the rent is not paid.

Substantial evidence should precede any action by the landlord. Clear evidence must exist that the tenant has left; e.g., all possessions are gone and the door is left open. Evidence should be cumulative in support of taking any action. Such evidence might include the fact that the tenant informed the landlord of his/her intent to leave, the mail has remained uncollected and a neighbour spoke with the tenant and saw the individual loading personal effects.

The landlord should also make attempts to contact the tenant and, at minimum, keep records of such attempts. Notwithstanding these guidelines, any landlord can take on substantial risk by re-renting a unit, or taking other action (e.g., disposing of any tenant's possessions) without an order by the Landlord and Tenant Board.

Access

The right to access or gain admittance to a rental premises is addressed in the *Residential Tenancies Act*. Matters concerning access should be clearly understood by all salespersons involved in the showing and/or rental of residential property. The right of quiet possession by tenants is well established in both common and statutory law. Consequently, practitioners must be knowledgeable of and demonstrate prudence regarding entry requirements.

The Act sets out selected access-related issues:

- The landlord may not restrict reasonable access by election candidates (or their authorized representatives) for any federal, provincial or municipal office.
- The landlord cannot change the entry locking system to a residential unit without providing replacement keys to the tenant. The tenant can apply to the Landlord and Tenant Board for an order to regain possession of their unit if they have been illegally locked out.
- The tenant cannot change, or have someone change, the entry locking system to a residential unit without the landlord's consent.

For additional discussion regarding salesperson entry for sale or rental purposes, see the topic below titled *Entry: Rights of Landlord*.

Animals

Any provision in a tenancy agreement that forbids animals (frequently referred to as the *no pet* provision) is in violation of the Act. In other words, a *no pet* provision in a tenancy agreement is void. However, exceptions do apply; e.g., provisions in the Ontario Human Rights Code and pet restrictions in condominiums (subject to certain qualifications). A condominium declaration may contain enforceable provisions (e.g., no pet provisions) relating to the occupation and use of units and common elements.

Practitioners commonly encounter questions regarding pets in rental accommodation. Any tenant or landlord wishing detailed information or currently involved in a dispute concerning animals is strongly advised to contact the Landlord and Tenant Board and/or seek expert advice.

The landlord may make application for an order to terminate the tenancy and evict the tenant under selected circumstances concerning animals; e.g., where the animal causes substantial interference with reasonable enjoyment, causes a serious allergic reaction or the animal is inherently dangerous.

Assignment

Assignment provisions apply to all tenancies whether periodic, fixed, contractual or statutory, but not to the tenant of a superintendent's premises (which is specifically excluded under the Act).

- If a tenant requests an assignment, the landlord can either consent or refuse consent.
- If a tenant requests an assignment to a specific assignee, the landlord can consent or refuse consent based on that assignee.

A refusal regarding an assignee cannot be arbitrary or unreasonable. It should be noted that the landlord may consent to an assignment and subsequently refuse an assignment to a specific assignee. The landlord may charge reasonable out-of-pocket expenses in giving consent.

If an assignment is requested by a tenant and the landlord refuses or does not respond within seven days of the request, the tenant may give notice of termination within 30 days of the request.

If an assignment is made, the terms and conditions of the tenancy agreement continue to apply. Both assignee and tenant (now former tenant) are liable to the landlord and have rights under the tenancy agreement as follows: (1) the former tenant for the period up to the assignment; and (2) the assignee for the period following assignment.

Care Home

Various matters concerning the operation of care homes fall under the provisions of the *Residential Tenancies Act*. A care home is generally described as a residential complex in which residents receive care services including health, therapeutic or rehabilitative services, or services that assist with daily living activities.

The Regulations set out a range of such services as a guideline including nursing care, assistance with bathing, feeding, dressing, ambulatory and personal hygiene assistance and personal emergency response services. Practitioners do not commonly encounter situations involving care homes. Certain key provisions, however, should be reviewed for general knowledge:

- A written tenancy agreement involving a care home must be provided setting out care services and meals including the related costs.
- Every tenancy agreement must have a statement outlining that the prospective tenant:
    - has the right to seek third party advice; and
    - may cancel the agreement within five days after the agreement has been entered into.

- The *Residential Tenancies Act* contemplates that a landlord may have both care-related as well as non care-related tenancies within the same residential complex. In such instances, the former are referred to as care attached units and fall under the provisions set out for care homes.
- An information package must be provided to all prospective tenants setting out particulars including, but not limited to, alternative packages of care services, information regarding staffing and emergency, fire and medical response systems. The Regulations set out minimum requirements concerning materials to be provided in the package.

Not all rehabilitative or therapeutic accommodation fall under the general provisions for care homes.

Condominium Conversion

The *Residential Tenancies Act* provides for tenants' security of tenure in the event that a residential complex is converted to condominium. The landlord cannot demand that tenants move out in order to convert a rental building into a condominium.

The tenant, in most instances, can continue to live in the rental unit after the property becomes registered as a condominium. As such, the tenant is protected under the *Residential Tenancies Act.* The Act sets out various exceptions and qualifications that should be read in detail.

Expert advice is required concerning all matters involving condominium conversions. Practitioners should also be reminded that local municipalities may have restrictions concerning such conversions.

Entry: Rights of Landlord

Right of entry by the landlord is broadly divided into two scenarios: entry with written 24-hour notice and entry without notice.

Entry With Written 24-Hour Notice Entry by the landlord with proper written notice is permitted provided that the notice sets out the reason for the request and the day and time of the requested entry. The landlord may enter between 8 a.m. and 8 p.m:

- to carry out repairs or do work in the rental unit;
- to allow a potential mortgagee or insurer of the residential complex to view that particular rental unit;
- to allow a potential purchaser to view the rental unit;
- to inspect for purposes of ensuring that the property is in a good state of repair and meets health, safety, housing and maintenance standards, consistent with the landlord's obligations; or
- for any other reasonable reason specified in the tenancy agreement.

Entry Without Written Notice Entry is permitted without written notice in the following specific situations:

- in the case of an emergency or the tenant consents at the time of entry;
- if the tenancy agreement provides for regular cleaning by the landlord and if:
    - entry is made at times specified; or
    - between 8 a.m. and 8 p.m. when no times are specified.
- if the landlord wants to show a prospective tenant and if:
    - the landlord and tenant have agreed to a termination or either has given notice of termination;
    - the landlord enters the rental unit between 8 a.m. and 8 p.m; and
    - the landlord, before entering, makes a reasonable effort to inform the tenant of his/her intention to enter.

Exemptions

Various rental situations are specifically exempted under the Act. The following is descriptive in nature only to highlight the scope of exemptions. Exact wordings in the *Residential Tenancies Act* should be accessed when analyzing specific circumstances.

- Accommodation for the travelling or vacationing public.
- Seasonal or temporary accommodation; e.g., hotel, motel, lodge, campground, trailer park and tourist home.
- Farm employee whose occupancy is conditional on continued employment.
- Non-profit housing cooperatives.
- Penal or correctional facility.
- Accommodation subject to selected Acts. Specific exemptions include accommodation that is subject to the *Public Hospitals Act, Private Hospitals Act, Community Psychiatric Hospitals Act, Mental Hospitals Act, Homes for the Aged and Rest Homes Act, Nursing Homes Act, Ministry of Correctional Service Act, Charitable Institutions Act* and *Child and Family Services Act*. Exemptions concerning municipal, provincial and federal housing programs are detailed in the Regulations.
- Emergency shelter.
- Accommodation provided to students by an educational institution under specific circumstances.
- An employee with accommodation in the same building or project used in part or in whole for a non-residential purpose and accommodation is contingent on continuing employment.
- Occupants sharing a bathroom or kitchen facility with the owner, the owner's spouse/same-sex partner/child/parent or the spouse or same-sex partner's child/parent and where any of these individuals live in the same building. Roomers/boarders who occupy a room in a rooming, boarding or lodging house and share facilities with each other (i.e., not related to each other as detailed above) are not exempt from the provisions of the Act.
- Premises occupied for business or agricultural purposes with living accommodation attached and under one lease.
- Accommodation involving rehabilitative or therapeutic services subject to certain restrictions.

A landlord or tenant may apply to the Landlord and Tenant Board to determine if the *Residential Tenancies Act* applies to their particular rental unit or rental complex. Practitioners are also reminded that certain rental units are partially exempted.

Mobile Home Park/Land Lease Community

A mobile home park or land lease community is a community in which the landlord retains possession of the land, structures, services and facilities for the common use and enjoyment of the tenants. A land lease home is a permanent structure, as opposed to a mobile home. For purposes of the Act, the terms mobile home park and land lease community are used interchangeably.

Practitioners are increasingly involved with mobile and land lease homes as a consequence of the aging Canadian population and certain pricing advantages that are associated with land leases. As with care homes, the *Residential Tenancies Act* covers various issues concerning this topic. A summary of the most relevant items follows:

- a tenant has the right to sell or lease the mobile home or land lease home without the landlord's consent;
- any agreement that requires the tenant to use the landlord as an agent is void;
- the landlord may act as an agent of the tenant in negotiations for the lease or sale of the mobile home or land lease home with a written agency contract for the purpose of beginning those negotiations;
- the tenant, in selling his/her mobile or land lease home, may place a sign in the window of the home unless prohibited by the landlord. The landlord can only prevent such signage if all of the following conditions are met:
    - the landlord's prohibition regarding signs applies to all tenants;
    - the landlord provides a bulletin board for placement of for sale advertisements; and
    - the bulletin board is provided to all tenants free of charge and located in a prominent place accessible to the public at all times.

Rent

The *Residential Tenancies Act* provides that no charge of rent or increase of rent is allowed greater than the lawful rent permitted. Lawful rent for a new tenant is the first rent charged to that new tenant, subject to certain qualifications outlined in the Act; e.g., selected provisions relating to rent premiums and discounts.

The topic of lawful rents has understandable complexities. As a general statement, the landlord can only increase rent in accordance with the Act if 12 months have elapsed since: (1) the last rent increase; or (2) since the day the rental unit was first rented by the tenant. Special provisions apply to existing tenants previously falling under the *Rent Control Act, 1992*.

Following are selected points regarding rent increases:

- The landlord must give at least 90 days notice on an approved form for any rent increase. This includes an increase involving higher operating costs or capital expenditures.
- An increase is void if the notice is not provided in accordance with the Act. A new notice must be issued.
- No landlord may increase the rent by more than the guideline except in accordance with the Act.

- Note: An added cost relating to the addition of a parking space or a prescribed service, facility, privilege, accommodation or thing agreed to by the tenant and landlord is not deemed to be an increase for purposes of rent increases under the Act. If the parking space or prescribed service is no longer provided, the rent must be reduced accordingly.

Rent Deposit

A rent deposit cannot be more than the lesser of the amount of rent for one rental period or one month. Any reference to a security deposit is automatically deemed to be a rent deposit for purposes of the Act and the maximum rent deposit is one month's rent.

Practitioners should be aware of certain important requirements regarding rent deposits:

- If the lawful rent increases, the landlord may require the tenant to pay the appropriate additional amount concerning the rent deposit.
- The landlord is required to pay the tenant interest annually on the rent deposit. Such interest is calculated on the percentage change from year to year in the Consumer Price Index for Ontario for prices of goods and services as reported monthly by Statistics Canada, averaged over the 12-month period that ends at the end of May of the previous calendar year, rounded to the first decimal point.
- The rent deposit is applied to the last rent period prior to the termination of the tenancy.
- A tenant is not required to provide a landlord with postdated cheques or agree to automatic debit payments from an account, to a credit card or similar automatic withdrawal for rent payment. Any landlord stipulation to that effect in a tenancy agreement is in violation of the Act.
- The landlord must provide receipts relating to rents and rent deposits upon request by the tenant.

Rent Guideline

Increases in rent are not permitted for a tenant or assignee except in accordance with the Act. The Minister for the Ministry of Municipal Affairs and Housing determines and publishes a rent guideline for the following year no later than the 31st day of August of the current year.

The rent guideline is the percentage change from year to year in the Consumer Price Index for Ontario for prices of goods and services as reported monthly by Statistics Canada, averaged over the 12-month period that ends at the end of May of the previous calendar year, rounded to the first decimal point.

RELATED PROVISIONS

Increases above the guideline can be effected in various ways. The Act sets out detailed procedures, some of which are summarized below for illustrative purposes. Practitioners should advise landlords and tenants to access the Act directly and/or seek expert advice.

- The landlord and tenant may agree to increase rent if new or additional services are provided. The Regulations set out various items that fall under the parameters of a service. The Act also provides flexibility on related issues; e.g., rent adjustment for increase/decrease in unit size and discontinued services.

- Landlord and tenant may agree to increase rent if capital expenditures are provided in exchange for a rent increase, subject to certain qualifications and restrictions. If the rent increase application is for capital expenditures or security services, there is a limit of three percent above the guideline for a maximum of three years. Once the capital expenditure is fully paid for, the rent must go down for any tenants who were living there at the time of the increase.
- The Act sets out provisions for rent increases based on capital expenditures relating to the rental property that are incurred by the landlord. The landlord must make application to the Landlord and Tenant Board for such an increase.
- If the rent increase application is for capital expenditures or security services, a limit of three percent above the guideline for a maximum of three years is permitted. Once the capital expenditure is fully paid for, the rent must go down for any tenants who were living there at the time of the increase.
- The landlord may also apply to the Board for an order to increase rents relating to certain extraordinary costs involving such areas as municipal taxes, utilities and certain services. The Act also provides for reductions if taxes are lowered (below a prescribed level), utility costs associated with the increase are subsequently reduced or services are discontinued.

Procedures and calculations relating to rent guidelines are complex. Expert advice is strongly recommended.

Subletting

Subletting provisions apply to all tenancies whether periodic (e.g., month-to-month), fixed (e.g., lease with exact term), contractual (specifically detailed by contract) or statutory (provided under the Act, for example a fixed tenancy becomes a periodic tenancy if the tenant remains following the term).

The Act sets out various requirements and restrictions concerning subletting. Selected items are highlighted for descriptive purposes only. Practitioners should access the Act directly for exact wordings.

- Subletting provisions do not apply to the tenant of a superintendent's premises.
- The landlord cannot arbitrarily or unreasonably withhold consent to a sublet.
- The landlord may charge reasonable out-of-pocket expenses relating to the consent.
- The tenant remains entitled to benefits and liable for breaches under the tenancy agreement during the subtenancy period.
- The subtenant is entitled to benefits and is liable to the tenant for breaches of the subtenant's obligations.
- The subtenant has no right to occupy the rental unit after the end of the subtenancy.
- The tenant may apply to the Tribunal for an order for compensation from an over-holding subtenant, if the subtenant is in possession of the rental unit at the time of the application.
- Various rights given to the landlord concerning termination apply to the tenant/subtenant relationship as if the tenant were landlord and the subtenant were tenant (e.g., damage, reasonable enjoyment and too many persons).
- If a subtenant overholds and the original tenant has vacated the rental unit, the landlord may negotiate a new tenancy agreement with that person.

- The unauthorized occupation shall be deemed to be an assignment with landlord consent if:
    - a new tenancy agreement is not entered into within 60 days; and
    - no application is made to evict the person or the subtenant.

Tenant Selection

Regulation 290/98 under the Ontario *Human Rights Code* sets out permissible landlord practices including tenant credit references and rental history information. A landlord may request credit references and/or rental history information, an authorization to conduct a credit check and a guarantee for the rent, in addition to a rent deposit, in order to assess and subsequently select or refuse a tenant.

A landlord may request income information only if items detailed above (credit references and rental history) are also requested.

- If such details are obtained, income information must be used in conjunction with that information to assess and subsequently select or refuse a tenant.
- If such details are requested but not obtained, the income information can be considered on its own merit when selecting or refusing a prospective tenant.

A final provision under this regulation warrants emphasis:

> *Nothing in this Regulation authorizes a landlord to refuse accommodation to any person because of race, ancestry, place of origin, colour, ethnic origin, citizenship, creed, sex, sexual orientation, age, marital status, family status, handicap or the receipt of public assistance.*
>
> Source: Sec. 4, Ontario Regulation 29/98: Business Practices Permissible to Landlords in Selecting Prospective Tenants for Residential Accommodation.

Termination (By Landlord)

Termination of a tenancy agreement is only possible in accordance with the Act. A notice of termination must identify the rental unit, the date of the tenancy termination and be signed (by the person giving the notice or his/her agent). In the case of the landlord, the notice must also set out the reasons and details respecting the termination.

The Act outlines appropriate notices to be used based on a range of circumstances. A notice of termination is not required if the tenant and landlord agree to terminate. Practitioners should consult the Act directly on such matters.

BEFORE END OF PERIOD

The landlord may proceed with a notice of termination either before the end of the tenancy period or at the end of the term, based on specific reasons set out in the Act. Notice periods and procedures vary. Reasons for termination include:

- Non-payment of rent.
- Termination for cause (illegal act, misrepresentation of income, damage, interference with reasonable enjoyment of other tenants, impairing of safety and too many persons occupying the rental unit).
- The Act also provides for termination for repeat of selected causes.

A change under the *Residential Tenancies Act* from the previous Act is of particular note. A shorter notice period is now provided to landlords in the case of tenants who cause wilful or excessive damage to a rental unit or building. This notice period (reduced from 20 to 10 days) also applies to tenants who cause a disturbance in a small rental building where the landlord also resides.

AT END OF PERIOD/TERM

Termination procedures at the end of the term depend on the reason for termination. Possession and sale of property are most frequently encountered by real estate practitioners.

Demolition, Conversion of Use, Extensive Renovations	The notice period is 120 days subject to certain qualifications regarding such activities.
Possession Required	A landlord may, by notice, terminate a tenancy if possession of the rental unit is for residential occupation by the landlord, the landlord's spouse or a child or parent of one of them. This also applies if the person provides or will provide care services to the landlord, the landlord's spouse, or a child or parent of the landlord or the landlord's spouse. Termination is 60 days after notice and is the day a period of the tenancy ends, or in the case of a fixed term, the end of the term. Upon receiving a notice, the tenant may then terminate earlier than the date provided in the landlord's notice of termination, but not earlier than ten days following notice.
Sale of Property	A landlord of a residential complex, containing no more than three residential units, may give notice if: • The landlord has entered into an agreement of purchase and sale to sell the complex; and • The purchaser, the purchaser's spouse, a child or parent of one of them, or a person who provides care services to the purchaser, the purchaser's spouse, or a child or parent of the purchaser or the purchaser's spouse requires possession of the complex or a unit within the complex. • The termination is 60 days following the notice and is the day a period of the tenancy ends, or in the case of a fixed term, the end of the term. Upon notice, the tenant may terminate earlier than the landlord's notice, but not earlier than ten days following notice. The same provisions apply to a condominium.

Other Specified Reasons	**Rent** The tenant persistently fails to pay rent on the due date. **Qualifications** The tenant ceases to meet qualifications in selected government owned, operated or administered rental units, federal or provincial non-profit housing projects, non-profit housing co-operative non-member units, education institution rental units and religious institution charitable non-profit units. **Tenant/Employee** An employee's employment has been terminated and the rental unit was provided during the employment. **Condominium** The tenancy arose pursuant to an agreement of purchase and sale for a proposed unit and the agreement of purchase and sale has been terminated.

Termination provisions by landlords are complex. Practitioners should refer to the Act regarding both procedures and applications to the Tribunal.

Termination (By Tenant)

Termination of a tenancy agreement is only possible in accordance with the Act. A notice of termination must identify the rental unit, the date of the tenancy termination and be signed by the person giving the notice or his/her agent. A notice of termination is not required if the tenant and landlord agree to terminate.

Practitioners should be particularly aware of notice periods relating to terminations by tenants. The tenant may give notice at the end of a rental period or at the end of a tenancy for a fixed term.

DAILY OR WEEKLY TENANCY	MONTHLY OR YEARLY TENANCY	FIXED TERM TENANCY
28 days before effective date of termination; i.e., last day of the rental period.	60 days before effective date of termination; i.e., last day of the rental period.	60 days before specified expiration date to be effective on the expiration date.

Case Synopsis

CANADA TRUSTCO MORTGAGE CO. V. PARK
ONTARIO SUPERIOR COURT OF JUSTICE SEPTEMBER 2002

This case, under the previous *Tenant Protection Act*, determined whether a mortgagee in possession can terminate a residential tenant's lease by giving notice on behalf of a buyer who is purchasing the property under power of sale.

The Ontario Rental Housing Tribunal dismissed the landlord's application (landlord was the mortgagee in possession) to terminate the tenancy on a date prior to the end of a fixed term tenancy. The landlord appealed the decision and the court agreed to hear the appeal, even though the tenant had already vacated, because of the great importance of the issue.

There is a conflict between the *Mortgages Act* and the *Tenant Protection Act* in this regard.

The *Mortgages Act* states a landlord in possession may give a notice "effective at least 60 days after it is given regardless of any fixed term of tenancy".

The *Tenant Protection Act* states "the date for termination specified in the notice shall be at least 60 days after the notice is given and shall be the day a period of a tenancy ends, or where the tenancy is for a fixed term, the end of the term".

However, the court also noted that the *Mortgages Act* states; "In the event of a conflict between this Part and any other provision of this Act or any other Act, this part prevails unless the provision or the Act states that it is to prevail over this Part".

The court also noted that the *Tenant Protection Act* states "if any provision of the *Tenant Protection Act* is in conflict with a provision of another Act, the provision of the *Tenant Protection Act* shall apply".

The court also noted that to allow the mortgagee to terminate the fixed term tenancy would place the mortgagee in a better position than any ordinary owner of a property and in a better position than the buyer of a property who has completed the purchase of a property in a power of sale situation. All of such similarly situated people could only recover possession at the end of a fixed term tenancy.

Therefore the court decided the provision of the *Tenant Protection Act* prevails and a mortgagee in possession can not obtain the early termination of a fixed term tenancy. The appeal was dismissed.

Case Questions

1. In what way did the court help to define the relationship between mortgagees, owners and tenants?

2. What effect can such a case have on future decisions of courts?

Case Synopsis

MACKO V. WASIK
AUGUST 2003

CASE LAW

This case heard under the previous legislation (*Tenant Protection Act*) is a review of an earlier Order by the Ontario Rental Housing Tribunal (now referred to as the Landlord and Tenant Board), determining that the Buyer of a rental property was to pay $4,100 to a Tenant as moving expenses, plus a fine of $1,000 for violating the Act.

The Order initially found that the Buyer acted in bad faith by requiring the selling Landlord to give the Tenant notice to vacate for the Buyer's personal use, with no intention of moving into the property. The Notice for Vacant Possession was given to the Tenant by the existing Landlord's real estate agent. It was noted that the Tenant had been living in the unit for 19 years and the Tenant's rent was substantially below the market rent. When the initial decision was made, the Buyer was given the status of Landlord and this resulted in the Order.

The Buyer requested a review of the order based on the fact that the Buyer was not the Tenant's Landlord.

The Ontario Rental Housing Tribunal agreed with this interpretation and determined there was no authority to make an order against or to levy a fine against the Buyer.

The Review determined that the Order for the payment to the Tenant and the fine was to be made against the existing (selling) Landlord, and not the Buyer of the property.

While there was no evidence that the Seller was aware of the Buyer's bad faith, and the Seller claimed she was not aware, the Tribunal found that the Seller was the Tenant's Landlord and was liable. The Tribunal reported determined that "to relieve the landlord/vendor of liability in these circumstances would be to acknowledge a gaping hole in the protection the legislation is meant to provide."

If the bad faith had to be that of the landlord/vendor, the tenant would fail because the landlord did not know the true intentions of the purchaser. The purchaser would also escape as the legislation only authorizes orders for payment of money against the landlord. The tenant would be remediless.

Sections 51 and 52 confer on the owner, or the soon-to-be owner, the right to live in his or her property. This right trumps security of tenure even though the tenant is innocent of any misconduct as a tenant. Other than some notice and filing requirements, all that is required is that the owner, or prospective owner, possesses a genuine intention of moving into the rental unit and making it his or her home. Thus, it is the good faith of the purchaser that is at issue. If the purchaser is acting in bad faith, then the document has been served in bad faith.

Section 32(9) of the Act clearly allows an application to be brought against the landlord/vendor when the purchaser has not moved into the unit.

None of the above is designed to make the landlord/vendor ultimately liable for the malfeasance of the purchaser. In a prospective proceeding before the courts, I expect the vendor would recover against the purchaser. But in the first instance, the tenant should be able to proceed before the Tribunal and recover against his former landlord.

The *Tenant Protection Act* protects the tenant in this scenario. It is up to the landlord/vendor to protect himself when the purchaser enlists the landlord/vendor for service of the notice of termination. Perhaps some sort of warranty that survives closing should be obtained from the purchaser to the effect that the purchase shall save harmless the vendor from consequences of applications such as this.

The Tribunal will hold the landlord/vendor liable for the bad faith of the purchaser in these circumstances."

Case Questions

1. What are the requirements for the buyer to be able to obtain vacant possession from the existing tenant?
2. What advice did the Tribunal give a Listing salesperson for this situation?

CHAPTER DISCUSSION

1. RESIDENTIAL TENANCY

a. You list a home occupied by a tenant who has one year and six months remaining on the lease. Are you selling a rental property or can a buyer obtain vacant possession? Explain.

b. You obtain an offer on the property in the situation described above, and the buyer requires vacant possession on closing in two-and-a-half months. What should you do?

CHAPTER DISCUSSION 

1. RESIDENTIAL TENANCY (continued)

c. You have just obtained a new listing on a very saleable property. The home is rented on a month-to-month basis. You call the tenants to inform them there will probably be some showing activity this weekend. They mention that they have some family members from Vancouver visiting for the weekend, and request that you delay showing the property until next week. Comment.

d. You obtain a listing from a mortgagee of a residential property in a power of sale situation. The home is rented to a tenant with almost one year remaining on the lease. Can a buyer obtain vacant possession on closing? Explain.

KNOWLEDGE INTEGRATION

Notables

- The listing and sale of properties involving residential tenancies must be dealt with in accordance with the *Residential Tenancies Act*.
- The *Residential Tenancies Act, 2006* replaced the *Tenant Protection Act, 1997*, but many provisions flowed from the previous legislation into the new statute.
- Significant changes involved creation of new Landlord and Tenant Board, amendments concerning annual rent increase guidelines and selected notice periods.
- Tenancies can be fixed, periodic, tenancy at will or tenancy at sufferance.
- Landlords must proceed cautiously regarding abandoned property. A unit is not considered abandoned if the tenant is still paying rent.
- A *no pets* policy is void under the *Residential Tenancies Act*.
- The Act contains provisions that relate to care homes, mobile home parks and land lease communities.
- Landlord rights of entry can be grouped under two categories: Entry with 24-hour notice and entry without written notice.
- Various increases above the rent guideline can be effected as a result of increases in taxes and utilities, as well as capital investment in the property.
- Corresponding reductions in rent are also provided for in the Act should costs reduce in relation to taxes and utilities, or capital expenditure has been paid.
- The *Human Rights Code* sets out various requirements concerning tenant selection criteria.
- Detailed provisions are set out in the *Residential Tenancies Act* concerning termination of a tenancy agreement either before the end of the tenancy period or at the end of the tenancy period.
- The time period for tenancy termination depends on the term; i.e., daily or weekly, monthly or yearly, or fixed term.

Chapter Mini-Review

Solutions are located in the Appendix.

1. A residential landlord can apply to the Landlord and Tenant Board for a rent increase, when utility costs have risen significantly. But if such costs subsequently reduce, the Act does not set out any provisions for a subsequent reduction relating to these costs.

   ○ True ○ False

2. It is unlawful for a tenant to make payments by way of post-dated cheques.

   ○ True ○ False

3. A landlord has a right to gain immediate access to the rented premises under certain circumstances.

   ○ True ○ False

4. Accommodation for the travelling and vacationing public is exempt under the *Residential Tenancies Act*.

   ○ True ○ False

Chapter Mini-Review (continued)

5. The notice period for termination by a landlord for non-payment of rent is 30 days.

   ○ True ○ False

6. A landlord has a statutory right to show a rental property to a potential tenant, if the landlord and tenant have agreed to a termination or either has given notice of termination to the other.

   ○ True ○ False

7. A mobile home park owner can prevent a real estate brokerage from placing a for sale sign on a home located within the park, if that owner meets specific requirements set out in the *Residential Tenancies Act.*

   ○ True ○ False

8. The rent guideline is established each year based on the Consumer Price Index (CPI) for Ontario.

   ○ True ○ False

9. If a subtenant overholds and the original tenant has vacated the rental unit, the landlord may negotiate a new agreement with that subtenant.

   ○ True ○ False

10. A landlord is not permitted to change the entry locking system for a residential unit until the end of the residential tenancy term.

    ○ True ○ False

11. According to the *Residential Tenancies Act,* an information package must be provided to all persons taking possession of a mobile home in a mobile home park, or a home in a land lease community by the owner of that park or community.

    ○ True ○ False

12. A landlord must allow a tenant to have pets in a residential unit, otherwise he or she would be in violation of the pet provision set out in the *Residential Tenancies Act.*

    ○ True ○ False

Active Learning Exercises

Solutions are located in the Appendix.

Exercise 1

Brown rents the lower part of a duplex from Jones on a lease for one year, expiring on December 31, 2008. Neither gives notice to the other and Brown continues to occupy the apartment and pay rent which Jones accepts. Jones' son will return on July 31, 2009 from a year-long trip to Europe, and Jones wants his son to take over Brown's apartment.

a. What is the minimum notice that Jones must give to Brown?

b. Can notice be given to take effect July 31, 2009, or does the 31st of December have to be the termination date? Why?

c. Jones gives the necessary notice, however, Brown does not vacate on the 31st of July, what can Jones do?

d. Assuming Brown has otherwise been a good tenant, what will likely happen?

Exercise 2

Green rents an apartment from Jones on a monthly tenancy at a rate of $600 a month. On the 30th of June of this year, Jones notifies Green that as of the 1st of September, the rent will be increased to $675, and requests that Green submit post-dated cheques for a period of one year.

a. What information must be included in Jones' notice to Green?

b. Does Green have any grounds to refuse to pay the increase?

c. In order to have Green comply, what must Jones do?

Exercise 3

Dave Developer owns a large apartment building in which there are several deluxe units facing the west. He also owns the vacant land to the west of the building on which he has started construction of an entertainment centre which is to include a bowling alley, a video arcade and a nightclub. One of the tenants of one of the west apartment units has a lease for three years but informs him that she is leaving at the end of this month, claiming that the landlord has broken the covenant for quiet enjoyment because of the construction noise, the dust and general disturbance to her. She also claims that the future use of the adjoining premises will interfere with her enjoyment of her apartment because of the noise of cars and people below her window.

Assume that she does leave and does not pay her rent, and the apartment is vacant for four months until it is rented to another tenant. Is she liable to the landlord? If so, for how much?

■ Exercise 4

A tenant signs a lease stating that there are to be no pets of any kind, including cats. The tenant moves into the apartment and buys three kittens. A neighbouring tenant complains to the landlord that the noise of the mewing kittens during the night is unacceptable. There are other tenants in the building who have pets but they were there before the new lease form was prepared. What can the landlord do about the noisy kittens?

■ Exercise 5

Which of the following pairings is correct with respect to the minimum time required for termination of a residential lease by a tenant? Check any or all.

- ☐ Fixed term of one year or longer—sixty days before expiry.
- ☐ Monthly tenancy—sixty days before last day of monthly tenancy.
- ☐ Weekly tenancy—twenty-eight days before last day of the weekly tenancy.

APPENDIX

SOLUTIONS

CHAPTER 1
HISTORY AND CONCEPTS OF PROPERTY OWNERSHIP

Case Law

DEBORA V. DEBORA

1. *In what way is a matrimonial home treated differently from the other net family property in the event of a marriage breakdown?*

   In addition to the spouse's right of possession to the matrimonial home, it receives special treatment in the calculation of the net family property. The entire value of the property, less any mortgage, of course, is added to the net family property.

2. *Describe 2 other provisions in the Family Law Act that could have prevented the full value of the cottage from being included in the net family property.*

   The Act provides that a marriage contract can determine ownership of an asset in the event of a marriage breakdown. Also, a different property can be designated jointly by the spouses as the matrimonial home and this would prevent the cottage from falling under the definition of a matrimonial home.

MCLENNAN V. MEYER

1. What proactive strategy would you recommend to buyers planning on purchasing land with shoreline, a natural watercourse flowing through the property or wetland located on the property?

   Your proactive strategy could include the following:

   - Include a condition in the offer to fully investigate the shoreline, natural watercourse or wetland.
   - Advise the buyer to seek further information regarding regulatory procedures concerning watercourses and any associated alterations.
   - Seek assurances from the seller that no near-water alterations have been made.
   - Buyers are well advised to obtain photographs at time of closing in the event of future watercourse changes.

2. What relevant questions should a listing salesperson ask a potential seller whose property includes, or is impacted in some way by, a natural watercourse?

   Questions could include:

   - Are there any disputes concerning the watercourse; e.g., with adjoining neighbours, or regulatory actions being taken?
   - Are there any pending applications to alter the watercourse?
   - Does the water follow a natural course or have changes been made during the seller's ownership?

Chapter Discussion

1. HISTORICAL BACKGROUND

a. What significant rights for the landholder became recognized by the royal courts as the concept of "*tenure*" evolved into the concept of "*estates*" in land?

When the feudal system was established in England, the tenants were totally dependent on the pleasure of the Crown and the King's Lords to maintain their tenancy. As time passed, society recognized the fairness of increasing the rights of the tenants. Families who occupied and worked the land for many years eventually acquired more security of tenure. Significant rights that were acquired included the right to bequeath the property to their heirs and to give away, sell or lease their interest in the property. Once these rights were recognized, it was said that land became "*alienable.*"

b. "*History only tells us what happened and it has little importance in my day-to-day real estate business.*" Comment.

History not only tells us what happened in the past, but it sets the foundation for our legal system. The legislature of Upper Canada, now Ontario, adopted the laws of England as a basis for legal decisions. Precedents from English courts from hundreds of years ago are being quoted in Ontario courtrooms today.

The law of property ownership, agency, contracts etc., are based on this tradition of English law. A knowledge of this history is essential for an understanding of the way law is created and modified, and directly applies to the sale or lease of real estate in today's market.

2. CONCURRENT OWNERSHIP

List the main similarities and differences between joint tenancy and tenancy-in common.

There are significant differences between joint tenancy and tenancy in common. The right of survivorship applies to joint tenancy. When one joint tenant dies, that person's interest in the property automatically and instantaneously transfers to the surviving joint tenant(s). Under tenancy in common, the interest transfers to the estate of the individual. The four unities are not required for tenancy in common. The interests of tenants in common do not have to be equal and do not have to be acquired from the same person or at the same time. If one of the joint tenant's sells or mortgages their interest, the four unities have been violated and that portion of the interest reverts to tenancy in common.

Joint tenancy and tenancy in common are similar in that they are both forms of concurrent ownership and there is an undivided interest with joint possession. The joint owners can not point to their share of their property. They have an interest in the entire property.

Obviously, the concept of "*survivorship*" with joint tenancy and the absence of survivorship for tenancy in common gives individuals two distinct choices for the ownership of property, depending on the circumstances and the relationship between the individuals.

CH1 DISC

Chapter Discussion

3. THE FAMILY LAW ACT

According to the *Family Law Act*, what special provisions for the matrimonial home do not apply to the balance of the family property?

While the *Family Law Act* provides an equal distribution of family assets, subject to certain exceptions, there are additional provisions for a property that falls under the definition of a matrimonial home. Each spouse has an equal right of possession of a matrimonial home. The spouse who owns the property cannot dispose of or encumber the matrimonial home without obtaining the consent of the other spouse or a court. This provision requires real estate salespeople to obtain the required consent when listing property and negotiating an Agreement of Purchase and Sale. There are additional special provisions for the matrimonial home, however, the involvement of real estate salespeople should be limited to the obtaining of the required signatures. Real estate salespeople must not, under any circumstances, make any comments or give advice related to such issues as the *Family Law Act*. Parties must be advised to seek independent professional advice.

CH1 MINI

Chapter Mini-Review

1. A life estate involves an interest in land granted to someone for a lifetime period.

 True  False

The life estate interest ceases on the death of the named person.

2. The concept of concurrent ownership applies to joint tenancy, but not to tenants in common.

 True  False

Concurrent ownership can involve either joint tenancy or tenants in common.

3. An owner having riparian rights relating to a watercourse abutting his or her property has a right to access the water and alter the shoreline to suit personal needs.

 True  False

The owner's riparian rights do not extend to shoreline alteration, but the owner does have a right to an increase in shore area provided that it occurs through natural growth.

4. Even if a wife is the only registered owner of the matrimonial home, the husband is entitled to live there.

 True  False

The husband, as a non-owner, has a right to possession of the matrimonial home under the *Family Law Act*.

5. If there is no marriage contract and a marriage breakdown occurs, the husband is entitled to claim half of the increase in value of his wife's rental property that she owned before they got married.

 True  False

Family property is equally divided subject to various exclusions. The division of assets can be disrupted when a valid domestic contract exists that excludes specific property owned by either partner.

CH1 MINI

6. If I own a house that my husband and I live in as our matrimonial home, he automatically owns half based on requirements set out in the *Family Law Act*.

 True  False

The *Family Law Act* does not directly address ownership. This statute requires equalizing at time of marriage breakdown and provides for the non-owner right to possession of the matrimonial home.

7. A husband and wife own a matrimonial home as joint tenants. Upon the husband dying, the interest in this home would automatically transfer to his wife.

 True False

Joint tenancy has the right of survivorship.

8. Property inherited or received as a gift is excluded under the net property family concept.

 True  False

This is one of several exclusions to the net family property concept.

Active Learning Exercises

CH1 EX

Exercise 1

a. The interest conveyed is called "*fee simple with conditions*." The interest immediately terminates as soon as the condition is violated.

b. The property reverted to the estate of John Smith and then to his heirs, Joseph and Mary. The owners are now Mary and the developer.

Exercise 2

a. Yes, a property held under a life estate can be leased.

b. The wife, who is the owner of the life interest, is entitled to the rent.

c. If the wife dies next year, the lease would automatically terminate. An individual can not convey an interest greater than the one that exists.

d. Both the wife and the son had an interest that is insurable, so hopefully, the building was insured. The wife now has a life estate in the land.

e. The wife and the son would have to come to an agreement as to the disposition of the proceeds of the sale and both would have to sign the listing and the Agreement of Purchase and Sale. If the property is a matrimonial home, the spouse(s) would have to sign.

Exercise 3

a. Mary and David would both have to agree to the transaction and both sign the listing.

b. Mary, David, Bill and Sarah would all have to sign the listing, obviously after coming to an agreement as to the disposition of the proceeds of the sale.

APPENDIX

CH1 EX

c. Both Mary and David must sign the listing. If either is married and the property is a matrimonial home, the spouse(s) to which this applies must also sign.

d. Mary, Sarah and Adam must sign.

Exercise 4

When at least one property is designated by both spouses as the matrimonial home, this relieves other properties from falling under the definition of a matrimonial home. The spouses may have a reason for not wanting the right of possession to apply to the other property or properties. In addition, properties that fall under the definition of a matrimonial home are not treated in the same way in the calculation of net family property. This designation does not prevent the other property from being included as net family property, however a marriage contract may apply to this situation. Real estate salespeople are cautioned to refrain from commenting on such legal matters. Parties must be advised to seek independent professional advice.

Exercise 5

The way the scenario is described, these properties seem to fall under the definition of a matrimonial home, since they live in the properties on a regular and recurring basis. While the issue of possession would have to be resolved, unless there are unusual circumstances not described in the information provided, the marriage contract would apply to ownership and her interest would be 10%.

Exercise 6

For the property on First Time Drive, Richard is the owner and he would sign the listing. Susan has never lived there and the property is not a matrimonial home so she does not sign. For the property on Better Street, Susan must sign as owner and Richard signs as non-owner spouse of the matrimonial home.

Exercise 7

She is involved. The property appears to be a matrimonial home and therefore she is entitled to notice so that she may protect her interest.

Exercise 8

Smith and the other neighbours along the creek have riparian rights. Smith cannot alter the quantity and quality of water flowing to the down-creek neighbours. Any diversion of water would likely cause immediate objections from the neighbours.

CHAPTER 2
LEASEHOLDS AND PROPERTY INTERESTS OTHER THAN OWNERSHIP

Case Law

RIDGELY V. NIELSON

1. *How large must an easement be for the salesperson to be concerned?*

   A salesperson should be cautious and not make the decision that an easement is too small to be an issue.

2. *What steps should a salesperson take to avoid such a loss of a sale?*

   If a salesperson is aware of an easement, whatever the size, there should be an acknowledgement clause in the Agreement describing the easement and obtaining the buyer's agreement to accept it.

   A salesperson should also look for potential problems when inspecting a property, for example, the lots may be narrow and it may be obvious there is a mutual drive. Also, documents can be requested and reviewed during the listing process. For example, a survey may disclose an easement.

COUNTRY STYLE FOOD SERVICES INC. V. 1304271 ONTARIO LTD

1. *In this instance, the Court found that the landlord had negligently misrepresented facts to the franchisee. What is the difference between fraudulent and negligent misrepresentation?*

   A fraudulent misrepresentation is a misrepresentation made with the knowledge of its falsity and reckless disregard for the truth. The purpose is to induce the other party to enter a contract. A negligent misrepresentation exists when there is a special relationship between the parties establishing a duty of care and a misstatement is made with the intention that it be relied upon. The individual may not know that the information is false, but should have known, given his/her particular knowledge and/or expertise. The innocent party may have grounds for damages if he or she relies on this false statement.

2. *What evidence supported the franchisee's claim that the landlord made a negligent misrepresentation?*

   The original site plan that was later revised was part of the head lease and was included with the franchisee's sub-lease. Changing the site plan to the detriment of the franchisee was very similar to the concept of "derogation of the grant" by the landlord.

CH2 DISC

Chapter Discussion

1. *LEASEHOLDS*

Under common law, the creation of a lease imposes various duties on the parties involved. Briefly describe the main duties of both Landlord and Tenant.

Landlords Duties

- Duty of quiet enjoyment. The landlord must give the tenant exclusive use of the property and must not interfere with the tenant's exclusive use.
- Derogation from the grant. The landlord may not do anything to prevent the tenant from using the property as intended. This seems to be the same as quiet enjoyment but it extends beyond the basics of quiet enjoyment. For example, it may have to do with the way the landlord permits other parts of the property to be used. If the landlord rents one unit to a tenant whose business is diamond cutting and then rents the adjacent unit to a tenant with heavy equipment that causes vibrations to the neighbour's diamond cutting equipment the landlord may be found to have derogated from the grant and the landlord would be liable in this situation.
- Duty to comply with the terms of the lease.

Tenants Duties

- Duty to pay rent and other charges as agreed.
- Duty to maintain the property and to not damage the property or commit or permit waste on the property, for example, cut down trees etc. (unless, of course, the agreement with the landlord permitted this action).
- Duty to use the property legally.
- Duty to comply with the terms of the lease.

2. *A STUDY OF HISTORY*

A study of the history of landlord and tenant relations provides an interesting insight into the way law changes over time in society. Provide at least three examples from Ontario statutes to show how the law relating to tenancy has changed dramatically to reflect the needs of modern society.

Many of the questions or case studies in this workbook have valid answers that we could never anticipate and list in the answers supplied. This question is an example of such a topic. There are statutes like the Statute of Frauds that require agreements to be put in writing and the *Registry Act* and *Land Titles Act* requiring documents to be registered for purposes of public notice. Perhaps the most interesting examples to illustrate how dramatically the law has changed over the years are related to residential tenancy. It has not been too many years since landlords could demand huge damage deposits, seize personal belongings for non-payment of rent and demand post-dated cheques for rent etc. The subject of rent control must surely be on the top of anyone's list for the answer to this question.

Chapter Discussion

3. ELEMENTS OF A LEASE

Briefly describe the main basic elements for a lease to be enforceable.

- The names of the parties. The requirements under contract law obviously apply; e.g., the requirement for the parties to be competent.
- A description of the leased premises.
- A statement of the consideration.
- The legality of use; another issue related to the required elements of a contract.
- The commencement and expiration dates.
- The rights and obligations of the parties.

For a lease to be a valid agreement, there must be a meeting of the minds and these elements of a lease are required for such an agreement. See Section 2, Chapter 5, Contract Law.

4. DEROGATION FROM THE GRANT

Using a specific example, explain the meaning of the term "*derogation from the grant*".

This concept was explained and an example provided above in the answer given for landlord's duties under lease.

5. OTHER INTERESTS IN PROPERTY

You are listing an older two-storey home in an established part of the city. The seller mentions the property has a "*mutual drive*".

a. What two provisions with reference to the mutual drive would you expect to find in the deed to this property?

For a mutual drive; a right to travel on a portion of the neighbour's property is appurtenant to the property, however, the neighbour also has the same right to travel on the subject property. The term "*mutual*" describes the situation. These rights would be carefully described in the deed for the subject property. The deed for the subject property would describe a "*right-of-way*" over the neighbour's property and would be encumbered with an "*easement*" in favour of the neighbour.

b. As listing salesperson what steps would you take in the marketing of this property as a result of your knowledge of the mutual drive?

The mutual drive would obviously affect the value of the property, but from a legal standpoint, the mutual drive would have to be mentioned on the listing and clearly described in the Agreement of Purchase and Sale. The standard pre-printed portion of the agreement requires the buyer to accept minor easements and utility easements that do not materially affect the use of the property, however, a mutual drive would go beyond this and would have to be mentioned in the agreement or the buyer may have cause to object to the title.

Chapter Discussion

6. CHARACTERISTICS OF AN EASEMENT

List the major characteristics required for the creation of an easement.

There must be a dominant tenement and a servient tenement, separately owned. The easement is terminated if the ownership of both properties is merged.

There must be a benefit to the dominant tenement. If the purpose for the easement ceases to exist, the easement will no longer exist. For example, an easement for access to a coal chute for delivery of coal would no longer exist if the use of coal was discontinued.

The dominant tenement and servient tenement need not be adjoining but must be reasonably close.

7. RESTRICTIVE COVENANTS

With the introduction of zoning by-laws in the twentieth century, does this make the concept of a restrictive covenant obsolete? Explain.

Interestingly, the concept of a restrictive covenant was created before zoning by-laws because individual property owners wanted to have some control over the use of land in their neighbourhood. Many of the potential problems addressed by restrictive covenants are now controlled by local government with zoning by-laws. For example, if a property owner is in the middle of a subdivision, it is unlikely that the by-laws would permit a fast food outlet next door.

However, even within areas strictly controlled by zoning by-laws, an individual property owner may want to be more restrictive and place limitations when selling nearby property. The zoning by-law may permit a use the seller may want to prevent. This is why they are sometimes called "*private*" deed restrictions. The zoning may permit a six storey building but the deed restriction may state a maximum of three storeys. It is sometimes possible to have a deed restriction removed by the court and it would be invariably argued by the applicant that the zoning by-law is not as restrictive, therefore the deed restriction should be removed for the benefit of the community.

Deed restrictions can also serve other purposes, for example, the commercial seller wants to prevent competition in the area. They are also widely used by developers to create a distinctive style or conformity of development. Therefore, even though the municipality may have similar goals with zoning by-laws, deed restrictions are still widely used.

Chapter Discussion

8. ENCROACHMENT

A few days ago you placed a sold sign on one of your listings. Today you received a call from the seller's lawyer who informs you that the seller's detached garage is an encroachment on the neighbour's property. For a property in the Registry system, what does this mean and how can it affect the transaction?

This could end up being a major problem. Hopefully something can be worked out so that the sale will not fall through, but it may not be easy to resolve. The adjoining owner may have the right to demand that the offending structure be removed. This may give the buyer the right to refuse to close, assuming there was nothing in the agreement requiring the buyer to take responsibility for this problem. An encroachment agreement between the two property owners may also exist to deal with the problem. The other issue that could affect the situation is related to the length of time the garage was on the property and whether the property was in the Registry or Land Titles system. The issue of title by possession will come up in the next chapter. You will see that it may support the seller's position if the neighbour takes a hard line and demands the removal of the garage. This matter is best left to the lawyers for the parties to resolve.

9. FIXTURES AND CHATTELS

Many items do not readily fall into the category of either chattels or fixtures. Build a list of items that may cause problems or result in disputes either before or after an Agreement of Purchase and Sale is arranged.

Just when you thought you had heard everything on this topic you will encounter another dispute related to fixtures and chattels. Such things as rose bushes, plants, shrubs, rocks, birdhouses, doorknobs, etc. have been the subject of disputes. There are more obvious items that frequently cause problems, such as drapery tracks and rods, blinds, carpets (Is it attached or just lying on the floor?), appliances, fireplace and pool accessories, light fixtures, mirrors, shelves, etc. What about things that are not attached; remotes for the garage door, the keys to the house? They are not attached, the usual definition of a fixture. Most real estate salespeople have a favourite story about fixtures and chattels. This is an area where a professional salesperson can anticipate potential problems and eliminate them by adding information to the Agreement of Purchase and Sale. Salespeople quickly learn that they do not want to lose all the good will they have built up by finding just the right house to be lost because of a dispute over a lawn ornament.

Chapter Mini-Review

1. Living accommodation intended for the travelling or vacationing public is regulated by the *Residential Tenancies Act.*

 True  False

This type of accommodation is excluded under the *Residential Tenancies Act*.

2. A lease must include a description of the legal purpose for which the premise is to be used.

 True  False

The requirement to identify the legal purpose is one of several elements necessary to make a lease legally enforceable.

3. An agreement to lease sets out material matters regarding a proposed tenancy arrangement, which can then be included in a formal lease document.

 True  False

The agreement to lease sets out material matters and is then a reference document when drafting the lease.

4. The term *dark space* refers to a situation in which a commercial tenant moves out of a rented premise while still paying the rent.

 True  False

Dark space can pose a problem to a landlord and, consequently, most landlords now require a continuous use clause within the lease.

5. A license to occupy a space, such as a concession in a retail shopping centre, is legally considered to be a contractual arrangement that involves the conveyance of an estate in land.

 True  False

A license is not a conveyance, but rather a right or permission granted to an individual to another.

6. A restrictive use clause within a commercial lease can be used to ensure a proper mix of tenants within a shopping centre, but cannot be used when leasing other retail establishments.

 True  False

A restrictive use clause is not limited to shopping centres, but can be used in many different retail tenancies.

7. An easement, once granted, attaches to the land and binds subsequent owners.

 True  False

An easement is a right enjoyed by a dominant tenement over a servient tenement, which runs with the land and binds subsequent owners.

8. A restrictive covenant might involve a prohibition on the use of clothes lines and satellite dishes within a particular subdivision.

 True  False

These are two of many restrictive covenant examples that might be included when a subdivision is registered, which run with the land and are assumed by subsequent buyers.

CH2 EX

Active Learning Exercises

Exercise 1

Wording of such a clause may vary, but will contain the essential elements required:

The lease will contain a clause providing that the lessee may use the premises as a restaurant, including the sale and consumption of alcohol, providing that the required licenses are obtained. The installation of equipment for the processing and cooking of food, including stoves and deep frying units is to be permitted. The use of video, mechanical or computerized games will not be permitted. Nor will live entertainment, including musical or other performances be permitted.

The lease will also contain a clause stating that no other part of the property described in Schedule C shall be leased as a restaurant or for any use in competition with the business of the lessee.

NOTE: If you are taking the course by correspondence, you must understand that a review of the suggested answers is an integral part of the course. You may feel that you do not have adequate detailed information to answer some questions, but you are encouraged to "give it a try" and after reviewing the answers, you will likely have a higher comfort level with your understanding of the course material. This is an ongoing learning process, and reviewing the answers is a part of this process.

Exercise 2

Trade fixtures are items that a commercial tenant adds to the property for business purposes such as stoves, pizza ovens, walk-in coolers, printing presses and other equipment related to the business (the list is endless). To avoid disputes, there must be an agreement between landlord and tenant defining permissible alterations and improvements. Trade fixtures can be removed by the tenant unless otherwise agreed.

Exercise 3

a. Terry Tenant is responsible for paying rent under the terms of the lease. The landlord can claim the following:

- any arrears from the period prior to June 30th.
- the rent payable up until November 15th.
- the landlord's reasonable costs of re-renting.
- any deficiency in rent paid by the new tenant, compared to the amount payable under the original lease, up until the end of the term.

b. The landlord has an obligation to take reasonable steps to mitigate the damages even when the tenant is in breach of the terms of the lease. If the landlord refuses to permit a satisfactory tenant to take over the lease, it will be unlikely that the landlord will be able to enforce a claim for unpaid rent and costs.

Exercise 4

a. The dominant tenement is Whiteacre.

b. The properties will merge and the easement will no longer exist.

c. The owners of each property could mutually agree to terminate the easement. However, the purpose for the easement may cease to exist if, for example, a new road or other change occurs that makes the access unnecessary. The easement may cease to be used and be intentionally abandoned.

Exercise 5

The agreement would include the legal description of the property, including an accurate description of the part of the property to which the easement applies and the purpose of the easement. Of course, the agreement would have to be signed by the parties. The other issue that will not come up until Section 2, Chapter 5 is that under contract law, the neighbour must receive some form of consideration for giving the easement. This could be easily accomplished in the agreement.

Exercise 6

a. You could create some degree of protection by including a restrictive covenant(s) in the deed to the lot being sold. A good starting point would be to review the zoning by-law to determine what may be permitted and to what extent you want to add restrictions.

b. There are a number of areas where you could add restrictions; set-back from street and side lot lines, total building coverage, building height, fences, exterior design and colour, minimum construction cost, restrictions on materials, restrictions on other structures and parking (e.g., mobile home), restrictions on trees and landscaping, location of pool, single family use, restrictions on home occupants, etc. Restrictive covenants must be limiting and not require anything to be maintained. They can be created in such a way that addresses these issues.

Exercise 7

The greatest concern is the right-of-way along the back of the property. This is not a "*minor*" easement and it must be mentioned in the Agreement of Purchase and Sale. The Bell easement along the front would probably qualify as a minor easement but there may be concerns about the location of the driveway (if there is one). The owner of Lot 10 can not park on the driveway running along the back of the property since it is a right-of-way for the neighbour's garage and cannot be blocked. The location of the hedge and the fence on the easement may also be a problem. Other concerns include the wire fence on the west side. Depending on how long the fence has been up, the neighbour may have a claim on that part of the property west of the fence (see Chapter 3 for information regarding possessory title). The same problem may exist at the back of the property if the cedar hedge has been up for more than ten years. The garage may also be an encroachment. While some of these concerns may be easily dealt with, they have the potential to create serious problems for any transaction. They must be addressed by the salesperson and resolved by agreements reached in the Agreement of Purchase and Sale.

Exercise 8

a. White is right. Jones does not own lots A and B and cannot grant an easement to lots D and E over A and B.

b. Black cannot claim this right. The easement ceased to exist when Jones bought A and B and owned all three lots. The answer would likely be different if the lots did not front on the street. There is a legal principle that someone cannot sell property and create landlocked property (create a situation where there is no access to a road).

c. Before River Street opened, the easement could not be blocked and the fence must come down.

d. Once River Street is opened, the purpose for the easement probably no longer exists and the easement is terminated.

CHAPTER 3
THE RECORDING ACTS

Case Law

FIFE V. COHAN

1. *How long must a property owner have continuous use of a right of way to claim the right by prescription (under the Registry system)?*

   At least 20 years.

2. *If the issue in this case was the ownership of a strip of occupied land, rather than a right of way, what would be the required time frame for continuous use for title to be granted?*

   At least 10 years.

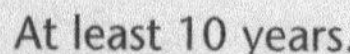

Chapter Discussion

1. THE RECORDING ACTS

List and briefly explain the major differences between the two systems of land registration in Ontario.

REGISTRY	LAND TITLES
The registry system registers documents. The Registrar or the system does not take any responsibility for the content or validity of these documents. If the form of the document, including the way it is completed, is correct, it can be registered. Therefore, an individual, usually through their lawyer, must examine the documents registered and trace the chain of title to make a determination as to who holds an interest in the property. This is called "*searching title*" for the property and rather than going back to the original Crown Patent, it is considered acceptable to find a good root of title at least forty years old and trace the chain of title from then until now. For example, if a mortgage is found to be registered on the property, a discharge registered later would be required to clear it from the property. This system is tedious and repetitious. A property may sell frequently, and this same process is repeated each time, with basically the same information being reviewed, usually by a different lawyer. The Registry system recognizes possessory title, provided that certain requirements are satisfied. An uninterrupted possession of ten years is required, with a minimum of twenty years for a right-of-way.	The Land Titles system is considerably more efficient. The Registrar is responsible for the content of the document and Title is tracked when documents are registered. It is said that while the Registry system registers deeds, the Land Titles system registers titles. The Land Titles system, unlike the Registry system, is based on the mirror, curtain and insurance principles. The title is not searched beyond the last transfer of title and an insurance fund is maintained to compensate anyone who suffers a loss as a result of the system. Since the system registers title, the acquisition of title by possession over time is not recognized in Land Titles. Electronic registration of title is being implemented and the shortcomings of the existing systems are being eliminated. It is a huge task due to the number of individually owned properties in each Registry and Land Titles office and the volume of documents involved. In terms of the standardization of documents for both systems, the Registry and Land Titles systems were brought a little closer together with the passage of the *Land Registration Reform Act*. For example, for hundreds of years, mortgages were registered in the Registry system. It was called a charge in Land Titles. Now we have a Charge/Mortgage of Land.

Chapter Discussion

1. THE RECORDING ACTS (continued)

Explain, in full, any differences in the meaning of the following terms.

DEED	TITLE
A deed is a document.	Title is a concept, implying ownership of property or an interest in property.

You may have a deed to your property but a buyer would not accept it at face value as proof of ownership. It may be proof of title or it may not be. The buyer searches title to determine whether the deed is a valid indication of title. You may have a deed to a property but if, for example, the mortgagee just issued a final order of foreclosure, or if the municipality has just completed a tax sale, the deed may be worthless. And, as previously mentioned, the neighbour or some other party may be able to make a claim for the title to all or part of the property (possessory title). A variety of legal documents fall under the definition of a deed, for example mortgage documents and many leases.

AGREEMENT OF PURCHASE AND SALE	AGREEMENT FOR SALE
An Agreement of Purchase and Sale is the standard document normally used for the sale of a property. After it has been negotiated, the necessary requirements for closing are completed and the sale is finalized on the completion date, at which time the title, payment, mortgages and possession are conveyed to the parties in accordance with the agreement.	An Agreement for Sale is quite different. While it is also a contract to sell property, it usually extends over a longer period of time and possession is turned over to the buyer, but not title until all of the terms of the agreement are fulfilled. For example, it may be a contract for the buyer to make monthly payments for ten years, at which time the buyer will obtain title. The contract probably also states that any breach of the agreement results in termination, forfeiture of possession and forfeiture of anything previously paid. An Agreement for Sale can be confused with an STB mortgage, since payments are usually made over an extended period of time, but no mortgage is created and the buyer does not have the protections under mortgage law if a default occurs. An Agreement for Sale is sometimes used in a business situation or with a developer where, for example, a lump sum payment is required some time in the future when financing is arranged. However, due to the risks involved, it is not commonly used.

MORTGAGE	CHARGE

Same thing, really. In Registry, the owner mortgaged the land. In Land Titles, a charge was registered against the property. Now we have a Charge/Mortgage of Land.

ABSTRACT OF TITLE	CHAIN OF TITLE
The abstract is the written documentation. Registry offices maintain abstract books, in which the documents related to a particular property are recorded. The abstract is the written history.	The chain of title is the actual transfer of title or ownership from party to party. When a title is searched, the *"chain of title"* is searched for a period of at least 40 years as the interest is transferred from party to party.

Chapter Discussion

1. THE RECORDING ACTS (continued)

Explain, in full, any differences in the meaning of the following terms.

RIGHT-OF-WAY	EASEMENT
There is no difference between the two terms, except that from the point of view of the dominant tenement, there is a right-of-way and from the point of view of the servient tenement there is an easement.	
The right-of-way is a benefit appurtenant to the dominant tenement.	The easement is an encumbrance on the servient tenement.

Describe the main responsibilities and activities of the solicitors in the completion of the transaction.

THE BUYER'S SOLICITOR	THE SELLER'S SOLICITOR
After completing the chart, review *Closing Procedures* in the Chapter.	

2. COMPLETION

a. Once the Agreement of Purchase and Sale has been arranged, what role should the real estate salesperson have in the completion of the transaction?

A real estate salesperson should be careful not to interfere with the roles of the solicitors after the agreement has been reached. The greatest responsibility at this point is to get the documentation to the lawyers and let them do their work. A lawyer would not expect a salesperson to interfere by engaging in unnecessary communication with the parties or re-opening the negotiations.

The salesperson would have a role in the removal of conditions and the satisfying of any reasonable requests from the parties, but anything beyond that may be considered interference by the lawyers who have been given the responsibility of representing their clients.

b. "It is possible for a seller or buyer of real property in Ontario to complete the purchase themselves without the assistance of a solicitor." Comment.

While, hypothetically, it is possible for an individual to complete a transaction without the assistance of a lawyer, there are too many documents to create and a number of pitfalls that could give grief to an unrepresented party. Issues related to title and title searching, financial matters etc. can be quite complex. For example, you will see in a later chapter that under certain circumstances, a buyer could be liable for some of the seller's income tax! This is not something a typical buyer would be aware of. Real estate salespersons should not get involved in this issue with their clients and should always advise unqualified individuals to obtain independent professional assistance.

Chapter Mini-Review

1. A quit claim deed can be an expedient method to resolve a mortgagor's financial difficulties by vesting all rights associated with the property to the mortgagee.

 True  False

A quit claim deed can be effective in this situation, but the mortgagee should be cautious because any existing problems are transferred along with the rights.

2. Under land titles, the curtain principle states that the register of title accurately and completely reflects current facts about a property title.

 True  False

The description provided describes the mirror principle, not the curtain principle.

3. The Charge/Mortgage of Land can only be used to register mortgages under land titles and not registry.

 True  False

The Charge/Mortgage of Land is used in both land titles and registry.

4. While the basis for modern land description was originally based on lots and concessions, this approach is no longer used as electronic registration requires that properties be identified by lot and plan number.

 True  False

Legal descriptions based on lot and concession are widely used in rural areas.

5. Title insurance policies are primarily designed for two target markets: lenders and owners.

 True  False

Policies and scope of coverages for these two audiences will vary by lender.

6. A survey is not required when a buyer obtains title insurance.

 True  False

Title insurance may eliminate the need for a survey, but that will depend on the property and the title insurer.

7. The seller's solicitor must undertake a title search of the property and provide a list of outstanding encumbrances to the buyer.

 True  False

The buyer's solicitor, not the seller's solicitor, undertakes a title search of the property being purchased.

8. Non-title search items could include compliance with zoning and the existence of any work orders.

 True  False

The two examples highlighted are non-title search items. The range of such items will vary by property and individual circumstances.

9. The seller's lawyer is responsible for preparing a draft Transfer/Deed of Land in preparation for closing a residential transaction.

 True False

The seller's lawyer also prepares the statement of adjustments.

10. The electronic conversion of land registry records is driven by two systems: Teraview and Teranet.

 True  False

The two systems are POLARIS and Teraview. Teranet is the company that owns and operates the Teraview software.

Active Learning Exercises

Exercise 1

The Land Titles system is far more efficient than Registry. Since the title information is kept current, it is not necessary to complete a lengthy search every time a property sells. There are fewer hidden problems such as, for example, a claim of possessory title.

Exercise 2

It may be appropriate in certain business transactions or in high risk situations where the seller does not want to take back a mortgage. An Agreement for Sale is more often used for the sale of lots or land, since it is easier to finance a property with a building on it. It is not frequently used. Most often it is used as a "*last resort*" method of financing a sale.

Exercise 3

a. Maybe. But there is not enough information to come to a decision.

b. Issues of title by possession are often open to debate. There are a number of requirements for title by possession to be recognized over and above the ten year minimum time period. Even the time frame is not totally clear. The property seems to have been used for four years without a fence and then fenced for nine. At least ten years fenced would carry more weight. Was the possession open and continuous? Did the possession take place with the knowledge but not the consent of the owner of the property? These are requirements for possessory title to be recognized.

c. There would be no debate if the property was in the Land Titles system. There is no title by possession in Land Titles.

d. She would have no claim.

e. Her son, the real estate broker, should not have made statements about legal matters, even to his mother. He should have advised her to speak to her lawyer.

Exercise 4

This is another example of an issue where parties should be advised to seek professional advice. One possibility would be to get declarations from family members and neighbours that would help to confirm the issues of ownership and the boundaries of the property.

Exercise 5

Real estate salespersons must be careful they do not encourage parties to use the services of a particular professional. Even if their opinion is sought, they should not make a specific recommendation.

CHAPTER 4
AGENCY REPRESENTATION

Case Law

MALPASS V. MORRISON AND NELSON

1. *Is it likely that the outcome would have been different if it were not dual agency (multiple representation)?*

   It is impossible to predict, however, the court did address the dual agency aspect of the case in the decision and made it clear there is potential for conflict of interest in a dual agency situation. Dual agency holds the salesperson to the highest possible standard.

2. *In what key areas did the Buyer's testimony conflict with the testimony of the Salesperson?*

   The salesperson testified the buyer was aware it was a three bedroom home. The buyers testified they were not aware the fourth bedroom in the basement was illegal.

MONTOUR ET AL V. CENTURY 21 CARRIE REALTY LTD. ET AL

1. *While this case is not entirely about agency, what can be learned by this case about agency?*

   As in the previous case, because of the potential conflict of interest, a salesperson is held to the highest possible standard.

2. *How could the salesperson have avoided this situation?*

   The salesperson should have obtained clear proof that the buyer was aware of the local improvement charge, either by putting an acknowledgment in the offer or some other form of documentation signed or initialed by the buyer.

ESBIN REALTY CORPORATION V. DAUSON PROPERTIES LTD. & THE NOIK GROUP OF COMPANIES

1. *Did the brokerage have any contact with the tenant during the listing period?*

   No. The tenant was already renting in the mall and contacted the landlord directly to express an interest in relocating to a larger unit. While the listing was in force, there were negotiations between landlord and tenant concerning the vacant space that was listed with the realty corporation.

2. *What if the tenant's initial contact with the landlord about the vacant space had taken place during the holdover period of the listing? Would the brokerage have had a claim for commission?*

   No. The holdover clause in the listing applies to prospects who were introduced to the property while the listing was in force. There is a very slight possibility the court could have ruled the tenant was introduced to the property during the listing period but it was the fact that there were negotiations between landlord and tenant during the listing period and the landlord did not inform the brokerage or involve the brokerage in the negotiations that helped the court to decide the listing agreement had been violated. The agreement states the landlord will inform the brokerage and involve the brokerage in the negotiations if the landlord is approached by a prospective tenant during the listing period.

Chapter Discussion

1. CREATION OF AGENCY

Provide an example, related to real estate brokerage, where an agency relationship is created by ratification.

Agency is created most frequently by express agreement, where there is a definite understanding established between the agent and the principal. If a real estate brokerage obtains a listing or enters into a buyer representation agreement with a buyer, each of these examples obviously fall into the category of an express agreement. But, what if a buyer is unwilling to consider creating a buyer representation agreement and says "*Give me a call if you find something in that neighbourhood for under $200,000?*" You do, in fact, find a property that meets these requirements, give the buyer a call, show the property and the buyer decides to make an offer. The buyer signs a representation agreement and an offer to purchase, and ratifies the fact that you were acting as his agent even before he recognized the relationship.

2. DUTIES OF THE AGENT

List the common law duties of the agent to the principal and give three examples from the *Real Estate and Business Brokers Act* where the common law duties of the agent to the principal are codified more specifically in statute law.

When an agency relationship is created, the agent owes the principal a number of duties which include good faith and full disclosure, obedience, competence and accounting. Usually, the agency relationship has been created because the principal does not have the resources and/or expertise to undertake the task and the principal expects the agent to act in the principal's best interests. It is often said that the agent "*stands in the principal's shoes.*" The agent has been placed in a position of trust and a fiduciary relationship exists between him/her and the principal.

Since the *Real Estate and Business Brokers Act* regulates the activities of brokerages, brokers and salespersons, it is not surprising that specific sections relate to these duties. For example, the general principle of accounting is more specifically covered by the requirements related to the Trust Account and Trade Record Sheet. It could be argued that the prohibition against a net listing (where the brokerage keeps everything over a specified minimum price as commission) is an issue of good faith, along with the requirement for disclosure in certain circumstances when purchasing listed property. There are a number of qualifications for registration as a broker or salesperson. These requirements support the general principle that an agent must be competent.

Chapter Discussion

3. DELEGATION

a. For many years it was standard practice for the duties of the agent to the principal to be delegated automatically to co-operating brokerages under the MLS® system. This practice has changed in recent years. Explain.

For many years, it was standard practice on the MLS® system for the co-operating brokerage to accept an offer of sub-agency from the listing brokerage. This meant that the selling brokerage's client was the seller, even though the selling salesperson had probably never even met the seller(s) and may have some sort of established relationship with the buyers. After all, the buyer has probably chosen to work with that salesperson to find a property. With the shift to buyer brokerage, there is an expectation that the co-operating brokerage will be representing the buyer and in this case, the listing agent's duties to the seller are not delegated to the co-operating brokerage.

b. An agent can bring a principal into legal relations with third parties. Therefore, a principal can be held liable for the statements and conduct of the agent. Does the transition to buyer representation increase or decrease this potential for liability for the seller of a property? Explain.

Advocates of buyer representation argue that the transition to buyer representation greatly reduces the liability for a seller. A principal is generally responsible for acts done and representations made by an agent on behalf of their client. Therefore, the seller is responsible for representations made to third parties. Under sub-agency, this extends to representations made by co-operating brokerages.

This is not the case with buyer brokerage, and in fact, a whole new area of responsibility is created for the co-operating brokerage who is now accountable to a buyer client.

4. DUTIES OF THE PRINCIPAL

Provide an example related to real estate brokerage that illustrates the meaning of "*indemnification*" of the agent by the principal.

The principal owes the agent the duties of remuneration and indemnification. It is widely understood that the principal must pay the agent, but what about indemnification? Basically, the principal must take responsibility for acts done by the agent in the lawful exercise of the agent's authority. The agent is not responsible for performance of any agreements arranged on behalf of the principal. For example, if the seller refuses to close a sale at the last moment and the buyer is stranded in a hotel room, the buyer's complaint and recourse is against the offending seller, not the agent who sold the house. The law protects the agent in this regard. If agents were responsible for what they arranged on behalf of their client, no one would be willing to act as an agent. If a sale closes and the dishwasher is missing from the kitchen, the buyer's recourse is against the party with whom they had the contract, not the agent. This example points out an interesting aspect of this principle; if the agent fails to fulfil his/her duties, indemnification comes into question. If the agent fails to include the dishwasher in the Agreement of Purchase and Sale, but told the buyer it was included, who is likely to pay?

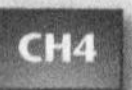

Chapter Discussion

5. THIRD PARTIES

Describe the duties of an agent to the third parties to a transaction.

Since the agent must promote the interests of the client, the primary duties of the agent are to the principal. However, there are legal duties to third parties. An agent must not provide the third party (who may be referred to as a customer) with false or incorrect or unverified information or misrepresent facts to the third party. If an agent knowingly concealed a hidden defect this would also result in legal liability. This is an interesting area to compare law and ethics. One of the functions of a Code of Ethics is to set a high standard. The Code of Ethics requires a real estate practitioner to obtain and disclose facts known to be pertinent (material) to both client and customer. From a common law standpoint, the agent may be able to say "*He didn't ask me if the landfill property across the road was a former dumpsite, so I didn't tell him.*" From an ethical standpoint, and interestingly enough from a buyer-brokerage standpoint, there is no way this should happen.

6. TERMINATION OF AGENCY

From the examples below, list the term that best describes the method of termination of the agency relationship.

a. The sellers send the brokerage a registered letter stating they no longer want to sell the property and that the brokerage will not be permitted access to the property. Revocation (breach of contract)	b. The brokerage requests a price reduction. The seller refuses. The brokerage suggests that the property should be taken off the market because it will not sell at the listed price. The seller agrees. Mutual agreement
c. The property is sold for 99% of list price. Completion (performance)	d. The first mortgagee obtains a Final Order of Foreclosure. Impossibility of performance

7. THE TYPICAL REAL ESTATE TRANSACTION

Seller Smith selects Salesperson Lee of ABC Realty Inc. to list his home. Lee places the property on the local MLS® listing service. Salesperson Martin of XYZ Real Estate Ltd. arranges an appointment to show the property to Mrs. Jones who has signed a buyer representation agreement with XYZ Real Estate Ltd. Seller Smith sells to Buyer Jones.

Chapter Discussion

7. THE TYPICAL REAL ESTATE TRANSACTION (continued)

a. Provide a step-by-step description of the forms of agency disclosure that would be used for this typical transaction. Be specific as to the type of form, the nature of the disclosure and the timing for each step, from the beginning of the scenario to the final sale.

There would be a series of agency disclosures for a typical transaction. At initial contact and prior to the listing being signed, Salesperson Lee would review an agency disclosure form, such as "*Working With A REALTOR®*", with the seller. There would be further information about agency in the Listing Agreement. Salesperson Martin would review the agency disclosure form with the buyer at the initial contact and clauses related to agency would be included in the buyer representation agreement. In most real estate boards in Ontario, it is assumed that the co-operating brokerage represents the buyer. Prior to any offer being presented, the salespeople and their respective clients should sign a Confirmation of Co-operation and Representation.

b. What duties are owed by Salesperson Martin and XYZ Real Estate Ltd. to Buyer Jones?

Salesperson Martin and XYZ Real Estate Ltd. owe the buyer the primary agency duties of good faith, full disclosure etc.

c. What duties are owed by Salesperson Martin and XYZ Real Estate Ltd. to Seller Smith?

Salesperson Martin and XYZ Real Estate Ltd. owe the seller the third party duties of fairness and the requirement not to give false information or misrepresent facts.

CH4 MINI

Chapter Mini-Review

1. The relationship between employer and employee is a good example of agency.

 True  False

An employer/employee relationship is not an example of agency, but is best described legally as a relationship between master and servant.

2. Agency is created by ratification if the principal accepts the benefits of the agent's previously unauthorized act.

 True  False

This is a true statement. Ratification is one of several methods outlined in the text by which an agency relationship can be created.

3. All registrants in Ontario must adhere to disclosure requirements set out in the Code of Ethics of the Canadian Real Estate Association (CREA).

 True  False

All registrants must adhere to disclosure requirements under REBBA 2002. Only those registrants who are members of organized real estate must adhere to the CREA Code of Ethics.

4. An agency relationship established by way of a listing agreement would probably be terminated by impossibility if the structure being offered for sale was destroyed by fire.

 True  False

Termination by impossibility is correct, but it should be noted that the listing agreement may provide for a continuation of the authority to sell the vacant land.

5. Unintended or implied dual agency (referred to in REBBA 2002 as *multiple representation*) can occur when a registrant unwittingly represents two parties in the same transaction.

 True  False

The salesperson may do so innocently, but unintended or implied dual agency (multiple representation) can have serious legal ramifications.

6. An agent must obey the principal's lawful instructions and is subject to detailed and direct control or supervision by that principal when either marketing that principal's (seller's) property or locating suitable property for a buyer as the principal.

 True  False

In agency involving real estate brokerages, the principal typically exercises little control over how the property is marketed or how a suitable property is located.

7. An agent can accept a finder's fee for referring the buyer to a mortgage broker without disclosing this fact to the seller client, provided that such fee is a minimal amount of money.

 True  False

REBBA 2002 requires disclosure regardless of amount (or other indirect financial benefit) received.

8. Under REBBA 2002, a buyer representation agreement must be in writing and signed by the buyer or seller client.

 True  False

REBBA 2002 requires that the brokerage put the agreement in writing for submission to the client, but no requirements exists that it must be signed by that client.

Chapter Mini-Review (continued)

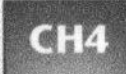

9. A brokerage cannot represent more than one client in the same transaction without receiving informed, written consent from the respective clients.

 True  False

Informed consent by the clients is required as per the General Regulation (Sec. 22), as well as selected provisions set out in the Code of Ethics.

10. REBBA 2002 only contemplates two types of agreements: representation agreements and service agreements.

 True  False

REBBA 2002 contemplates various types of agreements *other than representation agreements*. A service agreement is presently the only widely used alternative to the representation agreement.

Active Learning Exercises

Exercise 1

a. The brokerage is agent for the buyer and there are conflict of interest issues here. The letter of opinion is such a serious conflict of interest that it is very unlikely this would actually happen. The lender is not going to let the brokerage involved in the sale provide a letter of opinion to set value for mortgage purposes. It may be just slightly possible if someone who is working for the firm is an appraiser and has nothing to do with the sale, but this is extremely unlikely. Receipt of payment for the appraisal, along with the "*finder's fee*" of $500.00 conflicts with agency law, since the brokerage is receiving payment without the knowledge and consent of the client. And why is the lender paying this fee? Was the representative acting in the buyer's best interests, or using that particular lender in the hopes of benefiting personally?

b. The letter of opinion should not have been done. The representative is exposing the firm to the possibility of a claim of conflict of interest. At the very least, the buyer client must be informed of this and the fee, if the buyer does not already know. For the "*finder's fee*," immediately inform the buyer in writing.

Exercise 2

a. Yes. Bill is confused. Under sub-agency, his client is the seller, not the buyer. His confusion may have been passed on to the buyer. The buyer may think she is being represented and is providing information that must be given to the seller. The most serious problem is that Bill has no understanding of agency obligations and what he has told the listing brokerage must be told to the seller.

b. Explain to the seller what has taken place, including the comment about the $165,000, but caution the seller that there is no guarantee the buyer will actually increase the offer. As part of your duty of competence, you must also inform the seller of the implications of making a counter offer (See Section 2, Chapter 2). In this case, the initial offer no longer exists and cannot be accepted later, unless the buyer is willing to let it stand. The buyer may cool off, especially if the offer comes back at exactly the same price that the buyer previously mentioned.

CH4 EX

Exercise 3

a. The cheque must be deposited within five business days of receipt.

b. Discuss this with the seller and if this is what the seller wants, make whatever arrangements are required to follow the seller's lawful instructions. It would be appropriate to note this requirement on the listing information.

Exercise 4

This would be the case if there is no "*Commission Trust Agreement*" set up. Now that RECO insurance is mandatory, the brokerage has an obligation to maintain a Commission Trust Account. The deposit would be held in the brokerage's statutory trust account until completion at which time it would be transferred to the commission trust account. The trustee could not use this money to pay creditors as it is being held in trust for the listing salesperson and the co-operating brokerage.

Exercise 5

a. X loses.

b. Brokerage Y is acting as a sub-agent, so the seller is the client. Y has a secret interest in the transaction which makes it impossible to faithfully represent the principal. Undisclosed interest, conflict of interest. An agent cannot deal with the client in this way without the full knowledge and consent of the client, if at all. The listing brokerage will lose this one, even though it was due to the conduct of the sub-agent.

c. This is a really interesting slant on the situation; one that would be suggested by advocates of buyer brokerage. The selling brokerage's legal position shifts dramatically. Now the seller is not the client. The selling brokerage is openly representing the buyer and the seller cannot claim conflict of interest. There are still issues about complying with the *Real Estate and Business Brokers Act*. It is another example of how the Code of Ethics sets a very high standard, since disclosure is required in this situation, but the seller no longer has the right to expect good faith and full disclosure from the selling brokerage. The legal situation has certainly shifted.

Exercise 6

a. It is impossible to tell. Neither the name listed as owner, nor the individual signing are the actual owners of the property. The owner may not have authorized the sale and may not be willing to recognize the agreement. These circumstances may also benefit the buyer if the buyer is looking for a way out of the agreement.

b. Mr. Jones may be liable if he exceeded his authority and if a loss results.

Exercise 7

a. No. The courts would probably find that the brokerage has not provided the service described in the listing agreement unless the brokerage found a buyer ready, willing and able to buy the property.

b. Yes, the situation is quite different if it is the seller who refuses to close. It may be held that the brokerage has fulfilled the task as set out in the listing and is entitled to be paid for the service.

c. Normally, the deposit is released after closing. This deal is not going to close. The brokerage would have to obtain written releases from all parties or obtain a direction from a court before the money is released.

Exercise 8

a. You would be acting for the buyer so it would not be appropriate to go out and get listings for the properties. It would be advisable to establish a representation agreement with the developer before approaching the owners. Ideally, there would be advantages to approaching the owners individually and sign up as many as possible before news of the development circulated, but this is probably totally unrealistic, given the circumstances. Before anything is done, a strategic plan would have to be created and the lawyer for the client would be involved.

b. The agreement would have to be set up as an offer from the buyer. There would have to be changes in the typical policy of the brokerage holding the deposit in trust; the deposit would probably be turned over to the seller or lawyer for the seller. The statement on the offer in the acceptance clause referring to the seller directing the lawyer to pay the unpaid balance of commission would be deleted. Depending on how the issue of confidentiality unfolds, the offers may have to be conditional on the buyer obtaining all properties. The lawyer may have additional clauses and conditions, particularly with respect to obtaining approvals. The use of the Option to Purchase form is a possibility.

c. This is another interesting issue. Since this is a major project and it is a buyer representation situation, it may be appropriate to explore the possibility of paying the brokerage in some way other than a percentage. A percentage works well when the brokerage represents the seller; the more the buyer pays, the more the brokerage receives. This case illustrates that this method of payment is a bit of a contradiction for buyer brokerage. The *Real Estate and Business Brokers Act* permits an agreed upon amount.

Exercise 9

You are already representing the initial seller. You would have to fully inform your seller and obtain permission from the seller before you could consider acting for Penny. There are risks and you may want to decline this offer to avoid the possible problems related to conflict of interest.

CHAPTER 5
CONTRACT LAW

Case Law

RE/MAX GARDEN CITY REALTY INC. V. 828294 ONTARIO INC.

1. *What did the court mean by stating the irrevocable direction lacked consideration?*

   There was no consideration from the agent to the seller in return for making the irrevocable direction for the lawyer to pay the commission. The agent has not given or promised anything in return for this direction. However, the direction was held to be made under seal and this makes consideration unnecessary.

2. *What other irrevocable term of the agreement lacks consideration and requires a seal to give it force?*

   The buyer (usually it is the buyer) is agreeing to make the offer irrevocable for a specific period of time but is not receiving any consideration for this promise. Therefore the offer has to be made under seal for there to be any hope of the irrevocability having any force.

3999581 CANADA INC. V. 1394734 ONTARIO INC.

1. *On what basis did the original trial judge disallow the Buyer's claim?*

   There is a long-standing legal principle, especially for residential properties, that basically says "*what you see is what you get*". It means that if you viewed the property and were satisfied with what you observed, then minor discrepancies cannot be objected to. In this case the buyer walked on the property and the original trial judge stated the property was "*immediately identifiable and quantifiable by a casual inspection because of its observable and obvious boundaries.*"

2. *If this were a case about a home in a residential neighbourhood with a similar percentage discrepancy in the size of the land, is the outcome of the case likely to be the same?*

   No. The buyer could readily quantify the loss because fewer units could be built on the development property and on this basis the court determined a reduction in the price was warranted.

GESNER V. ERNST

1. *While the common law of contract makes a distinction between patent and latent defects, REBBA 2002 does not make this distinction. What does the REBBA Code require with respect to this issue?*

   The REBBA Code requires the registrant to disclose all material facts to both client and customer that are known or ought to be known by the registrant. While common law makes a distinction between latent and patent defects, the REBBA Code does not.

2. *If a Buyer wants the seller to provide a warranty concerning the property or a part of the property, what should be done by the salesperson?*

   The salesperson should include a carefully worded warranty in the Agreement.

Chapter Discussion

1. OFFER AND ACCEPTANCE

Describe in some detail the step-by-step requirements for an offer and acceptance to create a binding agreement.

For a binding agreement, there must be a meeting of the minds between the parties. If there was confusion, misunderstanding or lack of essential terms, there would not likely be an agreement. The offer must be complete and definite in its terms. If a buyer offered $100,000 for the seller's property and the seller accepted, would there be a binding agreement? What if the buyer wanted to close at the end of the month and the seller wanted to remain in the property for a few more months until a new home is built? What if the seller wanted the buyer to assume a mortgage so that a discharge penalty would be avoided, but the buyer wanted to pay cash? The Agreement of Purchase and Sale form is designed to establish terms adequate to create a meeting of the minds. The offer must be accepted exactly as offered. Any change, addition, new condition or alteration would result in a new offer back to the original offeror and would not be considered an acceptance. A counter offer would destroy or eliminate the original offer; the party who made the counter offer could not then decide to accept what was originally offered. The original offer no longer exists, unless the original offeror is willing to re-submit it. The offer must be accepted within any stipulated time period and acceptance must be communicated back to the offeror. If someone makes an offer for a stipulated time period and that period has expired and, if the offeror has not been informed the offer was accepted, there is no agreement. This is a general common law principle and there can be exceptions to this rule based on what is considered legal or understood or written into the agreement with respect to the method of communication of acceptance. Also, keep in mind there are often clauses written into agreements designating someone, for example, an agent to be authorized to give and receive notices related to an agreement. For a real estate agreement, the Statute of Frauds requires that an agreement to sell an interest in real estate be in writing (have written evidence) but this is not a requirement under the common law of contracts.

2. CONSIDERATION

a. For consideration to be valid, certain characteristics must be present. Describe these requirements for consideration to be valid.

Consideration must have some value but need not be equal to what is being received. It can be the act or the promise to give something. The basic requirement is that there must be some form of exchange in the contracting process. The offeror will not be held to their promise unless they are receiving something in return. Consideration must be lawful. Consideration cannot be an illegal act or a promise to do something illegal. Consideration must be present or future. You can not say *"Remember what I did for you in the past, now you must do this for me"*, but you can say *"If I do this for you, will you do this for me?"*

CH5 DISC

Chapter Discussion

2. CONSIDERATION (continued)

b. For a typical Agreement of Purchase and Sale, describe the consideration being exchanged in the transaction.

The buyer normally gives a deposit and promises to pay the balance on closing. The seller promises to give vacant possession of the property and title in return.

3. IRREVOCABILITY

An offer is irrevocable until 10:00 p.m. on February 10, 20xx. Is it really irrevocable? Discuss.

At the time of the offer, the buyer has not yet received or been promised anything by the seller, and therefore, generally would not be bound to the offer or to the promises in the offer. However, the offer is stated to be irrevocable and signed under seal, therefore it can be argued that the promise is irrevocable. There is an ancient legal principle that is still valid today that confirms a promise made under seal is binding on the promisor, even if not receiving anything in return. In ancient times, when something was sealed, it became the property of the recipient. Since only the recipient could break the seal, it could not be withdrawn. There are court precedents that uphold the validity of the seal and even confirm that the pre-printed seal on the Agreement of Purchase and Sale is recognized as a seal. It would be a good idea to make sure the party signing understood the implications of the seal and possibly even have that party add a seal to the document if you want to get formal. There is no universal agreement on whether the irrevocability has force, quite apart from the practical problem of trying to contract with someone who is trying to withdraw from the agreement even before it is created. For a document without the seal, it is not even debatable. It has no force until it is accepted and consideration is exchanged.

4. CAPACITY

The law protects certain parties who are not considered capable of entering into a binding contract. Who is protected? Explain.

Infants, under the age of eighteen, infirm, illiterate, intoxicated persons are not likely to be held to be bound to a contract.

5. LAWFUL OBJECT

For a contract to be enforceable it must have a lawful object. Provide at least six examples where the terms of an agreement would be unenforceable due to illegality. The examples must relate to real estate transactions.

This question shows the practical application of this course for real estate practitioners. An agreement to purchase a property would be void if, for example, it is determined a severance is required and cannot be obtained. A lease requiring a residential tenant to pay a three month security deposit, a contract between a group of brokerages agreeing to all charge the same commission rate etc., would be illegal and therefore unenforceable. There are many other examples of a lack of lawful object for a contract related to real estate.

Chapter Discussion

6. MISTAKE

If a mistake made in the contracting process is considered serious enough to have prevented a "*meeting of the minds*," no contract exists under law. Provide an example related to the sale of real estate.

For example, buyers think they are buying the lot on the north side of the road. The seller does not own that lot and the seller thinks he is selling the lot on the south side. Hope they catch the mistake before closing.

Buyer thinks they are buying a house with a backyard. The house is on a corner and, in fact, it should have been clearly stated that the lot was to be 110 feet by 65 feet instead of 65 feet by 110 feet. The house has a side yard, rather than a back yard. Hope they catch the mistake before closing.

Seller owns a lot of property and got confused when giving the real estate representative information on the mortgage. The property was sold with the buyer assuming an existing first mortgage at 6.25%. The mortgage doesn't exist.

7. MISREPRESENTATION

a. Explain the main differences between an opinion, an innocent misrepresentation, a negligent misrepresentation and a fraudulent misrepresentation.

An opinion is not considered to be a statement offered as a fact. It is merely an opinion, therefore cannot be classified as a misrepresentation. An innocent representation was not intentional and not something the individual should have known or suspected to be false. A negligent misrepresentation is a false statement that the individual reasonably should have verified before making the statement; stating a property can be used for a specific purpose when in fact it cannot and that should have been checked out. A fraudulent misrepresentation is a statement known to be false by the person making the statement or made with a reckless disregard for the truth to induce someone to enter into an agreement and a loss results. These categories can sometimes be arbitrary and a negligent misrepresentation can often be classified as fraudulent.

b. "*A real estate salesperson is considered to be a specialist in the marketing of real property and this makes it more difficult for the salesperson to claim that a misrepresentation made by the salesperson is innocent rather than negligent or fraudulent.*" Discuss.

For a real estate salesperson, the standard would be higher when determining whether a representation is innocent or otherwise. A special relationship such as representation can create a duty of care on the part of an agent. Real estate registrants have a duty of competence and must understand the need to verify information, even information given by the owner who may not realize the importance of providing only correct information to the buyer.

Chapter Discussion

8. RISK REDUCTION

The majority of lawsuits and Errors and Omissions claims against real estate brokerages involve some form of misrepresentation about a property or the service being provided by the brokerage. There are a number of steps that the brokerage can take to minimize the risk. Build a list of standard business practices that salespersons (brokerages) should follow on a day-to-day basis to minimize the risk of lawsuits and E & O claims.

A salesperson can take a number of steps to lessen the risk. For example, a salesperson should keep a complete and accurate paper trail, including documents, memos, journals, notes, etc. A salesperson should verify information, including information provided by the seller, and should not make statements of fact based on unsubstantiated information. A salesperson should obtain a completed SPIS (Seller Property Information Statement) from the seller and make sure a buyer is given a copy and acknowledges in writing receipt of the copy. Forms, such as the Agreement of Purchase and Sale should be completed with care and accuracy. If necessary, conditions should be used, to resolve issues between the buyer and the seller, etc.

Chapter Mini-Review

1. One of the essential elements of an enforceable contract is that the agreement must be definite and clear.

The requirement for definiteness and clarity is one of six required elements in an enforceable contract.

2. A voidable contract is one that is a nullity at law.

A voidable contract is one where the offended party may treat the contract as being at an end or enforce it against the offending party.

3. An infant's right to avoid a contract is extinguished at the moment of reaching the age of majority.

A minor may avoid a contract made during the age of minority for a reasonable period of time after majority, subject to certain qualifications.

4. All contracts with infants for the purchase of land are generally voidable by the infant.

Such contracts are sometimes void and not usually considered to be valid and binding on the minor.

Chapter Mini-Review (continued)

5. If a statement of opinion turns out to be false, it is either an innocent or fraudulent misrepresentation.

True  False

A misrepresentation can also be negligent, if there is a special relationship between the parties and the innocent party is misled by the information provided. A negligent misrepresentation can give rise to an action for damages.

6. Specific performance is a discretionary remedy for breach of contract and will not normally be granted if an award of damages would be adequate.

 True  False

Specific performance, as a discretionary remedy, would be considered under certain circumstances where some form of compensation is not adequate.

7. If a contract is breached and the injured party did part of what was promised to be undertaken, the injured party is entitled to quantum meruit as a remedy.

 True  False

Quantum meruit is a remedy for situations where part of the work has been performed but not all.

8. A buyer has a contract with a builder to construct a commercial structure. Following successful completion, the contract is effectively terminated by operation of law.

 True  False

The contract is effectively terminated by performance.

9. According to REBBA 2002, a copy of a written agreement regarding a trade in real estate must immediately be given to each of the other persons to that agreement upon signing.

 True  False

This requirement is set out in Sec. 12 of the Code of Ethics. Note: Requirements concerning copies of agreements *involving a conveyance of an interest in real estate* are addressed in Sec. 18 of the Code.

10. A salesperson who asks the seller client to seek expert advice, rather than making a statement about a situation that could ultimately prove incorrect, is complying with intent of Sec. 38: Error, Misrepresentation, Fraud, Etc. in the Code of Ethics.

 True  False

The salesperson is complying with Sec. 38 as his or her best efforts are being used to prevent error or misrepresentation.

11. When a seller's brokerage receives a written offer from a buyer and during the course of negotiations, receives a counter offer from the same buyer that is not accepted, the brokerage may retain the unaccepted counter offer as record of both offers

 True  False

A brokerage is required to retain a copy of each offer in its entirety. Every counter offer by a buyer is considered a new offer. If the buyer was working with a brokerage (i.e., the buyer was a client or a customer of a brokerage), then an equivalent summary document can be retained instead of a copy of the offer in its entirety.

CH5 EX

Active Learning Exercises

Exercise 1

The buyer is not correct. The offer was not accepted. The condition was added and the agreement depended on the condition precedent being fulfilled. It is a contract law issue, not a matrimonial home issue.

Exercise 2

a. No. The original offer no longer exists.

b. This is a very different situation. The offer was not rejected or countered. The salesperson would have to be careful to make it clear to the buyer that the original offer is still under consideration.

Exercise 3

This is a debatable issue. Did the agreement state it was binding when it was accepted? Are you the agent for the seller, authorized to give and receive notices on behalf of your seller client? Contract law requires the party who made the offer, the seller, to be informed of the acceptance within the required time frame. Real estate salespeople try to get the acknowledgement section of the offer completed before the irrevocable time expires to avoid problems with verifying the communication of acceptance.

Exercise 4

a. Under contract law, someone will not be held to their promise unless they receive or are promised something in return. At the point in time when the buyer makes the offer and it is not yet accepted, the buyer has not yet received anything from the seller. The only way for the promises in the buyer's offer to be made binding is to state the offer to be irrevocable and have the buyer sign under seal. There is a legal concept that a promise made under seal is binding on the promisor.

b. Yes, the printed black mark is a seal. However, it is recommended that the significance of the seal be explained to the party signing the document. Seals are frequently added to the document on top of the black printed seal.

c. It should be explained that the law binds someone to their promise if they sign under seal. It adds formality to the contracting process and verifies that the party is committed to what they are signing.

Exercise 5

Consideration requires there to be an exchange for an agreement to be binding. Someone is not bound to their promise unless they are receiving something in return. In a typical Agreement of Purchase and Sale, there is an exchange. A buyer is offering to buy a property and a seller is agreeing to sell. Even without a deposit and even if the agreement is not under seal, there is still consideration present. The contract is binding if all of the other elements are present.

Exercise 6

a. At the time that they entered into the agreement they had a lack of capacity and this was known by the salesperson. Very unlikely that a court would consider this a binding agreement.

b. No difference. They were drunk. Salesperson was negligent and may be liable. Listing brokerage loses again, even if blameless.

Exercise 7

a. Not clear who is the seller. The "*Limited*" was probably missing.

b. There probably is a contract but it leaves itself open to question. These types of unnecessary problems should be avoided.

Exercise 8

There was no contract. A contract is an agreement to do something lawful. This is a serious violation of a federal law—the *Competition Act* (price fixing).

Exercise 9

Not every breach makes the contract void. Students should be cautioned not to make assumptions or conclusions on matters that can be very complex. This can happen frequently for matters related to law. Basic concepts are presented and there can be additional issues that go beyond a basic law course. If only one term of an agreement is illegal and it is not essential to the agreement, that term may be unenforceable but it may not necessarily void the whole agreement.

Exercise 10

The listing is not valid because of the impossibility of performance. The intention was to market a building but it no longer exists. Some people would argue the brokerage still has a listing on the land. Maybe, but not likely, that is not what was intended. If they still want to sell the land, they should get a new listing signed. There would be different terms.

Exercise 11

The answer may surprise you after all that information about "*a meeting of the minds.*" The seller knew it was a listing, should have known there would be a commission and did not bother verifying the amount. The amount was not outrageous and the listing is probably valid.

Exercise 12

a. Yes, unless stated otherwise in the agreement. A contract and benefits under a contract are assignable.

b. This is a different situation. There is a personal obligation and the seller can insist that the buyer guarantee the mortgage.

Exercise 13

A clause could be put into the agreement permitting an inspection by someone who is willing to accept this responsibility.

Clauses may also describe warranties that survive until a specific time after closing, but this can sometimes cause disputes, with claims that there was no problem on closing and something happened later.

Exercise 14

- ☐ *This is a nice area for a young family.* **Probably an opinion, not a misrepresentation.**
- ☑ *This home has a dry basement.*
- ☑ *I have never seen any water or dampness in the basement.* **Could be a lie.**
- ☑ *This home has a new furnace.*
- ☑ *You can put an inground pool here, no problem.*
- ☐ *I think this is the best deal on the market today in this price range.* **Opinion.**

CHAPTER 6
THE AGREEMENT OF PURCHASE AND SALE

Case Law

DOL V. MARLENE MUSCLOW INSURANCE AGENCY LTD.

1. *How did the conduct of the Buyer compared to the conduct of the Seller play a part in the court's decision?*

   The court was not impressed with the buyer's attempt to gain maximum advantage from the mistake and the buyer's unwillingness to mitigate the situation.

2. *Comment on the conduct of the real estate salespeople in this case in relation to the decision of the court.*

   The real estate salespeople were not careful when documenting the terms of the agreement, as evidenced by the error in the lot dimensions and other mistakes. Even the name of the municipality on the Agreement was incorrect!

SELLATHURAI V. SRISKANDA

1. *If the warranty merged, what effect did that have for the Buyer?*

   If the warranty merged on closing, it would no longer exist after closing.

2. *Even if the decision of the court may have been based mainly on the issues of privity of contract and the Limitations Act, what lesson does this case illustrate for real estate salespeople?*

   Salespeople must understand there are important reasons for the wording of clauses and conditions and, while clauses can be worded in a variety of different ways, getting sloppy or cutting corners and omitting important details can result in drastic consequences.

Chapter Discussion

1. IDENTIFICATION OF THE PARTIES

You receive an offer on one of your listings with the buyers identified as "*Mr. and Mrs. Jim Jones.*" Do you have any concerns? Explain.

To avoid confusion and possible problems, the full legal names of the parties should be correctly listed on the document.

Chapter Discussion

2. PROPERTY DESCRIPTION

For a lot with a 48 foot frontage, in your opinion, how much of a discrepancy would the words "*more or less*" cover? Explain.

There should be no discrepancy at all. The term "*more or less*" is just there as a safeguard, not an invitation to be careless, and the exact measurements should be used. The term "*more or less*" may cover a minor discrepancy, but it is not to be relied upon.

Do the following legal descriptions look okay to you? Explain.

a. 15 Maple Street, Toronto.

Not okay, there are probably a dozen of them now that Toronto is amalgamated.

b. Part of Lot 23, Plan 249, more particularly described as Part of 2 on 15R2657.

Okay.

c. Part of Lot 19, Concession XII, being approximately 40 acres.

Probably okay, particularly if there is not a better description, for example, from a Reference Plan.

3. DEPOSIT

a. You receive an offer on one of your listings from a co-operating brokerage. A $10,000 deposit cheque is submitted with the offer and there is a clause in the offer stating the deposit cheque will be deposited in the bank "*after acceptance of the offer.*" The offer is irrevocable for ten days. Comment.

The *Real Estate and Business Brokers Act* requires the deposit to be placed in the Brokerage's Trust Account within 5 business days of receipt. If the offer states the deposit is to be deposited "*after acceptance*", this directly contravenes the Act. The "*Universal*" Agreement of Purchase and Sale resolves this dilemma for real estate brokerages.

The form permits the buyer to submit the deposit either at the time of the offer, or upon acceptance, therefore clauses like the one mentioned in the question are unnecessary.

b. During a listing presentation, the seller, an experienced investor, insists that the buyer's deposit be given directly to the seller rather than placed in the brokerage's Trust Account. Comment.

If this is what the seller wants, the buyer would have to accept this requirement of the seller and agree to this when submitting the offer. Changes would have to be made in the standard agreement to reflect this change. Of course, a buyer could make an offer indicating the deposit will go in the Brokerage's Trust Account, but the seller could then make the alterations in the form of a counter offer and request a cheque made out to the seller. If the deposit is being given to the seller, the seller will probably also want "*to be held in Trust*" removed from the Agreement.

Chapter Discussion

4. FIXTURES AND CHATTELS

The "*Chattels Included*" section of an offer describes *refrigerator, stove and fireplace screen.* Comment.

This is not adequate for the offer. After the sale closes, the buyer comments "*I don't remember the refrigerator having those rounded corners.*" The appliances should be described adequately for identification; manufacturer, model, colour, even serial number, if appropriate.

5. DATES AND TIME LIMITS

What basic guidelines would you follow in choosing a time for the title search to expire? Explain.

For a typical residential transaction, the time for title search should expire at least a few days after the conditions are fulfilled and at least a couple of weeks prior to closing to allow for time to clear up possible minor problems found in the title search. This can vary, depending on the other dates in the offer. If it is a long closing, it is not a great idea to provide two weeks before closing. If something serious shows up like a requirement for a severance, the extra time before closing can be helpful. The buyer's lawyer would get it done within a reasonable time after conditions are removed. For a commercial transaction, or a unique transaction, a title search probably should be done early on in the negotiations, to avoid a lot of work that may have been done for nothing if the buyer finds a problem that would terminate an agreement.

6. PRESENT USE

The property has a basement apartment rented at $425 per month. You have verified that this use is illegal. How would you deal with this issue in the buyer's offer? Explain.

This is an awkward situation. You should probably check with the seller's lawyer to find out how they want to have the offer written. If no changes are made, the buyers do not have to close if the present use is not legal. There are a variety of clauses available, such as "*The seller makes no warranty as to............*"

7. APPORTIONMENTS

In the Condominium—Resale Agreement, on what basis is the seller's contribution to the reserve fund adjusted? Explain.

For a typical transaction, the expenses for the property are apportioned as of the date of completion, with the buyer paying for the expenses for the date of completion. One exception is the reserve fund contributions for a condominium. The purpose of these funds is to pay for major future expenses of the condo corporation, and contributions are not adjusted. They stay in the fund.

 DISC

Chapter Discussion

8. SIGNATURES

What does the *Real Estate and Business Brokers Act* require with respect to the dating of signatures?

The Act requires a registrant to make all reasonable efforts to ensure parties signing the agreement date their signature in their own handwriting. A buyer or seller would not likely know that, so it is up to the salesperson to explain it and make sure it is complied with. There is also a prohibition against being involved in any falsifying of information or documents. If a brokerage is involved in any false dating, post dating, pre dating etc., there would be consequences.

9. ACKNOWLEDGEMENT

Salesperson Lee obtains an offer on one of his listings that is open for acceptance until 11:59 p.m. tonight. At a quarter to midnight the sellers sign their acceptance. It is late and Lee decides to call the buyers in the morning to give them the good news. Comment.

This is another scenario that points out the importance of communicating acceptance. Salesperson Lee is the listing salesperson. Assuming Lee is representing the sellers only, the buyers have not been advised of the acceptance and the offer is expiring in a few minutes. There are a number of ways the salesperson could have avoided being placed in this situation. It would be awkward if the buyers got cold feet and claimed that their offer had expired, and that, consequently, they were no longer bound by it.

CH6 

Chapter Mini-Review

1. A deposit relating to an agreement of purchase and sale is usually forfeited if failure of performance occurs.

 True  False

Alternatively, if performance occurs, the deposit typically represents part payment toward the purchase price.

2. A brokerage can only disburse the deposit in the case of a failed agreement if a mutual release is signed by all parties to the agreement.

 True  False

A brokerage can also disburse a deposit upon direction of the Court.

3. A representation is essentially the same as a warranty for purposes of real estate trading.

 True  False

A representation is a statement regarding some fact, while a warranty is an assurance that verifies, confirms or otherwise attests to a particular situation.

Chapter Mini-Review (continued)

CH6 MINI

4. A warranty might involve the seller confirming to the buyer in writing that the pool is fully operational and has no leaks, given that the agreement is being negotiated in the winter months.

 True  False

In this instance, the buyer would want to have this warranty survive and not merge at closing so that the pool could be checked in the warmer season to confirm the seller's assurances.

5. In the Agreement of Purchase and Sale (OREA Form 100) the heirs, executors, administrators, successors and assigns are bound by the agreement.

 True  False

A specific clause is included in the agreement setting out this requirement.

6. According to REBBA 2002, a registrant is only entitled to a commission or other remuneration if a written agreement is signed by the party paying the commission.

 True  False

The General Regulation (Subsec. 23(1)) also provides that the registrant is entitled to commission if the registrant has shown the property to a buyer or introduced the buyer and the seller to one another in relation to the buying or selling of an interest in real estate.

7. A registrant is obligated to use electronic signatures if either the buyer or seller makes a request that the agreement of purchase and sale be created and transmitted electronically.

 True  False

The use of electronic contracts is optional. All parties to the agreement of purchase and sale must agree to the use of electronic signatures. While agreement can be implied, it is recommended that the consent be in writing to avoid future disputes. If any party insists on using written signatures, registrants must oblige.

Active Learning Exercises

Exercise 1

This is a problem. The tax bill is not a reliable source of information for the lot size. You have to get a copy of the deed or survey. It is Saturday morning and, if this is not available from the seller's personal papers, there will be an unfortunate delay in obtaining an offer. Therefore, this question emphasizes the importance of doing a proper listing job and illustrates what can happen if a basic requirement such as verifying the lot size is not met. In these circumstances, you cannot draw up the offer unless the buyer is very understanding and permits the insertion of a clause eliminating the liability with respect to a possible discrepancy in the lot size. This is another situation that should have been avoided.

CH6 EX

Exercise 2

In a normal transaction, the deposit is made payable to the Listing Brokerage In Trust. On the sale of your client's house for $100,000 cash in a falling market you should get a deposit of $10,000.

(This is a falling market, so a substantial deposit would be appropriate, but there are practical considerations if the buyer will not agree. With a deposit of this size, it is customary to include a clause stating that the buyer gets the interest. This is done as an incentive for the buyer to give an adequate deposit.)

Exercise 3

The buyer would have to search the title before the conditional agreement becomes a deal. This is an unnecessary expense if the sale is not completed.

Exercise 4

Contact the seller or lawyer to arrange for the seller to have the window fixed and have some basic maintenance done. While the buyer would not likely be correct in refusing to close if the grass has not been cut, the buyer does have a point and the seller is responsible for the condition of the property until the deal closes.

Exercise 5

a. The agreement states the buyer will get clear title on closing.

b. Have the seller make the necessary arrangements with the seller's lawyer. If the buyers are not prepared to agree to an arrangement to solve the mortgage problem, the seller may have to pay it off and have the discharge available for closing.

Exercise 6

You cannot just write up the offer and forget about it. Hopefully you have a motivated buyer and you can explain it to him/her, and obtain his/her agreement to a clause in the offer that describes the problem and provides for the buyer's acceptance of the property.

Exercise 7

a. The radio antenna does not exist at this time. Apparently the buyer is planning to install one. If there is a deed restriction preventing installation of such an antenna, the buyer will have a problem. The deed restriction is being complied with at this time and would not be a valid objection to title. A zoning by-law may also prevent the installation of this antenna. Unless the buyer has stipulated a future intended use in the offer which includes the antenna, the buyer will not have any protection.

b. You can put clauses in the offer that will give the buyer the opportunity to verify if his plans for the property are legal.

Exercise 8

NOTE: This is another reminder that you are not expected to know everything from your reading. You may feel you do not have enough information to answer the question, but *"give it a try"*, based on the information provided and what you have learned from the course. Your answer may not be totally correct, but comparing your answer to the suggested answer is part of the learning process.

a. The sellers must give access to the property, but not necessarily for measurements. Of course, they can give them access if they want to co-operate. There is a court case that gives some support to buyers who want access. The agreement states that a buyer can cancel an agreement if there has been substantial damage to the property prior to closing. The judge reasoned: "*How can the buyers determine whether the property has been damaged if they are denied access?*" However, the question states that the buyer wants access for measurements, not to look for damage to the property. They do not have that right.

b. This is a wonderful opportunity for a buyer representative to show the buyer that it is advantageous to obtain representation. The best way for this situation to be handled is a clause in the offer to permit a pre-closing inspection. A typical buyer would not likely think of this and request the seller's agent include it in the offer. However, a typical buyer representative should certainly mention it and determine whether the buyer would like this included. It should be kept in mind, of course, for a hot property in a hot market, that it may not be a good idea to add too many clauses to the agreement.

CHAPTER 7
BULK SALES ACT AND REBBA 2002

Case Law

MOHN V. DREISNER ESTATE

1. *The Court addressed the statutory duty imposed by Sec. 33 (now Section 21 of the General Regulation) of the Real Estate and Business Brokers Act regarding sale of a business. Outline basic requirements for financial and related documents that must be provided including any waiver provision.*

   Section 21 of the General Regulation states that the following must be provided:

   - A profit and loss statement or statement showing the revenue and disbursements of the business during the preceding twelve months or since the acquisition of the business by the person disposing of it;
   - A statement of the assets and liabilities of the business; and
   - A statement containing a list of all fixtures, goods, chattels, rights and other assets relating to or connected with the business that are not included in the transaction. (Note: If this statement is not provided, such items are deemed included in the sale.)

   Section 21 of the General Regulation also contains a waiver provision regarding the first two requirements.

2. *What steps should a prudent salesperson or broker take regarding financial information when listing a commercial property?*

   Salespersons and brokers should ensure full compliance with Section 21 of the General Regulation. Further, the duty of a salesperson or broker extends beyond merely conveying information provided by the seller to the buyer. Practitioners are expected to take reasonable and prudent steps to satisfy themselves regarding the accuracy and completeness of such information. See *Code of Ethics, Section 21: Material Facts.*

Chapter Discussion

1. SALE OF STOCK IN BULK PROCEDURES

a. What is a "*sale of stock in bulk*"?

Many businesses sell products in volume. A sale of stock in bulk must be outside of the ordinary course of the seller's business. A sale of stock in bulk includes the sale of real or personal property, goods, chattels, fixtures or other items with which the person carries on a business.

b. Who does the *Bulk Sales Act* protect and what is the reason for this protection?

The *Bulk Sales Act* protects the creditors of the seller of the bulk products being sold so that trade creditors are not faced with debts (provisions are made for payment of the creditors).

c. Briefly describe the requirements of the *Bulk Sales Act* when a "*sale of stock in bulk*" occurs.

The *Bulk Sales Act* requires the buyer to demand and receive a sworn statement from the seller indicating the names and addresses of the trade creditors, the amounts owing and any security given. Any deposit money paid on the sale must not exceed 10% of the purchase price until the claims of the creditors have been resolved. The sale can proceed if the claims of the secured trade creditors do not exceed $2,500, or the trade creditors have been paid, or provisions are made for payment of the trade creditors or waivers obtained.

2. TAX CONSIDERATIONS

What other issues related to provincial and federal tax must be addressed in the sale of a business? Explain.

There are issues related to harmonized sales tax. There are other issues related to the value of the assets of the business and Income Tax implications for the seller and in the future for the buyer, but these matters should be left to the professional advisors for each party.

3. REAL ESTATE AND BUSINESS BROKERS ACT, 2002 REQUIREMENTS

You have just listed a business and the seller is reluctant to allow prospective buyers to have access to the financial statements of the business. Explain how you would deal with this.

If a seller is reluctant to allow a prospective buyer to review the financial statements of the business, many real estate brokerages will not get involved in the sale. A salesperson does not want to spend a lot of time on something that is not going to result in a commission and it is virtually impossible to sell a business if proper financial statements are not available. The salesperson should find out what the seller's reluctance is and try to resolve the problem. After discussion with the seller, the seller may agree to co-operate with respect to the financial statements. There may be a requirement to have work done to complete the statements. If the brokerage cannot convince the seller, the brokerage has to decide whether or not to get involved in the sale of this business. There is a requirement in the *Real Estate and Business Brokers Act* for the buyers to be given the financial statements, but also a provision for the buyer to waive this requirement if they are not going to be provided.

CH7 MINI

Chapter Mini-Review

1. The *Real Estate and Business Brokers Act, 2002* requires that a list of items included in the sale be provided to the buyer.

 True  False

The Act only specifies that items NOT included in the sale be provided.

2. An earnout arrangement when acquiring a business allows the buyer to pay the balance of the purchase price from cash flow generated by that business.

 True  False

An earnout arrangement can be very effective, as businesses are often difficult to finance through conventional lenders.

3. The *Agreement of Purchase and Sale – Business in Leased Premises Under the Bulk Sales Act* includes a provision that the seller covenants to deliver to buyer at or before the time of completion the written consent of the lessor to the assignment of the lease of the premises to buyer.

 True  False

This covenant is included under Clause 7: Seller Covenants.

4. A buyer acquiring a business and complying with the *Bulk Sales Act* remains responsible for debts owed under the business to trade creditors.

 True  False

The buyer would not normally be responsible for debts to trade creditors if correct procedures under the *Bulk Sales Act* are followed.

5. The buyer of bulk inventory must demand and receive a sworn statement setting out the seller's creditors.

 True False

This statement should include the names and addresses of the creditors, along with amounts owing and any security given.

6. Under REBBA 2002, a buyer must receive a statement of assets and liabilities, a profit and loss statement and a list of items not included in the sale prior to a binding agreement.

 True  False

The key here is the word *binding*. A seller may provide these statements/lists after an offer has been accepted providing the accepted offer is still conditional, e.g., conditional on receiving the statements/lists.

7. The *Real Estate and Business Brokers Act, 2002* requires the seller to provide financial statements for the business to the buyer.

 True  False

The buyer should receive financial statements, but if such are not available, the Act provides that the buyer may sign a waiver.

8. A profit and loss statement provided to a buyer by the seller of a business must cover the past 12-month period.

 True  False

The profit and loss statement could be for a lesser period if the person disposing of that business acquired it less than 12 months ago.

9. The waiver provisions allows the buyer to waive receipt of items and assets excluded from the sale.

 True  False

The waiver provision only relates to the provision of financial statements (i.e., profit and loss statement and balance sheet). Items not included must be provided.

APPENDIX

Active Learning Exercises

Exercise 1

a. There is a provision in the agreement, allowing either party to make a written request for a count of the inventory and payment of the inventory at cost.

b. Explain the provisions of the *Bulk Sales Act* and reassure the buyer that this issue will be taken care of by the lawyer.

Exercise 2

The provisions of the *Bulk Sales Act* will apply to the sale. You would have to obtain more information about the creditors and probably contact them to determine the extent of the problem and whether there is any point in proceeding.

Exercise 3

The amount is under $2,500, so there should be no problem. If you are not certain, get more information and check with the lawyer for the seller.

Exercise 4

a. There are alternatives for compliance with the *Bulk Sales Act* that do not require the involvement of a Trustee. If the business is selling for a lot more than the outstanding debts or if the buyer is credit worthy, the Act can usually be complied with by one of the alternatives that does not require a Trustee.

b. The creditor may be willing to make an arrangement with a credit worthy buyer to assume the obligation for payment of the amount owing on the stock.

Exercise 5

No it does not. As a buyer, you would normally expect to receive a list of items included. The Act actually requires a list of items excluded, so the buyer would probably receive both. This is dangerous for the seller if there is confusion with respect to this requirement because the Act goes on to state that if an asset of the business is not listed as excluded, it is deemed to be included in the purchase price.

Exercise 6

a.
- A Profit and Loss Statement for the preceding year. If the business was not owned for the year, a statement for the time period the business was owned is required.
- A Statement of Assets and Liabilities.
- A list of fixtures, goods, chattels, rights and other assets relating to or connected with the business that are not included in the transaction.

b. The seller must make a statement under oath indicating how the premises for the business are held, any subletting of the premises, all liabilities of the business and an explanation of why the buyer is not going to review the financial statements. This statement must be given to the buyer and the buyer may waive receipt of the financial statements by signing and delivering to the brokerage a statement that the buyer has read the statement under oath.

CHAPTER 8
THE CONSUMER PROTECTION ACT AND THE COMPETITION ACT

Chapter Discussion

1. CONSUMER PROTECTION ACT

a. There are two major categories of representations that are prohibited under the *Consumer Protection Act.* Describe these two main types of representations and give at least two examples for each category (examples must related to real estate).

The Act prohibits false, misleading or deceptive consumer representations and unconscionable representations in the selling of services. It does not apply to the selling of real estate, so if a salesperson lies to a buyer about a property, it will not fall under the act. Issues must relate to the selling of services, for example, telling the seller you can sell his property in less than two weeks for more than $200,000. This is not likely true, but you are just trying to get a listing. An unconscionable representation means you are taking advantage of someone. An example of this would be if you pressured someone into signing a service agreement such as a listing or buyer representation agreement.

b. A buyer learns that a number of statements made by a registrant at the time of the signing of the Buyer Representation Agreement were totally false. The buyer is convinced he would not have signed the agreement if his questions would have been answered truthfully. What can the buyer do? Explain.

If a buyer is convinced that the registrant made misleading statements to induce the buyer to sign the representation agreement, there are provisions in the Act that permit cancellation of the agreement. There are other provisions for prosecution of violators. Convictions under this Act would bring into question whether the individual has the qualifications to be registered under the *Real Estate and Business Brokers Act.*

2. THE COMPETITION ACT

You mention to another real estate salesperson in your office that the "*low downpayment*" advertisement he has been running in the newspaper for the last couple of weeks is an ad for a listing that has been sold for several days. He replies "*No problem. I am still getting lots of calls on that ad, so I am going to let it run for a while longer.*" Comment.

The *Competition Act* prohibits, among other things, misleading advertising directed at consumers. Advertising something that is not for sale would be a clear violation of the Act. This is usually called "*bait-and-switch*" advertising where one thing is advertised with the intention of selling something else to the consumer. The *Competition Act,* of course, also prohibits the price fixing of real estate commissions.

CH8 MINI

Chapter Mini-Review

1. "You told them there was hardwood under the carpet on the main floor. You know that is not true, so you have violated the *Consumer Protection Act*."

True  False

This situation involves the selling of real property (as opposed to the offering of services relating to real property) and, therefore, the *Consumer Protection Act* would not apply.

2. A consumer complaining about an unfair practice in relation to the *Consumer Protection Act* may rescind or cancel the contract.

 True  False

This is one of several alternative remedies that the consumer may pursue.

3. "It doesn't matter what they thought the ad meant. It is literally true and I am off the hook!"

 True  False

The *Competition Act* is concerned about the general impression given by an ad (i.e., misleading), not just the literal correctness of that ad.

4. An abbreviation widely used and understood in a local trading area would probably be acceptable and not misleading from a Competition Bureau perspective.

 True  False

The central issue is whether or not an abbreviation would confuse or mislead. If it is widely used and understood, then it would probably not be judged misleading.

5. An acceptable print size for disclaimers is 7 point, according to guidelines addressed in this chapter.

 True  False

The Competition Bureau has indicated that 7 point size is sufficient, but is viewed as a minimum.

6. An advertisement stating that new homes are available from as low as $300,000 within a particular subdivision is misleading if, in fact, all homes in that price range have all been sold.

 True False

The advertisement is false and misleading, as it gives the impression that this price point is still available.

7. If a brokerage offers a contest, Section 59 of the *Competition Act* requires that two disclosures must be made regarding the approximate number and value of prices and the closing date of the contest.

 True  False

Eight disclosures are required according to chapter materials, not two.

8. Certificates and coupons distributed by real estate brokerages may include disclaimers, but these must be consistent with the overall message being conveyed.

 True  False

This rule of consistency applies to the use of disclaimers in all published materials.

CH8 EX

Active Learning Exercises

Exercise 1

The Act applies to the selling of services. Obtaining financing would fall under this category, even if you are not representing the consumer or attempting to get a representation agreement signed.

Exercise 2

There are many examples but they must relate to a "*service.*"

> "*List with me, I have a buyer for this property.*"
> "*We charge the lowest commission rate in town.*"
> "*The real estate board rules require you to sign a six month listing.*" Etc.

Exercise 3

Cancellation is an option, however, there are other provisions for prosecution under the Act. Also, violations of the *Consumer Protection Act* could be considered cause for termination of registration.

Exercise 4

The seller would have good grounds for cancellation of the listing. It would make no difference if it is on MLS®.

Exercise 5

Another violation of the *Consumer Protection Act.* Cancellation, prosecution, report to Registrar of REBBA.

Exercise 6

Yes, she can cancel the listing. This is another violation of the *Consumer Protection Act.*

Exercise 7

Serious concerns. "*Hottest property....well below market.*" Can this be substantiated? "*New wiring and furnace.*" The word "*new*" is considered absolute by the Competition Bureau. A few days or months old would mean the Act has been violated. There are also violation(s) of the *REBBA Act.* Who is Albert? Also, advertiser must be identified as a brokerage.

CHAPTER 9
THE CONSUMER REPORTING ACT AND THE LAND TRANSFER TAX ACT

Chapter Discussion

1. CONSUMER REPORTS

Speedy Take-out Pizza is adding another location to their rapidly expanding business. You would like to do a credit check on the company before presenting their Offer to Lease to your client. Are there any requirements with which you must comply under the *Consumer Reporting Act*? Explain.

The *Consumer Reporting Act* defines a consumer as someone outside of their field of business. Speedy Take-out Pizza is expanding the business and the *Consumer Reporting Act* does not apply to this situation.

2. DISCLOSURES

Is it necessary to inform the consumer in every situation when a consumer report is being obtained? Explain.

It is not necessary to inform the consumer in every case. The consumer must be informed when the extension of credit or personal information is involved, or when information is used to the detriment of the consumer. In other circumstances, the consumer does not have to be informed. This is not widely understood because most parties who use this type of information add a statement in an application form for the consumer to give consent. This is going beyond the requirements of the Act.

3. PERSONAL INFORMATION

Using examples, explain the difference between credit information and personal information.

Credit information is factual. While you may think paying habits are very personal, they are considered factual credit information, not personal. Personal information would be defined as opinion, references and information about someone's character, reputation, health, mode of living, etc.

Chapter Discussion

4. RENTAL APPLICATIONS

The rental application form that you are using requests the names of previous landlords for reference purposes. Does the *Consumer Reporting Act* apply to this situation? Explain.

Yes. Rental applications usually involve both credit and personal information; information about income, paying habits and the names of previous landlords for reference purposes moves into the category of personal information.

5. LAND TRANSFER TAX

a. Everyone seems to have their own way of expressing the rate for provincial land transfer tax (and the municipal land transfer tax for Toronto). Set out the rate in the format that is the simplest and most understandable to you.

There are a number of ways to calculate the rate.

For properties from 0 to $55,000	***One half of 1%.***
For properties from $55,000 to $250,000	***1% minus $275.***
For properties over $250,000 that do not have the surcharge	***1.5% minus $1,525.***
For properties over $400,000 and the surcharge applies	***1.5%, minus $1,525, plus an extra 0.5% for the amount over $400,000.***

b. Is the provincial land transfer tax (and municipal land transfer tax for Toronto) something you should discuss with a prospective buyer-customer, and with a prospective buyer-client? Explain.

It does not matter whether the buyer is a client or customer. The Land Transfer Tax is a cost of closing and the salesperson should verify that the buyer is aware of the cost. Section 21 of the Code of Ethics states that parties should be aware of the material facts related to the acquisition of a property and this would include the nature and amount of the expenses they are incurring. Of course, if the buyer is a client and is not made aware of the cost, this omission would reflect badly on the agent's duty of competence.

Chapter Mini-Review

1. The *Consumer Reporting Act* applies when obtaining financial information on a business operation.

True ✔ False

A consumer, for purposes of this Act, specifically excludes a business, trade or profession.

2. You can obtain a consumer report to get information about your new neighbour.

True ✔ False

An individual cannot obtain a consumer report without proper reasons. Credit bureaus are only permitted to provide reports concerning a tenancy agreement, in connection with credit, in relation to other direct business needs and the updating of information already received.

3. If you deny a consumer a benefit because of information obtained in a credit report, you must give the consumer the name and address of the consumer reporting agency within 60 days of your refusal.

True ✔ False

When denying a consumer a benefit as a result of a bad credit report, you must notify the consumer of this fact and at the same time inform that consumer that he/she has 60 days from receipt of notice to request the name and address of the consumer reporting agency.

4. Credit bureaus compile various information about individuals beyond matters relating to credit, such as personal and political affiliations.

True ✔ False

Credit bureaus only compile credit-related information.

5. Consumers have the right to verify credit information being held on file.

✔ True False

The right to verify is complemented by the ability to dispute and alter incorrect data.

6. Certain types of transfers attract a *nil* land transfer tax rate.

✔ True False

A good example is a transfer of ownership to a spouse pursuant to a separation agreement.

7. If a home located in Southwestern Ontario has a selling price of $325,000. The land transfer tax on this conveyance would be $3,350.

✔ True False

True. $275 + $1,950 + $1,125 = $3,350.

8. If the provincial land transfer tax paid is $4,500, the refund to the qualified first time buyer purchasing that home would be $2,250.

True ✔ False

The refund limit is $2,000.

9. The municipal land transfer tax payable on a Toronto home selling for $380,000 would be $3,525.

✔ True False

True. $275 + $3,250 = $3,525.

10. The total land transfer tax payable on a Toronto home selling for $400,000 would be $7,100.

True ✔ False

False. The correct answer is $4,475 (provincial) + $3,725 (municipal) = $8,200.

Active Learning Exercises

Exercise 1

The purpose of the *Consumer Reporting Act* is to place some control on the collection and circulation of information about individuals. It also has provisions requiring that individuals be notified when information is being used to their detriment so they are aware and in a position to question incorrect information.

Exercise 2

The consumer must be notified that the application was rejected because of negative information. The consumer must be notified that they have sixty days to request the nature and source of the information. If they think there is a mistake, they can make efforts to correct the mistake.

Exercise 3

a. Get a credit report before accepting the offer or make the offer conditional on obtaining a satisfactory report.

b. The report is being used to the detriment of the consumer. Even though the mortgage is being provided, the rate is being increased. The consumer must be notified of this fact and that they have 60 days to request the nature and source of the information.

Exercise 4

In which of the following circumstances would a consumer have to be notified that a consumer report is being used?

a. When an employer is running a credit information report on a potential employee.

b. When a landlord is running a credit information report on a potential tenant.

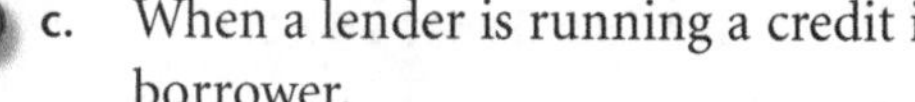

c. When a lender is running a credit information report on a potential borrower.

d. All of the above.

e. None of the above.

The answer is **c.** It is only credit information, not personal information, and the only one where the extension of credit is involved is **c.**

Exercise 5

a. Providing the agreement of purchase and sale was entered into after December 31, 2007, first time buyers of resale homes are eligible for a refund of up to $2,000. This includes duplexes, triplexes and fourplexes.

b. **$2,400** (4,400 – 2000 rebate)

Land Transfer Tax Payable: $4,400

$55,000 x .005	= $275
$195,000 x .01	= $1,950
$145,000 x .015	= $2,175
$395,000	$4,400

c. **$225** There will be no rebate in this instance. $45,000 x .005 = 225

Exercise 6

$36,950

$55,000 x .005	= $275
$195,000 x .01	= $1,950
$2,315,000 x .015	= $34,725
$2,565,000	$36,950

Exercise 7

a. $4,250

b. $11,225

c. $13,475

CHAPTER 10
INCOME TAX ACT (CANADA) AND THE EXPROPRIATIONS ACT

Chapter Discussion

1. CAPITAL GAINS

Build a list of factors that may be looked at in determining whether an individual has realized a capital gain or has earned business income.

Again it should be mentioned that this information is not included so that real estate salespeople can give advice about tax matters. Parties should be referred to professionals in that field for advice. For a disposition to be a capital gain, it must be outside of that individual's business. The individual's intentions and the frequency of transactions are taken into account. If similar transactions are frequent, it can be argued that the individual is in that business. The nature of the transaction and type of asset also has a bearing on it, and if it is a corporation selling the asset, so do the objects of the corporation.

2. BUYER LIABILITY

"*I am not paying legal fees. I am going to bring my certified cheque to the seller's lawyer and pick up the deed (and then put it in the freezer). There is nothing complicated about a real estate purchase.*" Comment.

This is a good time to mention this attitude. A buyer is not likely to know, and would be shocked to find out that it is possible to be liable for someone else's income tax.

3. THE AGREEMENT OF PURCHASE AND SALE

Within the pre-printed portion of the standard OREA Agreement of Purchase and Sale form, there are three alternatives for the buyer to be protected from having to pay income tax owed by the seller as a result of the sale. Explain the three alternatives.

This is the main reason why this topic is included in a real estate course. There is a clause in the Agreement of Purchase and Sale and a salesperson must be able to explain all of the clauses in the agreement to a buyer or seller. The clause states that the buyer can withhold whatever is necessary to cover liability for the seller's tax and the seller must still close the transaction. It goes on to say that there are two other alternatives that make it unnecessary to withhold. The seller can provide a statutory declaration that the seller is not a non-resident (this is what takes place for most transactions) or the seller can provide a certificate that they have paid any tax required for the transaction.

Chapter Discussion 

4. EXPROPRIATION

Do you feel there is a fair balance within the *Expropriations Act* between the rights of the public-at-large and the rights of private property owners? Discuss.

There are differing opinions on this topic. We give you full marks for your opinion, whatever it is.

5. COMPENSATION

a. List the various forms of compensation available under the *Expropriations Act.*

The property owner will be paid market value for the property, and also may be able to claim damages for disturbance, damages for injurious affection and costs of relocation.

b. Your city has decided to build an overpass for a railway in your neighbourhood. Unfortunately, the view from your living room in the future will be a concrete wall, you will no longer have access to the street from your driveway, and the noise and vibration from the trains will be significant. The project will not require the expropriation of any of your property. Can you expect any compensation? Explain:

While the railway overpass is not requiring any of your property to be expropriated, it will damage your enjoyment and use of your property, and you can take steps to make a claim based on injurious affection.

Chapter Mini-Review

CH10 

1. Provisions of the *Income Tax Act* provide that a buyer of a property may be held responsible for paying income tax owed by a non-resident seller.

 True  False

Section 116 of the *Income Tax Act* provides for the collection of capital gains payable by non-residents. If such amount is not paid, the buyer can be liable for the amount owed.

2. The non-resident seller may pay the applicable amount relating to the capital gain directly to the Minister of National Revenue.

 True False

The certificate is then presented at completion of the sale to confirm that the non-resident has paid the required amount directly to the Minister.

Chapter Mini-Review (continued)

3. The taxpayer's intention at time of purchase is irrelevant to the Tax Court in determining whether a gain is capital in nature or taxable income.

 True  False

The taxpayer's intention is one of several criteria used by the Tax Court to establish whether a gain is capital in nature or taxable income.

4. For purposes of qualifying as a principal residence, a family unit may only have one principal residence, which must be ordinarily inhabited in the year.

 True  False

The qualification process also involves other criteria beyond those stated in the question.

5. A capital loss occurs when the sale price exceeds the adjusted cost base plus the cost of sale expenses.

 True  False

A capital loss occurs when the adjusted cost base and costs of sale expenses exceed the sale price.

6. The *Expropriations Act* is a federal statute, which enables an expropriating authority to terminate the rights of property owners in Ontario.

 True  False

The *Expropriations Act* discussed in this chapter is a provincial statute not a federal statute.

7. The government's right to expropriate can override the rights of property owners in Ontario.

 True  False

This right is referred to as eminent domain.

8. An owner who has been served a Notice of Expropriation has the right to a hearing under the *Expropriations Act.*

 True  False

The owner has a right to a hearing, but he or she must notify the expropriating authority within the prescribed time limit.

Active Learning Exercises

Exercise 1

You should not get involved in advising a client, but you should at least know enough about the terms of the offer to be able to explain the terms and recognize when it would be advisable to encourage a party to the transaction to seek professional advice.

Exercise 2

A seller is taxed on the capital gain, but the liability shifts to the buyer if the seller is a non-resident of Canada. It is a lot harder to collect tax once the proceeds of the sale have left the country.

APPENDIX

Exercise 3

This is not something in which the salesperson gets involved. A statutory declaration is requested from the seller. This is standard closing procedure.

Exercise 4

a. The buyer has a problem. He/she may have to pay tax owed by the seller. Get legal and tax advice, but it may be a little late.

b. The buyer should have withheld enough funds from the sale to cover the maximum liability.

Exercise 5

a. Advise the seller to get legal and tax advice. Make sure that the buyer understands the potential problem.

b. This is not something to get involved in. Same answer as the previous question. Decline and advise them to obtain professional advice on these matters.

Exercise 6

This question gets back to the same issue about the fairness of expropriation. This individual should seek professional advice and take advantage of the protections available in the *Expropriations Act.*

Exercise 7

This is a tough question. There may be someone who is very attached to a property and is very reluctant to consider alternatives. The property may have been in the family for years or there may be other personal reasons. The *Expropriation Act* does not get into these personal issues. There is an underlying principle that the good of the public must prevail over the private property rights of the individual.

Exercise 8

There are provisions for a property owner to either continue with the transaction or cancel it, if the Expropriating Authority determines they no longer need the property.

CHAPTER 11
SHARED OWNERSHIP

Case Law

WATERLOO NORTH CONDOMINIUM CORPORATION V. WELDNER

1. *What primary document provides buyers with information concerning significant restrictions relating to a particular condominium unit?*

   Most significant restrictions are highlighted in the status certificate and related attachments. Practitioners should insert a condition in the agreement providing adequate time to review such documentation. However, salespeople can greatly assist in the process by being aware of important restrictions and inform the buyer accordingly.

2. *What information is readily available from condominium corporations that will assist a salesperson in providing better service to clients interested in specific projects?*

   The *Condominium Act* provides that *anyone* can request a status certificate for a specific unit. Salespeople are well advised to obtain current copies for complexes in which they specialize to ensure up-to-date information regarding attached documents including the declaration, by-laws and rules.

Chapter Discussion

1. CONDOMINIUM REGISTRATION

The buyer cannot obtain the deed to the unit until the condominium is registered. Explain.

It is not possible for someone to obtain a deed to a condominium before registration of the condominium. The deed would be for a unit that does not exist legally until registration. Before registration, all of the requirements must be met. If registration has not taken place, there is always the possibility, for whatever reason, that it will never be registered, therefore it will never exist.

2. CONDOMINIUM CORPORATION

a. A condominium corporation does not have limited liability. Explain.

One of the major reasons for creating a corporation when setting up a business is to limit liability. A typical business corporation can go bankrupt. For a condominium corporation, the unit owners are personally liable for the debts and obligations of a condominium corporation.

Chapter Discussion 

2. CONDOMINIUM CORPORATION (continued)

b. A six year old condominium project has had virtually no problems and no unusual expenses. The seller of a unit complains he has contributed more than $3,000 to the reserve fund that is being held by the corporation. Comment.

The reserve fund contributions remain with the condominium for future expenses and are not adjusted on closing.

3. CO-OPERATIVES

Compare and contrast the main features of condominium ownership and co-operatives.

A co-operative is very different from a Condominium. With a condominium, a deed is created. For a co-operative, the buyer obtains shares in a corporation and a contract providing the right to occupy a specific unit. This difference has a great impact on financing. A condo unit can be mortgaged. A co-operative can not.

Chapter Mini-Review

1. The owner of a condominium unit is personally responsible for the liabilities of the corporation.

   ✔ True ○ False

   The condominium corporation does not provide limited liability to its unit owners.

2. A minimum of 10% of the monthly common expenses must be deposited in a reserve fund when a condominium is first registered and until a reserve fund study is completed.

   ✔ True  ○ False

   The condominium corporation must undertake periodic reserve fund studies to determine if reserve funds are adequate or not and make appropriate adjustments to the common expenses.

3. A status certificate is only provided by a condominium corporation when an official request is received from either the buyer's or seller's lawyer prior to closing.

    ○ True  ✔ False

   A status certificate must be provided by the condominium corporation upon request by any person. A prescribed fee applies.

4. A buyer has forty-eight hours to cancel an offer to purchase for a new condominium unit.

    ○ True  ✔ False

   A buyer can rescind an agreement of purchase and sale within 10 days of receiving a disclosure statement (mandated under the Act) and receiving a copy of the agreement of purchase and sale executed by the declarant, whichever is later.

CH11 MINI

Chapter Mini-Review

5. A buyer has ten days to cancel an offer to purchase for a resale residential condominium unit.

 True  False

No such cancellation provision applies to resale condominiums.

6. The right to use an exclusive use common element parking space is granted by the condominium corporation.

 True  False

The condominium corporation owns the parking spaces as part of the common elements and grants the right to use specific spaces.

7. An equity co-operative owns the land and buildings with members being shareholders in the corporation.

 True  False

An equity co-operative has share capital that is held by the shareholders, as opposed to a non-profit co-operative that does not have share capital.

8. Land transfer tax does not apply to the sale of a co-operative, as the disposition involves a share and not real property.

 True  False

Land transfer does apply, as the government refers to such a disposition as a beneficial interest and is therefore taxable.

9. Timeshare involves the division of property rights into fractional interests based on time.

 True  False

The concept of fractional interest based on time has proven most attractive in recreational markets.

10. The *Consumer Protection Act* provides certain rights to buyers of timeshare ownership located anywhere in Canada.

 True  False

Certain rights are provided under the *Consumer Protection Act*, but they relate only to timeshare interests located in Ontario.

Active Learning Exercises

Exercise 1

A condominium corporation does not have limited liability. The unit owners are personally liable for the corporation. In addition, the shares of the condominium corporation attach to the unit. The shares cannot be bought and sold by investors.

Exercise 2

While value depends on many factors including location and for a multi-unit building, the reputation of the building, it is probably true to state that a condominium will generally have a higher value, due mainly to the issues of title and financing.

Exercise 3

The unit owners are personally liable.

Exercise 4

For a co-operative, the terms of the ownership contract, the restrictions on sale, the financing, the reputation of the developer and the building, the present condition of the building, the financial health of the corporation that holds title, and other issues, are all important matters when a unit is offered for sale.

Exercise 5

The answer is similar to the previous question. The terms of the ownership contract and rules and regulations for the project are important, as well as the reputation of the project and developer. Cost and financial issues are factors, as fees for services and maintenance can be substantial. With timeshare, other issues such as the actual time period in the year and the exchange network available (if any) must be considered.

CHAPTER 12
RESIDENTIAL TENANCY

Case Law

CANADA TRUSTCO MORTGAGE CO. V. PARK

1. *In what way did the court help to define the relationship between mortgagees, owners and tenants?*

   The court determined that a mortgagee should not have greater rights than the owner of a property or a tenant.

2. *What effect can such a case have on future decisions of courts?*

   Such a case can be considered as a "*precedent*", providing guidance for future decisions. However, while this decision was an appeal of an Ontario Rental Housing Tribunal decision, it was a decision of the Ontario Superior Court and not the Ontario Court of Appeal. It would more likely be a precedent if it had been a decision of the Court of Appeal.

MACKO V. WASIK

1. *What are the requirements for the buyer to be able to obtain vacant possession from the existing tenant?*

   The buyer must have a genuine intention of moving into the rental unit and the seller can then give the tenant notice on behalf of the buyer.

2. *What advice did the Tribunal give a Listing salesperson for this situation?*

   The tribunal suggested that perhaps some sort of warranty that survives closing should be obtained from the buyer. The warranty should be worded so as to protect the seller from the consequences of giving the notice to the tenant.

Chapter Discussion

1. RESIDENTIAL TENANCY

a. You list a home occupied by a tenant who has one year and six months remaining on the lease. Are you selling a rental property or can a buyer obtain vacant possession? Explain.

   You are selling a rental property. The lease has priority. The time frames for notice of termination apply to the end of a term of tenancy, not in the middle of a lease.

b. You obtain an offer on the property in the situation described above, and the buyer requires vacant possession on closing in two-and-a-half months. What should you do?

   If you find a buyer that wants vacant possession, you would have to obtain the agreement of the tenant to voluntarily terminate the lease. It is not unusual, in this situation, for the owner to offer the tenant an incentive.

Chapter Discussion

1. RESIDENTIAL TENANCY (continued)

c. You have just obtained a new listing on a very saleable property. The home is rented on a month-to-month basis. You call the tenants to inform them there will probably be some showing activity this weekend. They mention that they have some family members from Vancouver visiting for the weekend and request that you delay showing the property until next week. Comment.

You have a new listing and the tenants request a delay. This is a public relations issue. The good will of the tenant will be important in the marketing of the property, and you may want to consider working with the tenant on this one to start off on the right foot. Of course, this depends on circumstances, so if a buyer is leaving the area late Sunday, this may have to be explained to the tenants.

d. You obtain a listing from a mortgagee of a residential property in a power of sale situation. The home is rented to a tenant with almost one year remaining on the lease. Can a buyer obtain vacant possession on closing? Explain.

No, not without the co-operation of the tenant. The Ontario Superior Court has determined that the tenant's right of possession has priority.

Chapter Mini-Review

1. A residential landlord can apply to the Landlord and Tenant Board for a rent increase, when utility costs have risen significantly. But if such costs subsequently reduce, the Act does not set out any provisions for a subsequent reduction relating to these costs.

True False

The *Residential Tenancies Act* includes provisions for both increases and subsequent decreases in rent relating to such things as taxes and utilities.

2. It is unlawful for a tenant to make payments by way of post-dated cheques.

True False

Payment by post-dated cheque is not unlawful. However, the Act does provide that the landlord cannot require post-dated cheques.

3. A landlord has a right to gain immediate access to the rented premises under certain circumstances.

True  False

A landlord is permitted access without written notice under certain circumstances, such as an emergency.

4. Accommodation for the travelling and vacationing public is exempt under the *Residential Tenancies Act*.

 True  False

This is one of several exemptions provided for under the Act.

Chapter Mini-Review

5. The notice period for termination by a landlord for non-payment of rent is 30 days.

 True  False

The notice period is 14 days.

6. A landlord has a statutory right to show a rental property to a potential tenant, if the landlord and tenant have agreed to a termination or either has given notice of termination to the other.

 True  False

The landlord does have this right, but the showing must be between 8 a.m. and 8 p.m.

7. A mobile home park owner can prevent a real estate brokerage from placing a for sale sign on a home located within the park, if that owner meets specific requirements set out in the *Residential Tenancies Act.*

 True  False

The landlord's prohibition must apply to all tenants, a bulletin board must be available in a prominent location accessible to the public for the free placement of for sale advertisements.

8. The rent guideline is established each year based on the Consumer Price Index (CPI) for Ontario.

 True  False

The guideline is based on the CPI averaged over the 12-month period that ends at the end of May of the previous calendar year, rounded to the first decimal point.

9. If a subtenant overholds and the original tenant has vacated the rental unit, the landlord may negotiate a new agreement with that subtenant.

 True  False

The Landlord may negotiate a new agreement with the subtenant.

10. A landlord is not permitted to change the entry locking system for a residential unit until the end of the residential tenancy term.

 True  False

The landlord may change an entry locking system during the tenancy, but must provide replacement keys to the tenant.

11. According to the *Residential Tenancies Act*, an information package must be provided to all persons taking possession of a mobile home in a mobile home park, or a home in a land lease community by the owner of that park or community.

 True  False

The requirement to provide an information package relates to care homes, not mobile home parks or land lease communities.

12. A landlord must allow a tenant to have pets in a residential unit, otherwise he or she would be in violation of the pet provision set out in the *Residential Tenancies Act.*

 True  False

Generally, a landlord must allow pets, but certain important exceptions apply; e.g., a condominium in which a no pet provision is included in the condominium declaration.

Active Learning Exercises

CH12 EX

Exercise 1

a. The lease has expired, so the tenant is renting on a month to month basis. The notice period required is sixty days to coincide with the end of a month.

b. There is no lease. The notice can take effect at the end of any month, as long as the required notice is given.

c. Jones can apply for a court order within thirty days.

d. The judge will give the order for vacant possession as long as the judge is satisfied that the requirement is genuine and the son will be moving in.

Exercise 2

a. The notice must include the effective date, the amount of the increase and the percentage.

b. The notice period for a rent increase must be at least 90 days. The increase is greater than the amount allowed in the Rent Control guidelines. The tenant can also decline paying by post-dated cheques.

c. Jones must restrict the increase to the limit allowed or apply for a greater increase, if justified. Jones must give notice on the proper form and comply with the required time for notice.

Exercise 3

The landlord has not broken the covenant for quiet enjoyment. This is not derogation of the grant; the tenant can still use the apartment. The tenant is liable for the loss of rent, the costs of re-renting and any decrease in the rent to the new tenant.

Exercise 4

The clause stating that there are to be no pets is unenforceable. The landlord can try to obtain a court order to terminate the tenancy, but he/she would have to prove that the kittens were interfering with the other tenants.

Exercise 5

All are correct.

- ✔ Fixed term of one year or longer—sixty days before expiry.
- ✔ Monthly tenancy—sixty days before last day of monthly tenancy.
- ✔ Weekly tenancy—twenty-eight days before last day of the weekly tenancy.